The Kiln Book

Third Edition

materials, specifications & construction

Frederick L. Olsen

A & C Black • London

First published in Great Britain 2001
A&C Black (Publishers) Ltd
37 Soho Square
London W1D 3QZ

ISBN 0-7136-6060-0

Published in the USA
Krause Publications
700 East State Street
Iola, Wisconsin 54990-0001

A CIP catalogue record for this book is available from the British Library.

(copy for the title page of *The Kiln Book* 3rd edition)

The Kiln Book

Third Edition

Frederick L. Olsen

A&C Black-London

To Albert F., Jeanette L., Ingrid A., and Lee A.

Bernard Leach (1887-1979)

Bernard Leach's book's, his philosophy, and his pottery made an un paralleled contribution to ceramics. He brought potters and artists from all over the world together to exchange styles and technical and aesthetic ideas, to the benefit of all of us.

During my last visit with Leach in 1978, though he was blind, he pantomimed the throwing of a pot with such feeling, grace and sensitivity that I saw the pot formed, fired and finished in my mind's eye. It was a good pot and we both enjoyed it. He was a friend, a Sensei to many of us, and we count ourselves fortunate to have learned from him and to have shared with him.

Bernard Leach and Frederick Olsen; St. Ives, England; March 16, 1965

THE FIRING

By Gary Snyder

Bitter blue fingers

Winter nineteen sixty-three A.D.
    showa thirty-eight

Over a low pine-covered spaly of hills in Shiga

West-south-west of the outlet of Lake Biwa

Domura village set on sandy fans of the sweep
    and turn of a river

Draining the rotten-granite hills up Shigaraki

On a nineteen fifty-seven Honda cycle model C

Rode with some Yumanashi wine "St. Neige"

Into the farmyard and bellowing kiln.

Les & John

In ragged shirts and pants, dried slip

Stuck to with pineneedle, pitch,
    dust, hair, woodchips;

Sending the final slivers of yellowy pine

Through peephole white blast glow

No saggars tilting yet and segers bending
    neatly in a row—

Even their beards caked up with mud & soot

Firing for fourteen hours. How does she go.

Porcelain & stoneward: cheese dish, twenty cups.

Tokuri, vases, black chawan

Crosslegged rest on the dirt eye cockt to smoke—

The hands you layed on clay

Kickwheeld, curling,
    creamd to the lip of nothing,

And coaxt to a white dancing heat that day

Will linger centuries in these towns and loams

And speak to men or beasts

When Japanese and English

Are dead tongues.

John Chappell, Domura, Japan, 1963

Daniel Rhodes (1911 - 1989)

Clay and *Glazes, Stoneware* and *Porcelain* were the standard text books all of us used in our college ceramic courses, so when I was told by Tomimoto Sensei that the legendary author Daniel Rhodes was coming to Kyoto to do research on Tamba Potteries, and I was to assist him, I was thrilled. This beginning affiliation led to a close personal and professional friendship for 27 years. Daniel's inscription in my copy of his book, *Kilns,* was "If we put the best part of this (*Kilns*) together with the best part of yours, we'd have a dynamite book." Daniel was a dynamite person, author and artist.

Daniel Rhodes attending kiln opening at Olsen studio, Feb., 1987.

F. Carlton Ball (1911 - 1992)

"At last, art potters have a book that explains the construction of a kiln in the smallest detail. Expert potters, as well as students, have asked me how to build a high-temperature kiln, a raku kiln, a chamber kiln, a salt glazing kiln. Many have asked how to repair a kiln and have posed endless questions involving the intricacies of firing pottery. Now, at last, I can say with confidence that there is a complete and expert source: Frederick Olsen's *The Kiln Book* explains everything one must know to start the process of understanding the firing of pottery.

"Olsen is a practicing artist potter. His kilns must perform properly in order for him to make a living from his pottery. He is an accomplished teacher and, therefore, understands what pottery students want to know. He has traveled around the world, stopping here and there to make pots, build kilns, fire the other potters' kilns, take kiln measurements, and study kiln building. Olsen is a highly skilled and talented artist, potter, and teacher. *The Kiln Book* fills a longtime need and I recommend it to all potters."

— *F. Carlton Ball, Professor of Ceramics, USC, retired.*

Preceding is an excerpt from the original Forward for *The Kiln Book* back in 1973, which I cannot thank Carlton enough for. Throughout my years in clay, Carlton remained a close personal friend up until his death. His unrelenting ability to motivate, excite and teach over 30,000 students the wonders of clay without losing his enthusiasm, and the love for teaching, are a benchmark few will reach.

F. Carlton Ball and author; Incline Village, Nevada, 1987.

Contents

Foreword

When I returned to the University of Southern California from a sabbatical in the early 1960s, I approached Fred Olsen with the idea of actually going to Japan. He had been experimenting with Japanese-style tenmoku glazes and was already an expert in the art of throwing stoneware and porcelain. It was a chance for Fred to compare the American materials and kilns with Japanese supplies and firing methods, and to further his glaze studies.

In those days it was not so simple to acquire sponsorship to live in Japan, but a Japanese English professor managed it through the Kyoto City College of Fine Arts. Fred's story of his time in Japan is another book in itself, but suffice it to say that the experience changed his life. He learned Japanese, worked with two famous cobalt calligraphers and ceramic artists in Tomimoto Kenkichi and Kondo Yuzo, was the subject of an hour-long documentary on NHK television, and was in general a fine help to Tomimoto-sensei as well as being his faithful student.

When Tomimoto died, I advised Fred to continue his travels around the world and attend some exhibitions his mentors had scheduled for him. Fred did tour, stopping in many countries to visit friends and make new acquaintances, and build various kilns along the way. Returning to California more than three years later, he received a master of fine arts degree for the work he accomplished abroad and accepted an invitation from Carlton Ball and me to teach a kiln-building class in our ceramic department at USC.

The rest is beginning to feel like history. Fred wrote the first of his several kiln books in the 1960s as a course syllabus while he taught at USC. The work was published by our local ceramic supplier, Ernie Sherrill, as the first paperback edition of *The Kiln Book* in 1973. Fred went on to update and improve the book for a second addition in 1983. Now he has made a major revision for the new book published by Krause Publications.

Along the way, Fred has developed a business, selling his Olsen kiln kit for updraft gas kilns and wood furnaces of varying sizes. He has given lectures and workshops all around the globe, and has frequently been the "Kiln Doctor" at the annual conferences of the National Ceramic Educators Council of America. In recent years he has been invited to build anagama derivative wood-fired kilns in many remote locales. Among his memorable

Susan Peterson and the author have been friends and colleagues for four decades.

stops: the International Ceramic Center in Denmark; a "singing kiln" with two stacks at an art school in Canberra, Australia; Janet Mansfield's sheep ranch in Glugong, Australia, for a car-shaped anagama; and Denmark again for Nina Hole's large site kiln sculpture.

This revised edition of *The Kiln Book* was a monster undertaking. Fred has been at this so many years that his experience in kilns and kiln building and firing is astronomical. In this edition of the book he has particularly expanded his chapter on "Fuels, Combustion, and Burners" a great deal, and included a new chapter on "Specialty Kilns and Innovative Ideas," encompassing some of the experimental kilns that he and others have built recently. He has also added advice on new safety devices and important ways of using them.

The Kiln Book is the only book from which potters have actually been able to construct real kilns. He knows the dimensions for combustion, the flue areas for fast-fire, and after all these years is still experimenting with new ideas for furnaces and firing techniques. He discusses conventional updraft, downdraft, crossdraft gas and alternative fuel-fired kilns, talks about electrics, anagama, noborigama and groundhog kilns, and gives specific instruction in all cases.

Fred is a ceramic artist as well, so he understands the problems from our vantage point. There is no question that this is the right book for all who will build or use kilns, no matter what kind.

Hallelujah, Fred, you've done it again.

(Susan Peterson is a retired professor and ceramic artist who founded five ceramic art departments, including the University of Southern California in 1955 and Hunter College, City University of New York, in 1972. She has written 10 books, including *Shoji Hamada, a Potter's Way and Work,* and *The Craft and Art of Clay.* Her studio is in Carefree, Arizona.)

Acknowledgments

I wish to thank a number of people who, over the years, helped me to write *The Kiln Book* and to do the revisions for the second edition and for this new millennium edition.

In Japan, Professor Tomimoto Kenkichi, Professor Kondo Yuzo, Yutaka Kondo, Mutsuo Yanagihara, Teruo Fujieda, Kenji Kato, Kei Fujiwara and his son Yu, Takichi Kawaii; in Australia, Les Blakebrough, Marion Chappell; in Denmark, Neils and Herman Kalher; in Spain, Luis Estepa Pinilla; in England, John Chappell; in India, Mansimran Singh.

The teaching, friendship and encouragement of F. Carlton Ball in the beginning and throughout my years in ceramics have made a singular contribution to the book. It was at his instigation that I began writing it in 1966 while teaching kiln building at University of Southern California. I give special commendation to Susan Peterson for 40 years of support, advice, friendship, and for writing the Foreword for this new edition.

My continued thanks to the old cast of Westwood Ceramics, David Massey, Carole Brammer, Ann Wolcott, Brian Johnson, Bruce Dedmen, the original publishers of *The Kiln Book* and to the National Endowment for the Arts for their financial grant in 1977 which allowed me to research firsthand the information on wood kilns of Spain, France and England.

I would like to express my appreciation for the workshop venues where I was able to build prototype kilns; Janet Mansfield (Gulgong racer) and Allen Watts, Fergus Stewart (Tiwi kiln) in Gulgong and Cambera, Australia: Alfred Schmidt and Chuck Wissinger (fireworks kiln) in Alberta, Canada; Nina Hole and Clay Today (church kiln) in Skaleskor, Denmark.

I owe appreciation for my friends, Nils Lou, Jack Troy for their new books which motivated me to revise and update my book once again to keep it a definitive work.

The Kiln Book has become a tool for so many people around the world that this new edition, with a new format and publisher, has new information, new kiln designs, pictures, updated materials and techniques, should further the usefulness of this book for you past readers and the new readers to come. This is still the only way I have to say thank you.

Introduction

In January of 1961, I became an assistant to Tomimoto Kenkichi, Japan's greatest potter, calligrapher and creative artist. My first meeting with him was at the Kyoto City College of Fine Arts just after I arrived. I was throwing as Professor Tomimoto came into the studio. He stopped, looked at what I was throwing, and said "Baaaaah" three times, then left, mumbling in English, "Western people just can't throw and shouldn't bother to come to Japan." I was determined to stay anyway.

A few weeks later, Professor Kondo Yuzo, who was Tomimoto's apprentice of almost 14 years and who is today one of Japan's greatest potters, specializing in blue and white porcelain, explained to me that I must forget my Western training and begin to study pottery all over again. Professor Kondo also informed me that Tomimoto had asked him to begin my studies, so I had my first introduction to the traditional approach to pottery. A few months later I was invited to live and work at Tomimoto's studio, where I stayed for three years.

Professor Kondo made arrangements for me to have my pottery fired in the Koyama chamber kiln in Kyomizu and for Mr. Koyama to instruct me in the firing of the kiln. After four months, I was allowed to stack and fire my rented space in the chamber kiln without supervision. For the next three years, I fired three chamber kilns a month and learned by experience the nature of wood-fired climbing kilns.

During the fall of 1962, English potter John Chappell stopped by Tomimoto's studio and asked me to give him a hand building his new kiln. For the next two months, on the days I could spare, I'd travel out to Domura where John was working and help. It was John who became my first actual kiln-building teacher. He introduced me to construction techniques, the oil drip system for firing, and the art of designing a kiln for a specific purpose. I asked John where he had learned to build and design kilns and he replied, "Just as you are — by helping to build them." John believed that, whatever you needed for your pottery or work, you built or made yourself. This, of course, is learning the hard way through experience and mistakes; in the case of kiln building, I found it the only way.

I subsequently traveled throughout Japan, Asia, the Middle East and Europe, collecting data on kiln designs and proportions, and taking photographs, for I knew I would eventually write a book on kiln building. Over the years I have made many trips abroad collecting information on kilns, firings, techniques and have developed new ideas concerning kilns which can be found in this third edition. I have planned *The Kiln Book* to

Tomimoto Kenkichi, 1886-1963

provide basic information on: (1) the materials used in kiln construction; (2) the methods of kiln construction; (3) the principles used in designing kilns; and (4) layouts and procedures for building each type of kiln. Further, and most importantly, I hope this book instills the confidence you need to successfully build your own kiln.

The book is organized as a step-by-step guide to building a kiln of your own design. Read through the entire book first, and choose the type of kiln to fulfill your specific needs. Then, design your kiln (Chapter 3), select the refractory materials (Chapter 1), and so on. Bricklaying techniques, fiber construction, etc., are found in Chapter 2; these chapters make for rather dry reading (how can you get excited about a brick?), but the information contained in them should more than compensate. The remaining chapters provide examples of different types of kilns, both traditional and innovative, and perhaps one will be similar to the one you plan to build. These kilns have been successfully built and used, but there is no guarantee of their success when copied. There are so many variables involved in kiln building and firing that experience, common sense and one's mistakes (remember to make all critical areas adjustable) determine the success or failure of any kiln.

Kongo Yuzo (1902 - 1985) and author, Kyoto, Japan 1962.

Chapter 1

Refractory Materials and Applications

Refractory materials (or refractories) are defined as materials, usually nonmetallic, that can withstand extreme temperatures. In other words, they have a high resistance to fusion. Refractories are also capable of resisting one or more of the destructive forces of abrasion, which can be pressure, thermal expansion and/or the chemical attacks of either acid or base slags or fluxes at high temperatures.

A refractory's capacity for resisting destructive forces depends upon the material's composition and intended use. For example, a high-silica brick would not be used in a salt-glaze kiln because it would react with the basic flux of soda and would slag. High silica (up to 90 percent) does not withstand the heating and cooling processes with the same stability as other materials.

Refractory materials are divided into five main groups:

1. Oxides
2. Carbides
3. Nitrates
4. Borides
5. Elements (see Glossary)

A comparison (see Table 1-1) of the melting points of these refractory substances shows that carbides can be extremely refractory, and that materials most often used by the potter/kiln builder are least refractory (these are in the kaolinite and fused mullite group).

The refractory materials listed in Table 1-1 are, for the most part, special materials. They are used primarily for extreme high-temperature conditions. An exception, silicon carbide, which is used where strength and heat transfer are needed, has proven suitable for pottery use. Silicon carbide offers high strength over a wide temperature range, high resistance to thermal shock (in short-cycle kiln operations), abrasion, erosion, chemical attack, and high thermal conductivity[1]. Silicon carbide refractories, especially the oxide-bonded group, have a poor to fair resistance to oxidation. As silicon carbide is oxidized and SiO_2 is formed, there is an increase in volume. If uniform, it grows in all dimensions, but normally it is

Table 1-1
Temperature Ranges of Refractory Materials

Material	Formula	°C	°F
Harnium carbide	HfC	3890	7030
Tantalum carbide	TaC	3870	7000
Zirconium carbide	ZrC	3540	6400
Carbon	C	3500	6364
Tungsten	W	3410	6170
Fused thores (oxide)	ThO_2	3300	5970
Titanium carbide	TiC	3140	5680
Zirconium boride	ZrB_2	3060	5540
Titanium nitrate	TiN	2950	5350
Titanium boride	TiB_2	2900	5250
Uranium boride	UO_2	2760	5000
Fused zirconia oxide	ZrO_2	2700	4900
Fused magnesia oxide	MgO	2620	4750
Lime	CaO	2570	4658
Boron carbide	B_4C	2400	4440
Silicon carbide	SiC	2300	4170
Chromium oxide	Cr_2O_3	2275	4127
Spinel	$MgO \cdot Al_2O_3$	2135	3875
Aluminum oxide	Al_2O_3	1900-2000	3450-3630
Fosterite	$2MgO \cdot SiO_2$	1910	3470
Mullite fused oxide	$3Al_2O_3 \cdot 2SiO_2$	1840	3340
Kaolinite	$Al_2O_3 \cdot 2SiO_2 \cdot 2H_2O$	1785	3245
Cristobalite	SiO_2	1728	3142

1. Norton's Crystolon 63 oxynitride bond greatly increases the resistance of silicon carbide to soda slags in incinerators.

not uniform and distorted growth occurs. It is, therefore, unwise to use silicon carbide from the oxide-bonded group in oxidation firing.

For the most part, the materials of concern to the kiln builder/potter fall in the range of kaolinite and mullite refractories.

The most common refractory material found in nature is clay. Pure kaolin has one of the highest melting points (3,245°F) of the natural clays and, because of its availability, refractory qualities and cost, it is the bulwark of the refractory business. Mullite, one of the sillimanite group of minerals found in nature, has become an important material as a raw additive to a refractory and as a synthetic material formed in the refractory during firing. The primary source of mullite is the Kyanite Mining and Manufacturing Company in Dillwyn, Virginia. It is produced from kyanite, a raw material which, when calcined, converts to mullite.

The advantages of mullite in refractory materials are its long, crystal needle structure, which interlocks and gives it strength, its high fusion point and its excellent thermal-expansion characteristics.

True mullite refractories (75 percent mullite) are for extremely specialized uses and are expensive. For the kiln builder/potter, refractory materials containing 30 percent mullite, such as bricks and kiln furniture, are extremely reliable at cone 10 temperatures. Refractory materials consisting predominantly of mullite must meet the following requirements: (1) alumina content of 56 percent to 79 percent; (2) maximum 5 percent content of other metallic impurities; (3) maximum deformation of 5 percent.

From the various kaolinite clays, such as Missouri flint fire clay, kvanite from Virginia, Lincoln fire clay from California, etc., refractories produced by various manufacturers are available throughout the country, and sources of supply can be found in the Yellow Pages of any telephone directory.

Refractory materials, as they are used in kiln building, fall into five categories:

1. Firebrick
2. Insulating firebrick
3. Castables
4. Mortars
5. Special materials

FIREBRICK

Firebrick is a broad term covering any type of refractory brick. More specifically, it refers to a brick made of fire clay. The chemical and physical properties of firebrick vary greatly, depending upon its intended use and the various materials which may be added to its basic kaolinite composition. The American Society for Testing and Materials (ASTM) has established a general classification for firebricks based upon temperature destruction (Table 1-2). The four classes are:

1. **Super-duty**, 33-34 + PCE (3,173°-3200°F; 1,745-1,760°C)
2. **High-duty**, 32-32 1/2 + PCE (3,092°F; 1,700°C)
3. **Intermediate-duty**, 28-31 PCE (2,0300-3,056°F; 1,2770-1,680°C)
4. **Low-duty**, 28 down PCE (2,939°F; 1,615°C)

The pyrometric cone equivalent (PCE) is the temperature at which the material in a cone form will bend simultaneously with a standard pyrometric cone. I have found that, for potter's kilns, low and intermediate bricks are sufficient, except in the firebox of certain designs and with certain fuels, where high-duty firebrick should be used.

All refractory manufacturers produce a wide variety of bricks in the super duty, high duty, intermediate duty, and low duty categories. These are available in basic refractories, such as magnesite, lime and chrome; in straight fire clay composition; in semisilica bricks to extreme silica bricks (90 percent); in high-alumina composition bricks; and special fused mullite refractories.

Here are the applications of the four basic firebrick classifications:

Super-duty brick is highly refractory and has great resistance to spalling (chipping). It is fired to extremely high temperatures to decrease porosity and increase hardness and resistance to abrasion. Recommended uses for super-duty brick are boilers, furnace walls and arches, forge furnaces and all extreme heat conditions.

High-duty firebrick possesses excellent spalling and slagging resistance. It can be used everywhere, except where extreme conditions warrant a super-rated brick.

Intermediate-duty brick is suitable for furnaces, boilers, incinerators and kilns where a moderate condition of temperature range and destructive forces is present. For a potter who works in the range of cone 10, intermediate brick is well suited.

Low-duty brick is generally used as a back-up brick. However, if a low-duty brick has a PCE rating of 28, it is certainly capable of withstanding cone 10 temperatures in a kiln. On the other hand, it would not be wise to use it in a firebox or in an extreme hot face area.

Firebricks are usually manufactured by one of two methods — the dry press (DP) process or the stiff mud (SM) process. The dry press process uses the exact minimum quantity of water (moisture) with a properly blended body to provide a bond under extreme pressure application. The dry press machine is automatically fed the mixture of clay and moisture into the press molds; using extreme pressure, and de-airing the mixture at the same time, presses out the firebricks. This process ensures greater uniformity in texture and dimension, and produces a firebrick with

Table 1-2
Fire Clay and High-Alumina Refractory Brick Classes and Types

Class	Type	PCE	Panel Spalling Loss (max. %)	Hot Load Subsidence (max. %)	Reheat Shrinkage (max. %)	Modulus of Rupture (Min. PSI, Kgf/mm³)	Other Test Requirements
FIREBRICK CLAY							
Super Duty	Regular	33	8 at 1649°C (3000°F)	—	1.0 at 1599°C (2910°F)	600 (0.422)	—
	Spall Resistant	33	4 at 1649°C (3000°F)	—	1.0 at 1599°C (2910°F)	600 (0.422)	—
	Slag Resistant	33	—	—	—	1000 (0.703)	Bulk density Min. 140 lb/ft.³ (2243 Kgm/m³)
High Duty	Regular	31 1/2	10 at 1599°C (2910°F)	—	—	—	Bulk density Min. 140 lb/ft.³ (2194 Kgm/m³) or max. porosity of 15%
	Spall Resistant	31 1/2		—	—	500 (0.352)	
Semi-silica		31 1/2	—	1.5 at 1349°C (2460°F)	—	300 (0.211)	Silica Content Min. 72%
Medium Duty		29	—	—	—	500 (0.352)	—
Low Duty		15	—	—	—	600 (0.422)	—
HIGH-ALUMINA BRICK							
50% Al₂O₃		34	—	—	—	—	Alumina content 50 ± 2.5%
60% Al₂O₃		35	—	—	—	—	Alumina content 60 ± 2.5%
70% Al₂O₃		36	—	—	—	—	Alumina content 70 ± 2.5%
80% Al₂O₃		37	—	—	—	—	Alumina content 80 ± 2.5%
85% Al₂O₃		—	—	—	—	—	Alumina content 85 ± 2.0%
90% Al₂O₃		—	—	—	—	—	Alumina content 90 ± 2.0%
99% Al₂O₃		—	—	—	—	—	Alumina content 97%

SOURCE: ASTM Chart C27-70

a general ability to stand thermal expansion without spalling.

The stiff mud process employs a pug mill, which automatically adds sufficient moisture to develop proper plasticity. This permits extrusion through a modern, de-airing combination auger machine. The extruded column is cut and re-pressed into the shapes desired. This process produces very dense brick that can withstand abrasive conditions and slagging. After the blocks have been cut from the column of the clay body, special shapes can be made in hydraulic and steam presses.

There are other processes used in the making of refractory shapes and specialty items, including a pneumatic ramming process (for shapes not practical to press), a slip-cast process (kiln shelves, setter tiles, IFB (insulation fire brick) shapes and special shapes needing uniformity in body), a high-pressure extrusion process (tubes, pins and pieces of uniform cross section), and a hand-molding process.

The standard size for firebricks and insulating bricks in the 9" series is 9" x 4 1/2" x 2 1/2". In Europe, the standard size in the 9" series is 9" x 4 1/2" x 3". Upon special request, the European standard can be obtained here in the U.S. I personally feel the European standard is the best size. The reason is that 4 1/2" + 4 1/2" = 9" and 3" + 3" + 3" = 9" and the total length is 9". Therefore, in combinations — laying bricks on their edges, their sides, or flat — even top surfaces can be achieved. However, with the 2 1/2" measurement, a total of three bricks stacked flat equals only 7 1/2", and an even top surface can only be attained at high multiples (Fig. 1-1).

Thus, with the 2 1/2" brick series, tying every fourth to sixth row is impossible in a 7" or 9" wall.

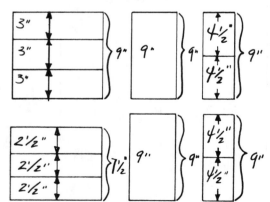

Fig. 1—1: *Firebrick (top) 9" x 4 1/2" x 3", (bottom) 9" x 4 1/2" x 2 1/2".*

This presents a minor problem when using a 7" wall made of insulation brick within a kiln frame. The back-up (rowlock), which should be tied to the hot face brick (stretchers) every fourth to sixth row, has to be tied on every ninth row when it matches evenly. This creates a great loss in total wall strength and stability (Fig. 1-2).

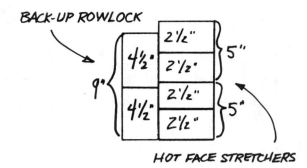

Fig. 1—2: *Rowlock must be tied every ninth row with 2 1/2" series, causing loss of stability and wall strength.*

Figure 1-3 shows the most common bricks used in kiln building. All bricks in the 9" x 4 1/2" x 2 1/2" and 3" series are standard sizes and can be ordered from various manufacturers. (Wider sizes, called "large 9 inch," including 9" x 6 3/4" x 2 1/2" and 9" x 6 3/4" x 3", straight and wedges, are used mainly for breaking joints. Longer sizes, including 12", 13 1/2" and up to 18", are available. These longer bricks have widths of 4 1/2" and 6", which are the most common widths and considered standard.)

SQUARE-EDGE FIRE TILE

Square-edge fire tile (Fig. 1-4) can be used as flooring for kilns and also for kiln shelves. For example, in my chamber kiln, I use 12" x 18" x 2" super-duty square-edge tiles for shelves. Other available sizes are:

2" x 12" x 12"	2 1/2" x 12" x 12"	3" x 12" x 12"
2" x 12" x 15"	2 1/2" x 12" x 15"	3" x 12" x 15"
2" x 12" x 18"	2 1/2" x 12" x 18"	3" x 12" x 18"
2" x 12" x 24"	2 1/2" x 12" x 24"	3" x 12" x 24"

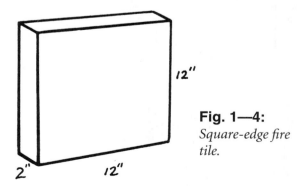

Fig. 1—4: *Square-edge fire tile.*

LARGE 9" SERIES

The large 9" series bricks are recommended in place of soaps for breaking joints.

Fig. 1—3:
9" x 4 1/2" x 2 1/2" series:

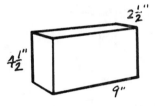

9" Straight: 9" x 4 1/2" x 2 1/2"

Small 9": 9" x 3 1/2" x 2 1/2"

Soap: 9" x 2 1/2" x 2 1/2"

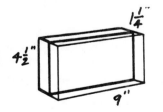

Split brick: 9" x 4 1/2" x 1 1/4"

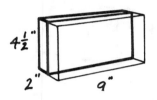

2" Brick: 9" x 4 1/2" x 2"

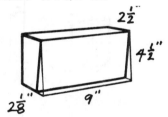

No. 1 Arch: 9" x 4 1/2" x (2 1/2" x 2 1/8")

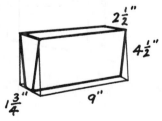

No. 2 Arch: 9" x 4 1/2" x (2 1/2" x 1 3/4")

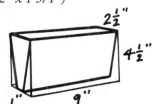

No. 3 Arch: 9" x 4 1/2" x (2 1/2" x 1")

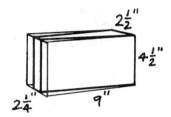

No. 1 Wedge: 9" x 4 1/2" x (2 1/2" x 2 1/4")

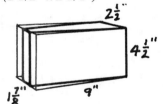

No. 1 Wedge: 9" x 4 1/2" x (2 1/2" x 1 7/8")

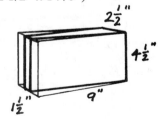

No. 2 Wedge: 9" x 4 1/2" x (2 1/2" x 1 1/2")

Fig. 1—3: (continued)
9" x 4 1/2" x 2 1/2" series:

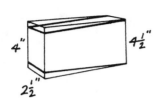

No. 1 Key: 9" x (4 1/2" x 4") x 2 1/2"

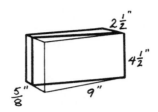

Neck brick: 9" x 4 1/2" x (2 1/2" x 5/8")

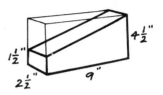

Edge skew: 9" x (4 1/2" x 1 1/2") x 2 1/

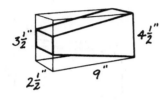

No. 2 Key: 9" x (4 1/2" x 3 1/2") x 2 1/2"

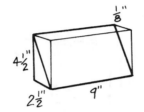

Featheredge: 9" x 4 1/2" x (2 1/2" x 1/8")

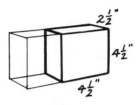

Bat brick: 4 1/2" x 4 1/2" x 2 1/2"

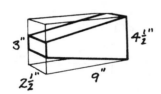

No. 3 Key: 9" x (4 1/2" x 3") x 2 1/2"

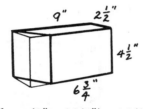

End skew: (9" x 6 3/4") x 4 1/2" x 2 1/2"

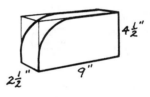

Jamb brick: 9" x 4 1/2" x 2 1/2"

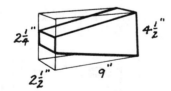

No. 4 Key: 9" x (4 1/2" x 2 1/4") x 2 1/2"

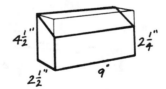

Side skew: 9" x (4 1/2" x 2 1/4") x 2 1/2"

Fig. 1—3: (continued)

9" x 4 1/2" x 3" series:

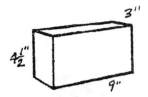

9" Straight: 9" x 4 1/2" x 3"

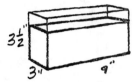

Small 9": 9" x 3 1/2" x 3"

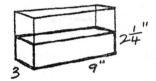

Soap: 9" x 2 1/4" x 3"

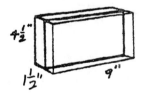

Split brick: 9" x 4 1/2" x 1 1/2"

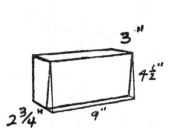

No. 1 Arch: 9" x 4 1/2" x (3"- 2 3/4")

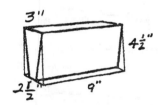

No. 2 Arch: 9" x 4 1/2" x (3" - 2 1/2")

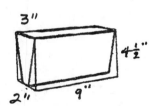

No. 3 Arch: 9" x 4 1/2" x (3" x 2")

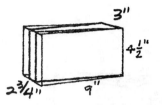

No. 1 Wedge: 9" x 4 1/2" x (3" - 2 3/4")

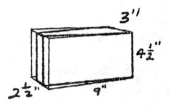

No. 2 Wedge: 9" x 4 1/2" x (3" - 2 1/2")

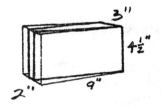

No. 3 Wedge: 9" x 4 1/2" x 3" - 2")

Fig. 1—3: *(continued)*
9" x 4 1/2" x 3" series:

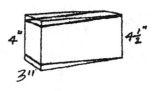

No. 1 Key: 9" x (4 1/2" - 4") x 3"

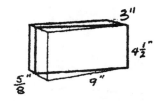

Neck brick: 9" x 4 1/2" x (3" - 5/8")

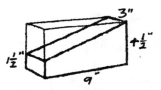

Edge skew: 9" x (4 1/2" - 1 1/2") x 3"

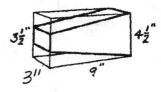

No. 2 Key: 9" x (4 1/2" - 3 1/2") x 3"

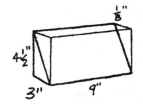

Featheredge: 9" x 4 1/2" x (3" - 1/8")

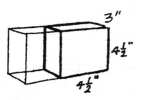

Bat brick: 4 1/2" x 4 1/2" x 3"

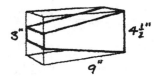

No. 3 Key: 9" x (4 1/2" - 3") x 3"

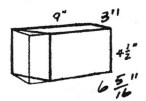

End skew: (9" - 6 5/16") x 4 1/2" x 3"

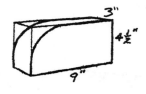

Jamb brick: 9" x 4 1/2" x 3"

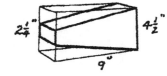

No. 4 Key: 9" x (4 1/2" - 2 1/4") x 3"

Side skew: 9" x (4 1/2" - 2 11/16") x 3"

Large 9" Straight, 9" x 6 3/4" x 2 1/2" (Fig. 1-5):
No. 1x Wedge, 9" x 6 3/4" x (2 1/2"-2 1/4")
No. 1 Wedge, 9" x 6 3/4" x (2 1/2"-l")
No. 2 Wedge, 9" x 6 3/4" x (2 1/2"-1 1/2")

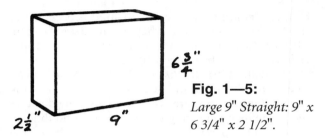

Fig. 1—5: *Large 9" Straight: 9" x 6 3/4" x 2 1/2".*

Large 9" Straight, 9" x 6 1/2" x 3" (Fig. 1-6):
No. 1 Wedge, 9" x 6 3/4" x (3"-2 3/4")
No. 2 Wedge, 9" x 6 3/4" x (3"-2 1/2")

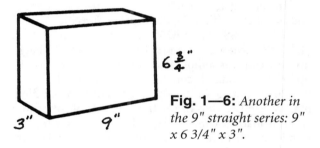

Fig. 1—6: *Another in the 9" straight series: 9" x 6 3/4" x 3".*

SPECIAL SHAPES

Straight 13 1/2" x 4 1/2" x 2 1/2" (Fig. 1-7):
   No. 1 Arch, 13 1/2" x 4 1/2" x (2 1/2"-2 1/8")
   No. 2 Arch, 13 1/2" x 4 1/2" x (2 1/2"-1 3/4")
   No. 3 Arch, 13 1/2" x 4 1/2" x (2 1/2"-1")

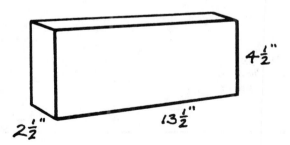

Fig. 1—7: *Straight 13 1/2" x 4 1/2" x 2 1/2".*

Series 13 1/2" x 6" x 3" shapes (Fig. 1-8):

No. 1 Wedge, 13 1/2" x 6" x (3"-2 3/4")
No. 2 Wedge, 13 1/2" x 6" x (3"-2")
No. 3 Wedge, 13 1/2" x 6" x (3"-2 1/2")

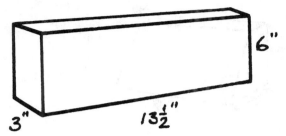

Fig. 1—8: *Special shapes are available in the 13 1/2" x 6" x 3" series.*

Standard circle brick, 4 1/2" lining (Fig. 1-9). For complete circle brick sizes, see Estimating Data in the Appendix.

Fig. 1—9: *Standard circle brick.*

Rotary kiln and cupola blocks, 6" lining (9") x 6" x 4" (Fig. 1-10). For complete block sizes, see Estimating Data in the Appendix.

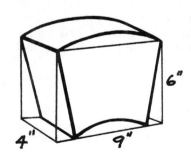

Fig. 1—10: *Rotary kiln and cupola blocks.*

STANDARD BRICK SKEWBACKS

The most commonly used skewback assemblies for building kilns (from 10 to 100 cubic feet in size) are assemblies that give a rise to the arch per foot of span. To make this assembly, a standard featheredge is used. Thus, for a 4 1/2"-thick arch with a rise of 1 1/2" per foot of span, the skewback consists of one 9" x 4 1/2" x 2" brick series, and one 9" featheredge 2 1/2" series (Fig. 1-11).

For an arch that is 9" thick, with a rise of 2 5/16" per foot of span, the skewbacks consist of two 9" end-skew 2 1/2" series, two 9" side-skew 2 1/2" series, and

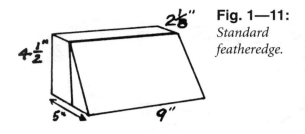

Fig. 1—11:
Standard featheredge.

one 9" x 2 1/4" x 2 1/4" soap (Fig. 1-12). (For special-purpose skewbacks, see the Appendix.)

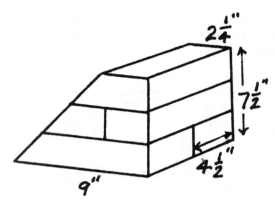

Fig. 1—12:
Skewback assembly for 9"-thick arch.

INSULATING FIREBRICK (IFB)

Insulating bricks are produced from high-quality refractory clays containing a carefully selected organic filler which, upon firing, is burned out. This method of production is called the burnout process. A.P.

Green manufactures an insulating brick, Greenlite, without the aid of artificial burnout materials. Greenlite is manufactured in a new process from multicellular lightweight aggregate having a string-ribbed internal structure.

Insulating firebricks (IFB) are made by either the casting method or a type of stiff-mud process. After the blocks are produced, they are fired in the kiln. They are then ground and cut into standard and special brick shapes by sizing machines.

Insulating bricks store or absorb very little heat. Therefore, the time and fuel needed to obtain the desired temperature are reduced. This provides further benefits by allowing close control in holding or changing temperature. Insulating bricks have low heat conductivity, or flow of heat through the brick (approximately one-sixth to one-third that of dense brick). This reduces heat loss through the kiln walls.

Insulating bricks weigh 65 percent to 85 percent less than dense firebrick. They reduce the need for heavy-duty foundations or structural steel work.

Insulating firebrick is classified by temperature and number (Table 1-3); appropriate uses are:

16 — (882°C, 1,620°F): Used up to 882°C (1,620°F), when exposed to 1,093°C (2,000°F) back-up. Brick in this temperature range is strictly a back-up brick, although it could be used in a raku kiln.

20 — (1,093°C, 2,000°F): Used in kiln building, mainly as a back-up brick. It has good cold-crushing and hot-load-bearing strength. However, its composition is similar to the 23, the only difference is 0.6 percent more calcium oxide and 0.1 percent more alkalies (Na_2O) and the melting point is the same at 2,750°F.

23 — (1,260°C, 2,300°F): Used in cold spots of cone 10 kilns; an excellent choice for kilns not exceeding cone 6. (Unofficially, can be used in cone 10 kilns, but not at temperatures exceeding cone 10).

Table 1-3
Insulating Firebrick

Common Refractory Type		Group Identification No.	Reheat Change not more than 2% when tested at		Bulk Density not greater than	
°F	°C		°F	°C	lb/ft³	hg/m³
1620	882	16	1550	845	34	545
2000	1093	20	1950	1065	40	641
2300	1260	23	2250	1230	48	769
2600	1427	26	2550	1400	54	865
2800	1538	28	2750	1520	60	961
3000	1649	30	2950	1620	68	1089
3200	1760	32	3150	1730	95	1522
3300	1816	33	3250	1790	95	1522

SOURCE: ASTM classification C155-70.

24 — (1,316°C, 2,400°F): It is called 24 HS (heat storage). Has the same melting point as the 23 and 20 brick. I have never used this brick because of the 25 brick .

25 — (1,371°C, 2,500°F): A brick formulated to fill the gap between 23 and 26 temperature and price range. It resembles the 23 brick in texture and insulating capabilities. Thermal Ceramics (Morgan Refractories of Great Britain) offers a JM-25 (Johns Manville brick made in the Milan, Italy plant by Thermal Ceramics) and a K-25 (Thermal) insulation firebrick. The JM-25 is a bit coarser and easier to cut, shape, and mortar and is very strong. The 25 IFB is a good choice for high-fire ceramic kilns for the potter.

26 — (1,427°C, 2,600°F): The 26s are excellent for cone 10 kilns. They are coarser, easier to cut and shape and to mortar because they do not absorb the mortar as readily as the 25/23 IFB bricks. I have used Thermal K-26 in my anagama style kiln for over 16 years and they have resisted the slagging effects of the wood ash superbly — in fact, better than the same rated hard brick.

28 — (1,538°C, 2,800°F): An excellent brick for fireboxes and kiln floors, because of its high spalling resistance.

30 — (1,649°C, 3,000°F): Used in extremely high-temperature kilns, such as forge furnaces and ceramic kiln furnaces for cone 15 porcelains and refractory materials.

32 — (1,760°C, 3,200°F) and

32 — (1,860°C, 3,300°F): Used in extremely high-temperature kilns.

Information used to estimate the number of bricks required for walls, arches, etc., can be found in the Appendix.

CASTABLES

Castable refractories are composed principally of alumina or aluminum-silica aggregates, using hydraulic-setting cement, so that, when tempered with water, they will develop structural strength and retain their cast form. Castables are furnished in dry form to the job site, then mixed with water and poured or cast in place in a manner similar to that used for concrete. Castables should be mixed in a mortar box or paddle mixer, using clean, cool water for at least six minutes. I have also used cement mixers successfully. Foreign materials may lower strength or prevent proper setting.

An exact water ratio must be used and the material mixed and installed within approximately thirty minutes after adding the water. A vibrator is recommended to remove air pockets after the castable is placed in deep forms like wall units or deep platform units. However, over-vibration can force the binder and fines to the surface. If the castable is poured next to a porous surface, the surface should first be waterproofed to prevent absorption. This can be done using oil, grease, plastic, shellac or wax-resistant ceramul as a coating. Depending upon the weather, castables will set up in eight hours or less, but should have at least twenty-four hours of water curing to assure proper hydration of the binder and to remove heat generated by chemical reaction. The castable surface should be covered with damp cloth and then plastic, creating a damp situation to ensure a proper curing process. The hotter the temperature, the quicker the set; the cooler the temperature, the slower the set. Castables should never be cast in freezing weather nor allowed to freeze until properly cured.

Castables can be poured like concrete or applied by gunning or slap-troweling. Gunning is done with a pneumatic gun that shoots the castable mixture at high velocity and pressure to form dense homogenous coatings. There are two types of guns: dry and wet. In the dry type, the water is mixed at the nozzle. The wet type combines water and the dry castable in the hopper, then forces it through the hose and out the nozzle. Slap-troweling applies force, or throws the mixture into place with the use of large trowels, similar to plastering or gloved hands for forcible placement. Overworking the castable can cause problems with slumping, especially over arch or dome forms. Therefore, do not overwork or smooth out the surface

Table 1-4
Typical analysis of Johns-Manville JM 26, 28 insulating brick

	JM 26	JM 28
SiO_2	57.40	39.00
TiO_2	1.70	1.25
Fe_2O_3	0.80	0.50
Al_2O_3	39.70	59.00
CaO	0.20	—
MgO	0.10	—
Na_2O	0.10	0.19
K_2O	0.10	0.06

of the castable. The castable mixture for best slap-troweling is achieved through trial and error. One test for the proper mixture is the "ball in hand" method. Mix a ball of castable and toss it a few inches into the air, then catch it. If it breaks up, it's too dry. If it flattens out, it's too wet. If it retains its shape, it is about right.

Castables come in two types, heavy or dense, and lightweight insulating. Estimating and use data for these two types of castables are as follows:

The heavy castables are designed to withstand greater abrasion, mechanical spalling and slagging, while the light castables are mainly designed for their insulating value. Castables have a wide range of material composition: from high alumina (53 percent), aluminum silicate (36-46 percent), to a chrome base (28 percent) that fills just about all the requirements for its various uses.

Kaolite 2500 LI and Kaolite 2600 LI permanent linear change, in percentage fired at 2,500°F for five hours, is -.05 to +0.5 and -0.5 to +1.5, respectively. Both of these castables are high strength, light weight, very insulating with low thermal conductivity and are excellent for kiln ceilings, arch/domes and special shapes. In Australia, the Thermal Ceramics insulating castable I have used is called Coolcaste 140.

The ASTM has designed maximum service temperature classes for castables (Table 1-5).

Castables have a variety of industrial uses. They are used to make furnace hearths, large sprung arches and domes, monolithic tops in furnaces, tunnels, kilns, linings and special shapes where the cutting and fitting of brick would be costly. The lower-temperature insulating castables are excellent for back-up insulation and can be used over kiln arches very successfully.

If a castable is used for the door of a kiln where less than four square feet is involved, reinforcing bars are generally not required. When stainless reinforcing bars are used, they should be spaced on 24" centers running or tied into the door frame. The maximum diameter bolts or rods used is 1/2", and it is advisable that they be made of stainless steel.

MORTARS

Mortars, or refractory cements, bond small units into a strong, stable and relatively gas-tight structure. The type of mortar and the type of brick used, plus the method in which the mortar is applied, determine the success of the bond. The requirements for high-temperature mortars are greater than those for the refractory bricks to be bonded.

The mortar must withstand all the destructive forces, thermal expansion, spalling, slagging, etc., that the brick withstands, but it also must convert itself into a part of the structure. Therefore, care must be taken to choose a mortar with similar chemical properties to the brick, balanced in characteristics, in order to ensure a strong bond.

The primary functions of mortars are to: (1) bond the brickwork into a solid monolithic structure, having

	DENSE CASTABLES		INSULATING CASTABLES		
	Interpace Super Shasta Kast 1,760°C (3,200°F)	Kaocrete 28-LI 1,538°C (2,800°F)	Interpace Litecrete 70 1,260°C (2,300°F)	2500-LI 1371°C (2,500°F)	Kaolite 2600-LI 1427°C (2,600°F)
Pounds required to cast 1 cubic foot	115-120	126	70-75	74	81
Quarts of water used to mix one bag Vibrating	—	6.5-7	—	19-20	12 to 14 U.S. QTS./75# BAG
Ramming	—	3-4	—	—	—
Casting	5-6	7-7.5	14-16	20-21	12 to 14 U.S QTS./75# BAG (1 QTS= 0.9463 liter)
Bag weight (pounds)	100	100	75	50	75 (1 lb. = 0.4535 kg)

Table 1-5
Maximum Service Temperture Classes of Castables

REGULAR OR HEAVY CASTABLES

Test Requirements	Classes of Alumina-Silica-Base Castables						
	Class A	Class B	Class C	Class D	Class E	Class F	Class G
Permanent linear shrinkage not more than 1.5% when fired for 5 hr. at these temperatures	1095°C (2000°F)	1260°C (2300°F)	1370°C (2500°F)	1480°C (2700°F)	1595°C (2900°F)	1705°C (3100°F)	1760°C (3200°F)

LIGHT OR INSULATING CASTABLES

Test Requirements	Classes of Insulating Castables				
	Class N	Class O	Class P	Class Q	Class V
Permanent linear shrinkage not more than 1.5% when fired for 5 hr. at these temperatures	925°C (1700°F)	1040°C (1900°F)	1150°C (2100°F)	1260°C (2300°F)	1760°C (3200°F)
Maximum bulk density lb/ft³ (kgm/m³) after drying at 220 to 230°F (105 to 110°C)	55 (881)	65 (1041)	75 (1201)	95 (1522)	105 (1682)

SOURCE: ASTM Chart C410-70

Chemical Analysis:	Kaolite 2500-LI	Kaolite 2600-LI
(Percentage fired basis, ASTM C 573-81)		
Alumina (Al_2O_3)	44.0	46.0
Silica (SiO_2)	35.0	36.0
Ferric oxide (Fe_2O_3)	0.9	1.4
Titanium oxide(TiO_2)	1.8	1.7
Calcium oxide (CaO)	17.0	14.0
Magnesium oxide (MgO)	0.2	0.2
Alkalies, as (Na_2O)	1.3	0.7

greater resistance to mechanical and thermal shocks and stresses; (2) make a gas- or airtight kiln; (3) provide a flat surface between irregular bricks; (4) prevent penetration of slag through the joints.

Mortars are classified into three groups: (1) ready mixed, air-setting mortar; (2) dry air-setting mortar; (3) dry heat-setting mortar.

High-temperature mortars are classified by ASTM according to the fire clay grade and to the service temperature:

1. Super-duty class: 1,600°C (2,910°F)
2. High-duty class: 1,500°C (2,730°F)
3. Medium-duty class: 1,400°C (2,550°F)

The requirements for mortar to be classified as being of ASTM quality, C178-47 include three standards: The mortar shall be free from grit and of such quality and workability that it will spread satisfactorily with a trowel, either as it comes from the container, or after a moderate amount of tempering with water. It must convert to a dipping consistency with the addition of water. It must remain easily workable for six months after purchase and opening of the container.

Air-setting mortars are finely ground aggregates, either wet or dry, and contain a bonding agent to give them air-setting properties at room temperature. Upon air drying, they set to a tough monolithic structure. Air-setting mortars develop maximum strength above 816°C (1,500°F) and also develop a strong bond throughout the entire brick joint, rather than near the hot force area. The air-setting bond, with the heat developed ceramic bond, ensures a structure of exceptional strength with well-bonded seams. The mortar thickness for insulation bricks should be 1/32" and no greater than 1/16" for hard brick.

Air-set wet mortars are packaged ready for troweling straight from the drum. In laying firebrick with troweled-on mortar, the joints must be maintained for proper bending strength. Approximately a 1/16" layer of mortar troweled on the bricks and tapped in place, with the excess troweled away, should produce the proper tightness.

Heat-setting mortars are composed of ground raw or calcined refractory materials similar to the bricks they are intended to mortar. Heat-setting mortar requires heat to develop a ceramic bond (sintering) between the bricks and it does not have air-setting (chemical bond) properties. It will provide joints with minimum shrinkage, since only the mortar that is close enough to the hot face, or reaches setting temperature, will actually bond. Heat-setting mortar is used in arches, domes, and walls where a lot of different kinds of bricks with different thermal characteristics are present. During the first firing the bricks are free to move and equalize internal stresses before the mortar reaches setting temperature.

When using 2600 and 2800 insulation bricks, the mortar must be thinned with clean water to a dip consistency that allows the brick to submerge one quarter of the way down and/or to a malted milk consistency, but not so thick as to ooze out when laid. When using 2000 and 2500 insulation bricks, which are lighter, the mortar must be thinned with clean water to a dip consistency that allows the brick to submerge one-third way down and/or to creamy consistency. Care must be taken to make the mortar thick enough as not to dry out before laying due to the porosity of the brick. To mix mortar to the proper dip or butter joint consistency, thoroughly dry-mix the mortar on a clean surface (in most cases the mortar is thoroughly mixed as it is in the bag). I recommend mixing the mortar with warm water one hour before

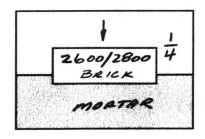 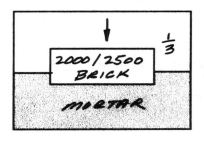

Fig. 1—13: *Proper mortar consistency for 2600/2800 bricks (left) and 2000/2500 bricks (right).*

using. For dip consistency, use 24 U.S. quarts per 100 lbs. of mortar; for butter joints, use 14 U.S. quarts per 100 lbs. of mortar. Always mix a full bag.

Pre-dunking 2000 and 2500 bricks in water before dipping in mortar could lead to problems. Most of the mortars use sodium silicate as the bonding agent and flux to fuse the mortar to the bricks at a certain temperature. The problem occurs when there is too much water in the mortar mixture or in the waterlogged pre-dunked bricks: Sodium silicate can leach out and form sodium crystals along the brick joints. When the kiln is fired for the first time to high temperature, the crystals form a salt glaze that can eat into the bricks, causing slagging in the joints. Building kilns in extremely humid conditions can cause the sodium silicate to leach to the surface. If this happens, scrape off crystals before firing — do not use a wet rag to wipe them off. I have found that Thermal Ceramics "smooth-set" mortar has a tendency to leach out sodium crystals even under normal conditions, and especially when there is an excess of water in the mortar or in the bricks. I have been told this problem has been resolved in the newer "smooth-set" mortar. "Air-set" mortar, which has a tendency to dry more quickly, provides less chance for the sodium silicate/cement to leach out. Most companies will recommend the proper mortar for each style brick.

Should insulation bricks be mortared or just laid up dry? I have seen both results and recommend mortaring. The trouble with dry laying is that individual bricks tend to spall, grind smaller (especially if 2600 and 2800 bricks are used), and move. In an arch, they may fall out in time. The main reason for dry laying is that it allows the kiln to be torn down or moved. It also makes for less work. However, I have found that I lost a lot of bricks to cracking and, when rebuilt, the kiln was worse for wear.

Caution: Do not re-mortar over dried mortar. Scrape off the old, then mortar again. When resealing a mortar can, it is advisable to pour a little water over the surface of the mortar first for long periods of "in-use time." Approximately 300-400 lbs. of mortar are required to thin trowel or dip joint 1,000 bricks.

It might be interesting to point out here that there are mortars made of only fire clay and grog that can do a sufficient job. I have used a fire clay (60 percent) and fire clay grog (40 percent) as a successful mortar. In 1962, in Domura, Japan, John Chappell used two parts sand, two parts grog (stoneware), and one part stoneware clay for a mortar when building his kilns out of an intermediate-duty fire clay brick. Richard Hotchkiss, in building his raw clay chamber kiln, used 50 percent Lincoln fireclay and 50 percent sand or basically made a slip out of his brick body. It might be noted that Richard's chamber kiln is still firing after thirty years. However, the bonding strength and durability of these mortars does not meet the requirements of standard prepared mortars.

SPECIAL MATERIALS

PLASTIC FIREBRICK

Plastic firebrick, sometimes called ramming mix or plastic moldable, is a refractory material that can be pounded or rammed into place (plastics have a greater workability than ramming mixes). Ease of application and extremely low shrinkage and expansion have made plastic firebrick a major material in the repair of damaged masonry arches or linings. Plastic firebrick can also be used to make special shapes on the job, simply by ramming it into place and shaping.

Fire clay plastics and ramming mixes are classified in Table 1-6. Highalumina plastics and ramming mixes are classified in seven types, as shown in Table 1-7.

CERAMIC FIBER PRODUCTS

Ceramic fibers (alumina-silica) are found in a variety of lightweight products, such as bulk fibers, blanket, strip, paper, mesh, spray mix, castables, ramming mix, tamping mix, cement (mortar), wet felt, board, and vacuum-cast shapes. Their main purpose is to provide insulation up to 1,260°C (2,300°F.) The major suppliers of these products are consolidating into larger and more efficient multi-national operations. For instance, Morgan Refractories of Great Britain now owns Babcock and Wilcox, and John Manville (Cerafelt, Cerablank, Cerafiber), which became Thermal Ceramics (Kao-

Table 1-6
ASTM classification of fire clay plastics and ramming mixes

ASTM Class	PCE Minimum	Shrinkage (linear maximum)
High Duty*	31	3%
Super Duty*	32 1/2	2.5%

*15% water calculated on basis of wet weight.

Table 1-7
ASTM Classification of High-Alumina Plastics and Ramming Mixes

ASTM Class (% alumina)	PCE Minimum	Alumina Content (%)
60	35	57.6-62.5
70	36	67.6-72.5
80	37	77.6-82.5
85	—	82.6-87.5
90	—	87.6-92.5
95	—	92.6-97.5
100	—	97.5 and over

wool, Saffil, Kao-bloc, Superwool and Supermax in the U.S., Australia, Europe, and South America); the old Carborundum company is now Unifrax (fiberfax); R.H.I., an Austrian Company, owns General Refractories, A.P. Green, North American refractories and Harbison-Walker Refractories. For the most part, these new companies make similar products with corresponding properties.

Among the furnace types using ceramic fiber products: air-heating furnaces, forging furnaces, coil-annealing furnaces, petrochemical process heaters, billet preheating furnaces, steel-casting stress-relieving furnaces, and brick kiln linings.

These fibers are produced by sending a high-pressure blast of steam against the molten alumina, silica, flux, and/or kaolin mixture 1,982°C (3,600°F) while it is being poured. The process produces a fluffy white ceramic fiber. The basic fiber has a normal use limit of 1,260°C (2,300°F) and a melting temperature of 1,760°C (3,200°F). The fiber lengths vary from an average of 4" to 10" long. One of the bulk fibers, Kaowool (made from alumina-silica kaolin), has excellent insulating qualities and high tensile strength, and it is extremely resistant to thermal shock. The chemical analysis of the ceramic fiber Kaowool is as follows:

alumina	Al_2O_3	45.1%
silica	SiO_2	51.9%
iron oxide	Fe_2O	31.3%
titania	TiO	21.7%
magnesia	MgO	trace
calcia	CaO	0.1%
alkalies as	Na_2O	0.2%
basic anhydride	B_2O	30.08%

The three interesting products that can be used by the potter are fiber blanket, fiber board, and fiber module.

Fiber blanket is made from the basic fiber in 3-, 4-, 6-, and 8-pound per-cubic-foot density, and comes in 2-foot and 4-foot widths, 25 feet long. The blankets come in standard 1/4", 1/2", 1", 1 1/2", and 2" thicknesses. Fiber blanket is a highly efficient insulator up to 1,093°C (2,000°F). Fiber blankets are more or less self-supporting, will not separate, sag or settle, have low heat storage and are extremely resistant to thermal shock. However, at 1,260°C (2,300°F) plus, they have approximately 5.2 percent linear shrinkage. Once the fiber blanket has been fired to cone 10, for instance, the surface shows marked embrittlement and sintering and damages easily: the edges have a tendency to curl toward the heat flow or flame direction. Newer high-temperature blankets can be used in reducing atmospheres and at 1,316°C (2,400°F) temperatures. How well these materials hold up will depend upon rapidity of firing, temperature, method of construction, and abuse. Linear shrinkage at 1,427°C (2,600°F) will be from 3-4 percent and could be greater if temperature rise is extremely fast. Thermal Ceramics has a new synthetic vitreous fiber blanket called Superwool 607 for continuous use with a limit of 1,832°F (1,000°C). This is a breakthrough in blanket technology for health reasons because it was designed for enhanced solubility in body fluids. According to the Health Hazards Summary statement provided by Thermal Ceramics, "Rats have been exposed 6 hours/day, 5 days/week during two years at an average concentration of 200 fibers/cc (200 to 300 times higher than the concentrations found in manufacturing plants). Preliminary findings indicate: no formation of fibrous tissue; no significantly elevated tumor incidence over the negative (air) control group; and reversible cellular changes similar to the effects observed after the inhalation of inert dust."

The new Superwool 607 is a calcium-magnesium-silicate raw material. For kilns operating around bisque temperature (1,000°C) this blanket can ensure a health safety factor not found in other fiber products. Another similar synthetic vitreous fiber blanket from Thermal Ceramics called Supermax 612 blanket operates at a higher temperature 2,195°F (1,200°C), but does not have the same health characteristics as the Superwool 607 blanket. It will be only a matter of time before all of these products will have the health factor of the Superwool 607, but until then follow the safety precautions listed on the carton the material comes in or ask for the Material Safety Data Sheet (MSDS).

Fiber board is vacuum-molded from the basic fibers into rigid boards. These boards come in 2-by-3-foot panels, running from 1/2" to 1 1/2" thick. Depending upon the composition of the basic fiber, some boards will handle temperatures up to cone 10. The higher the board or blanket density, the higher the service temperature will be.

Fiber modules are fabricated from fiber blanket into standard 12" x 12" blocks, 3" to 8" thick and also 16" x 16" blocks, 3" to 12" thick. There are 24" square modules and split sizes such as 12" x 24", 6" x 12" etc. available. They can be made from pre-cut 12" strips, edge grained, or a single long strip, accordion pleated and edge grained, then slightly compressed by a gauze-type wrap into blocks. Most modules are compressed by one-third, then banded to hold the compression for installation. Fiber modules have a service temperature range up to 1,538°C (2,800°F). The blocks were designed to improve on blanket and board applications in kilns.

Almost all refractory fiber products, when fired to temperatures above 1,093°C (2,000°F), will have excessive linear shrinkage, from 2.3 percent to over 5 percent at 1,316°C (2,400°F). Linear shrinkage is due to the crystallization of the fiber at high temperatures. Fiber products are recommended for a clean oxidation atmosphere. Atmospheres containing heavy reduction, fuel residues from wood, coal, or oil, or volatile glaze materials can cause greater linear shrinkage.

The linear shrinkage of Kaowool M Board, as shown in Fig. 1-14, is typical of most refractory and silica fiber blankets and boards. There are a few new products that have a better shrinkage and high-temperature ratio. One of these is Johns-Manville (now Thermal Ceramics). Fiberchrome, which at 1,482°C (2,700°F), shrinks 3.7 percent and has less sintering

and embrittlement of its surface than have the refractory and silica fiber products. A typical chemical analysis (percentages) for Fiberchrome is:

SlO_2	55.0
Al_2O_3	40.5
CR_2O	34.0
FE_2O_3	0.21
NA_2O	0.15

Fiberchrome and similar products would be more advantageous for high fire and a reduction atmosphere.

Among the advantages listed by manufacturers of fiber blankets and boards are low thermal conductivity, light weight, low heat storage, mechanical and thermal shock resistance, faster cool-downs and heat-ups, and easy repair.

My personal experience, and that of other potters, has uncovered a number of disadvantages, as well:

— Sintering and embrittlement of the surface, which is extremely open to abrasion and impact.

— Once fired, the loss of resiliency leads to sealing problems with the door, especially when using blanket products.

— High linear shrinkage, which causes all joints to open up and curl into the chamber.

— High cost of material compared to IFB refractories for the same high temperature (cone 10).

— Surface of the fiber blanket tends to crack and develop tears.

— Can cause extreme irritation of the skin, throat, and lungs.

Table 1-8 compares a 7" fiber kiln wall to an IFB 7" kiln wall. There is little advantage in using fiber insulation rather than regular insulation bricks at 1,204°C (2,200°F).

The methods of using fiber blanket, module block, and board in construction of kilns can be found in Chapter 2.

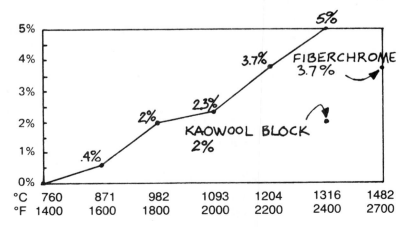

Fig. 1—14: Shrinkage of Kaowool M Board and Johns-Manvill Fiberchrome. (From Babcock/Wilcox, Kaowool-M-Fiber Product Catalogue, Oct. 1, 1974).

Castables, ramming mixes and tamping mixes are examples of other fiber materials that have kiln-building possibilities. Castables contain an inorganic hydraulic binder which, when tempered with water, develops structural strength and retains its cast form. The amount of water required for the desired density should be added slowly to the dry material and mixed until thoroughly wet. It can then be poured and finished as other castables, however, at least 18 hours of air-curing time is needed, after which the cast can be force-dried at temperatures up to 2,040°C (400°F).

Ramming and tamping mixes also contain an inorganic binder which achieves bonding strength through drying. This material can be used to form small arches, and catenary arches in small kilns. The material is rammed or tamped into the catenary or arch mold form to a thickness of 2" or greater, then allowed to air cure. The average range of rammed density varies between 25 lbs. per cubic foot and 38 lbs. per cubic foot.

If a kiln is greater than 9 cubic feet, whether catenary arch or sprung arch, the ramming or tamping mix should be reinforced with a steel mesh embedded in the ramming mix. Also, the thickness of the catenary or arch should be increased to at least 4" to ensure proper strength and structural support. Consult the manufacturer or his representative as to the feasibility of using materials in the designated kiln size and configuration.

Table 1-8
Comparison of fiber wall to insulation brick wall in a kiln with hot face temperature of 1204°C (2200°F).

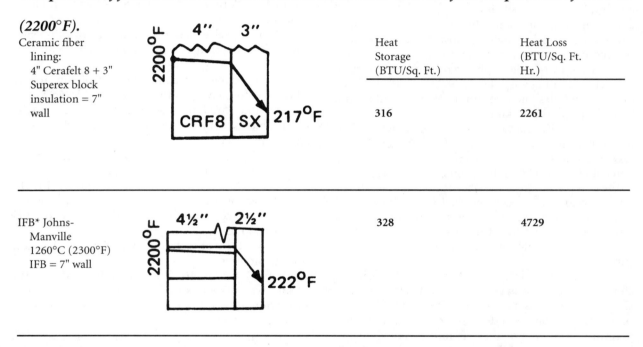

	Heat Storage (BTU/Sq. Ft.)	Heat Loss (BTU/Sq. Ft. Hr.)
Ceramic fiber lining: 4" Cerafelt 8 + 3" Superex block insulation = 7" wall	316	2261
IFB* Johns-Manville 1260°C (2300°F) IFB = 7" wall	328	4729

*If JM-20 (1093°C; 2000°F) back-up rowlock brick were used, the 7" IFB wall would be a better insulator.

Chapter 2

Methods of Kiln Construction

The laying of firebrick in kiln construction is a specialized masonry skill. There are rules that must be followed to ensure a strong, monolithic structure that will function efficiently at high temperatures and be durable.

STRAIGHT-WALL CONSTRUCTION

There are three vital rules in straight-wall construction: (1) An unsupported wall 4 1/2" thick cannot be higher than 3 feet; (2) an unsupported wall 9" thick, tied by alternate header and stretcher courses, cannot be higher than 8 feet; (3) an unsupported wall 13 1/2" thick, tied by alternate header and stretcher courses, cannot be higher than 12 feet.

There are five basic methods of laying straight walls: header course, stretcher course, alternate header and stretcher, rowlock course, and soldier course.

HEADER COURSE

In a header course, bricks are laid lengthwise across the wall with the 2 1/2" x 9" side butting against the next brick (Fig. 2-1). All header courses develop a reasonably stable wall with minimum hot face exposure (4 1/2" x 2 1/2") and the back side of the brick subject to relatively low temperature. Header courses are good for bricks facing near temperature limits.

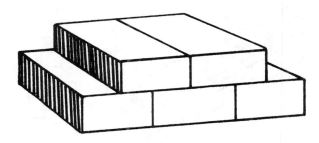

Fig. 2—1: *Header course, with bricks laid across the wall.*

A wall laid mainly of headers, which normally consists of three or four rows of header courses to one row of stretcher courses (Fig. 2-2), has the advantages of an all-header wall but has greater rigidity.

Fig. 2—2: *Alternating four header rows with one stretcher row gives greater rigidity.*

STRETCHER COURSE

Stretcher courses are laid lengthwise, running with the wall so that the 2 1/2" x 9" surface becomes the hot face (Fig. 2-3). An all-stretcher wall is not rigid and is not recommended for over 3 feet in height unless it has other means of support.

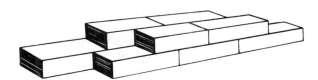

Fig. 2—3: *Stretcher course, with bricks running along the wall.*

A wall laid mainly of stretchers, which normally consists of three to four rows of stretcher courses to one header row, as shown in Fig. 2-4, is a much stronger wall and has an important advantage. In a kiln where bricks are subject to slagging or other erosive action, such as occurs in a wood-fired kiln or salt-glaze kiln, the exterior face can be easily repaired by replacing the 4 1/2" x 9" hot-face brick with another, or a 4 1/2" skin wall (ram mix) tied into the remaining bricks.

ALTERNATE HEADER AND STRETCHER COURSES

Alternate headers and stretchers in walls of 9" and 13 1/2" thicknesses are extremely stable. This is considered good practice in bricklaying.

Fig. 2—4: *Alternating four stretchers with one header makes it easy to replace a hot-face brick.*

It is also considered good practice to have alternating joints on each row, which means no joints run in a straight line above each other (Fig. 2-5).

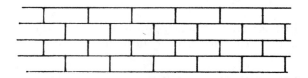

Fig. 2—5: *Alternating joints produce a stable wall.*

This alternate header and stretcher wall is sometimes referred to as "English bond" and is the most common method of construction using dense firebrick. To begin a 9" wall, a 9" x 6" large brick, a 4 1/2" bat and straight bricks are used to set up the joint pattern for subsequent rows (Fig. 2-6).

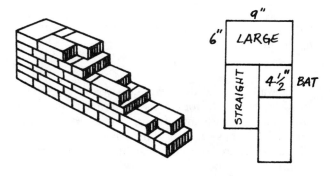

Fig. 2—6: *Layout for base of 9" alternate header and stretcher wall.*

ROWLOCK AND SOLDIER COURSES

In a rowlock course, bricks are laid on their sides (2 1/2" x 9"), side-to-side or end-to-end (Fig. 2-7). In a soldier course, bricks are laid on end (4 1/2" x 2 1/2"), side-to-side or end-to-end (Fig. 2-8).

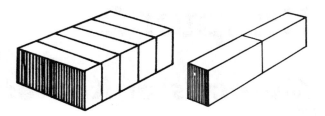

Fig. 2—7: *Rowlock course; (left) side-to-side; (right) end-to-end.*

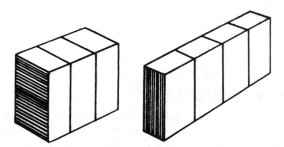

Fig. 2—8: *Soldier course: (left) side-to-side; (right) end-to-end.*

WALL CONSTRUCTION
13 1/2" WALLS

There are three usual methods for laying 13 1/2" walls:

1. One may use standard 9" x 4 1/2" x 2 1/2" bricks with 9" x 6" x 2 1/2" bricks. The 13 1/2" wall (shown in Fig. 2-9) has no joints running through it. Also (shown in Fig. 2-9) alternating header/stretcher with stretcher/header, use 9" x 6" x 2 1/2" brick for staggering joints.

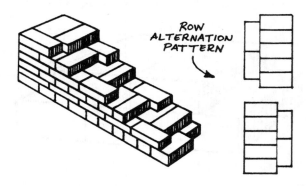

Fig. 2—9: *Method 1 for laying a 13 1/2" wall.*

2. In the second method, the wall is laid with four rows of hot-face stretchers backed by headers, and one row of headers, which, in turn, is backed with stretchers (Fig. 2-10). The advantage of this construction is that is makes for easier repair.

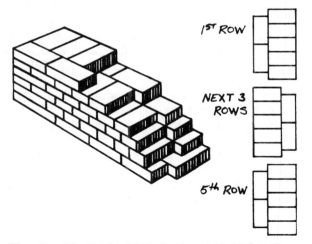

Fig. 2—10: *Method 2 for laying a 13 1/2" wall.*

3. In the third method of laying a 13 1/2" wall, every fifth-row header course has a 13 1/2" brick in it, with alternating joints on each row.

This type of construction makes an extremely stable wall that is easy to repair. It is also good for setting sprung arches.

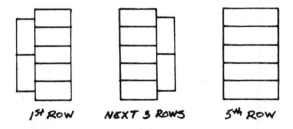

Fig. 2—11: *Method 3 for laying a 13 1/2" wall.*

FLUES

When building flues into the kiln wall, the normal distance between flues will be 9", or one brick. The average size of flues will be one brick standing on end (9" x 4 1/2"). (If using the 2 1/2" brick series, four rows of bricks will cause the flue holes to be 4 1/2" x 10". Three bricks of the 2 1/2" series will be sufficient in almost all cases; however, it is better to err in having flues too large, rather than too small.) All flue holes should be built on a header course, with the flue opening directly above a header (Fig. 2-12). The reason is that the header brick becomes a knockout brick, in case the flue is too small. In building the 9" flue separator, alternate header and stretcher courses should be used.

CURVED WALLS

Curved walls are found in domed, downdraft, and beehive kilns. The reason curved walls are used is that they are much stronger and more stable than a straight wall. The curve creates a wedging action, which keeps the brick from falling inward. The only limiting factor on height is the compression strength of the bottom bricks. This is why many early kilns with walls 18-22 1/4" thick (in some cases up to 3 to 5 feet) could carry the thrust of the dome without reinforcing supports.

Materials choices for curved walls:
— 4 1/2" wall thickness-circle (arch brick can be used, but is not recommended)
— 9" wall thickness-key (or combination of circle and key brick)
— 13 1/2" and greater wall thickness-key (or combination of circle and key brick; wedge bricks not recommended)

Curved walls are laid with the same alternating joints straight walls (Fig. 2-13).

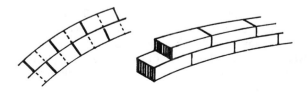

Fig. 2—13: *Joints are alternated in curved wall construction.*

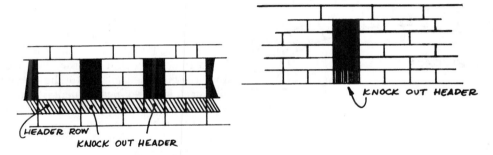

Fig. 2—12: *All flues are built on header courses.*

DIVISION OR COMMON WALLS

A division wall is the common wall between two chambers. In a normal chamber wall, the temperature drops from the inside out, whereas a common wall may be subject to hot-face temperature on both sides. Thus, the division must be made of good quality refractory material. The common wall also supports the thrust of two arches (Fig. 2-14).

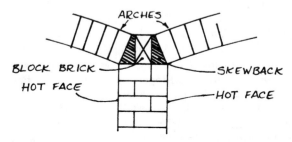

Fig. 2—14: *A common wall supports the thrust of two arches and has two hot faces.*

It is good practice to build common walls 4 1/2" greater in thickness than the ordinary kiln wall; and a common wall should never be less than the width of the two skewbacks used.

ARCHES

SPRUNG ARCHES

Kiln arches perform two duties — forming roofs for the kiln chamber and forming doors and openings. Sprung describes the arch of a cylinder, and is the most common arch used in kiln building.

The arch rests on a skewback on both ends. Skewbacks determine the arch rise and tie the arch to the wall (Fig. 2-15). The force of the arch is down and out against the walls. If the skewbacks fail, the arch will move; therefore, the walls and skewbacks must be rigidly constructed. Standard sizes have been developed for arch, wedge, and key bricks, because dense firebricks are molded to size and fired, thus they cannot be easily machined. These special sizes are called No.

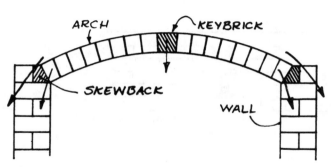

Fig. 2—15: *An arch rests on skewbacks, exerting its force down and out.*

1, No. 2, and No. 3, and, when used by themselves, turn a circle. Arches are built using a combination of No. 1, 2, and 3 bricks with straights to turn almost any given circle. For the combinations of arches and straights in a given radius, see Estimating Firebrick Arches in Appendix.

The following list gives shapes and combinations of brick for the arch thickness specified:

— **4 1/2"**: Arch brick, or combination of arch and straight.

— **6 3/4" or 7 1/2"**: Large 9" arch, or combination of large 9" arch and large 9" straight.

— **9"**: Wedge brick, or a combination of wedge and straight. (Construction of key brick, or combination of key and straight, is not common, as the load is placed on the narrow face. This construction is only used when special conditions make it desirable.)

— **Over 9"**: Necessarily constructed of special wedge brick. However, 13 1/2" wedge bricks are standard from some manufacturers.

There are four major types of sprung arches: Bonded arches, ring arches, ribbed arches, and straight arches.

Bonded arches. The bonded arch is the most commonly used arch and is considered the best. The joints are staggered, tying the whole arch into a single unit (Fig. 2-16). If one or several bricks fail in a bonded arch, the bricks on either side absorb the load and the arch remains in place.

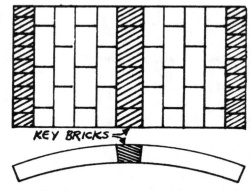

Fig. 2—16: *Joints are staggered in a bonded arch.*

Ring arches: The ring arch is, as the name implies, one where each row of bricks across the arch is a ring of brick (Fig. 2-17). If one brick in the ring fails, the whole ring drops. It is difficult to replace a ring of brick. I used a ring arch on a chamber kiln and found that, during firing, the rings expanded open almost 1/2". Perhaps if the kiln had been tied together with steel, it would have helped. A bonded arch, however, doesn't have this problem. The main advantage of a ring arch is the ease of laying, especially when using a combination of standard shapes.

Ribbed arches: The ribbed arch is primarily used in open-hearth furnaces. The ribs give the arch stabil-

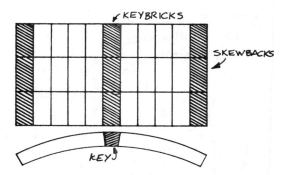

Fig. 2—17: *Ring arches expand during fire and, if one brick fails, the whole ring fails.*

ity and strength after the intermediate bricks have eroded (Fig. 2-18).

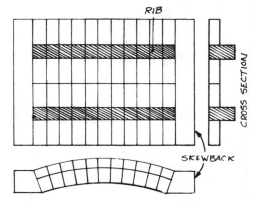

Fig. 2—18: *Ribs provide stability and strength against erosion.*

Straight arches: The straight arch is a bonded arch made with standard 9" x 4 1/2" x 2 1/2" straight bricks and is used when one doesn't have arch brick available or when one wants to produce a freeform arch (see Fig. 2-19).

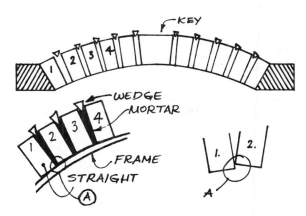

Fig. 2—19: *Proper laying and wedging technique for a sprung arch.*

The important factor in using straights to make a sprung arch is to set the corners of the brick carefully (see Fig. 2-19, point A). Brick 1 is laid onto the arch frame. The inside edge of brick 2 must be above and touching the outside edge of brick 1. In other words, each brick acts as a lip for the brick on top of it. The arch is laid from both sides simultaneously, then the key brick is cut to fit. The arch is sprung off the form by starting at the bottom and working up both sides, driving wedges (bits and pieces of small refractories) into the gaps between the brick rows and spreading them apart, while driving the bottoms into a tighter fit. If, however, one over wedges or drives too big a wedge too deep, it will part the bricks on the bottom. This could also result in weakened brick. When mortaring the arch bricks, care should be taken to apply the mortar in a wedge form, thus helping to set up the proper wedge.

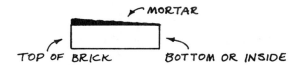

Fig. 2—20: *Applying mortar to form a wedge.*

The key brick must be pounded down below its neighboring bricks, thus ensuring a strong key (Fig. 2-21).

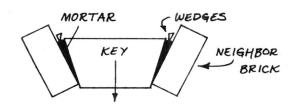

Fig. 2—21: *The key should be forced below neighboring bricks.*

SUSPENDED ARCHES

A suspended arch is mechanically held together and supported in place, and does not tie directly into the side walls. The support is usually a metal framework fitting into holes or grooves, or around specially shaped bricks, and held together by rods, pipe, tee bar, and so forth (Fig. 2-22). The most common thicknesses for suspended arches are 4 1/2" and 9".

The advantages of using a suspended arch are readily seen in top-loading electric or gas kilns. Repair to these arches is quite easy, unless sidewall bracing is required. Also, it is easy to accommodate thermal expansion, both horizontally and vertically, which reduces break-causing stress in the bricks.

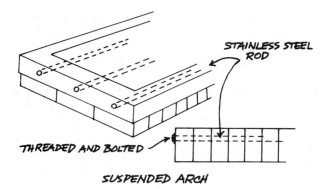

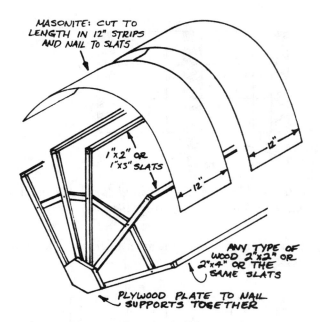

Fig. 2—22: *Metal framework for a suspended arch.*

The disadvantage is that it usually costs more for the additional metal framework and connection rod assembly than is the case with a sprung arch.

CORBEL ARCHES

A type of arch seldom mentioned is the corbel. This particular arch can be used to span portholes or flue holes where other lintel shapes are too small (Fig. 2-23). Use the corbel arch to span up to 24".

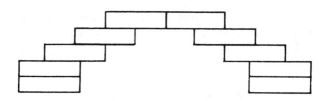

Fig. 2—23: *Corbel arches can be used to span flues or portholes.*

I have seen small, 10- to 16-cubic-foot kilns with corbel arches. This is not a good practice for the following reasons: (1) structural instability; (2) the uneven inside surface causes irregular heating and flame turbulence; (3) bricks are subject to greater erosion; and (4) the design is generally poor.

FRAME CONSTRUCTION

To begin building an arch, one must have a wood frame, which can be constructed in a number of ways. The first method produces a one-use arch form that is good for freeform arch construction (Fig. 2-24). Another method produces a reusable arch form for standard skewback arches (Fig. 2-25).

To make an arch support for a standard skewback arch using a featheredge, you need to know two things: the span (the distance between the two supporting walls) and the rise of the arch (Fig. 2-26). A featheredge will give a rise of 1 1/2" per foot of span.

Fig. 2—24: *Building a one-use arch form.*

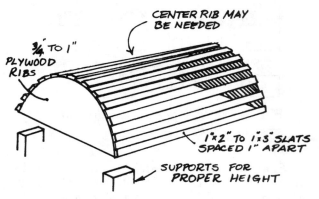

Fig. 2—25: *Building a reusable arch form.*

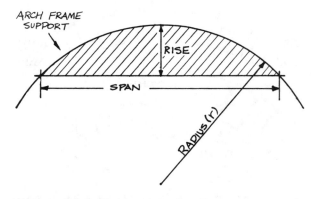

Fig. 2—26: *Support for a standard skewback, using a featheredge.*

Use this formula to find the radius of the circle:

$$1.0625 \times span = radius\ (r)$$

A catenary arch usually has a rise-to-span ratio that exceeds the 1 1/2"-3" range considered good practice. The catenary arch is formed by first deciding upon the span, then forming the curve with a perfectly flexible, inextensible cord suspended by its end (Fig. 2-27). The catenary arch is self-supporting. It contains the walls and sprung arch all in one curve.

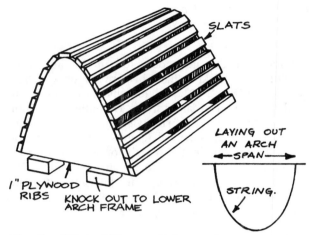

Fig. 2—27: *Building a self-supporting catenary arch.*

DETERMINING ARCH

Because a standard featheredge can be used as the skewback, the minimum rise for an arch is usually 1 1/2" per foot of span. Anything less can result in structural difficulty. The maximum rise has generally been set at 3" per foot of span. The greater the rise of the arch per foot of span, the sturdier the arch will be. I have raised an arch with a 6" rise per foot of span with very good results, so no hard-and-fast rule can be applied.

When using dense bricks, standard-size arch, wedge, and key brick can be used in combination with straights to turn any given radius. Insulating bricks, however, are sized and shaped after firing to a given radius, thus simplifying construction and increasing strength because of the radius involved. Standard shapes can be used, which reduces the cost.

DOMES AND CROWNS

Domes and crowns differ from sprung arches in that an arch describes a portion of a cylinder, while a dome or crown describes a portion of a sphere. A crown describes two sphere arches that meet at dead top center, but originate from different axes. A dome has a single radius (See Fig. 2-28). A crown generally has a flue in the top, while a dome is usually plugged. The rule of thumb for the rise of domes and crowns is 2 1/2"-3" per foot of span. Bricks are laid the 4 1/2" way.

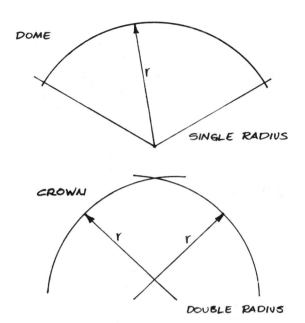

Fig. 2—28: *A dome or crown describes a portion of a sphere.*

EXPANSION JOINTS

During the heating and cooling of a kiln, firebrick will expand vertically and horizontally along a wall, and at a 90° angle to the wall. Each foot of refractories along the wall will expand from 1/16" to 3/32" when heated and cooled. If a kiln is built without an allowance for expansion, the bricks will destroy themselves through mechanical and structural spalling. In many cases, kilns with steel frameworks have been built with no tolerance for expansion and contraction. The walls have buckled, sagged, and cracked, and the frame has bent and bowed.

In free-standing kilns, such as a chamber kiln, expansion joints are not used, except perhaps when the side wall is fitted to the arch. Corner joints and joints where the common wall ties into the side wall are mortared with just a bit more space between bricks. The walls are then free to expand as a structural unit, since they are not tied by steel. If such a kiln is reinforced with tie rods, the rods should be bolted taut when the kiln has reached temperature. This allows for normal expansion.

In an enclosed steel frame, or when a kiln is backed by rigid steel, the bricks must be given proper expansion joints (Figs. 2-29 and 2-30).

Figure 1/16" gap per 1 foot of wall. If the kiln wall is 5 feet long, then the gap should be 5/32" on each end. However, do not have the expansion joint going through the wall but built into the corner joint (Fig. 2-31).

In an insulating firebrick kiln within a steel framework, the expansion joint can be eliminated

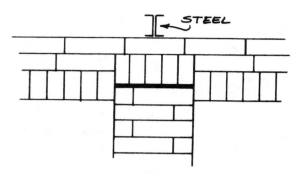

Fig. 2—29: *Division wall expansion joint (hard bricks).*

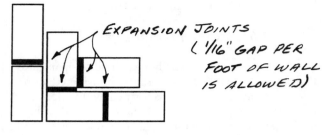

Fig. 2—31: *A gap of 1/16" per foot of wall is allowed. The gap can be filled with a 1/4" fiber pad mortared to the brick end.*

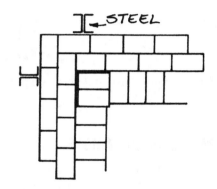

Fig. 2—30: *Floating corner expansion joint (hard bricks). Note that only the 9" hot-face row requires an expansion joint, which is filled with expansion-joint board or a ceramic-fiber filler.*

completely with walls under 4 feet and less and have a flexible wall backing like sheet metal or expanded steel mesh (Fig. 2-32). Wall lengths of over 5 feet can, and in most cases should, use 1/4" fiber pads mortared to the end of the brick when building the corner joints. However, 5-feet wall lengths in a flexible frame, if built properly (not too tight or wedged into the frame), can get by with no expansion joints. Walls well over 5 feet long use vertical expansion cuts in the wall, filled with a ceramic fiber product such as wool, strip, blanket, or board (Fig. 2-33).

SKEWBACKS

Arch stability is dependent upon the rise and thickness of the arch and structural support of the skewbacks. Skewbacks can be built from the standard 9" series shape. A rise of 1 1/2" per foot of span is obtained when the skewback is formed by standard 9" featheredges of the 2 1/2" series. A rise of 1.608"

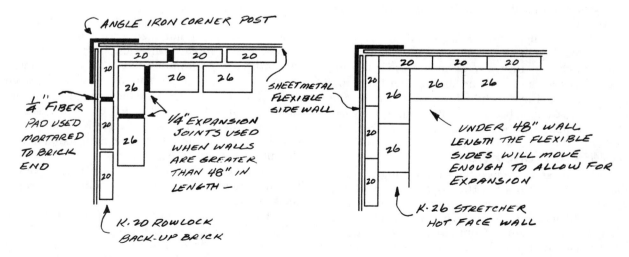

Fig. 2—32: *Expansion joint is eliminated in an IFB kiln with steel framework, with a wall 4" or less.*

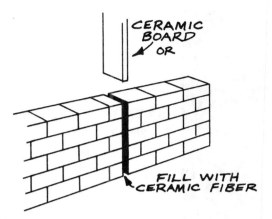

Fig. 2—33: *Vertical expansion cuts are filled with ceramic board or fiber.*

(19/32") per foot is obtained when the included angle of the arch is 60°. Special skewbacks for arches with included angles of 60° are available in sizes 4 1/2" thick, 9" thick, and 13 1/2" thick (Fig. 2-34). A rise of 2.302" (2 5/16") per foot is obtained when standard 9" side and end skews of the 2 1/2" series are used.

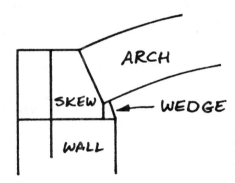

Fig. 2—34: *Special skewback for 60° arch.*

The skewback is the structural member that transmits the stress of the arch to the supporting wall, and to the framework, if any. When the skewback, wall, and arch form an acute angle, steel supports must be used to hold the stress of the arch and the skewback in place (Fig. 2-35A). In Fig. 2-35B, the

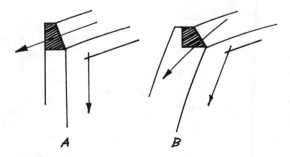

Fig. 2—35: *Distribution of stress created by the arch.*

angle is greater and the arch stress is brought down the slanted wall. It remains self supporting.

The placement of the skewbacks is very important to the success of the arch. If straight bricks are used to build a skewback, the lip of the throw brick (first brick off the skewback) should be resting on the wall (Figs. 2-36 and 2-37).

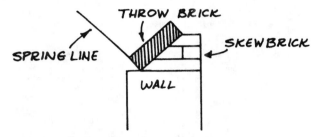

Fig. 2—36: *Lip of the throw brick must rest on the wall.*

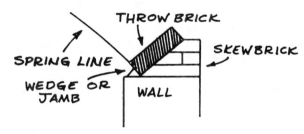

Fig. 2—37: *A wedge fits under the throw brick.*

In both these cases, the throw brick catches the wall. In Fig. 2-37, a wedge or joint (specially cut to fit) fits under the throw brick. The reason for catching the throw brick on the wall is to prevent slippage. It is considered bad practice to have the spring line of the arch flush with the wall (Fig. 2-38).

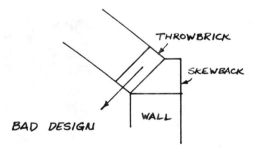

Fig. 2—38: *In this poor design, the spring line of the arch is flush with the wall.*

RAW CLAY CONSTRUCTION

Raw bricks are made in a single or multiple wood-press mold. A long wood trough can be made with piano hinged sides with sizing slots for the cutting wire to slide through to cut the brick sizes. The

Fig 2—39: *Brick making in trough mold, cut and sun dried.*

mold should be at least as long as the kiln width. Clay is packed into the mold, then sliced, the sides dropped and the bricks removed to dry. Various sizes can be made to conform to the kiln's dimensions. When the bricks are bone dry, they can be laid using soft fireclay brick mix as the mortar to level and seal the joints. The mortar is not in a troweling or dipping consistency, but soft, soft clay. Then follow the same construction techniques as using regular brick.

In the illustrated six-chamber raw brick kiln built in 1971 by Richard Hotchkiss, Rimas VisGirda and a workshop group used a Lincoln 60 fireclay base (50 percent — a California fireclay, at Lincoln, California) and coarse sand (50 percent) for the brick clay. Three sizes of raw clay blocks were made: 9" x 10" x 18", 9" x 10" x 9", and 9" x 5" x 5". The kiln was started with the uppermost chamber 6, building up the front and back walls to the desired height, an arch form was installed. At the same time the arch was being laid, the lower chamber front wall was begun and the process continued down to the first chamber. Since the blocks are dry, they could be readily shaped by an axe to follow the curve of the arch form and to make the key block row. Generous amounts of soft mortar were used to level, tilt and seal the joints of the blocks. Each successive arch was strapped with rope to keep from spreading until the next arch was finished which buttressed the upper arch. The side walls were bricked in leaving a door on one side and stoke holes and spy holes on both sides. Average chamber size was 5' x 5' x 6' tall. As each chamber was finished, a fire was started in them to dry them out, and the two upper chambers were being fired to bisque before the rest of the kiln was finished. The chimney was built with commercial firebricks to 12' and then 18' of a scavenged piece of hydraulic water pipe was placed on the brick work. Caution must be taken in the initial firing so as not to blow out the blocks from a rapid temperature increase. The kiln is still being fired by Hotchkiss and Tom Orr.

Fig 2—40: *Start of straight wall with flue holes.*

Fig 2—41: *Soft thick mortar, especially on arch.*

Fig 2—42: *Building arch following form cut to fit.*

Fig 2—44: *Constructing side wall, notice rope brace.*

Fig 2—43: *Setting key bricks cut to fit with an axe.*

Photos provided by Rimas VisGirda

Fig 2—45: *Building stoke hole and entrance door.*

Fig 2—46: *6th, 5th, 4th chambers, building down.*

Fig 2—47: *Bisquing in upper chambers, building below.*

Fig 2—48: *Firebox firing, May '97.*

CASTABLE DOME CONSTRUCTION

Using a castable like Kaolite 2,500 or 2,600 LI is relatively an easy procedure with the most important factor being the proper mixing of the material for a minimum of six minutes into the "ball-in-hand" consistency. The placement of the individual batch must be done within 30 minutes. Each subsequent batch follows the same time requirements and can be placed butting next to or on top of the previous batch. The casting must be done in one session.

Preparation of the walls to receive the castable is no different than that for an arch. The transition from the vertical wall to the castable is done by using a skewback section. This can be done by wedging bricks to slope in for two to three rows with last row being a featheredge laid down or perhaps with arch bricks. It is best to use a 2,500 or 2,600 IFB for the featheredge and the brick below.

sand for the final smoothing and shaping. Plastic is used to cover the dirt form and the skew brick to receive the castable. Remember, no porous surface must come into contact with the castable.

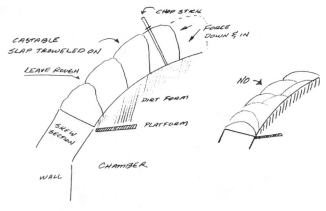

Fig. 2— 51: *Castable slap troweling.*

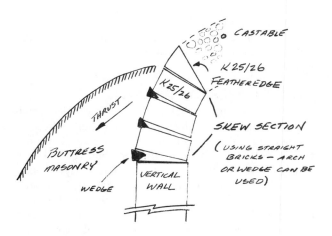

Fig. 2—49: *Wall section.*

Next, a platform is built up to the featheredge level using sufficient bracing and material to carry a lot of weight, but also easily collapsible. The irregular dome form is shaped with dirt, then capped with wet

When the castable reaches a proper consistency it is hand or trowel slapped down onto the form, starting at the skewbrick and working all around the form and then laying up. Always keep the receiving edge slanted in and down so it can catch the next layer. Build the thickness as you apply the castable. Do not make a thin layer then add more on top the next time. Do not overwork it, it will slump down with too much laboring on it. For most castings covering 10 to 12 feet in diameter, a 6" thickness is best. For small diameters, a 4 1/2" thickness is adequate. Chopsticks are a good thickness indicator. Do not smooth the surface with a trowel at any time.

Once the casting is completed, cover with damp towels and cover over with plastic. Let cure for 24 hours and then uncover. It is now ready for a capping mix (dirt, sawdust, cement mixture like an adobe mix). Before the platform is removed, make sure the

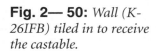
Fig. 2— 50: *Wall (K-26IFB) tiled in to receive the castable.*

side walls are extremely well buttressed with masonry. Once the platform is removed and the dirt dug out, the side walls must hold the weight of the casting. The casting will look rough on the outside, which is normal. It will be smooth on the inside because of the plastic, until the first firing, then it will resemble a course brick.

I have not used expansion joints in casting irregular domes, but relied on the material to stress itself. (Perhaps this is not the recommended procedure by ceramic engineers, but it has worked for me.)

Fig. 2— 52: *Slap troweling castable onto the form. Notice ledge to receive next batch.*

FIBER CONSTRUCTION

The construction of a fiber-lined kiln is relatively simple. However, there are several major factors to consider when working with fiber, one is shrinkage. At 1,093°C (2,000°F), fiber blanket or board will shrink by a factor of from 3.5 percent to 5 percent. Thus, special care must be taken in the design stages of a kiln that will be fired to cone 10 (1,305°C; 2,381°F). The metal shell, stud pattern, layering procedures, and choice of materials must all work together. Another factor the potter or kiln builder must keep in mind is the higher cost per cubic foot of a fiber-lined kiln over that of a brick kiln. Also, general maintenance must be performed more frequently and is more costly than maintaining insulation firebrick (IFB); the durability of fiber interiors against knocks and abrasions is considerably less than that of IFB.

(**Caution**: Fiber irritates the skin, eyes, nose, throat, and lungs, not only during construction, but also when loading and repairing the kiln. Always wear a dust respirator and protective clothing and gloves. Follow manufacturers' recommendations when using fiber materials.)

ANCHORING SYSTEM LAYOUT

The most important factor in fiber construction is the design of the kiln frame or metal shell to accommodate the welded stud anchoring system. This system is laid out to meet the hot-face blanket or board laying scheme without regard for the underlying blankets or boards used as backup. In most cases, the stud anchors are welded to a fabricated metal shell in recommended spacing for certain temperatures. Instead of a metal shell, a metal frame with metal spars corresponding to the stud spacing scheme, or even a flexboard backing instead of metal spars, could be used. Flexboard backing requires a stud anchor that screws into place instead of being welded. The anchor studs used per square foot should follow manufacturer's instructions. Examples are given in Tables 2-1 and 2-2.

Fig. 2—53: *Finishing the casting.*

Table 2-1
Thermal Ceramics

	24"-wide blanket	48"-wide blanket
Wall	1.5	1.0
Roof up to 1900°F	1.8	1.5
Roof, 1900°F	2.3	1.9

Table 2—2
Johns-Manville anchor stud spacing in inches and corresponding studs required per square foot.

	1010°C to 1204°C (1850°F to 2200°F)	1204°C (2200°F) and over
Wall	12" (1.56 studs/sq. ft.)	9" (2.1 studs/sq. ft.)
Roof	9" (2.1 studs/sq. ft.)	6" (4.0 studs/sq. ft.)

Vertical walls will generally require fewer studs per square foot than the roof. Also, the higher the firing temperature, the more studs required per square foot. However, the distance between the stud and the edge of the blanket or board should be 2 3/4" in each case. The stud anchor system best suited to stoneware temperatures is shown in Figs. 2-54 and 2-55.

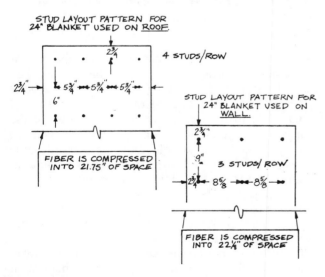

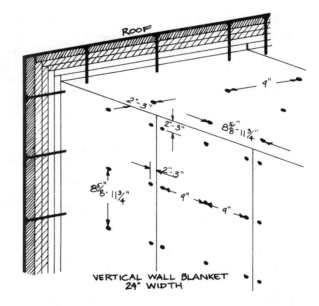

Fig. 2—55: *High-temperature layout for walls, based on 22 3/4", with an allowance of 1.2" for shrinkage.*

Fig. 2—54: *High-temperature layout for roof, based on a 22 3/4" measurement; allowance for 1.2" of shrinkage.*

Most fiber product manufacturers say to use a 23 1/2" measurement in the layout pattern for the studs. However, if the fiber material used for high-temperature firing (cone 10) has a shrinkage rate of 3.7 percent to 5 percent or more, then using the 23 1/2" measurement results in the joints opening up 1 1/2" or more. This will tear the fiber and cause holes around the middle anchor studs, as well as along the edge studs, which shortens the life of the studs and fiber material. Thus, depending upon the material used and its shrinkage rate (test fire your material to find out), use a measurement from 22 3/4" to 23" to allow for shrinkage.

ANCHOR STUDS

The anchor stud perhaps best suited for high-temperature firings is the threaded ceramic anchor from Johns-Manville, now Thermal Ceramics. A metal threaded stud base is welded to the frame and the ceramic stud screws onto the stud base (Fig. 2-56). The ceramic anchor washer slips onto the stud and turns 90° to lock. This system is recommended for temperatures up to 1,427°C (2,600°F).

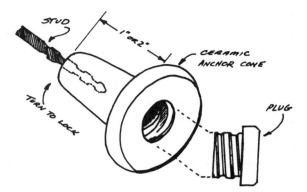

Fig. 2—58: *Kao-Lok ceramic stone anchor.*

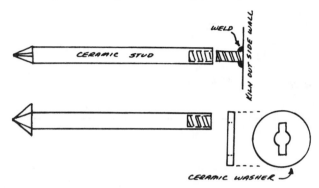

Fig. 2—56: *Johns-Manville threaded ceramic stud anchor system.*

Thermal Ceramics' Kao-Loc high-temperature anchoring system is similar in design, but the ceramic stud slides into a metal sleeve base and is pinned. The metal sleeve is welded to the kiln's outside wall or skin. A ceramic washer holds the fiber blanket or board in place (Fig. 2-57).

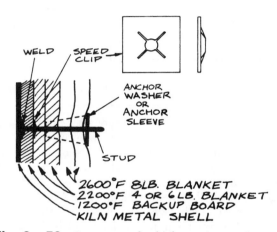

Fig. 2—59: *Correct method of securing anchor stud with a metal dip washer.*

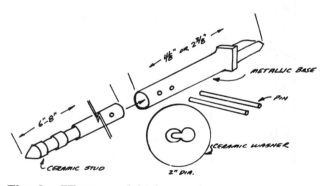

Fig. 2—57: *Kao-Lok high-temperature anchor.*

I have not used either of these systems, but I have used the Kao-Lok ceramic cone anchor system (Fig. 2-58). It uses a high-temperature inconel stud welded to the frame, and a ceramic cone is pushed down on the stud and turned 90° to lock. Then the end of the ceramic cone is stuffed with fiber to protect the metal stud from oxidation. However, this system leaves much to be desired because of the leakage of the packing and eventual destruction of the anchor stud. Continual repacking of the ceramic cone itself and around the cone exterior is required. The manufacturer has since tried to improve the anchor cone by adding a screw-in plug. The user still must pack the anchor cone body with fiber to protect the metal stud, then dip the threads of the plug in mortar or Kaowool cement before threading the plug into place. I found that while it did slow down the destruction of the anchor studs, it didn't last long in twice-daily cone 10 firings. The conduction of heat by the ceramic cone causes shrinkage of the fiber materials around it, especially the back-up lower-temperature materials, leaving a gap wide enough for eventual destruction of the anchor stud.

A third method is to use the high-temperature inconel metal stud with a metal clip washer, turning it 90° to lock in place, then cementing a fiber blanket patch over the anchor stud and washer. This system will work fine if the patch stays in place. It will not leak after its 5 percent plus shrinkage. However, I would not use this system above 1,204°C (2,200°F).

Another system used by some fiber-kiln builders is wiring the fiber blanket or board in place. I will not discuss this procedure. You can see in Fig. 2-60 that the flat ceiling and side walls are collapsing and that wiring does not work too well.

Fig. 2—60: *A collapsing fiber ceiling; wiring fiber blanket or board in place is not recommended.*

LAYER CONSTRUCTION

Kiln linings for high temperatures (above 1,204°C; 2,200°F) should consist of 1" to 2" back-up block insulation; two inches of 1"-thick 4-to-6 pound 1,204°C (2,200°F) fiber blanket or board; and two inches of 1"-thick 8-pound high temperature blanket or board. In this layered system, great care must be taken to stagger joints on each layer of different-temperature blankets or boards. Even greater care must be taken to stagger the two hot-face blanket or board joints in relation to the blanket or board beneath (Fig. 2-61).

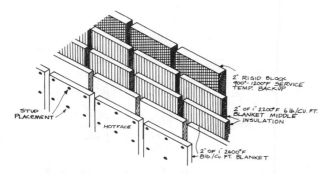

Fig. 2—61: *Vertical layer butt joint construction; rotate 90° for horizontal butt joint construction.*

Back-up insulation: Whatever the back-up block or flat insulation board used, it should have a service temperature limit of 482 to 649°C (900 to 1,200°F) and be rigid, with a 12-to-15-pound density. Also, the rigid block back-up insulation should have a linear shrinkage of less than 1 percent. Most blocks come in 1", 2" and 4" thickness, and in 24" by 36" or 48" length. The blocks can be held in place on the studs with speed clips.

Middle layer: In most constructions, fiber blanket is used for the middle and hot-face layers. Choose

4-to-6 lb./cu. ft. density blanket or board with a service temperature of 1,204°C (2,200°F). Lower service temperature blankets could be used, but I wouldn't go below 1,038°C (1,900°F). The first layer impaled is staggered to the block lying underneath. The second layer is then staggered again to the blanket beneath it, just as in bricklaying with alternating joints.

Hot-face layer: Use two layers of 1" 8-pound blanket for high temperature, such as Thermal Ceramics Kaowool (1,427°C (2,600°F) Blanket or Cerachrome Blanket. Again, care must be taken to stagger joints and make sure the hot-face blanket is impaled on the studs with the proper dimensions. For high-firing kilns, 6" walls are the maximum needed. Anything over this would not be economically justifiable. Minimum wall thickness is 4" and consists of two layers of 1" 1,427°C (2,600°F) 8-pound blanket, a 1" layer of middle insulation, 4 to 6 lbs. blanket and one inch of back-up block insulation. Instead of a blanket hot-face, Thermal Ceramics Indo-Form 1,427°C (2,600°F) board, or any 1,427°C (2,600°F) board, can be used in a 1" layer backed up with 1,427°C (2,600°F) blanket in a 1" layer, then the normal middle and back-up block. The board has a tendency to warp and curl at the edges after numerous firings. Therefore, it is necessary to follow the same stud layout as for high-temperature blanket, even though less may be recommended.

Do not try to use one stud and anchor to hold down the butt joints of the hot-face blanket (see Fig. 2-62).

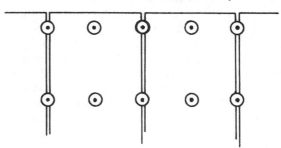

Fig. 2—62: *Erroneous placement of anchor studs between blankets.*

CORNER CONSTRUCTION

The corners are critical areas in fiber construction. I do not recommend a labyrinth corner joint for the hot-face layers at high temperatures; instead, use an around-the-corner joint. When using the board hot-face, the corners will be labyrinth joints, but the layer beneath should be a corner joint (Fig. 2-63).

The overlapping corner joint can be used with a stud layout which has overlapping blanket joints (Fig. 2-64). An overlapping system can save studs, but

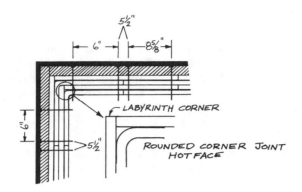

Fig. 2—63: *Corner construction combines labyrinth and around-the-corner joints.*

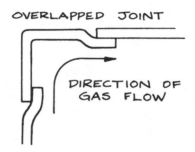

Fig. 2—64: *Overlapping joint construction, appropriate in selected layouts.*

reduced wall thickness results, and this may not be good in high-temperature firings.

DOOR JAMB SEALS

Ceramic fiber blanket cannot be abraded, or it will quickly be destroyed. Therefore, all door jamb seals using ceramic fiber blanket must be designed to allow the closing action of the door to be perpendicular to the seal. The easiest door design is the simple hinge door. The suspended sliding door and the guillotine door can be used, so long as the last action for cinching down to the jamb is a perpendicular action. One thing to remember is that ceramic fiber blanket or board has no resiliency and cannot take compression. For a door to seal, it must have some compression on the jamb, which by the very nature of sealing itself is destroying the fiber blanket. If the blanket material has a 5 percent shrinkage at high temperature, then any part of the door seal that is close to, or connected with, the hot-face will shrink and thus cause an opening in the seal. This is compensated for in the next firing by compressing the door a little tighter. This goes on until the seal is completely destroyed, and oxidation and warping of the door frame begin.

Typical door seals used in fiber kilns now on the market, and the problems associated with them, are illustrated in Figs. 2-65 and 2-66.

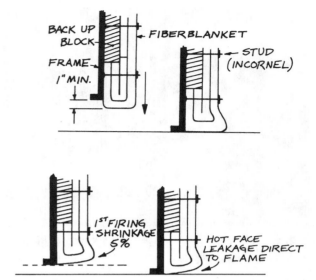

Fig. 2—65: *Standard bottom seal for hood or guillotine door. The problem is evident in the lower diagram.*

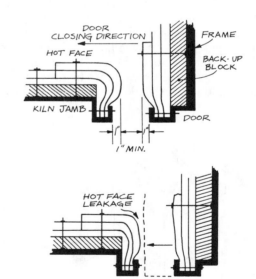

Fig. 2—66: *A standard door seal. At bottom, you can see the problem: 5 percent shrinkage and compression cause eventual destruction of seal, necessitating replacement.*

Points to consider when designing door jambs or other sealing jambs:

1. The actual sealing area should be built so that it may be easily replaced with new fiber, which means the sealing area cannot be connected to the door hot-face area.

2. In high temperatures, the actual seal should be a considerable distance from any hot-face area, thus keeping the actual seal cooler, and reducing both shrinkage and the chance of failure.

3. Use a doorstop to prevent over-compression of the door on the seal. Thermal Ceramics recommends seal compression at 25 percent or 30 percent of original thickness; in no case should it be compressed to less than 50 percent of original thickness.

MODULE BLOCK CONSTRUCTION

Module blocks are made by laminating edge-grain strips of fiber blanket or board, either 3", 4", 5", or 6" thick, and 12" long, into 12" by 12" blocks. The module blocks are held in slight compression either by a gauze-type wrap or an expanded metal backing. The gauze-wrapped blocks are designed for veneering over an existing refractory lining, and it is important that the lining surface have porosity in order for the veneering mortar to adhere.

The first step is to clean and back-fill all uneven areas with veneering cement. Trowel each module just before application with a 1/4"-thick bed joint of veneering cement on the cold-face or common side. Hold the module in place with perpendicular pressure for about 10 to 20 seconds, thus allowing the cement time to set (Fig. 2-67). Module application usually begins in a lower corner. Work out and up from there.

The modules that are bonded with waterproof chemical setting mortar to a metal backing are used in new applications with the welded-stud fastening system. Each module requires its own stud and lock fastener to hold it in place.

ACCORDION MODULAR WALL AND FOLDED WALL CONSTRUCTION

Folded-over and the accordion-folded fiber blanket construction techniques require a 33 percent compression of the material and held in that compression until fastened to the backing structure of the kiln wall or ceiling (Fig. 2-68). The backing structure can be expanded metal mesh, wire reinforcing steel mat or sheet metal. A sufficient gauge, grid pattern and mesh patterns must be selected to be ridged and allow for easy anchoring within the kiln frame. I prefer expanded metal mesh or wire reinforcing steel mat because the fastening can be done from the backside. The most common fastening attachment of the studs or anchors to the backing material is by spot welding. Other methods can be used, such as tying if using high-temperature wire, and hooking if using heavier gauge rod.

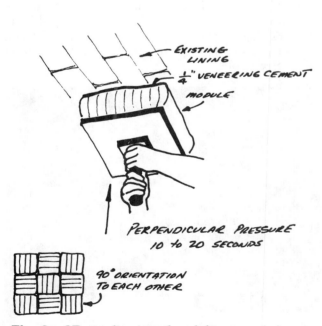

Fig. 2—67: *Application of modules over existing refractory lining.*

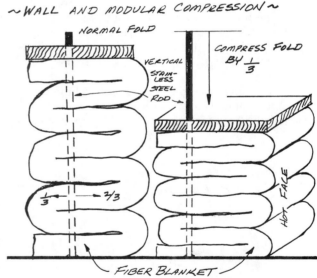

Fig. 2—68: *Wall and modular compression.*

In some high-temperature applications, each module is oriented 90° to the one next to it, which helps to protect against shrinkage.

When the modules are fired, the gauze burns away, allowing the module to distend to provide a tight, uniform lining. In ideal circumstances, the shrinkage and distention are nearly equal, so that a tight seal between each module is produced.

Folded-over construction is cut double the wall width and to the length of the wall. It is then folded in half and placed with the cut edges to the back or to the front for an edge grain and impaled on 10-mm stainless steel vertical rods (Fig. 2-69). Edge lining fiber was installed around the perimeter before the folded fiber was impaled — this would later be folded over for a seal. See the construction photographs from a large kiln built at the Tasmanian School of Art, in Hobart, Australia, under the direction of Les Blakebrough.

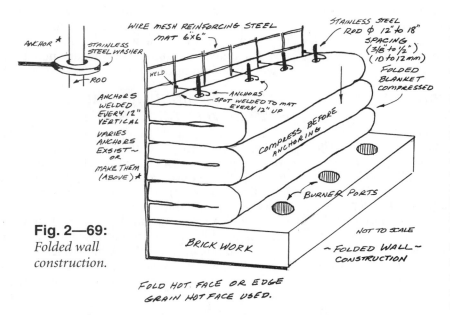

Fig. 2—69: *Folded wall construction.*

When a predetermined height is reached, in this case 30 cm (12"), the fiber is compressed to 20 cm or 1/3 compression. A specially designed hydraulic ram press applied downward pressure on a full width and length board with cutouts for the rods to evenly compress the fiber. This was done until the height of the wall was reached. The vertical rods were tacked back to the metal frame in 30 cm intervals up the wall. (See Fig. 2-69 and Fig. 2-70). This is an extremely strong construction.

Using the accordion modular technique, the blanket is cut to its width with a predetermined length for the number of folds necessary to compress to a 12"

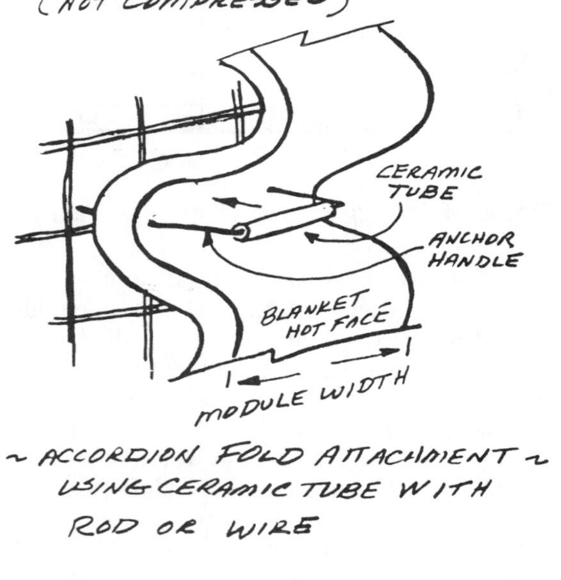

module. It is then accordion folded to the width of the wall unit and compressed 30 percent with the folded edge out. The wall attachment mechanism is built into the unit, such as vertical rods with anchor pins attached. It is held in compression by bands, gauze or a metal holder that can be removed once installed and fastened. A row of vertical modules will be attached to the backing frame, across the width of the wall. Once all are secure another row on top can be started. The bands, gauze or metal holder on the lower row can be removed once the top row is completed. Pressure must be applied to the opposite direction of the fold when installing. For vertical folds, downward pressure must be applied when installing the module above. Butt corners are used (Fig. 2-73). Proper respiratory protection should be worn as well as full body clothing, gloves, hat and eye protection. I know this sounds excessive for us that are not dealing with fiber construction day in and day out, but for those who work in fiber construction, take all the precautions.

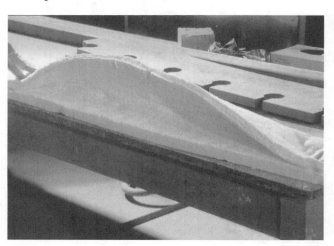

Fig. 2—71: *Blanket cut to double width and folded over, edge grain out (notice compression board behind the blanket).*

CONCLUSIONS

Ceramic-fiber furnace linings and kiln linings have proved successful in a variety of applications, mostly under 1,204°C (2,200°F). They are especially well suited to continuous firing operations or long-soaking firing applications in a neutral or oxidation atmosphere.

Fig. 2—70: *Accordion fold attachments.*

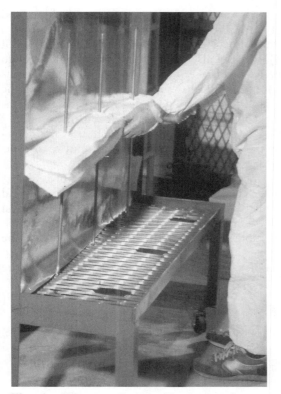

Fig. 2—72: *Impaling the blanket on the vertical rods.*

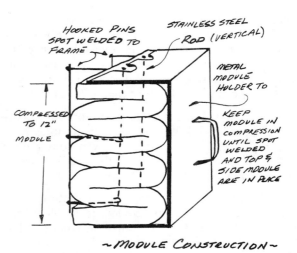

~MODULE CONSTRUCTION~

Fig. 2—73: *Compression folded and handed modular construction.*

Fig. 2—74: *Building up the wall, with compression every 12" (notice edge-flap that will be folded over when done).*

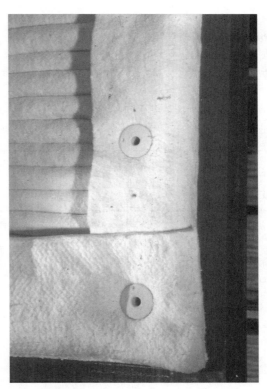

Fig. 2—75: *Securing the edge-flap to the wall for a compression seal.*

The disadvantages of fiber linings in high-temperature: High shrinkage; inability to withstand direct mechanical abuse, no resiliency; the catalyzation of the anchor metal studs in a reducing atmosphere (however, the systems are improving), curling and warping of the edges (this, too, is improving with the newer materials), crystallization of the surface after numerous firings, the presence of minute particles of silica/alumina fiber dust which irritate the skin and lungs (wear long sleeves, gloves, and a face-nose-mouth mask when working with fiber products or loading fiber kilns), negligible fuel savings compared to IFB kilns in the short firing cycle of 6 to 12 hours that most potters use, and higher cost per cubic foot than IFB kilns.

In recent years, new, more durable high-temperature fiber blankets, boards, and modules have appeared. I have not used the new modular fiber blocks, so I cannot evaluate their effectiveness under normal operating conditions.

This was due to improper construction techniques used, however the construction technique described in the folded wall construction has proven to be an excellent method. The accordion-folded modular technique is being used by an Italian kiln company called Job Forni to build excellent kilns with excellent construction technique and good durability. (The veneer block and weld-on modules described in the previous section were not used). I have also seen unsuccessful attempts to veneer fiber blanket onto hard brick linings. I caution you that all fiber products must be used in the application they were designed for to achieve maximum benefits and life. Thus, before using any fiber products, check with the manufacturer to determine the applicability of those products to your kiln.

In summary, for high-temperature, short-duration firings, such as a potter or a school would use, insulation firebrick kilns are still the best choice today. Once the new fiber products', which are soluble in body fluids, service range can be extended to stoneware/porcelain temperatures, then the choice could be equal, depending upon the design and price.

Table 2-3
Chemical analysis of typical module blocks

	1427°C to (2600°F) Kaowool modules Veneering (%)	1427°C (2600°F) Kao-bloc Weld-On (%)	1649°C (3000°F) Kaowool or Kao-bloc Saffil modules (%)
Alumina (Al_2O_3)	54.9	55.5	95.0
Silica (SiO_2)	44.8	44.9	5.0
Trade inorganics	0.3	0.1	-

Chapter 3

Principles of Design

Six critical factors must be considered before you begin to design a kiln. This chapter reviews those considerations, then discusses the nine principles of good kiln design. These basic principles are then incorporated into the four distinct types of kilns discussed in succeeding chapters on crossdraft, downdraft, updraft configurations and multi-directional draft configurations.

PRELIMINARY CONSIDERATIONS

Kind of kiln: Will you build an updraft, downdraft, crossdraft, circular dome, or salt glaze kiln? Will the kiln be 10, 20, 25, 45, or 150 cubic feet or larger? You must carefully calculate your requirements before you begin the design.

Clay to be fired: The type of clay you plan to fire will determine the type of kiln you need, its size, the fuel to be used, and so forth. Kilns may be planned and built specifically to fire terra cotta clay, sewer pipe clay, earthenware, stoneware, porcelain, or any of a number of possibilities. In fact, the potter should know the clay and ware so well that he can design the kiln to enhance the pottery and to control the effects of firing.

Atmospheric conditions: The chamber shape will depend on whether the kiln is intended for oxidation, reduction, or perhaps middle fire. Burners and dampers can greatly affect the ability of the kiln to oxidize or reduce. This, in turn, affects clay bodies and glazes and their outcome.

Available fuel. It would be foolish to build a wood-burning kiln in the city; it's a romantic idea but impractical. Therefore, the relative availability of natural gas, propane/butane, oil, wood, coal/coke, and electricity must be considered. Since propane/butane and electricity are available almost anywhere, and are clean burning, they can be used anywhere except where natural gas is provided. Natural gas is a perfect fuel for use in cities or highly populated neighborhoods; however, before one proceeds, ascertain the amount of gas available to the site. Wood, coal/coke, and oil should be reserved for use in the country.

Location of kiln. Whether city, suburb, backyard, garage, manufacturing area, or countryside, all locales tend to "self design" a kiln. By this I mean that each location tends to dictate what kind of kiln is feasible, a wood kiln in a garage is not the best idea, nor is an anagama in the suburb. Many areas will have building code restrictions that affect what kind of kiln you can use. Be sure to check local regulations before spending any money.

Shelf size. Be sure your kiln is designed to accommodate one of the standard shelf sizes.

DESIGN PRINCIPLES

Once the basic requirements are determined, as outlined in the preceding section, the nine principles covered here become an integral part of every kiln design.

PRINCIPLE 1

A cube is the best all-purpose shape for a kiln. The best design for an updraft kiln has the arch on top of the cube, not contained within (Fig. 3-1). This allows for the best stacking space. Also, the volume of the arch serves as a collection area for the flue gases. Increasing the height of the cube chamber with a fixed width decreases the efficiency of even-temperature firing (Fig. 3-2). I do not know what the ratio factor is between increasing height and uneven temperature. From experience in firing an updraft kiln (2' x 3' base x 5'-plus-high stacking space) with burners in the floor, I have found from 1/2 to 1 cone difference between top and bottom, no matter what firing schedule was used. However, on the same kiln 1 foot

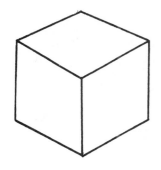

Fig. 3—1: *A cube is the best all-purpose chamber shape.*

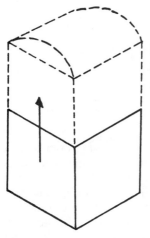

Fig. 3—2: *Increasing the height of a cube chamber decreases firing efficiency.*

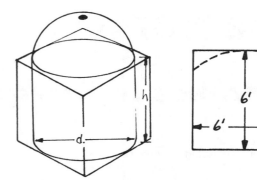

Fig. 3—4: *Diameter and height should be nearly equal in circular or round-dome kilns.*

shorter (2' x 3' x 4') it can be dead even top to bottom. In a similar kiln (3' x 3' x 5' stacking space), I found a constant 1/2 to 1 cone difference in the firing temperature between top and bottom but if the width and length was increased to 4 feet, the temperature evens out perfectly. My conclusion is that equal height and width is extremely important to even temperature when using floor level burners. From my experience, the same findings also apply to the downdraft and crossdraft kiln design. Increasing the length of the cube has no effect on the even firing efficiency of the kiln, hence the development of tunnel kilns (Fig. 3-3), and other long tube-type kilns used commercially. In circle or round-dome kilns, (Fig. 3-4), the diameter and height should be nearly equal, depending upon whether it is an updraft or a downdraft kiln. Most small downdraft kilns tend to include the dome in the height measurement, while updraft beehive types tend to add the dome to the height measurement. (See Appendix for estimating data on arch construction.) For firing tall kilns (Fig 3-2), the burner becomes important and should be placed up the sides of the kiln (See Chapter 9). There are other specialty kiln designs, not based on the cube, like the tube, groundhog and derivative kilns, but follow other principles listed here.

PRINCIPLE 2

The chamber shape is determined by heat direction and ease of flame movement to allow a natural flow. Two important rules to remember are: (1) the flame and heat direction should follow the arch (Fig. 3-5), and should not be at right angles to the arch (Fig. 3-6); and (2) the flame movement and heat direction should have only two right angles to negotiate within the chamber, usually located at the firebox inlet flue and bagwall and at the exit flues. Right angles can cause irregular heating or hot spots, which could lead to refractory failures and firing inefficiency. Fig. 3-6 also depicts the basic groundhog kiln design which is an effective kiln design (see Chapter 4). Nevertheless the fact remains it produces hot areas along the crown following the directional arrow, which leads to cool areas along the bottom back side wall and refractory failure at the back wall. If the design runs contrary to the arch then the transition should be curved or shaped from the firebox up into the volume and then into the chimney wall or chimney flue. This is possible with the use of lightweight insulation castables as done in the Gulgong racer, or with brick work as in the Ellington kiln. (See Gulgong racer and Ellington new kiln, Chapter 4.) Kilns that run contrary to this principle are the Nils Lou Minnesota flat-top kiln design and some professionally made gas-fired pseudo-downdraft kilns. They show

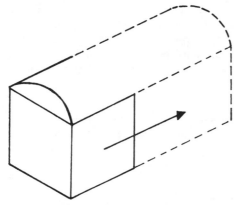

Fig. 3—3: *Increasing length does not affect firing efficiency.*

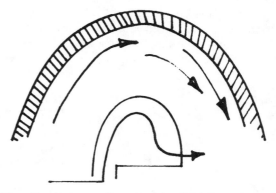

Fig. 3—5: *Heat direction should follow the arch.*

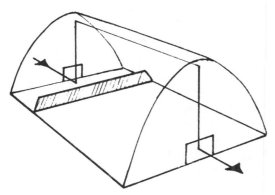

Fig. 3—6: *Configuration forces heat direction to flow at right angles to the arch (see groundhog kiln design).*

that any shape can be fired if there is sufficient heat produced and a correct flue-to-chimney ratio is used. The box, which is the easiest shape to build, becomes their primary kiln shape. There is merit to this style of design and they do work and should be researched. However, a more traditional approach based on natural draft is used here.

Three kiln chamber cross sections with proper heat direction and flame movement are shown in Fig. 3-7.

PRINCIPLE 3

A specific amount of grate area or combustion area is needed for natural draft. Grate area (firebox or fuel combustion area) depends upon the fuel used, following these approximate guidelines to get started:

Wood: 10 times greater than the horizontal section of the chimney, or put another way, the grate combustion area to chimney cross section area at the base ratio is 10 to 1.

Coal: 1 square foot of grate to every 6 to 8 square feet of floor space.

Oil: 1 square foot of combustion area to every 5 square feet of floor area.

Gas: 4 1/2" minimum channel combustion space between ware and wall, usually the length of the wall.

This is the most difficult principle of kiln design to apply, but it is the real heart of the kiln, for it determines the draft rate. When in doubt, be generous. Better a grate area too large than one too small. It is also better to have a chimney area on the large side instead of too small.

When designing kilns the fireboxes or combustion area and chamber are usually designed first, then the chimney matched to the size of the grate area or combustion area and chamber. If your calculations come out short of brick sizes, then opt for increasing the area up to match the brick sizes. To give examples of the wood guideline, I will use the fastfire downdraft and a crossdraft design.

The fastfire kiln has two fireboxes under the floor equaling 810 square inches of grate area which is divided by 10 giving a chimney of 81 square inches or 9" x 9". If the fastfire grate area is 1,215 square inches dividing by 10 gives a chimney of 121.5 square inches or 9" x 13.5" (Fig. 3-8). A crossdraft with a firebox of 60" side by 36" deep gives a grate area of 2,160 square inches divided by 10 equals a chimney of 12" x 18" or to match brick sizes, would be built as 13.5" x 18" (Fig. 3-9). I have found that over the years I have tended to use a larger ratio of about 7 to 1 (firebox-to-chimney ratio) in wood kilns because it allows for a more forgiving firing technique, fires faster when needed, adjusts for altitude, and allows for more adjustability in altering flues, chimney height and dampering. The groundhog kiln uses approximately a 4-to-1 ratio (Fig. 3-10).

In natural-draft kilns the inlet flue areas must be equal to exit flue areas for the simple reason, "what comes in must go out." If exit flues are too restricted, this will slow down the flow and retard combustion efficiency, thereby affecting the temperature increase. The combined area of the inlets should be equal to the chimney section. If the latter is 162 square inches, then the inlet flue area should be about 162 square inches. Since the normal flue size is a brick size (9" x 4 1/2"), four flues of this size would equal 162 square inches, adequate for a chimney with a cross section of 162 square inches. At the point where the exit flues enter the chimney, they should be restricted so that

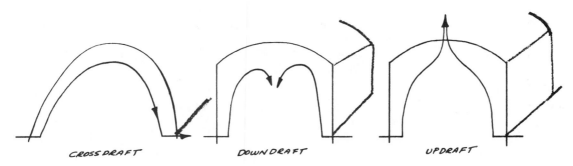

Fig. 3—7: *Cross sections of three chambers showing proper heat direction.*

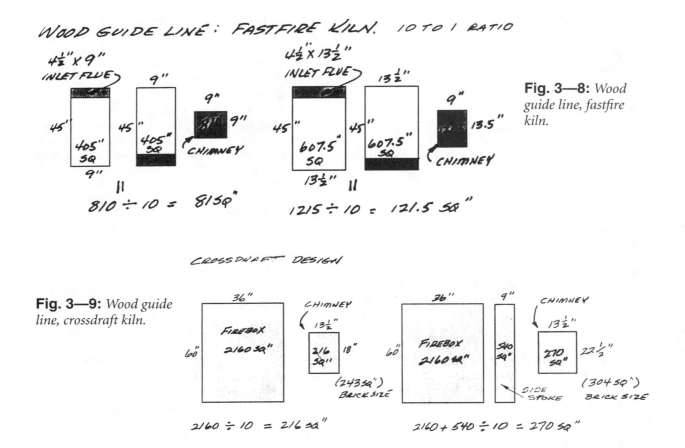

Fig. 3—8: *Wood guide line, fastfire kiln.*

Fig. 3—9: *Wood guide line, crossdraft kiln.*

the chimney cross-section is larger than this flue area. This can be done by using a flue collection box behind the chamber and in front of the chimney. In the fastfire design the exit flue is restricted because of the direct connection into the chimney.

If the chimney cross section is made much larger than the inlet and exit flues in a natural draft kiln, tapering of the chimney must be done to ensure proper draft.

To make matters simple without jeopardizing the kiln design, make the inlet and exit flue areas and the chimney cross-section area all equal, with the chimney point of entry slightly smaller. It is far better to make these areas too large than too small, for they can easily be altered by plugging them up.

When using pressurized gas as a fuel, the inlet flue area should equal the exit flue area. An example: For an updraft gas kiln with 10 bottom burner ports with 2 1/2" diameters (inlet floor flues) which will equal approximately 4.9 square inches per hole or a total of 49 square inches, the exit flue in the arch should equal approximately 49 square inches. See Fig. 3-12. This is a safe rule of thumb to use, remembering in the case of a downdraft or pseudo downdraft one can block the exit flue. In the updraft the exit flue or

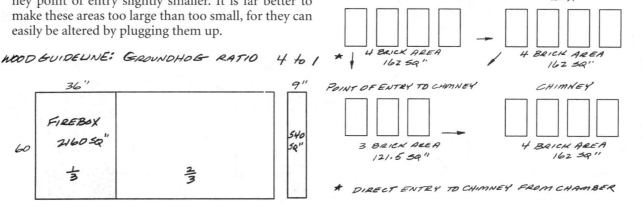

Fig. 3—10: *Wood guide line, groundhog kiln.*

Fig. 3—11: *Flue-to-chimney relationship.*

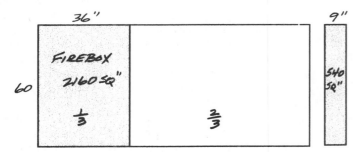

Fig. 3—12:

flues (if two holes are used) can be made smaller by about 5 percent, but the option to enlarge if needed is possible. Remember, making a hole smaller is a whole lot easier than enlarging.

For a downdraft or crossdraft kiln using pressurized gas (forced draft), the inlet flues can be the size of the burner tips or slightly larger since the oxygen is supplied through the burner with secondary air pulled in around the burner port hole. In most cases, the inlet flue will be brick-size then reduced in size to add adjustability to the flue. If a combination of wood was to be used also, then an auxiliary air source must be provided. Exit flues should be built brick-sized (can be reduced in size if needed) and follow the natural draft relationships from flues to chimney. The difference with forced draft is that the height of the chimney is reduced by at least 25 percent.

PRINCIPLE 4

The taper of a chimney controls the rate of draft. Tapering reduces atmospheric pressure and increases the speed of draft, thereby controlling the rate of draft, which ideally should be 4 to 5 feet per second for natural draft kilns. The draft rate is measured periodically throughout the firing of the kiln, and, in the beginning, it will be very slow. The 4 to 5 feet per second is the rate of draft at most efficient operation, usually after 1,093°C (2,000°F) in cone 10 kilns. The draft rate measurement in feet is determined by the inside circumference of the chamber up the front wall, over the arch, down the back wall, through the flues and up the chimney (which is 45 feet in Fig. 3-13). For this kiln to fire at the proper draft rate, gases would take about 10 seconds to travel from X to Y. One way to determine the draft rate is to throw an oily rag into the firebox and count the number of seconds it takes for the smoke to come out the chimney. If it is too slow, tapering the chimney could increase the rate. A kiln chimney that is between 16 and 20 feet, with a base section of 12" x 12", would normally taper to a minimum of 9" x 9". In a natural draft kiln, seldom would a chimney be less than 9" x 9" at its base cross section.

PRINCIPLE 5

For natural draft kilns there should be 3 feet of chimney to every foot of downward pull, plus 1 foot of chimney to every 3 feet of horizontal pull. The height of the kiln chamber in Fig. 3-11 is 6 feet. Therefore, there are 6 feet of downward pull (dp); and for every foot, 3 feet of chimney are added: Thus, 3 x 6 = 18 feet of chimney. Then add 1 foot of chimney for every 3 feet of horizontal pull (hp), which in Fig. 3-14 equals the chamber width (5 feet), plus 1 foot of collection box, plus a 1-foot-wide chimney, totaling 7 feet. Thus, 7 / 3 = 2.3 feet; added to 18 feet, we find that this kiln requires a 20.3-foot chimney. To calculate chimney height for any natural draft kiln chamber: *When using pressurized gas, the draft is forced and does not need the same height requirements as natural draft does to pull the draft through the kiln.*

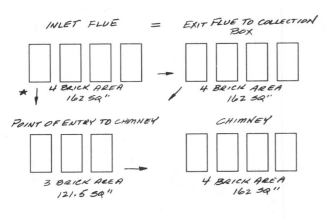

Fig. 3—13: *Inlets and outlets must be approximately equal.*

Fig. 3—14: *An updraft gas kiln must have equal inlet and exit area.*

PRINCIPLE 6

Chimney diameter is approximately one-fourth to one-fifth of the chamber diameter. If a chamber is 5 feet in diameter, then the chimney must be at least 1 foot in diameter. This principle when used with Principle 3 can give a more specific chimney dimension for natural draft kilns.

PRINCIPLE 7

A tall chimney increases velocity inside the firing chamber. Too high a chimney can cause irregular heating by pulling the heat out of the kiln, not allowing it to build up within the chamber, thereby prolonging the firing. On the other hand, too short a chimney can protract the firing by decreasing the draft rate, which allows build-up in the firebox and does not pull enough oxygen into the kiln to allow proper combustion for temperature increase.

PRINCIPLE 8

The height of the chimney of a chamber kiln should be equal to the slope of the kiln. This is a useful guideline for determining minimum chimney height for a chambers kiln. To line up the chimney height, place a line along the chamber tops as shown in Fig. 3-15.

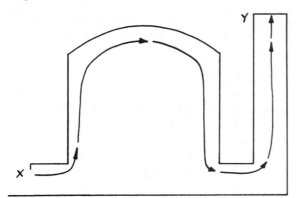

Fig. 3—15: *It requires 10 seconds for gases to travel from x to y (45 feet) in this kiln.*

PRINCIPLE 9

Critical areas of a kiln should be planned and built to be altered easily. If in doubt as to flue sizes, grate area, or chimney size, bigger is better. Plugging excess space with bricks is an easy matter. Also, for ease of construction, all dimensions should be based on the standard 9" x 4 1/2" x 2 1/2" brick, or the large standard, 9" x 4 1/2" x 3". Perhaps 80 percent of the time, normal flue dimensions will be one brick standing on end (9" x 4 1/2"). These should be spaced 9" apart.

There will be no uncorrectable problem in the kiln if you remember to make flues adjustable, planning so that you can add or knock out a brick, make the chimney entrance flue adjustable, and build the chimney so that the height is readily adjustable.

HIGH-ALTITUDE ADJUSTMENTS

Building a kiln at high elevations necessitates adjustments to compensate for decreased oxygen per cubic foot of air. The difference is very apparent in hot desert elevations over 3,800 feet, and in mountain elevations from 5,000 to 10,000 feet. Outside air temperature, as well as elevation, has a direct effect on the amount of oxygen present. For instance, in Aspen, Colorado, the elevation is about 8,600 feet. However, at an outside air temperature of 22°C (72°F), the density of oxygen per cubic foot of air is equivalent to the amount found in air at 10,000 feet. Thus, kiln firing is more efficient at night, when the air cools and becomes denser, and more oxygen is present.

There are five steps in the procedure for making appropriate alterations to a natural draft kiln to compensate for high altitude and low air density.

1). Design the kiln according to standard principles, figuring out the chimney diameter, the inlet and exit flue sizes, and the chimney height.

2). Increase the chimney diameter by roughly 50 percent (so it works into the closest bricklaying combination). Thus, a chimney with a diameter of 9" would be increased to a diameter of 13 1/2" (Fig. 3-16).

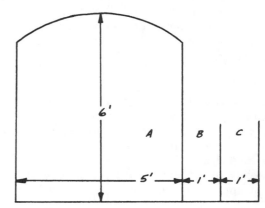

Fig. 3—16: *Three feet of chimney length are added for every foot of downward pull, plus 1 foot of chimney for every 3 feet of horizontal pull: A, chamber; B, flue collection box; C, chimney.*

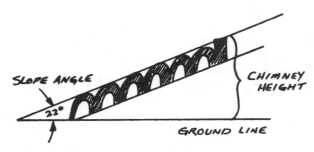

Fig. 3—17: *Slope of the kiln determines chimney height.*

3). Increase the inlet and exit flues by 50 percent. If you have three inlet and exit flues measuring 9" high and 4 1/2" wide each, increase the height by 4 1/2" to make them 13 1/2" high by 4 1/2" wide (Fig. 3-17).

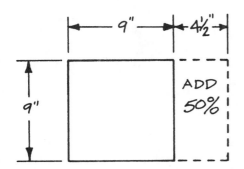

Fig. 3—18: *Chimney diameter is increased by 50 percent in high-altitude adjustment.*

4). Increase the chimney height by at least 30 percent to pull the greater volume of air needed.

5). It is not necessary to increase the grate area in relation to the chimney (for wood) or to the floor area (for coal and oil). Remember, it is not more fuel that is needed, but more oxygen to burn the fuel.

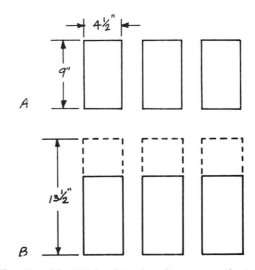

Fig. 3—19: *High-altitude adjustments for inlet and exit flues: A, normal; B, flue height increased by 50 percent.*

Chapter 4

Crossdraft Kilns

Crossdraft kilns have a flame movement from the inlet flues on one side of the kiln chamber to exit flues along the opposite side. The four most common types are: the single-chamber kiln, the chamber kiln, and the tube kiln (Fig. 4-1).

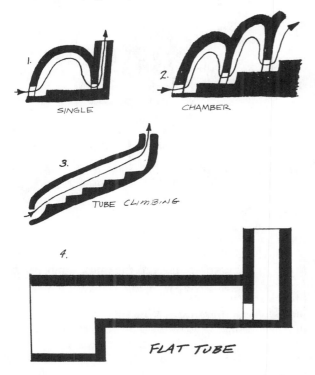

Fig. 4—1: *The four most common crossdraft kilns.*

Crossdraft kilns originated in the Orient. The exact location and time is impossible to determine, but it is probably safe to assume that China, Korea, and Japan simultaneously developed similar crossdraft kilns known as bank or hole kilns. The hole kilns were in use during the Asuka period in Japan, the Sui period in China, and the Silla period in Korea. In Japan they were called anagama; ana meaning hole or cavity and gama meaning kiln.

The late Tomimoto Kenkichi related his theory on the development of the anagama. Through the centuries, potters realized that the more enclosed the primitive pit kiln became, the hotter the firing and the more durable the pottery. Firing temperatures were increased by banking up the sides with clay as shown in Fig. 4-2.

Fig. 4—2: *An enclosed pit kiln, forerunner of the anagama.*

While the potters around the eastern Mediterranean Sea (Asia Minor) and the Middle East built the walls up to form a simple beehive updraft kiln, Oriental potters proceeded in a different way. Their pottery villages were always built upon the clay source. (China, Korea, and Japan have vast amounts of stoneware clays ready to use right out of the ground, while in comparison, the Middle East has very little usable clay.) Utilizing the banks and hills of clay, they hollowed out holes large enough for a man to crawl into. The main cavity was widened and then tapered back into a chimney flue leading up to the surface. After the hole and cavity were hollowed out, the firebox, floor, and walls were shaped in the clay and allowed to dry. A small fire of increasing intensity was built in the entrance or firebox and allowed to burn for weeks until the inside walls were bisqued. This transformed the chamber into a monolithic structure.

When the anagamas were fired, glaze deposits (wood ash slag) formed on the chamber walls and roof. As the kilns became hotter and were fired longer, the accumulated wood ash slag dripped onto the pots. The resultant marking was considered a defect at first, but in time it came to be appreciated, and became the first style of wood ash glazes.

As the anagama developed, the kiln became too large to be dug out without breaking through the ground. Thus, according to Tomimoto, the single chamber kiln matured into the tube or bank kiln. The art of brick making and the design of the conical tatami bricks made possible the spanning of an arch and the elevation of half the kiln above the surface level.

Fig. 4—3: *Inside the anagama, looking out.*

Fig. 4—4: *Looking into the anagama chimney.*

TAMBA TUBE KILN

Tamba is one of the original earthenware kilns of Japan. For the past 600 years, the Tamba kilns have remained virtually the same. Tamba family names, clays, glazes, and techniques are unchanged. The 23 kilns of Tamba are now protected as cultural properties of the Japanese government and are the best known Mingei (folk) potteries.

During the early Kamakura Period (1185-1392), migrant Korean potters built the Tamba kilns and began to make stoneware pottery in Tachikui. A problem confronting the Tamba potters was how to fire the large container pots (averaging between 13" and 24" in height) in lots of as many as 500 at a time. The Korean solution was to extend the Anagama to approximately 120 feet and bring half of the kiln out of the ground, creating in principle a chimney-full of pots.

There were no kiln shelves at this early time and saggaring such large pots was impossible. Instead, saggar setters were used to level the pots, which were arranged in rows between the side stoke holes.

The Tamba kiln allows for ease of flame movement through the tube. The chamber flues are equally

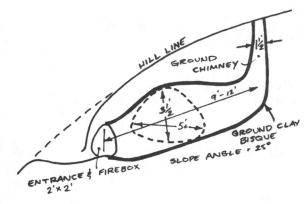

Fig. 4—5: *The anagama.*

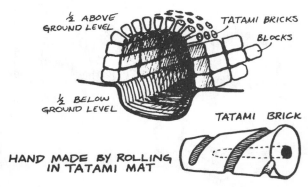

Fig. 4—6: *The tube kiln.*

spaced with a slight restriction at the chamber exit. The firebox or, Dogi, is about 6 feet deep and 5 feet across at the entrance flues to the first chamber (Fig. 4-16). A small fire is started in the entrance of the firebox and gradually increased in intensity as large pieces of wood are used. When the coals have accumulated sufficiently, a long iron rod is used to rake them down. The firebox stoking lasts roughly 36 hours, which brings the first three or four side-stoke holes up to about 1,000°C (1,832°F). Eventually, the firebox becomes the air supply and stoking is done in the upper stoke hole and side stoke holes. The long firing of the firebox thoroughly dries out the whole kiln and the greenware, and also starts the draft pulling. Today a majority of the Tamba kilns use an oil burner with a blower to fire the firebox. This saves considerable effort and shortens the total firing time.

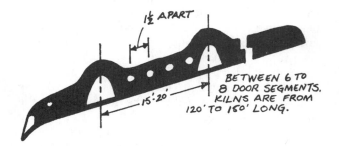

Fig. 4—7: *Cross section of the Tamba tube kiln.*

Fig. 4—8: *The Tamba tube kiln.*

Fig. 4—9: *Tamba tube kiln, showing a doorway (center) and stoke holes (right).*

Fig. 4—10: *Saggar setters.*

Fig. 4—11: *Inside the Tamba tube kiln.*

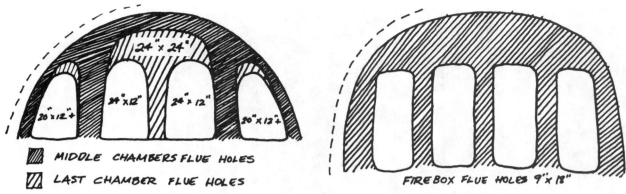

Fig. 4—12: *The Tamba tube kiln chamber flues.*

Fig. 4—13: *Firebox flues.*

Fig. 4—14: *Another view of a Tamba doorway.*

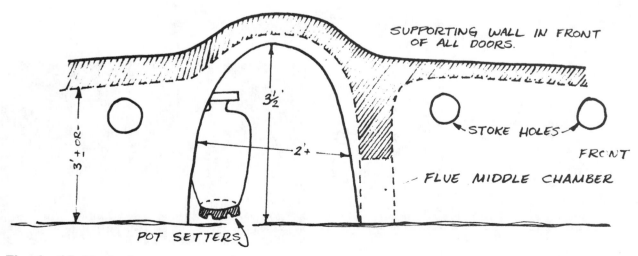

Fig. 4—15: *Tamba doorway construction.*

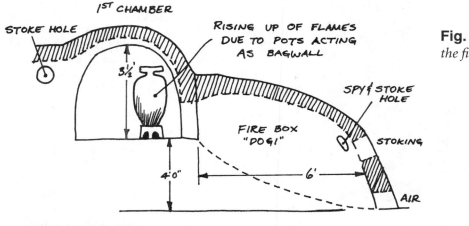

Fig. 4—16: *A cross section of the firebox.*

Fig. 4—17: *Oil burners with blowers are used today to fire the Tamba tube kilns.*

Fig. 4—18: *Stacking arrangement.*

Proper stacking of the kiln is extremely important to ensure that the pots will not be knocked over when the side holes are stoked. The pots are carried into the chamber by a man who must crawl into the kiln and place the pots on setters. Between every second or third stoke hole a 9" space is left. This allows room (himichi) for the wood to fall and combust. These holes are stoked simultaneously on both sides of the kiln, until the himichi is filled and a 12" flame is coming out of two or three stoke holes ahead. The flame is allowed to die down, whereupon the stoking is repeated until temperature is reached. On the third or fourth stoking, an iron rod is used to rake down the coals and allow more space for wood. Wood explodes upon entering the kiln and causes a tremendous burst of heat.

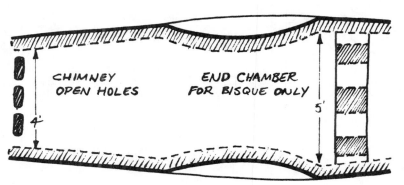

Fig. 4—19: *An overhead view of the Tamba end chamber.*

Fig. 4—20: *Exit holes of the Tamba end chamber.*

If too much time is allowed between stokings, temperature cannot be maintained or increased. The timing must therefore be perfect. It takes from 14 to 18 hours to side stoke the kiln, and approximately 200 bundles (15" x 15" x 30") of split kindling and small pieces of wood. During the firing of the last segment, the firebox and first segment are almost cool enough for unloading. The air for combustion is coming up through the firebox, causing tremendously fast cooling in the first segments, and the shattering of quite a few pots. When the firing is finished, the exit or chimney flues are plugged and the firebox sealed. Even so, within a half day the front part of the kiln is being unloaded.

The interesting and beautiful effects of flame flashing and wood ash deposits directly on the pots have long been admired, even though some blotting and glaze defects occur. The technique of side-stoking

segments up the length of the kiln was an important innovation in kiln design because it led to the segmenting of the tube chamber into separate, connected chambers. The Tamba kiln design is of little value to contemporary potters, except when miniaturized and used as a special-effects kiln. The value of the kiln historically is its transition to the climbing kiln.

Korean Gilgama

The gilgama that You-sup Bae, third generation Ongi potter, built for the 1988 Portland NCECA conference is based upon the primitive Silla Dynasty kiln. At one time in South Korea there were thousands of Ongi production kilns. Less than 196 kilns were operational in 1988. Most of the Ongi potters then were over forty years of age, over fifty at this writing, and the question is how many are still working a dying tradition? The gilgama can best be described as a bricked version of the hole kiln, or anagama. (Fig. 4-21 drawing and Fig. 4-22 & 23.) The kiln was bricked up in a teardrop form using a herring bone brick laying technique (Fig. 4-24) butting into the back wall which contains two 4.5" x 9" exit flues. (Fig. 4-25). The firebox was built spaciously to handle the longer 3' - 5' lengths of slab wood. A 20 percent slope was used which is standard for most kilns of this style. After the kiln was bricked, the floor step (18") was built and the chamber floor sloped up.

When the kiln reaches temperature and the fire color is clear throughout, Mr. Bae began to brick up the firebox door, leaving enough room to do the final stoking. Once the firebox is totally stuffed with wood, the bricking up of the door is finished and totally sealed by using a wood form around the door and filled with dirt. At the same time the chimney flues are closed and covered with dirt (Fig. 4-26 and 7).

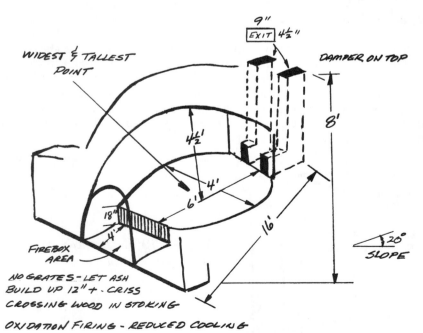

Fig. 4—21 drawing:
Gilgama — Silla Dynasty kiln.

Fig. 4—22: *Overall side view of gilgama, Mr. Bae firing.*

Fig. 4—23: *Front view, firing in oxidation.*

Fig. 4—24: *Stacking chamber.*

Fig. 4—25: *Exit flues of chimney.*

To check for methane gas leaks, Mr. Bae took a burning newspaper to ignite the gas where it was leaking. Once found, the leak was plugged with mud. In order to achieve the desired black ware, the kiln must be tightly sealed to cool in a smoky, reducing (carbonized) atmosphere.

LA BORNE TUNNEL KILN

Before the chamber kiln was developed, the tube kiln was enlarged into what was to become known as the tunnel kiln. Large tunnel kilns were used in China, Korea, Southeast Asia, and also in Europe. The European tunnel kilns were similar to the Oriental tunnel kilns. However, they were not segmented in their design and stacking in order to fire up the side of the tunnel. They were fired from the firebox only. Typical examples of these kilns are the La Borne tunnel kilns.

La Borne was a major pottery village located in central France in a region known as Haut-Berry. Almost all the inhabitants were involved in making, firing, and selling domestic wares. The potteries were large, as were the dozen or so kilns used. World War II caused the potteries to close and they never reopened completely. La Borne as a traditional pottery has gone, but the kilns remain.

The La Borne tunnel kilns ranged in size from 50 to 80 cubic meters. Figure 4-28 shows a typical La Borne kiln layout. The pottery was loaded through the back of the kiln. When this entrance was bricked up it also served as the exit flue for the kiln (Fig. 4-29). The firebox was quite large because the total firing took place there. Usually, the grate was a bonded arch with a series of nine holes per row across the top, each measuring 5" x 5" x 5" x 7", although in some kilns a series of ring arches was spaced 4 1/2" apart along the length of the firebox. At the back wall of the firebox, a space, usually about two feet wide, was left

Fig. 4—26: *Covering exit flues with dirt.*

Fig. 4—27: *Mr. Bae sealing door with dirt.*

between the grate and the bagwall. This space allowed an unobstructed area for pre-heated air to enter and also a space where the coals could be raked through into the ash pit. Without this space, the kiln could choke if the grate were to clog. The bagwall was rebuilt after each firing with greenware bricks arranged in a checkerboard pattern. The spaces between bricks acted as inlet flues, and the bagwall was always leaned away from the flame (Fig. 4-30). The bagwall bricks were a product used in local build-

ing construction. Not all potters rebuilt the bagwall after each firing, however. The kiln's calcined dirt floor was arranged in tiers for the stacking of saggars and pots. High-fire pots were placed in the first third of the kiln, middle fire pots were stacked in the next third, and earthenware in the last third. The kiln ranged in temperature from about 1,300°C (2,372°F) towards the firebox to 1,200°C (2,192°F) in the middle, and about 1,100°C (2,012°F) in the rear of the kiln.

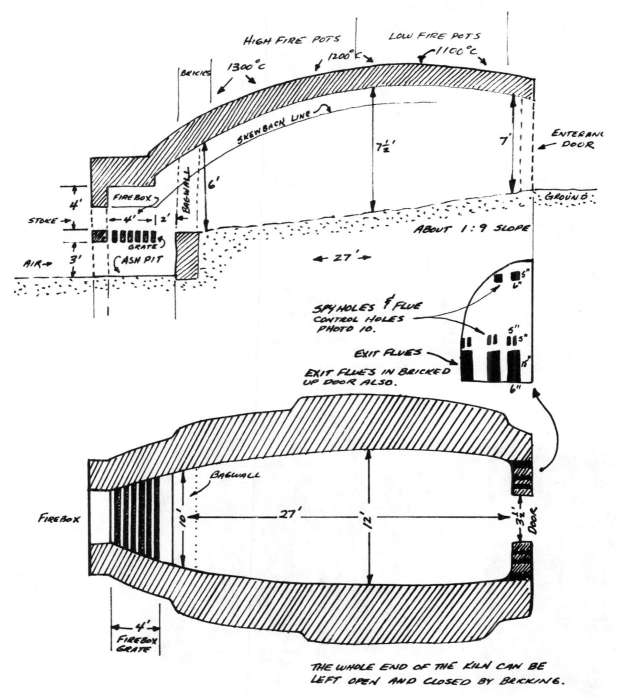

Fig. 4—28: *La Borne tunnel kiln.*

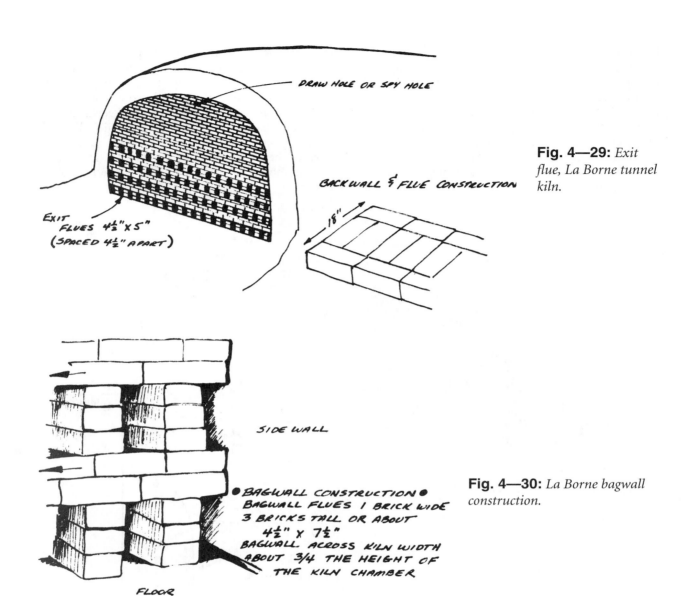

DRAW HOLE OR SPY HOLE

EXIT
FLUES 4½" X 5"
(SPACED 4½" APART)

BACKWALL & FLUE CONSTRUCTION

18"

Fig. 4—29: *Exit flue, La Borne tunnel kiln.*

SIDE WALL

• BAGWALL CONSTRUCTION •
BAGWALL FLUES 1 BRICK WIDE
3 BRICKS TALL OR ABOUT
4½" X 7½"
BAGWALL ACROSS KILN WIDTH
ABOUT 3/4 THE HEIGHT OF
THE KILN CHAMBER

FLOOR

Fig. 4—30: *La Borne bagwall construction.*

Fig. 4—31: *La Borne kiln shed and bundles of wood.*

Fig. 4—32: *La Borne firebox; the ash pit is open, but the stoke hole has been bricked up.*

The pre-firing (drying out) of the kiln and the greenware pots would take from 2 1/2 to 3 days. This period of slow burning and gradual accumulation of the ash pit coals was called bassinage. The next stage of the firing, called le petit feu, used split logs of oak and/or birch stoked at regular intervals. This stage of the firing could last up to four days, depending upon the kiln size and weather conditions. The last stage of the firing, called le grand feu, lasted about one day. Bundles of branches and twigs were tossed into the firebox, creating intense heat with a very long flame which gave a good reducing atmosphere and increased the temperature at the back of the kiln. Towards the end of the firing, the firebox was given a light salting between the final stokings.

GROUNDHOG KILN

A rectangular kiln, known as the "groundhog" because of its resemblance to the earth burrows created by some rodents, had its design roots in middle European crossdraft kilns such as the La Borne kiln in France (page 74), the Cassel kiln in Germany and the Newcastle kiln in England. Most American colonial potters followed the traditional methods of central Europe and England in producing their earthenware pottery fired in standard updraft kilns (see chapter 6). Sometime during the first decades of the 1700s southern colonial potters familiar with the La Borne, Cassel, or Newcastle kilns and knowledge of the kaolin and stoneware clay deposits in the mountains of Virginia and the Carolinas began making stoneware pot-

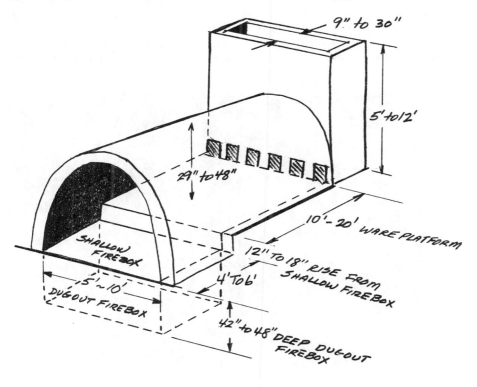

Fig. 4—33: *Basic groundhog dimensions.*

Fig. 4—34: *Heart Square kiln, built in 1987 (Ellington).*

tery. They used slip glazes and/or salt glazing methods for the finished surface and burned the ware in a rectangular crossdraft kiln — the groundhog kiln. For the better part of our history the Southern groundhog kilns of various regional styles burned the functional pottery used by the small town and country people along the Mid-Atlantic seaboard to northern Florida and inland to the Midwest and further on west.

The basic groundhog kiln floor plan is a rectangular shape with a full width chimney at one end and a full width firebox at the other end. To create the chamber volume of the kiln, imagine a cylinder sliced lengthwise at a center or less, then laid down placing the chimney at one end and the firebox at the other end. The average chamber height is from 29" to 48", and 7' to 10' wide and from 12' to 24' long. The chamber proportions range from 1/3 firebox area to 2/3 ware platform using the shallow firebox style and 1/4 firebox area to 3/4 ware platform using the dug-out firebox style with a full width chimney attached at the

back. The chimney height ranged from 5' to 10' depending upon the kiln size and length (Fig. 4-33 Basic Groundhog Dimensions). The kilns could be dug down into the ground utilizing the buttressing effects of the earth and covering the kiln with dirt for added insulation or built on the ground buttressing with rock work or other means of bracing. The groundhog kilns with dug-out fireboxes (approximately 48" deep) could use shorter chimneys than the shallow firebox style kilns. Loading entrances were either through the chimney or firebox. The shallow firebox kilns generally loaded from the front. The dug-out firebox kilns usually loaded from the chimney, however it was more of a potter's preference than a rule.

Regional styles of groundhogs vary from county to county and state to state, as is exemplified in the Hart Square dugout firebox groundhog in Vale, North Carolina (Fig. 4-34), and the Meaders shallow firebox groundhog in Cleveland (Mossy Creek), Georgia (Fig. 4-35).

The construction of the kiln was a simple matter of laying bricks over an arch form made from arch boards connected together with wooden slat runners or today using masonite, plywood, or milled 1-x-3s. (Refer to Chapter 2, Methods of Kiln Construction, Fig. 2-19 for brick-laying details.) It was not usual for the arch boards to be passed from one generation to the next or from one potter to another potter. When Kim Ellington built the Hart Square kiln in 1987, he used the arch boards from Burlon Craig's kiln (constructed in early 1930s), that were from the late 1800s (Fig. 4-36). An interesting feature of this kiln is that the arch entry into the chimney is a full arc, with the front wall of the chimney built on top of the arch (Fig. 4-37 drawing Hart Square groundhog). To carry the weight of the front chimney wall, two 9" x 9" support columns, 18" in from the sides, were constructed (Fig. 4-38). The distance between the two columns, about 66", acts as the entry to the ware chamber. The Hart

Fig. 4—35: *Cheaver Meaders' last kiln.*

Fig. 4—36: *Burlon Craig's Nineteenth Century arch boards used in the Hart Square kiln.*

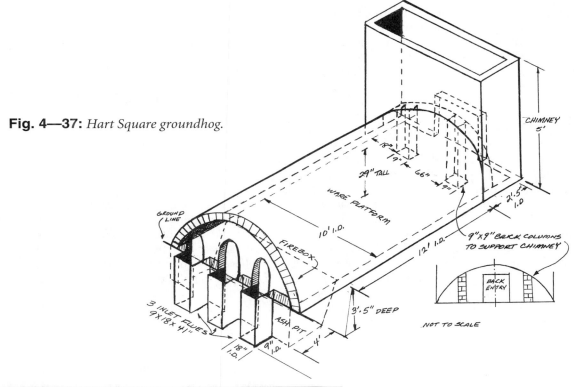

Fig. 4—37: *Hart Square groundhog.*

Fig. 4—38: *Interior supporting columns for holding up front chimney wall on top of arch. Notice ware platform and front stoke holes.*

Fig. 4—39: *Hart Square groundhog blasting.*

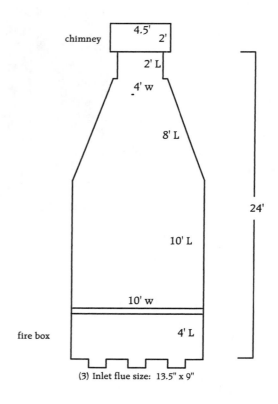

chimney   4.5'   2'

2' L

4' w

8' L

24'

10' L

10' w

fire box   4' L

(3) Inlet flue size: 13.5" x 9"

Fig. 4—40: *New hog kiln floor plan, dimensions.*

Square kiln burns hot according to Ellington, with cool areas along the rear side walls (Fig. 4-39). To deal with the cool areas, lower temperature glazes are used, however the clay body wasn't being vitrified enough to hold water, relegating the area to flowerpots or similar ware. This problem could have been aggravated by the two columns splitting the heat flow more towards the bigger center space, remembering the heat flow always seeks the easiest path to follow which is along the crown and, perhaps to some extent, the stacking arrangement. The problem could have been corrected by putting equally spaced exit flues along the back wall and then bricking up the ware platform entry with the exit flues. Adding a center damper, just above the chimney door, thus forces left and right heat flow to the outer sides of the kiln.

Kim Ellington's new hog kiln solves the problem in a different way by adding side stoke holes, funneling the back ware platform into the chimney and a having front entry to the ware platform (Figs. 4-40 & 14). The extended length of the new hog is feasible with the side stoke holes and also adds the ability to salt the back portion of the ware stacking. Notice the roller conveyor to bridge the firebox moat and ease the stacking of the kiln (Fig. 4-42 to 48).

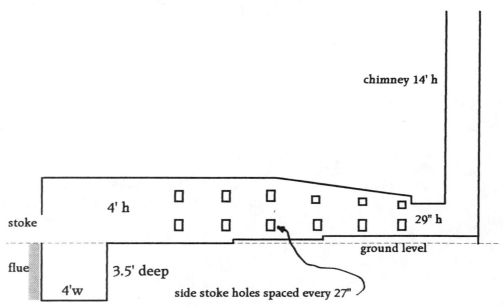

chimney 14' h

stoke   4' h

29" h

ground level

flue

3.5' deep

4' w   side stoke holes spaced every 27"

Fig. 4—41: *New hog kiln side view, dimensions.*

Fig. 4—42: *New hog kiln front view, dimensions.*

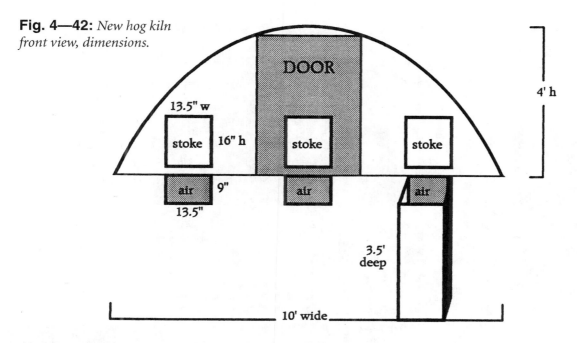

Fig. 4—43: *New hog foundation layout.*

Fig. 4—44: *Looking from ware platform into dugout firebox with vertical air channels.*

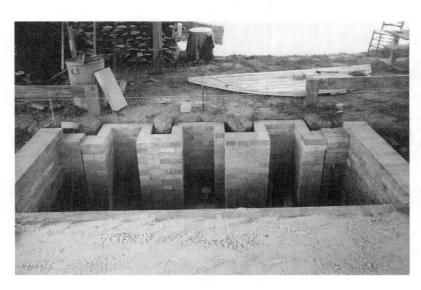

Fig. 4—45: *Arch form and buttressing form for concrete.*

Fig. 4—46: *Brickwork and taper to chimney.*

Fig. 4—47: *Finished kiln with side stock and salt ports.*

Fig. 4—48: *Front of kiln. Notice roller conveyor to span firebox for loading.*

Fig. 4—49: *Kim Ellington stacking green ware in kiln.*

(Figures (4-) 34, 36-43, 45-49 courtesy of Kim Ellington.)

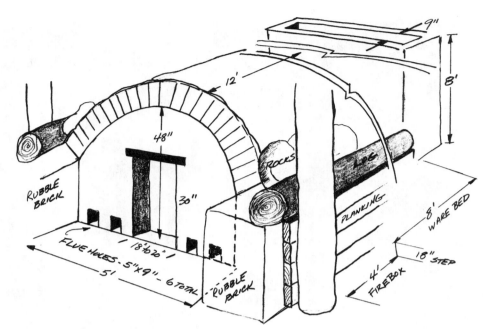

Fig. 4—50: *Cheaver Meaders' old kiln.*

Kim Ellington's firing schedule is as follows using saw mill slab wood:

6 P.M. – Start small campfires at the bottom of each inlet flue.

7 P.M. – Push the fires inside firebox — maintain 200° F in the kiln for next 12 hours.

7 A.M.– Start raising temperature at 100°F per hour.

3 P.M. – At 1,000°F, start raising temperature at 200°F per hour.

9 P.M. – Front at 2,200°F and neat 1,800°F. Start blasting by totally stuffing front stoke holes each time the flame retreats inside the chimney.

10 P.M. – Start side stoking. Cone 12 in front.

11:30 P.M. – Finish, cone 11 down at entrance to chimney.

The kiln requires approximately three cords of cured pine sawmill slabs and about a pickup truck load of thin pine slats for side stocking for a 30-hour firing.

The Meader kilns are a shallow firebox style groundhog based on 1/3 to 2/3 proportion with front entry. Cheaver Meaders' old kilns at the original Meaders set the style of kilns used by son Reggie Meaders and grandson David Meaders (Fig. 4-50 drawing). In 1994 Phil Cornelius and I flew back to Atlanta, Georgia and drove up to Lulu in White County to meet folk potters Reggie Meaders and son David. We were going to fire David's groundhog kiln, my first introduction to the legendary kilns (Fig. 4-51 drawing, Fig. 4-52). We met David late Friday night and drove over to his kiln behind his grandfather's (Cheaver Meaders) pottery. David had delayed the fir-

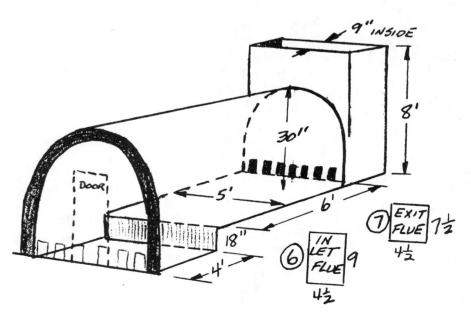

Fig. 4—51: *David Meaders' groundhog kiln.*

Fig. 4—52: *David Meaders' ground-hog, side view.*

Fig. 4—53: *Burning David's ground-hog kiln.*

Fig. 4—54: *Unloading—a buyer and Phil Cornelius.*

Fig. 4—55: *Reggie Meaders' kiln with butting front wall.*

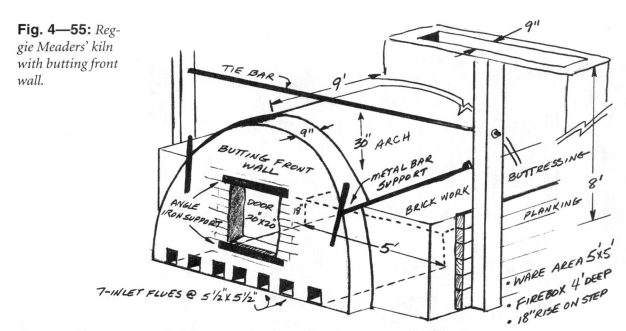

ing so we could put in a few pots, right up front on the ware platform. The firing went well, all night into the early morning before the tobacco spit glazes were melted, helped along of course by some fine white lightning home peach brew, which inspired the stoking to the highest degree of perfection. I later learned that one does not fire the groundhog, one burns it. David's kiln is approximately a 10'-long chamber with a 6'-long ware platform and a 4'-long firebox. The kiln is 5' wide and 4' tall at the firebox level (Fig. 4-53). The step between the firebox and platform is 18", leaving a 30" ware platform height (Fig. 4-54).

Reggie Meaders' kiln is smaller overall than David's kiln, but reflects his ideas on firebox proportions for he prefers a larger firebox area than is the norm. The basis for this larger firebox are intuition and his years of burning groundhog kilns. Which firebox design is best, shallow or dugout? They both do

the job and follow local styles and tradition. According to Reggie, "The closer the ceiling is to the pots the better the kiln burns, and besides, you don't have to heat up all that extra space and use all that extra wood." It must be remembered that kiln shelves and saggers were not used and the kilns were designed to meet the height requirements of the ware produced and were stacked directly on the ware platform (Fig. 4-55 drawing).

In some kilns where stacking on top of larger pots was done, the arch height was increased accordingly. Another observation made by Reggie from years of burning his dad's kiln, his brother Lanier's kiln and his own kilns, was that the heat always went to the top of the arch leaving the sides, especially the back sides, cooler. Similar situations occur in the Hart Square and groundhog kilns. Naturally, the heat will rise directly to the top of the arch and heat along the ridge line and

Fig. 4—56: *Blocking middle exit flues with bricks.*

Fig. 4—57: *Reggie's groundhog (with author).*

then slowly spill over down the sides of the arch, to the floor as the kiln gets hotter and hotter. Once blasting starts the kiln roars up to top temperature in 1 1/2 to 2 hours and then it's done, not leaving enough time for a complete spill over to the rear bottom sides.

Reggie tried many things to compensate for this cool area from blocking the ground inlet flues in the middle — it only caused uneven burning of the wood — to blocking the middle exit flues (Fig. 4-56), thereby forcing more heat to flow to the outside exit flue holes, which helped (Fig. 4-57).

The burning style of the groundhog kiln was to start slowly to dry out the greenware. Once the carbon was burned off the ware, stoking would increase to red heat, then blasting would begin until the back wall was shiny and the glazes melted, which went very quickly. Soaking the kiln at the end is not generally done. The groundhog kilns were designed to blast up to temperature, not for soaking, changing atmosphere or special effects. The shallower the arch, the less spill-over time required, the less area to get hot and the better the burning will be, unless the chamber length is too long.

Gulgong Racer

I like the groundhog kiln design because of its ability to fastfire on demand, the openness to the ware from the firebox, and the large, wide stacking platform. For those reasons I decided it would be the perfect vehicle (Olsenised, of course) for my Scotch cup kiln. It may be pointed our here that I have admired the small tea bowl kiln that Shino National Treasure potter Arakawa had at his studio near Tajimi, Japan, and have always wanted a special kiln for my Scotch cups.

At the 1995 NCECA conference in Minneapolis, Minnesota, I met with Janet Mansfield (potter and editor *Ceramics Art and Perception*) and we talked about her upcoming Claysculpt Gulgong event and my ideas for a new kiln which could be a good project for the Gulgong experience. When I arrived at Gulgong, Australia, each invited artist was to do a ceramic piece for a chosen site. Of course, my site would be the kiln shed. My dilemma was, could a kiln be a sculpture? (Fig. 4-59 drawing) Why should a kiln have to look like a kiln or what we perceive a kiln should look like? Can it have tires, hub caps, lights and an exhaust system? There is only one rule concerning a kiln — that it functions as a kiln should and reaches temperature with control. Therefore, my kiln design, based on the traditional groundhog kiln, became a cross between a Formula 1 racer and a sports car. It is known now as the "Gulgong racer." The irreverence towards kiln construction I exhibited

Fig. 4—58: *Gulgong racer side view.*

perhaps caused some concern as to the outcome, especially when I wanted to paint the kiln Ferrari red, but I ran out of time. This leads to rule two: The kiln doesn't care what it looks like on the outside.

The Gulgong racer's primary ware platform is 5' x 5' (150cm x 150cm) and 3' (90cm) tall. The firebox area is 5' wide and 3' deep and 4' (120cm) tall. The step between the two platforms was 18" (45cm). The side walls on the upper platform were only 1' high (30cm) sloping down to meet the firebox platform and the door entry arch. The kiln's crown was shaped using local dirt capped by a thin layer of wet sand smoothed to a final finished shape and covered with plastic. The kiln's crown was cast over the dirt form using Moral Coolcast 140, a product of Thermal Ceramics in Australia (See Chapter 2). The dirt that made up the form was dug out of the kiln's chamber and mixed with straw and cement for an adobe-style capping mix for the final shaping of the kiln's racing form. The 3-cubic-meter capacity kiln took four days to build by a number of hard-working participants. The kiln was stacked as the final adobe mix and hubcaps and lights were applied. At 4:45 p.m., a fire was started outside the kiln door and maintained throughout the night. By 7 a.m. the fire was moved into the firebox chamber. Seven hours later, at 2 p.m., cone 6 was down and the kiln was on a fast track up. The object of the stoking (blasting) was to melt the cones at the back wall of the kiln, all air supply was totally open. In less than 3 hours cone 10 was a puddle and the entire kiln was at temperature. The kiln was held at temperature and the air was reduced at the front for a more reducing atmosphere until the kiln was shut down at 12:30 a.m. The kiln worked perfectly even though the Gulgong racer was still steaming at the end.

As with most kilns I design, I try to have a variety of firing effects possible. To change the kiln to fire more like the front chamber of a Bizen-style kiln, it would be necessary to reduce the air supply at the front (after temperature was reached) to create a reducing condition. Open the passive air dampers to slow the draft rate and perhaps add dampers to the top of the chimney to choke the kiln. The Gulgong

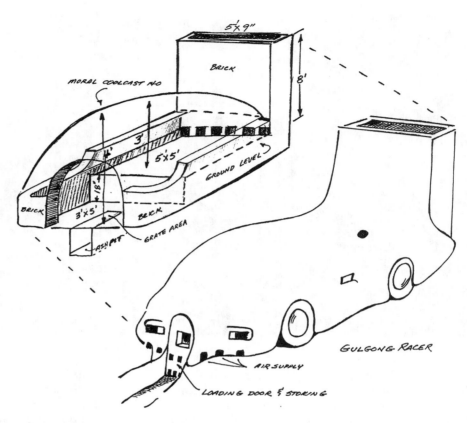

Fig. 4—59: *Gulgong racer drawing.*

racer would have to be choked or de-tuned for reduction operation. The only air should come from under the grate area in the door entrance. Then it is a matter of time and fluctuating temperature to build coals, flashing and the effects desired.

A series of photographs shows the step-by-step construction of the Gulgong racer (Figs. 4-60 to 79).

Fig. 4—60: *Layout exit flues into chimney.*

Fig. 4—61: *Exit flues, starting chambers walls.*

Fig. 4—62: *Firebox wall.*

Fig. 4—63: *Firebox and ash pit construction.*

Fig. 4—64: *Laying firebox walls and door arch.*

Fig. 4—65: *Sidewall, bevel for castable.*

Fig. 4—66: *Building platform to hold dirt.*

Fig. 4—67

Figs. 4—67-70: *Filling of dirt for shaping arch foam.*

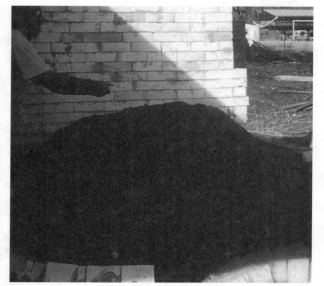

Fig. 4—68

Fig. 4—69

Fig. 4—70

Fig. 4—71

Fig. 4—72: *Finished casting.*

Fig. 4—73: *Covering with towels and plastic.*

Fig. 4—74: *Buttressing with concrete/rocks.*

Fig. 4—75: *Covering adobe mix.*

Fig. 4—76: *Gulgong racer ware platform 5' x 5' x 3 1/2' tall.*

Fig. 4—77: *Stacking the racer.*

Fig. 4—78: *Loaded.*

Fig. 4—79: *Firing below grates.*

CLIMBING CHAMBER KILN

In the central part of Honshu Island there lies the traditional capital and cultural center of Japan, the city of Kyoto. It is a beautiful city clothed in architecture of its past. Kyoto's thousands of temples and shrines, such as Ginkakuji, Kyomizu, Shisendo, and Hienjingo illuminate and enhance the city. Kyoto's traditional celebrations such as Diamongo and Gionmatsuri bring the old world life to the modern day. In the southeast sections against the mountains, quietly embedded in the narrow secluded streets between great temples, lay hundreds of the big Kyoto chamber kilns, which were filled every fortnight with the works of thousands of potters.

The early 60s were really the beginning of the decline of the chamber kiln, which suffered from the

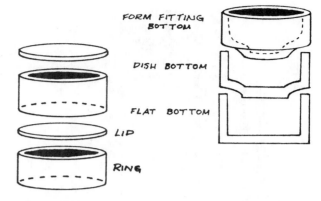

Fig. 4—82: *Saggars were developed to take advantage of the increased chamber space.*

Fig. 4—80: *The climbing chamber kiln*

Fig. 4—81: *Kyomizu climbing chamber kiln, Kyoto, Japan. I learned wood firing from firing this kiln every month for 2 1/2 years.*

lack of available wood and high firing costs. Today, because of smog ordinances, these southeast sections of Kyomizu, Gojo, and Sennuji have had to change to electric or gas kilns, ending an almost 600-year reign of the climbing chamber kiln.

The transition from the Tamba style tube kiln to the climbing chamber kiln is quite evident in the segmenting of the tube into distinctive chambers. This allowed for greater control in firing and also increased the stacking space per chamber. The development of saggars paralleled chamber kiln development. Saggars are fireclay containers or capsules that contain pots, enabling them to be stacked in the kiln. They were developed in China during the Sung Dynasty (960-1279) to assist in the firing of Tenmoku tea bowls in Chienyao, Hohnan and other sites and Celedon wares in the North. A great deal of knowledge regarding saggars and kiln design was brought to Seto, Japan, in 1265 by Toshiro, who apprenticed in Chien Yao, Fukien Province, China. (Fig. 4-80 and Fig. 4-81).

The largest chamber kiln was the Tobe Village Kiln (destroyed in July 1963). It had a total of 15,000 cubic feet; the largest of its seven chambers was 25' long by 10' tall by 10' wide and required 40 tons of wood to fire. The Kyoto style chamber kiln was the most advanced of all the chamber kiln designs and is the style of a chamber kiln dealt with here (Fig. 4-82 and Fig. 4-83 photo, Fig. 4-84, Fig. 4-85 and Fig. 4-86 photo, Fig. 4-87).

The Kyoto chamber kiln is narrower than other chamber kilns. Over the years, the kiln builders found that a taller and narrower chamber had a more even temperature distribution and provided more control over the reduction process. The chambers have a double-radius arch with the acute radius off-center towards the back. This causes a slight congestion in the draft flow by rolling over, as the arrow in the diagram shows, and creates a reduction atmosphere when the kiln is fired properly. To fire a reduction chamber, quick interval stoking must be used all the time to keep the wood coals stacked high in the firebox.

Fig. 4—83: *Fifth chamber stacking in the Kyomizu kiln.*

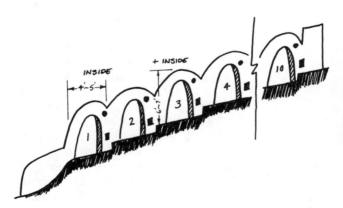

Fig. 4—84: *Cross section of the Kyoto chamber kiln.*

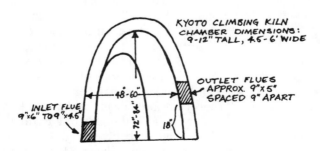

Fig. 4—85: *Kyoto chamber dimensions.*

Fig. 4—86: *Inside view of second chamber used for reduction only.*

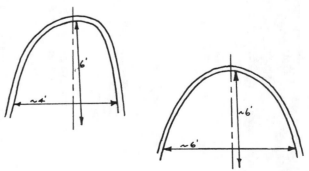

Fig. 4—87: *Comparison of the Kyoto chamber and a chamber typical of other climbing kilns.*

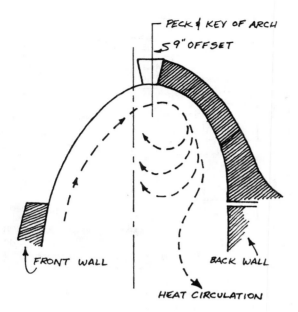

Fig. 4—88: *The offset peak encourages a reduction atmosphere.*

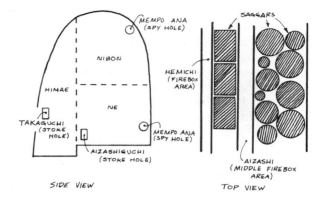

Fig. 4—90: *Vertical divisions of the Kyoto chamber kiln.*

The middle fire and oxidation chambers have a less radical arch, closer to a single radius arch, which releases congestion and facilitates oxidizing conditions (Fig. 4-88). In some kilns, such as the Tobe kiln (on Shikoku Island), and the Onda and Koishibara kilns (on Kyushu), the width of the chamber is almost equal to the height. This lends the kiln an oxidizing atmosphere, which makes reduction a little harder to achieve. In firing oxidation, the stoking is allowed to burn completely down before stoking again, thus maintaining a relatively clear atmosphere.

The floor area of the Kyoto chambers is divided into specific areas or sections, called Hana, Tsunaka, and Donaka (Fig. 4-89). These divisions refer to the stoking of the wood into their areas according to the length of the toss: a short toss for Hana, a medium toss for Tsunaka, and a long toss for Donaka. The chamber is fired (stoked) simultaneously from both sides. Thus, when the lead fireman yells "Tsunaka," one knows where to toss the wood.

A cross section of the chamber shows that it is also divided vertically into three sections (Fig. 4-90). The Himae is the front part of the chamber contain-

ing the firebox, a 9" trough next to the front wall and one row of empty saggers at the bottom, which act as a bagwall. The Himae is fired (stoked) through the Takaguchi stoke hole. The Nibon is the top half of the main stacking area and also is fired by the Takaguchi stoke hole. The Ne is the bottom half and is fired to proper temperature through the Aizashiguchi stoke hole, which is between the saggar settings.

It takes approximately 56 hours to fire a chamber kiln of seven chambers (such as the Suzuki kiln shown in Fig. 4-91) to cone 8-9. Each chamber is 14 feet x 6-1/2 feet x 4-1/2 feet. The firebox is stoked for 15 hours to a temperature of 1,000°C (1,832°F). Then the firemen begin stoking from both sides of the first chamber using a quarter bundle of wood (a bundle is 15" in diameter by 18" long) per stoking for the first hour or so. Gradually this is increased to half a bundle in the second hour and to three-quarters of a bundle in the third hour. By the fourth hour one bundle is used every 3-4 minutes to provide a reducing atmosphere. In the seventh hour (the last hour) up to two bundles may be used in each stoking. Chambers 1, 2, and 3 take approximately 75 bundles per side and seven hours of stoking for a reduction firing. Chambers 4, 5, 6 and 7 take approximately 60 bundles per side and five hours of stoking for an oxidation firing. It takes constant inspection to fire a chamber kiln and, perhaps most important, a constant rhythm must be

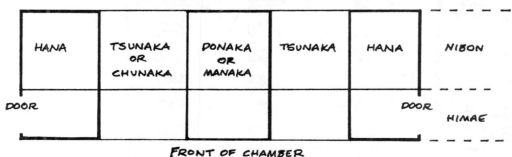

Fig. 4—89: *Chamber floor divisions.*

maintained. In the case of middle to oxidation firing, stoking must precede each complete burning down of the coals or temperature will not be increased. A feel for the amount of wood per stoking must be learned by experience. Too much wood and the kiln will choke; too little and the kiln will not increase in temperature.

Fig. 4—91: *The Suzuki cooperative kiln.*

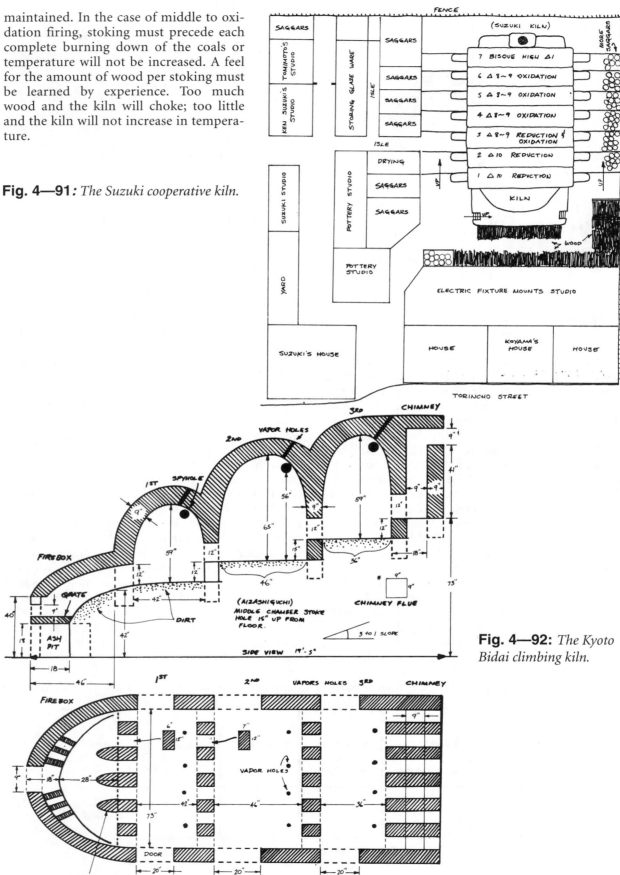

Fig. 4—92: *The Kyoto Bidai climbing kiln.*

KYOTO BIDAI AND KAWAII CLIMBING KILN

To construct the small Kyoto Bidai climbing kiln, a foundation was roughly dug in the side of a small slope. The wall foundation was laid up with large blocks (7" deep x 11" long x 9" wide) mortared together. The entire perimeter wall was structured up to the beginning of the arch curve. This included the chimney structure but not the firebox. The wall bricks (6" x 3 1/2" x 9 1/2" to 6" x 6" x 9 1/2") were laid with a thick fireclay mortar joint. The front wall leans slightly in towards the chamber up to a height of 38" and then the drastic curve begins for the arch (Fig. 4-93). The first chamber wall had to be braced with poles before the first arch was begun (Fig. 4-94). The peak of the arch was offset to the back of the chamber centerline in order to throw the force of the arch back onto the common wall and in turn to the chimney.

Fig. 4—94: *The first arch.*

This relieved the first chamber leading wall and the firebox arch. If the pressure had been too great, the first chamber wall would have been braced. The second and third arches (Fig. 4-95) were laid and properly wedged from the bottom to the top center on both sides (Fig. 4-96). After the three arches were completed, the firebox construction was begun without the use of an arch framing support (Figs. 4-97 and 4-98). When done, the whole kiln was plastered with a 3"-thick mixture of fireclay, dirt and straw, leaving the vapor and flame hole sticks in place to be fired out. A detailed description of this wood firebox and others can be found in Chapter 8. This kiln was built with odd-size bricks and blocks, compared to our standard sizes, which explains the odd flue sizes and spacing. Standard brick-size flues (4 1/2" x 9") spaced 9" apart can be used.

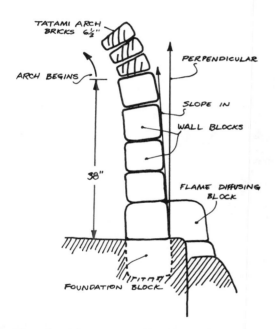

Fig. 4—93: *Front wall construction.*

Fig. 4—95: *Second chamber construction.*

Fig. 4—96: *Laying the arch.*

Fig. 4—97: *Chambers completed.*

Fig. 4—98: *Laying the firebox.*

Fig. 4—99: *Firebox construction.*

Kawaii Kiln

In the spring of 1984 Takichi Kawaii built a Kyoto style four-chamber kiln in the country outside of Kyoto, Japan. Takichi Kawaii, John Chappell and I were close friends in the early 1960s in Japan and we all traveled to Australia for exhibitions in the fall of 1963. In May of 1984 I went to Japan to visit my mentor and friend, Kondo Yuzo, who was ailing, and other old friends from my days of working in Kyoto with Tomimoto Kenkichi, including Takichi Kawaii (Fig. 4-100). The visit to Takichi's house was very enjoyable. We reminisced about old times, old pictures and events, and walked down the street and over to his uncle's Kanjiro, Kawaii, museum and studio. Takichi was anxious to have me see his new kiln and we made arrangements to drive out to the new studio (Fig. 4-101). I noticed that the construction technique had not changed since the Bidai kiln was constructed in 1962. The Kawaii kiln interior dimensions are 7' wide, 4' deep and 5'-8" tall with the chamber inlet and exit flues at 7" by 10", except the last chamber exit flues which are bigger at 9" by 10" (Fig. 4-102). There is a 12" to 15" step between the chambers. The dogi (firebox) is 5' tall with 18" to 24" grate bar length to span over the ash pit on to the firebox mound. There are two extra stoke holes on the sides of the dogi. Tatami mat bricks were used in the arches and the firebox. (See photographs). The Kawaii kiln and the Bidai kiln have a similar floor plan, in fact almost exact. Notice the bracing on the dogi (firebox) and front chamber to support the outward thrust of the weight of the arch. This bracing is a must on all similar chamber kilns.

Fig. 4—101: *Kawaii chamber kiln before earth mix plastering.*

Fig. 4—100: *Talkichi Kawaii and author at his studio in 1984.*

Fig. 4—102: *Second chamber, stoke hole built into door bricking.*

ASO PER GLUMSO KILN

I built a small chamber kiln at Clifford and Elsa (Gress) Wright's home in Aso per Glumso, Denmark, in 1964. This kiln, built on a 25° slope with a 16' chimney, had two 60-cubic-foot chambers and one 40-cubic-foot bisque chamber, which provided a natural draft rate of 4' per second (Figs. 4-103 and 4-104). The kiln was fired by an oil drip (diesel fuel) and wood. An interesting feature of this kiln is the firebox arrangement, which is actually inside the first chamber (Fig. 4-105). This was done to economize on bricks and to save on fuel and time by having all the direct heat in the first chamber from beginning to maximum temperature. I used a side-firing method with oil drip along with wood stoking that saved long hours of labor.

The stacking arrangement for the kiln was based on two and one-half shelves across the back with one row of saggars in front of them (Fig. 4-107). The back row of saggars consisted of two 15" saggar bungs

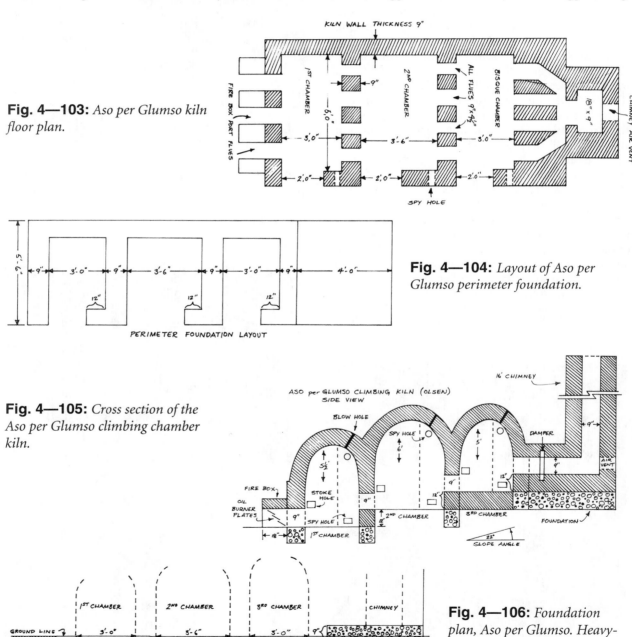

Fig. 4—103: *Aso per Glumso kiln floor plan.*

Fig. 4—104: *Layout of Aso per Glumso perimeter foundation.*

Fig. 4—105: *Cross section of the Aso per Glumso climbing chamber kiln.*

Fig. 4—106: *Foundation plan, Aso per Glumso. Heavy-duty foundation due to very soggy ground and high water table.*

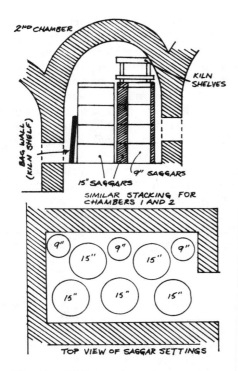

Fig. 4—107: *Stacking arrangement for the Aso per Glumso kiln.*

spaced between three 9" saggar bungs up to the height of 3 feet. On top of these saggars, two and one-half 18" x 12" shelves were laid for shelf stacking. The front row of saggars consisted of three bungs of 15" saggars stacked to 3 feet and then lidded for pots. In front of these saggars and resting lengthwise on edge against them, four 18" x 12" x 1 1/2" kiln shelves were set to act as the bagwall in the firebox. Each chamber had the same stacking arrangement, except the saggar bungs were not as high and closely stacked in Chambers 2 and 3, providing more shelving space for open stacking. This was done to ensure better oxidation firing conditions in these chambers. Loose stacking facilitates an oxidizing atmosphere, while tight stacking helps in gaining a reducing atmosphere. With

Fig. 4—109: *Front view of my first home studio built in 1965 (taken in 1998).*

Fig. 4—108: *Backyard and kiln site.*

proper stacking, the kiln held between 150 and 250 pots per chamber, depending upon their size.

An epilogue on my Aso per Glumso kiln – I am happy to say it was destroyed by vandals on New Years Eve back in the late '70s. I am happy because it took vandals to knock it down and not the fire. The kiln was used by various Scandinavian and foreign potters for over a decade. Today, the fine house/studio/kiln shed I built is occupied by pigs, sheep and bales of hay (Figs. 4-108 and 109). My good friends, writer/poet Elsa Gress and American painter Clifford Wright, who founded the Decenter International Art Center and contributed so much to the Danish art culture, have both passed on.

BIZEN KILN

The Bizen kiln is unusual in both function and design when compared to other Japanese kilns, and is only indigenous to the Imbe region of Okayama prefecture in central Japan. Its use is kept alive by a small group of potters working in the traditional style who particularly desire the special effects it enables them to achieve. (Fig. 4-110)

Before one can understand this type of kiln, however, one must first understand one of the important design factors for a kiln —the clay to be fired. The clay used for the commercial manufacture of Bizen ware is a semi-refined clay with an iron content of 4 to 5 percent that has been mixed 2/3 to 1/3 with a grey stoneware clay of the Shigaraki type. And for this commercial ware ordinary climbing chamber kilns are used. However, the special clays used by the artist potters are more challenging. One artist potter, Kei Fujiwara, uses a blend of three clays. The clay body is 60 percent groggy black clay, which has 10-plus percent iron and considerable organic materials in it. This clay is dug from under the rice paddies at a depth of seven feet and aged for a minimum of one year before use. To this clay is added 20 percent sea sediment clay, an alkaline clay dug offshore at a depth of 2 to 5 feet. The other 20 percent body addition is a yellow mountain clay that is very plastic and refined nat-

Fig. 4—110: *Kei Fujiwara's kiln firing.*

urally. Upon firing, this clay mixture has a tendency to bloat, blister, crack, and sag if fired too rapidly. Even under ideal firing conditions the normal loss averages 50 percent due to these faults. The commercial clay used is more reliable in that there is a smaller loss (20 percent) due to bloating, blistering, cracking and sagging.

All Bizen ware is unglazed ware. It relies totally on fired clay color, atmospheric conditions, fire flashing, the use of various design techniques, such as Hidasuki (use of straw), Matsuka (use of pine needles) and natural deposit of wood ash, and stacking methods, to obtain variation in clay color. It is only the artist potters, however, who are using riskier clays and exploiting all these techniques, who find the true Bizen expression.

The Bizen artist potter's kiln is designed to overcome the undesirable nature of the clay and at the same time to complement its natural beauty when fired. To accomplish this, the design offers (1) great chamber area of direct fire flashing, (2) low chamber draft, allowing for maximum amount of wood ash deposit, (3) variation in chamber design to give atmosphere variation, (4) maximum efficiency of wood consumption over a seven-day firing period with minimum stoking and draft, and (5) minimum loss of heat over gradual temperature increase.

The fire mouth (dogi) of this kiln is interesting for two reasons: (1) it is the most open fire mouth of all Japanese kilns and (2) the fire mouth itself is the first and most important chamber. There is no filler mound from the fire hole to the flue holes of the next chamber, but only a gradual incline that is stepped halfway (Fig. 4-111). The stepped portion of the fire mouth is actually made of shelves that stretch across the width of the fire mouth on which pots are stacked. It gives the pots a direct access to the flame flashing and intense reduction atmosphere that contains ash for deposit.

The average climbing chamber kiln wall is 9" to 10" thick and loosely constructed, with vapor holes

running the length of each chamber on top. However, the Bizen kiln walls average from 10" to 13" thick, are tightly constructed with no vapor holes and are insulated with overcoats of fireclay, straw and earth mixture. The thick, tight construction reduces heat loss and makes for more intense soaking over a gradual temperature rise with minimum fuel consumption. Kiln expansion and contraction are accommodated by an unusually long and gradual firing and cooling cycles.

Between the fire mouth and the first chamber there is a 24" draft flue that contains a small chamber called the himitsu, or secret chamber (Fig. 4-112). The flue holes leading into the himitsu are very small (3" x 6"), which increases the draft rate through it and to the first chamber. Small pieces such as tea bowls

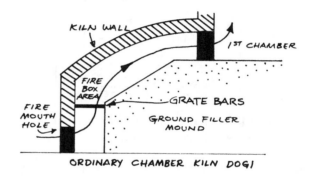

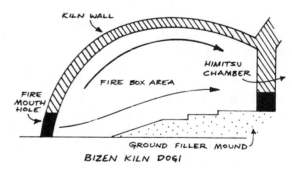

Fig. 4—111: *The absence of a filler mound and the use of the fire mouth as the first chamber provide an intense reduction atmosphere in the Bizen kiln.*

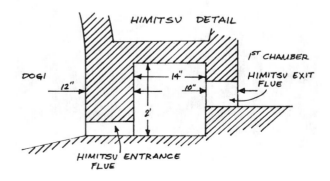

Fig. 4—112: *Cross section of the himitsu.*

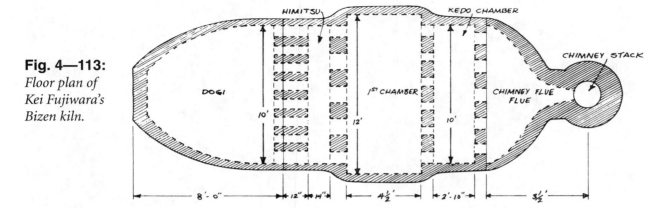

Fig. 4—113: *Floor plan of Kei Fujiwara's Bizen kiln.*

and sake bottles are stacked in the himitsu. It is very good for intense flame and ash flashing, due to the small flues and chamber size which forces the fire to pass through the ware at a fast crossdraft rate. Also, there is no rise in the entrance and exit flue levels to reduce the crossdraft.

The first chamber, ichi no ma, is the largest of the chambers (Fig. 4-113). The flue holes leading from the himitsu to the first chamber are average size (6" x 9"). This allows the fast draft produced by the himitsu flue holes to pass into the first chamber with ease, without causing back pressure in the himitsu. Once inside the first chamber, the draft slows down considerably because of the large chamber volume. This chamber has built-in side fire holes (takiguchi) that help raise temperature and create greater flame flash-

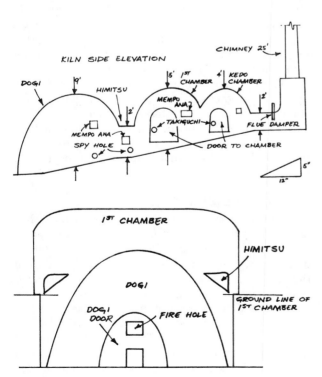

Fig. 4—114: *Front and side elevations of the Bizen kiln.*

ing, not only at the bottom, but also at the top of the chamber. The chamber's atmosphere is from middle fire to reduction, depending upon what is desired. Six-by-nine-inch flue holes lead out of the first chamber and into the second.

The second chamber, kedo, is considerably lower in height and smaller in width. No shelvings are used in this chamber; all wares are stacked on the floor and upon one another. There is a built-in fire hole that is sometimes used to add extra fire flashing for effect and also to raise the temperature if need be. The flue holes leading out of the second chamber are a bit bigger, 6" x 10", and lead into a single stack that runs for 3 1/2 feet before rising into the chimney. As in all previous chambers, there is a step or rise of 5" for every 12" between each chamber; however, between the last chamber (kedo) and chimney there is no rise. (Fig. 4-114)

The chimney for this kiln is approximately three times the total rise of the kiln, or 25 feet. The flue stack leading into the chimney is a 10" diameter opening, which is the same size as the height of the exit flues of the kedo chamber. There is a damper located at the flue entrance to the chimney, which is used to control draft rate and atmosphere conditions in the first and kedo chambers. The main function of the chimney is to create a greater pull at the start of the firing in the fire mouth and to slow down the overall draft rate later in firing. By closing the damper at the firing of the first or second chamber, one can back up the draft rate, creating a reduction atmosphere; opening it up allows an oxidation atmosphere. At the end of the firing the flue damper is closed to assure even, slow cooling.

STACKING OF BIZEN KILN

The fire mouth, or dogi, is loaded from the front through the fire mouth hole, which is quite large (3 1/2 feet by 2 feet) when open. It is stacked on the three step levels with posts and shelves reaching across the width and to the top of the chamber (Figs. 4-115 and 4-116). The first step's stacking contains the most pieces. The amount

Fig. 4—115: *Stacking arrangement in the dogi.*

decreases with each step because of the incline of the floor to the himitsu flue. Under each step's stacking, there are small air spaces (3" x 5") across the floor. There is also a 6" space between the top setter and the chamber roof to allow the draft to move freely over the top. The rest of the draft travels directly through the tightly stacked ware. Because of the tapering effect of the back of the chamber and the small himitsu flue holes, the draft is forced to move down and through the ware from the top, to enter the himitsu flue holes.

The himitsu is stacked by laying the pots on the ground and upon one another (Fig. 4-117). This

Fig. 4—116: *Detail of the stacking arrangement.*

Fig. 4—117: *Stacking arrangement in the himitsu.*

small chamber is stacked until the level of the pots reaches the middle of the himitsu entrance and exit flue hole levels. The himitsu is very difficult to load, and must be loaded before the fire mouth and the first chamber stacking. The pots are placed in this chamber by putting them through the fire mouth and first chamber flues and setting them on the floor. There is an opening in the side of the himitsu, which a small person could crawl through. Both methods of stacking are used.

The first chamber is also stacked by using posts and shelves that run the width of the chamber and within 6" of the top of the chamber. As in the fire mouth stacking, there are draft spaces beneath the first shelf stacking to allow an under draft. There is a 9" to 10" space (hemichi) in front of the stacking running the length of the chamber which is the firing trough for the side fire hole, or takiguchi.

The second chamber is stacked by laying the pots upon one another on the floor. The piling of pots fills about two-thirds of the chamber. There is a himichi left in front of the pots in case stoking is needed, for fire effect or to raise temperature. Sometimes it is fired to change the usual oxidation atmosphere to reduction.

FIRING OF BIZEN KILN

The total kiln firing takes exactly 7 days. It is divided into three main firing phases. The first phase, which lasts 2 1/2 days, is stoking the fire mouth air duct. The second phase is stoking the fire mouth from the fire hole; it lasts 4 days. The last phase, lasting 12 hours, is stoking the chambers.

The stoking of the fire mouth air duct is a very simple procedure. At the start, a small fire (similar to a camp fire) is built half in the fire duct and half out (Fig. 4-118). As it burns to embers, more sticks (about 12" to 15" long and 1" to 3" thick) are added. When the embers become sufficiently large, they are pushed into the fire mouth and more wood is added to the original embers.

Fig. 4—118: *The first stage of firing.*

After 2 1/2 days of this process, there is a large bed of hot glowing embers lining the inside of the fire mouth. This long ember building process completely dries out all the ware in the whole kiln and produces sufficient heat to ignite the wood used in the fire-mouth firing. This phase may be called the pre-heating period, since none of the ware is bisqued.

After a sufficient ember bed is formed, the stoking is done with huge pieces, ranging in size from 3' to 4' long and from 2" to 5" thick. They are not fed straight in, but pushed in diagonally along the inside fire mouth curve on both sides; when full, more pieces are loaded straight in. When they burn down completely, the process is repeated. After approximately 2 days of this, 1/4 and 1/2-size fireplace logs are used to stoke. On the fourth day, the huge sticks are used for stoking once again, along with the logs. The large logs burn slowly and with a low flame. With the addition of the huge sticks, ignition occurs almost instantly, creating large bursts of flames, and filling the atmosphere with natural ash. During this process, depending upon results desired, large amounts of pine needles may be thrown in that explode and splash the pots with their ash. When the proper temperature is reached at the end of 6 1/2 days, a soaking fire is maintained to finish off the first and kedo chambers. To determine the temperature, there are spy holes at the top and bottom, and on the side at the rear of the chamber to view saggar cones. However, fire color is usually the determining factor as to when the chamber is finished.

The himitsu is not stoked, but relies totally on the firing of the fire mouth for its effects and temperature.

The first chamber is fired through the fire hole or takiguchi, which is only on the one side of the kiln. The wood, small pieces ranging in size from 12" to 15" long and 1-2" thick, is liberally thrown in until a 12" flame is coming out the spy hole (mempo ana). The fire is allowed to burn down and then is rebuilt. This is done until the finishing temperature is reached, determined by fire color and saggar cones visible through the spy hole. If reduction is desired, the chimney flue is damped and more wood is thrown in to keep a continuous flame coming out the spy hole. This chamber is usually fired at a middle flame atmosphere (halfway between oxidation and reduction).

Depending upon the fire color and the saggar cones, the kedo chamber may or may not be stoked. Stoking is done with the same size wood as in the first chamber. After stoking, the fire is allowed to burn completely down before stoking again, thus maintaining an oxidation atmosphere. Again, depending upon results desired, pine needles may be stoked. Pine needles are added only to the fire mouth or kedo chamber. They produce better effects in the kedo, because there is no bagwall of tightly shelved pots and the pine needles, upon exploding, move directly over and through the pots lying on the kiln floor.

When the desired temperature is reached in the last chamber, all spy holes, fire holes and dampers are tightly closed. The kiln cools very slowly in about three days.

Visitors to Bizen usually raise the question: Why don't they alter the clay to a more manageable body, use an ordinary chamber kiln and cut down losses? As I mentioned, the commercial potters have done just that. Hamada Soji once told me, "If in your work you gain such a high perfection and technical skill that it no longer offers a challenge, you will have lost the interest and desire it takes to create." If such artist potters as Kei Fujiwara decided to improve their clay and thus change their kilns, they would defeat their purpose of challenging the Bizen expression.

Bizen — New Fujiwara Kiln

During the 1984 trip to Japan, I visited Kei Fujiwara. He was living in a beautiful new home that contained the studio, gallery, and kiln building with his son Yu Fujiwara and family. I was extremely fortunate Kei remembered me and invited me to visit with him, for he was 84 years old and extremely ill. As we talked, I could see the enthusiasm and the love of the Bizen expression in his eyes, but also some sadness in the commercialization of Bizen ware. We talked about Tomimoto, my visit in the 60s, the changes that have happened, San Jose and Herbert Sanders, his dislike of Las Vegas (so much so he spent most of his time in his room), my work — he liked a coyote platter I did — my home, and of Yu's success and that the old house has been replaced with a park with the old kiln as a memorial. Kei told me he only sleeps now and was ready to go on — he gave me two autographed

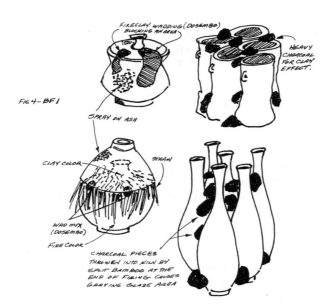

Fig. 4—120: *Side view from dogi looking up past the other chambers.*

Fig. 4—119: *Decoration styles.*

books on him in appreciation for my visit and that his old kiln was in *The Kiln Book*. Yu Fujiwara's kiln is clinically clean with smooth architectural lines and always maintained as an impressive structure (Fig. 4-120). The firing sequence has been modernized as well: Two days on gas alone up to 600°C — two days with wood and gas together up to 900°C — two days with wood alone to temperature and finish. Only southern Japanese coastal pine wood can be used to fire this kiln. I believe the kiln is fired in a mostly oxidizing atmosphere with special stacking techniques used, like blocking out areas on the pot with dosembo (fireclay wadding), spraying ash on, dumping charcoal in on top of the pots at the end, etc. (Fig. 4-119 drawing). My visit with Kei was on a Friday and Sunday I returned to have lunch with Yu and family to learn that Kei had been taken to the hospital. He died a short time later, before I returned to California.

Hollyweird (Anagama) Tube

In 1985 I built an anagama derivative kiln that had a Bizen style front chamber connected to a tube style second chamber at my Pinyon Crest home/pottery, jokingly named the "Hollyweird tube." The kiln was built from the chimney to the front because it had an existing chimney. Hard firebrick was used for the kiln's side walls construction and Thermal Ceramics K-26 I.F.B. Castable was used to cast the two large dome-shaped chamber ceilings (Fig. 4-HT1 drawing).

Overall length of the kiln is 20'. The front chamber is 8' long, 55" wide and 48" tall and the second chamber is 12' long, 55" wide, 3' tall and tapering down and into the 18"-by-18" chimney entrance flue with the chimney being 18" by 24" by 12' tall (Fig. 4-121 drawing). Three large exit flues connect the front chamber to the second chamber bisecting the second chamber firebox grate area, thereby providing air under the grate and over the grate for efficient burning in the main side-stoke firebox. A secondary air supply for this firebox is a 5" extruded clay tube with graduate air holes along the vertical side placed under the grate. Please refer to Chapter 8 for details. Air supply is regulated by a shutter or a plug on the outside end of the tube which passes through the ash pit side wall (Figs. 4-113, 114, 115).

The front firebox is just over 3' long and a full chamber width with a 18"-x-13 1/2" deep, dug-out ash pit (Chapter 8). The access to the chamber is through the firebox using the ash pit as a walk way, therefore the grate bars are removed after every firing. Grate bars are placed 3/4" apart using broken kiln shelves spacers and wedged in tight using a wadding to prevent shifting

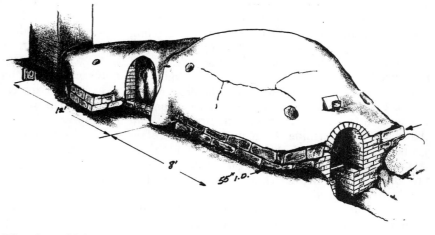

Fig. 4 — 121: *Hollyweird tube.*

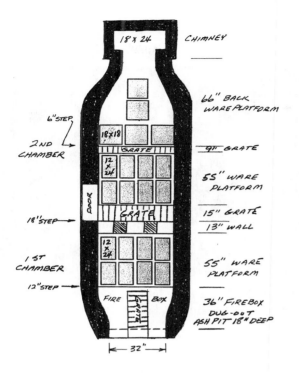

Fig. 4—122 drawing: *Hollyweird tube floor plan.*

(Wadding — 1. a mix of refractory fireclay with coarse sand and sawdust or rice hulls just enough to hold together best for separating pots, or 2. a mix of equal parts of kaolin and alumina best suited for separating kiln shelves, post and grate bars.) The tight spacing of the grate bars is to reduce the size of coals dropping into the ash pit thereby reducing the build up. If the coals build up to the bottom of the grate bars, the air supply can be choked off and the kiln will literally stop. To open the air supply, the coals are removed from the ash pit by raking, thus the term "raking the coals". During a normal 60-hour firing, the coals never have to be raked out of the ash pit. One large inlet (15" x 18") flue and one stoke hole (9" x 13 1/2") are built into the door bricking. A series of construction photographs details the building process.

Over the last 15 years the kiln has been fired on the average of twice a year, being held at cone 11-plus for 35 to 40 hours in the front chamber and 10 to 15 hours in the back chamber per firing, representing over 1,200 hours at top temperature with over 30 up-and-down cycles. The K-26 L.I. castable has held up perfectly, while the hard bricks have slagged, spalled and melted. When the kiln is finally retired, it will be precipitated by hard brick failure.

Fig. 4—123: *Overall view of Hollyweird tube during firing with Tom Gaines at firebox, Patricia Ferber and author stoking the back.*

Fig. 4—124: *Side view of Hollyweird tube. Notice secondary air supply tube at bottom right on door.*

Fig. 4—125: *Front view during cooling from 600°F. Ash pit door cracked open.*

Fig. 4—126: *Breaking into existing chimney and starting the walls and back tube section.*

Fig. 4—127: *Back section showing walls and back chamber inlet flues — IFB transition bricks.*

Fig. 4—128: *Front chamber section showing both firebox door arches.*

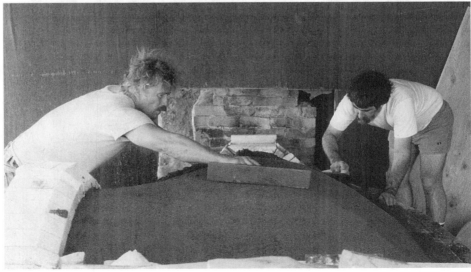

Fig. 4—129: *IFB transition walls slanted in and finished — building platform for supporting dirt.*

Fig. 4—130: *Conrad Calipong and author building up earth mound for front section.*

Fig. 4—131: *Laying plastic over dirt mound to create a non-porous surface. Vincent Seuz pictured.*

Fig. 4—132: *Vincent Suez and author shaping back chamber earth mound.*

Fig. 4—133: *Slap troweling 2,600 IFB—RFT castable 5" thick onto front chamber form.*

Fig. 4—134: *Entire casting covered with wet towels and plastic for a 24-hour cure period.*

Fig. 4—135: *Plastering with adobe earth mix to shape the final form of the kiln.*

SALT GLAZE CROSSDRAFT KILN

The basic plan for this crossdraft salt-glaze kiln was designed by John Chappell at Domura, Japan, in 1962. The floor plan (Fig. 4-137) is interesting because it is a tandem kiln with a common wall separating a two-chamber (40-cubic-feet each) kiln and a 50-cubic-foot salt glaze kiln. The two share a common chimney. A long, low chamber is excellent for

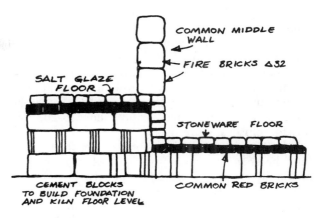

Fig. 4—136: *Foundation plan.*

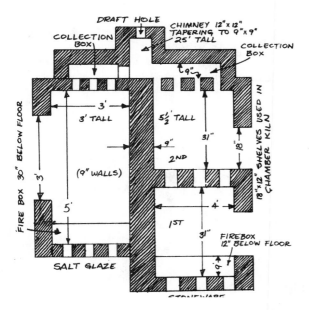

Fig. 4—137: *Floor plan of John Chappell's kiln.*

Fig. 4—138: *John Chappell working at the potters wheel in 1962 in Domura, Japan.*

salt glaze for it allows direct salting into the chamber above the pottery (Fig. 4-138).

The salt glaze kiln is built upon a concrete block foundation covered with common red bricks, followed by a layer of medium duty firebricks (Fig. 4-136). It is not advisable to use high silica bricks, and never high silica insulating bricks when building a salt kiln. High- or medium-high alumina bricks are best, but if not available, any dense medium- to high-duty bricks can be used. The only sacrifice is in the life of the kiln, for it will be subject to quicker slagging by the soda.

One thing I learned from John Chappell about kiln building was to use whatever materials are available, regardless of whether it is the best or not. Just build the kiln, fire it until it collapses or melts, and then rebuild it. Considering that in the early '60s we did not have money for more than second-hand bricks and the lowest-priced fireplace bricks, kiln builders were improvisational with a "just do it" mentality. John felt if his kiln reached 50 firings, it was well worth it. In November of 1963, with this attitude, I built John's salt kiln at the pottery of Col Levy in Australia. It was my first kiln and mistakes were made in the depth of the firebox, otherwise the kiln functioned as it should, producing my first all-salt-glaze exhibition for Berry Stern's Gallery in Sydney.

The entire kiln and arch were built with the cheapest new and used straight bricks I could find. The kiln was fired with free crankcase oil, and side stoked with wood. Figure 4-141 is a revised design of John's kiln using different fireboxes; for gas, oil drip or wood, and with fuel combinations possible. For further descriptions of the fireboxes, refer to Chapter 8.

It takes two to three firings with enormous amounts of salt to break in a salt glaze kiln. On the average, one pound of salt per cubic foot of stacking space is required for an excellent salting in a new kiln. As the kiln matures the salt requirements will diminish. The salt is best introduced into the kiln chamber on salt-filled split bamboo poles about 2 1/2" in diameter and as long as the kiln is wide. These are inserted and flipped. The bamboo halves can be used for as many as three firings before they completely burn away. Salting should begin when maximum temperature (cone 9-10) is reached. In the kiln illustrated in Fig. 4-140, there are four salt stoke holes. The firebox and first top hole can be salted with an interval of 5-10 minutes before salting the top and back salt stoke holes. If all four are salted at once, allow 15-20 minutes for temperature recovery.

The firebox salt is always tossed over the bagwall into the chamber, never just dropped in. The solid arrows in Fig. 4-140 indicate a pattern for the first salting. The next salting is indicated by the open-arrow pattern, at which time the top and back are salted and the salt is thrown towards the firebox. If a reducing salt is desired, the dampers are closed, the kiln salted, a short time is allowed to pass for the pressure to build up, and then the dampers are opened. If an oxidation atmosphere is desired, the dampers are left open and the fuel is cut back a little before salting. The temperature drops at least 56°C with each salting, so an interval is needed to build the temperature up again. I consider it bad design and bad practice to salt directly through the burner ports or flues, for the obvious reason of the firebox's temperature and its consequent susceptibility to slagging.

When this kiln is fired, the back is usually cold, so a side burner must be lit or wood stoking has to be done to even out the temperature. An overall chamber length of 48" would help to even up the firing.

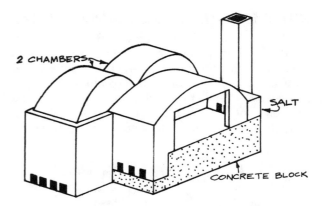

Fig. 4—139: *John Chappell's kiln.*

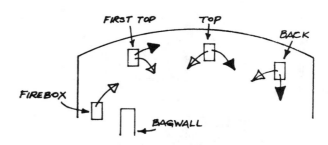

Fig. 4—140: *Salting pattern.*

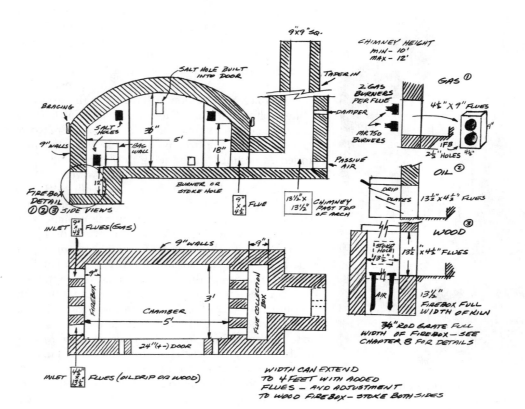

Fig. 4—141: *John Cappell's Domura design.*

Chapter 5

Downdraft Kilns

A downdraft kiln can be defined as a kiln which has draft movement starting with the inlet flues, circulates in the chamber, passes down through floor exit flues, and flows out the chimney (Fig. 5-1).

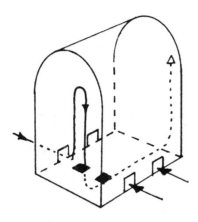

Fig. 5—1: *Air flow in a downdraft kiln.*

Downdraft kilns probably originated in Europe, perhaps in Germany after 1800. European porcelains had their beginning in the early 1700s when a man named Better in Germany developed a kiln that could reach the desired temperature of 1,300°C (2,372°F). For the next 100 years, considerable improvements in refractory materials were made, especially in saggars (which also played an important part in the Kyoto chamber kiln development). Coal and coke were introduced as a fuel, and new methods in kiln construction were developed to meet the higher temperatures. These included improved fireboxes, chimneys and draft systems that were being experimented with to increase efficiency. Better kilns, which would fire evenly, produce a more uniform quality and, of course, save on fuel and losses, were needed to meet the demands of industrialization. Thus the downdraft kiln was developed to replace the European bottle updraft kiln (see Chapter 6).

The downdraft kiln design offered inherently even temperature with the ability to control temperature distribution and atmosphere, economical fuel consumption, and the ability to expand the kiln to an extremely large size while retaining the firing characteristics of a smaller kiln.

The advent of the European downdraft kilns in Japan followed the Meiji Restoration in 1868. An Austrian chemist, Dr. G. Wagener, was a guest of the government and responsible for the establishment of national and prefectural ceramic research and training institutes in Japan. According to Tomimoto, he sent one of his students to Europe to learn about downdraft kiln construction and production methods. Upon the student's return to Japan, the production methods and downdraft kilns were introduced to the Seto and Tajimi areas in Gifu prefecture.

PROPORTIONAL RELATIONSHIPS OF EARLY NATURAL-DRAFT DOWNDRAFT KILNS

1. The height-to-width ratio is very important for satisfactory even firing (see Chapter 3, Principles in Kiln Design, Rule 1).

2. A downdraft kiln's proportional dimensions or multiples are as shown in Fig. 5-2 for natural draft.

3. The chimney must be placed at a right angle (90°) to the firebox inlet flues to provide a proper draft pull down through the middle of the chamber.

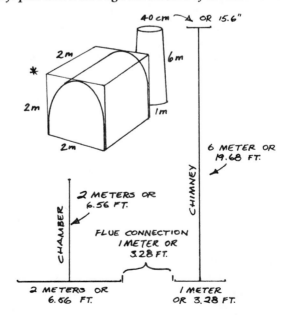

Fig. 5—2: *Proportions of early downdraft kilns. *Variance on 2m x 2m chamber to 1.7m x 1.7m with same chimney relationship.*

4. All rules in Chapter 3, Principles in Kiln Design, must be followed.

The proportional dimensions given here are based upon the analysis of Oriental kilns. These basic dimensions should be used as a starting point for designing a natural-draft downdraft kiln. In comparison to the nine principles of kiln design in Chapter 3, there are two minor discrepancies found in the proportional downdraft kiln dimensions.

First, Rule 5, concerning chimney height, states that for every foot of downward pull, add 3 feet of chimney; for every 3 feet of horizontal pull, add 1 foot of chimney. In comparison with downdraft chimney proportions, this would add an extra 1 1/2 ft. to the chimney. The two relationships between kiln chamber and chimney are so close that the proportional relationship can be used as the minimum and Rule 5 the maximum. In the case of forced draft, the chimney height can be reduced by about 1/4 or until a draft rate of 4 to 5 feet per second is achieved.

Second, Rule 6 states that the chimney diameter is 1/4 to 1/5 of the chamber diameter while the proportional dimensions give the chimney diameter as 1/2 of the chamber diameter. The reason for specifying such a large chimney base is that it will be able to accommodate additional kilns. This rule has generally been retained even though normally only one kiln is ever built. Remember, there is greater safety in having an oversized chimney diameter. To compensate for the extremely large bottom diameter, the chimney entrance flue is greatly restricted and the taper of the chimney is 2 1/2 to 1. If Rule 6 is followed, there is a saving in the number of bricks used in laying the chimney and the construction difficulty in tapering the chimney is eliminated. Thus, a more realistic proportional dimension can be derived that would be more in tune with modem forced-draft kilns.

Proportional relationships of modern forced or natural-downdraft kilns are shown in Fig. 5-3.

Notice that the chimney taper is 1 to 3/4 or 1 1/4 to 1. If forced-draft burners are used, the height of the chimney can be reduced by as much as 25 percent, but I know of no certain rule. The only way to determine this is to fire the kiln and adjust.

DOWNDRAFT TAJIMI STYLE KILN

Kenji Kato pottery, Tajimi, Japan. Mr. Kato's coal-fired downdraft kiln is approximately 250 cubic feet in size (Figs. 5-5). The kiln is fired in 50 hours to 1,300°C (2,372°F) in a very heavy reduction atmosphere and allowed to cool for three days or more. The firing cycle is quite slow due to the extreme thickness of the kiln walls and the fact that there are only two fireboxes. After 1,090°C (2,000°F) is reached, the reduction stoking rate is 10 to 12 shovels of coal every 20 minutes, while an oxidation stoking rate is 3 to 4 shovels every 20 minutes.

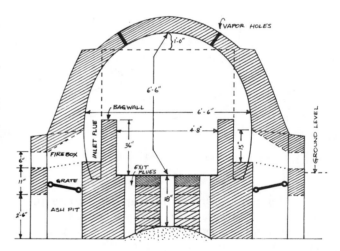

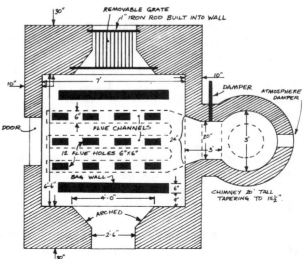

Fig. 5—5: *Cross section and floor plan of the Kato kiln.*

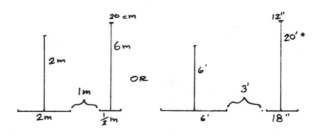

Fig. 5—3: *Proportions of modern downdraft kilns. For a 6 x 6 foot chamber, the chimney base must be at least 12" in diameter, the top 8" in diameter, and the height at least 20'. The distance between chamber and chimney can be smaller than 3' without affecting the chimney size.*

Fig. 5-6 illustrates how the chimney design could be changed using Rule 6 and the modem proportional relationships. The floor exit flues equal 432 square inches. The inlet flues from the firebox are a bit larger, around 500 square inches, but dampering the air supply when firing will equalize inlet and exit flues.

One of the most interesting features of this kiln is the bowed walls. They impart a curl to the circular, downward flame movement sooner than a straight wall (Fig. 5-7). This allows for a stronger natural flame movement to the center of the kiln.

The bagwalls are just a few feet shorter than the chamber length. They act as baffles, forcing the flames in equal directions into the chamber. For the bagwall to have its proper effect, it is important to have a large enough opening into the chamber from the firebox.

In stacking the kiln, the bottom shelves should be at least 4 1/2" off the floor. The shelves should be gapped and staggered about 2" apart in order to allow enough room for the draft to move easily through the floor (Fig. 5-8). Stacking too tightly could cause uneven temperature distribution and a hot firebox. Only experience and a few firings can reveal the best

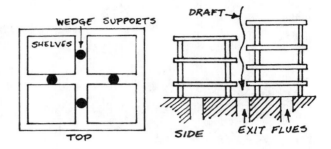

Fig. 5—8: *Proper stacking.*

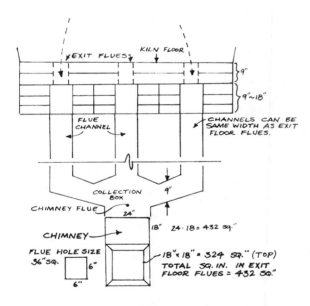

Fig. 5—6: *A possible change in chimney design, applying Rule 6 and proportional relationships.*

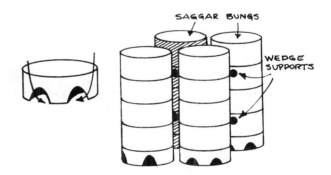

Fig. 5—9: *Saggar stacking.*

stacking arrangement. If saggars are used, the bottom saggars of each saggar bung should be fluted and spaced about an inch or more apart and wedged against one another (Fig. 5-9).

CIRCULAR DOMED NATURAL DOWNDRAFT KILN

Mansimran Singh, Dehli blue pottery, New Dehli, India. Circular domed downdraft kilns follow the same design and proportional dimension relationships as square or rectangular downdraft kilns.

Mr. Singh's coal-fired circular domed downdraft kiln is approximately 585 cubic feet in size (Fig. 5-11). It is fired from four fireboxes in about 19 hours. The firing atmosphere is primarily oxidizing to middle fire, but reduction takes place in some parts of the kiln. A typical firing schedule for a Cone 10 oxidation-to-middle fire is given in Table 5-1.

There can be 2 1/2 cones temperature variation between the top and the bottom of the firing cham-

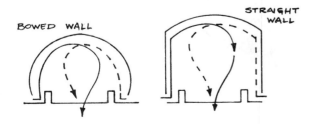

Fig. 5—7: *The bowed walls curl the flame sooner and move it more strongly.*

Fig. 5—10: *Mainstream Singh's domed kiln, New Delhi.*

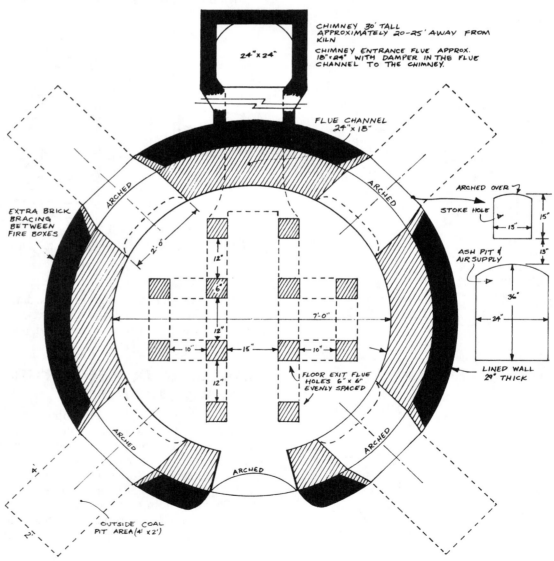

Fig. 5—11: *Floor plan for the Singh kiln.*

Fig. 5—14: *Exit flues in the floor.*

Fig. 5—15: *A view of one of the fireboxes.*

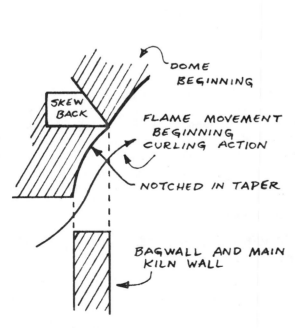

Fig. 5—16: *Wall recess.*

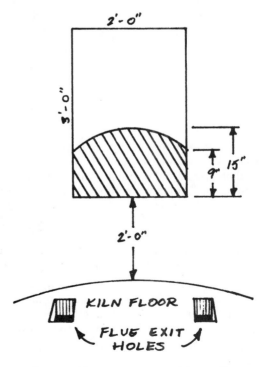

Fig. 5—17: *Front view of the wall recess.*

Table 5-1
Firing Schedule for Singh Circular Downdraft Kiln

Hour	Stoking for Each Firebox
1 to 3	1 shovel every 1/2 hr; firemouth open
4 to 6	2 shovels every 1/2 hr; brick up firemouth
7 to 12	3 shovels every 45 min.
12 to end	4 shovels every 50 min.; glaze tiles drawn
19	5 shovels every 50 min.; maximum firebox combustion

Total time of firing: 19 to 20 hours.

(Started by wood and kerosene, adding handfuls of coal)

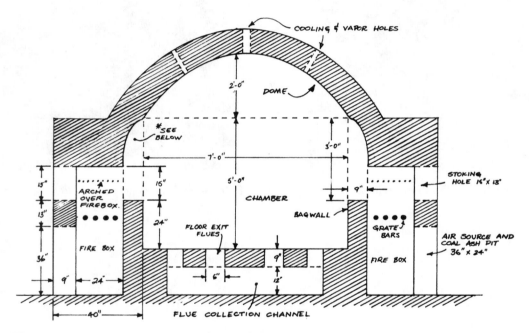

Fig. 5—12: *Cross section of the Singh kiln.*

ber. The variation depends primarily on weather conditions and the quality of the coal. Steam coal, Grade B, is usually used. Coal of poorer quality can lengthen the firing to 30 hours. Temperature differences can be accommodated by using glazes that mature earlier.

Notice that on Mr. Singh's kiln design the bagwall is actually the main wall of the chamber (Fig. 5-12). The wall is recessed, or notched, 9" deep by 2 feet wide and 3 feet in length with a firebox flue entrance of 15" x 24" opening into the chamber (Figs. 5-16 and 5-17). The beauty of this design is the elimination of a freestanding bagwall, which has a tendency to collapse. The notched area tapers into the dome, thus causing, as in Mr. Kato's bowed wall design, the circular downward flame movement. This design technique of using the kiln wall as the bagwall could also be used in a square or rectangular downdraft kiln.

Mr. Singh's downdraft kiln is stacked by using saggars. The kiln is stacked very tightly, up to within 6" to 8" of the dome. Because of the kiln's wall design, there is about 12" of space around the saggars up to the skewbacks. When using fuels such as coal, coke, or oil, the pottery must be protected from the residues of the ash produced and the sulphurous gases released. This is to ensure uniformity among pieces in sets, such as tableware.

DOWNDRAFT SALT KILN (SIDE-FIRED GAS)

Nils and Herman Kalher, Neastved, Denmark. The Kalher salt kiln has a 16-cubic-foot stacking space. It is constructed with high-alumina insulation refractories in order to withstand the slagging action of the salt.

Edmonton Fireworks Kiln

Following is a series of step-by-step construction photos of the Edmonton fireworks kiln built in 1998 using a multi-directional design. See Chapter 7 for details about this project and the similarly built Denmark church kiln.

Beginning of floor and walls.

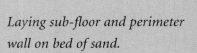

Laying sub-floor and perimeter wall on bed of sand.

Bricking fireplaces while working on main floor and sub-floor.

Walls and chimneys going up.

Spanning chimney flues on groundhog side.

Building walls, chimneys, and firebox arches.

Firebox arches finished. Builders tapering in (skewing) wall to receive castable while chimneys go up.

Building chamber platform and piling fillers and dirt on top.

Mounding dirt on top of kiln.

Finished dirt and sand mound.

Castable covered with wet towels and plastic while kiln walls are buttressed.

Buttressing finished. Time for 24-hour cure and start of adobe mix shaping.

After finishing adobe plastering, workers set chimney pipes and stack kiln on third day.

Decorating kiln with paint.

Author (left), Alfred Schmit, and Warren Mackenzie sitting in firebox of Edmonton fireworks kiln as it nears completion.

It's cone 10 inside the fireworks kiln, and pouring rain outside.

The rain didn't dampen the initial firing of the fireworks kiln.

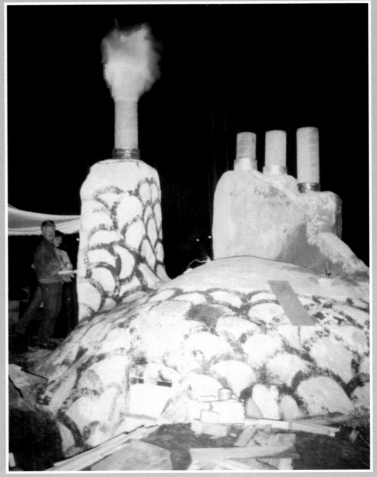

Lighting up the sky after the storm is finished.

Demonstrating chimney control on the other side.

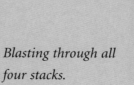

Blasting through all four stacks.

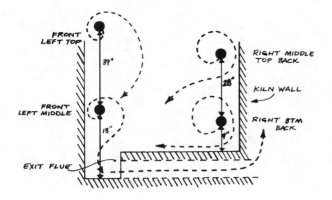

Fig. 5—18: *Flame movement in the Kalher side-firing salt kiln.*

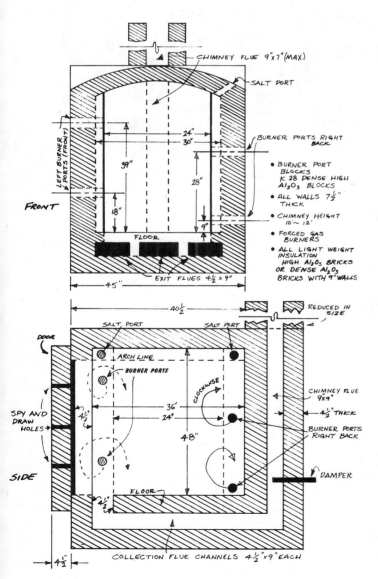

Fig. 5—19: *Front and side cross sections of the Kalher salt kiln.*

Fig. 5—20: *Exterior construction of the Kalher kiln, Neastved, Denmark.*

The interesting feature of this kiln is the side firing method used. By using side burners, a clockwise flame movement is developed in the upper hemisphere of the kiln. As the front burner flames shoot into the chamber, they roll down and over toward the center before being pulled down into the exit flue (Fig. 5-18). The back burner flames roll into the center and back down the wall before being pulled towards the exit flue. This rolling action gives even temperature distribution throughout the kiln. For the rotating flame pattern to work properly, the front burners must be high above the exit flue and the back burners lower and in between.

The salt ports are on the right side of the kiln. The back port salts directly above the right middle top burner and the front port salts directly into the flame of the left front top burner which provides an even salting of the kiln. The burners used are a forced air/gas type mounted into super duty port blocks. (See Chapter 8).

UNIVERSITY OF PUGET SOUND DOWNDRAFT KILN

The University of Puget Sound downdraft kiln was built by the students of a class I taught during the summer of 1971. The downward kiln was a part of a kiln complex which contained a two chamber wood kiln and salt glaze kiln (both crossdraft kilns), all using a common chimney. The downdraft kiln is about 75 cubic feet in size and was built with all medium- and low-duty straight bricks.

The kiln design is straightforward, using as few bricks as possible (Fig. 5-22). The walls are straight. A high rise arch was used to encourage a downward curling flame movement. Figures 5-23 through 5-37 point out some of the building stages of the kiln.

The inlet port flues are spaced evenly along the firebox wall (Fig. 5-23). Below them is a knockout row from which bricks can be removed if the port flues prove to be too small.

Fig. 5-24 (taken from the front of the kiln looking down past the door jamb) shows the laying out of the fireboxes on each side and the space for

Fig. 5—23: *Inlet port flues.*

Fig. 5—24: *Fireboxes and flue channels.*

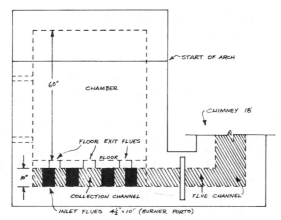

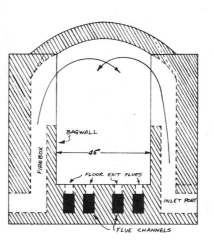

Fig. 5—22: *Cross sections of the Puget Sound downdraft kiln.*

Fig. 5—25: *Inside view of port flues, firebox and flue channels.*

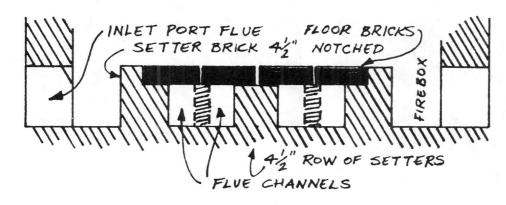

Fig. 5—26: *Channel supports and floor bricks.*

the flue channels beneath the floor. Fig. 5-25 shows the inside view of the port flues, the firebox, and the two main flue channels. Fig. 5-26 shows all three channel supports in place making four channels. It also shows how the floor bricks bridge over the flue channels.

Fig. 5-27 illustrates the use of one large flue channel down the center of the kiln floor. The channel should be at least 9" across and 9" to 12" or 3 to 4 bricks deep. One central flue channel can be used successfully in kiln floors ranging up to 4' in diameter, beyond which multi-floor channels should be used, spacing them evenly in the floor.

Once set and leveled, the bricks are mortared down. Before the arch is laid, the kiln walls (Fig. 5-29) are laid up past the makeshift skewback. The arch flame support is made from masonite bent to

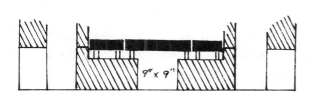

Fig. 5—27: *A central flue channel.*

Fig. 5—29: *Laying the kiln walls.*

Fig. 5—30: *The frame support is bent from Masonile (Photo by Jill Austin).*

Fig. 5—32: *Laying the arch (Photo by Jill Austin).*

Fig. 5—31: *The arch support is diagonally braced (Photo by Jill Austin).*

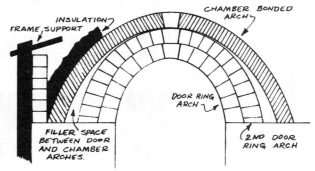

Fig. 5—33: *Cross section of the arch.*

the proper curve and nailed to supports of the chamber radius to secure its shape (Fig. 5-30). The frame support is installed and diagonally braced (Fig. 5-31). The arch is laid with straights from both sides simultaneously (Fig. 5-32) until the key brick can be cut and wedged into place. The arch is then wedged with bits and pieces of broken bricks which spring it off the arch frame and ensure its strength.

The door arch frame support is made to span the door jamb, and the door ring arch is laid in exactly the same way as the main chamber arch. Another ring arch, resting on top of the door arch, is then laid. The space left between the double ring arches of the door and the chamber arch is mortared in with cut bricks and wedged tight (Fig. 5-33).

Angle iron, 1/4" x 3", is placed at the four corners of the kiln and tied together by welding 1/2" around the bottom. Three angle iron braces are welded on the side walls; one 9" below the skewback, one on edge just at the skewback to make sure the skewback doesn't move (if it does the arch will drop), and one on top tying the frame together (Fig. 5-34). Two short

angle iron pieces are placed at the center of the door arch and on the back side of the kiln; they are welded together by a 1/2" to 3/4" rod across the top of the arch. Bracing runs diagonally from this short piece to each of the corners to tie together the angle iron kiln frame support (Fig. 5-35).

The first firing of this kiln was, as expected, terribly long. Moisture steamed from the kiln and concrete foundation throughout the firing. More than 36

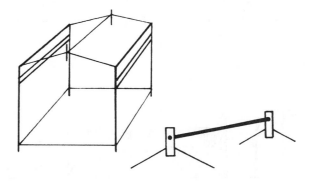

Fig. 5—34: *Angle iron and steel rod bracing arrangement.*

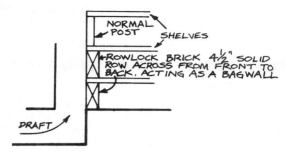

Fig. 5—37: *In this design the bagwall becomes the shelving support.*

Fig. 5—35: *Completed bracing in place (Photo by Ken Stevens).*

hours later, the firing was terminated; only one place in the kiln had exceeded Cone 9. The second firing went quicker and reached temperature, but one of the bagwalls fell, which caused irregular heating. (The bagwall, constructed with super-duty bricks, is loosely laid and should be supported against the shelving and firebox wall; see Fig. 5-36.) The floor flue holes were changed; the front ones were increased slightly and the back flue holes next to the chimney flue entrance were decreased slightly. Another consideration was that the burners were undersized for such a large (about 90-cubic-foot interior volume) hard brick kiln. They were the old pipe style burner. If 16 of the newer MR-750 rated at 75,000 Btu each, were used, eight per side, the kiln would have powered through the firing with no trouble. During a workshop at the University of Idaho at Boise, I built a similar 40-cubic-foot salt kiln using 12 MR-750 burners and the initial firing was about eight hours, standard for this size of hard brick kiln.

One improvement to eliminate any bagwall problems is to incorporate the bagwall into the shelf stacking arrangement (Fig. 5-37). (This change also decreases the size of the kiln, reducing the cost, yet provides the same amount of stacking space). For the first two or three shelf tiers bordering the firebox, rowlock bricks are used as a solid row from front wall to back wall. This is done for the next shelves on top until the desired bagwall heights is reached. The bricks can also be opened up to let some penetration through before switching to normal kiln post furniture. The first few rows of shelves will be limited to 4 1/2" rowlock or 9" soldier in height to make the bagwall. The space used by the rowlock or soldier row will be lost to stacking but gained when switching back to normal post. Looking at Fig. 5-37 and then at Fig. 5-38 you can see that by using this method of bagwall construction, the stacking space in the kiln can be increased by 33 percent. The kiln shelves incorporate the total 45" width plus the 9" used for the bagwall, giving a total of 54" of stacking space, using three 18" by 18" abreast. The space between shelves necessary for a downdraft is picked up

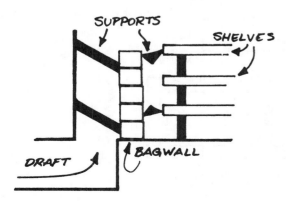

Fig. 5—36: *Bagwall support.*

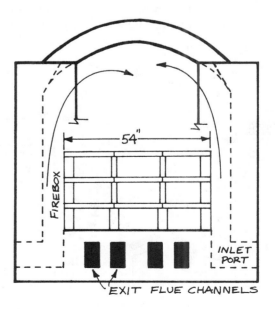

Fig. 5—38: *Cross section of the kiln using the stacking shown in Fig. 5—37.*

front to back. This same method of shelf/bagwall stacking is used in the next kiln design, a wood-fired downdraft.

FASTFIRE WOOD DOWNDRAFT

Since 1961, I have been firing wood kilns ranging in size from the huge Kyoto chamber kilns, to the Chinese style tube kilns in Vietnam, to my own small chamber kilns, to smaller 12 to 20 cubic foot fast-firing downdrafts which I call "fastfire wood."

There are many misconceptions in pottery. One is that extremely fast firing is bad for the pottery, glazes, furniture, and so on. A second is that wood kilns take an extremely long time to fire to Cone 10. It has been my experience that the speed of taking the kiln up to temperature causes no difference in the outcome of the bodies or glazes in either color or maturity. Granted, if the pots are saggared or tightly packed, a half hour of soaking time would be beneficial. I fire my pots in my Olsen 24 updraft gas kiln in an eight-hour firing and the same pots in a four-hour firing and I see no difference at all. Similar pots fired in 3 1/2 hours in my fastfire downdraft with wood show no difference as to melt and strength of the body. There is a difference in some glazes due to the fly ash that has been deposited on them, and a little warmer color of the clay body due to wood reduction.

Quick cooling can be dangerous. A slow cooling cycle is best, especially from 590°C down to 90°C.

An intermediate solution to the continuing problems of fuel shortages and rising costs is to have kilns capable of extremely fast firings and efficient fuel consumption. The illustrated fastfire wood kiln is an example of a finely tuned downdraft kiln capable of firing to Cone 10 in 3 1/2 hours using 1/4 cord of wood of any kind.

The bottom firebox section is made with straight, hard, refractory bricks. The actual kiln chamber and arch are laid with 1,260°C (2,300°F) insulation firebricks 4 1/2" thick, backed by flexboard (Fig. 5-40).

There are three important design principles that should be kept in mind when building an effective fastfire wood kiln:

1. The firebox area should be 10 times the horizontal cross section of the chimney. For fastfire, increase firebox area by 20 percent.

2. More than half of the firebox volume should be below the grate bars.

In other words, the grate level should stand at more than half of the firebox height, the larger lower half being the ash pit, and the upper portion the combustion area.

3. The chimney height should be three times the height of the kiln's chamber plus the height of the firebox, plus 1 additional foot for every 3 feet of horizontal travel of the flue gases. For altitudes over 4,000 feet, an additional 3 feet of chimney or more may be needed.

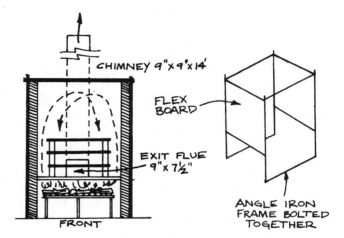

Fig. 5—40: *Construction details. Chimney: for high altitude, 13 1/2" x 13 1/2" for 3', then 12' with 12" O.D. flue liners.*

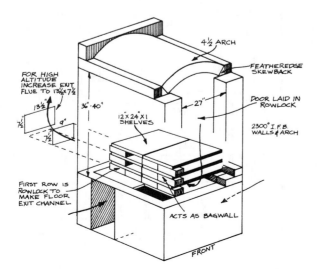

Fig. 5—39: *The fastfire wood downdraft kiln.*

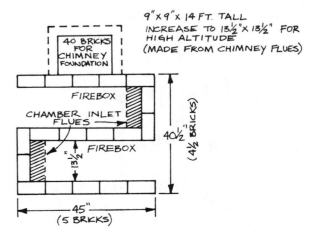

Fig. 5—41: *Top view of foundation layout.*

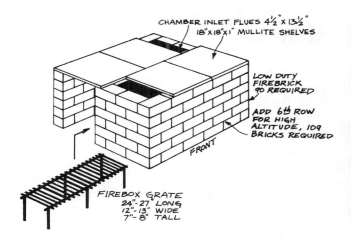

Fig. 5—42: *Firebox construction.*

Fig. 5—45: *Firebox entrance.*

Also increase chimney diameter by 50 percent and exit flue size (square inches of area) by 40 percent.

This fastfire wood design can be enlarged to almost any size between 12 and 120 cubic feet. It can be built with insulation bricks or hard bricks (hard bricks will lengthen the firing time). To establish the desired size, simply lay out the kiln shelves to be used and add 4 1/2" minimum on each side (except at the back), making sure the shelves have about a 1-inch gap between them (Fig. 5-46). If the dimensions seem big because of brick module, stay with them anyway. The kiln is better with a looser stacking.

The kiln can be designed to use wood, gas or oil. Oil drip plates or forced oil burners can be mounted in the firebox area. Gas ports can be built into the side

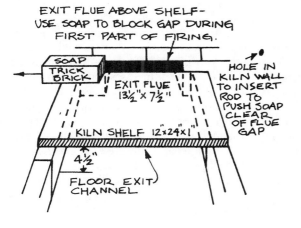

Fig. 5—43: *Shelf and exit flue channels.*

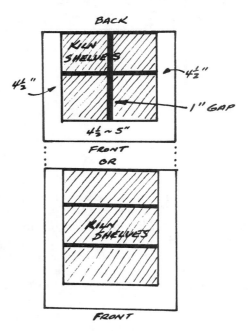

Fig. 5—46: *Top views of shelf arrangements.*

Fig. 5—44: *Flue channel.*

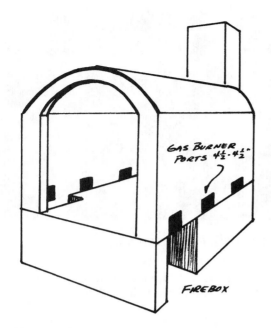

Fig. 5—47: *Gas ports.*

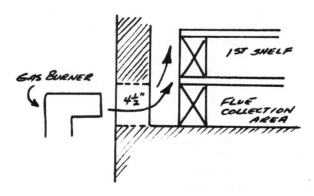

Fig. 5—48: *The shelf supports act as a bagwall.*

walls at floor level using removable bricks. Gas ports should be 4 1/2" x 4 1/2" (see Fig. 5-47). If gas is used, the inlet flues must be blocked and the firebox mouth bricked up and sealed with mud. The kiln stacking arrangement acts as the bagwall and flame deflector for the gas burners (Fig. 5-48). To determine the proper size and number of burners, refer to Chapter 7.

The door of the kiln is bricked up using either stretchers (4 1/2") or rowlocks (2 1/2"). Cone hole pull-out plugs are built in and an empty hole, about 2 1/2" x 2 1/2", is left open at the top center of the door.

FASTFIRE WOOD FIRING SCHEDULE

I gave a kiln building workshop at the Anderson Ranch, Aspen, Colorado, during the summer of 1977, where we built an 18-cubic-foot fastfire wood downdraft. The firing schedule in Table 5-2 is derived from that kiln. This firing took place on a warm, clear evening.

FIRING

Start one firebox and fire until a bed of coals is accumulated. Then start the other side (which will be around 540-590°C) and begin an alternating stoking pattern. Never full-stoke both sides at once. Fill the grate half full and let it burn down. In one hour or so the fireboxes will take only four to six kindling-size pieces every three minutes or so. When one firebox is stoked with its four to six pieces, the other side may need one or two to carry it through until its turn. Have a spy hole, preferably at the top, open at all times. Watch the flame that emerges from this spy hole, and also watch the chimney smoke. When the flame sucks back into the kiln and the chimney has cleared, it is time to stoke. Critical temperatures are around 590°C and 1,090°C, where care must be taken not to choke the kiln. I use a pyrometer when firing. As long as the kiln increases in stoking quantity and rate, it's perfect. If the kiln loses temperature, rake and clear some of the coals out of the firebox and beat down the wood on top of the grate so more oxygen is available. When Cone 9 is down on top, I insert a metal rod through the hole in the side wall and push the trick brick back to open up the exit flue above the first kiln shelf, thus sucking the majority of the draft directly to the back and bottom wall and evening out the temperature in the entire kiln. The kiln will use less than a quarter of a cord of wood for a 3 1/2- to 4-hour firing.

It takes time to work out the kiln's personality and organize an efficient firing schedule and stacking arrangement. Do not be discouraged if the first firing is not as expected. The next one will be better because of the first experience.

Construction Fastfire 36 - Brock

Construction photographs of the Brock 36 were taken during my 1995 kiln building workshop in McNaughton, Wisconsin, sponsored by Joan Slack De Brock. The first step in any kiln design is to lay out the kiln floor pattern using the kiln shelves available. In this kiln we used 12" x 24" shelves with a 12" x 12" corner shelf, for a 3' square for the ware platform. Next the inlet flues, exit flue, flue channel, and chimney walls were laid out around the ware platform. The resulting configuration became a seven-brick-wide and deep square pad which was laid on the concrete slab using a leveling portland cement. At the same time, the flue channel and chimney's pad was done.

Fig. 5—49: *Arch.*

The "S" firebox pattern and perimeter walls are laid on top of the pad (Fig. 5-49). Nine-inch perimeter walls, 13 1/2"-wide fireboxes with a 18" space between the fireboxes, 18" long by 9" wide flue channel into a chimney that was a 13 1/2" x 13 1/2" interior dimension. The "S" configuration, flue channel and chimney perimeter were built up six rows. In order to conserve bricks, dirt, sand, broken bits of bricks, was used to fill the flue channel, chimney base and channel between the fireboxes (Fig. 5-52). Kiln shelves were used to span the firebox channels (Fig. 5-53).

Fig. 5—50: *The completed fastfire kiln.*

Fig. 5—51: *Floor layout in S-form with chimney connection.*

Fig. 5—52: *Filling spaces with rubble and dirt to save on bricks.*

Fig. 5—53: *Laying kiln shelves as the floor.*

Fig. 5—56: *Setting the featheredges with back-up bricks.*

Next the perimeter 9" walls using IFB interior bricks and exterior hard bricks were built up 17 rows to the skewback level and the chimney continued up to the same level (Fig. 5-54). Three removable burner port flues were built into each sidewall at the inlet flue level so the kiln could be fired or preheated with gas. To ensure the door spacing, rowlock bricks were laid up to the 17th row (Fig. 5-55). An angle iron frame was cut and fitted to the corners of the kiln. An arch frame was built using the rise given by a standard

Fig. 5—54: *Building the side walls.*

Fig. 5—57: *Laying the arch using alternating arch and straight bricks.*

Fig. 5—55: *Wall built halfway up with rowlock door spacing.*

featheredge brick (1 1/2 per foot of span) and the formula radius = span x 1.0625 for the arc. Once the arc was drawn out on a board with the proper span marked, the arch boards were cut out and the frame could be built. Parallel featheredges plus back up bricks were placed on both sides of the kiln (Fig. 5-56). The arch was laid using No. 1 arch bricks and straights in alternation with the key brick ground to fit perfectly (Fig. 5-57). Before the arch frame supports could be removed, the metal frame had to be welded together around the kiln thus preventing the possibility of the arch spreading out and falling in (Fig. 5-58 and 59).

Fig. 5—58: *Finished arch.*

Fig. 5—59:
Welding up the frame to support the arch and brick work.

Fig. 5—61: *Barbecue on the "river of fire" flue channel.*

A metal plate was used for the flue channel cover leaving a gap for a vertical damper to be installed. The metal plate also provided a place to barbecue steaks and dogs over the "river of fire" (Fig. 5-61). The metal plate could also be used as a passive damper by opening it up or just cracking it a little. I first saw this type of passive damper on Ian Jones' anagama outside of Canberra, Australia. Principle 5 was used to calculate the chimney height.

The grates were made out of 3/4" rebar with the grate bars spaced 3/4" apart and 7" legs were used. When designing a pull-out grate, it should bisect the firebox height in half and be 3/4 the length of the firebox. It is necessary to have the bar spacing close together to limit the size of the coals passing through, thus eliminating the racking out of coals during the firing. Remember, when the firing is finished, the hot grates must be pulled out of the firebox and straightened and the fireboxes must be bricked up for slow cooling. Fig. 5-60 shows the first stacking for the first firing and Fig. 5-62 shows the firing results.

Fig. 5—60: *First firing stacking.*

Fig. 5—62: *Fired ware.*

First Firing Log:

Started at approximately 2:30 p.m. with a fire under the grates in the fire mouth. An hour later, fire on the grates.

4:00 p.m. — Kiln at 500°F.

5:00 p.m. — Kiln at about 1,000°F with flames moving up into the chamber.

6:00 p.m. — 1,250°F reducing flames out the door blow hole. Damper set at 1/4 open.

7:15 p.m. — 1400°F damper open to 1/2.

7:30 p.m. — Second fire box started. (Back firebox)

8:15 p.m. — 1600°F.

9:30 p.m. — 1820°F damper opened to 3/4.

10:00 p.m. — Cone 8 down on the bottom.

10:30 p.m. — Large flames at chimney, glazes melted. Cone 10 soft, begin soaking period to even out kiln.

12:30 a.m. — Cone 10 down everywhere.

12:45 a.m.— Kiln shut down and closed up.

Fig. 5—64: *Overall view of fastfire 120 kiln.*

Fig. 5—63: *Pot on head stokers.*

Fastfire 120 - Polizzi

Frank Polizzi proportionally expanded the fast-fire design out to 120 cubic feet of stacking space. The ware platform is 4 1/2' wide, 5 1/2' deep and 5 1/2' tall (top of the arch), with two underneath fireboxes, 18" wide and 24" tall. Bisecting the firebox in half was a grate made of thick gauge stainless steel tubing placed at 2" on center (giving a slot space of 1") and running 48" long. Arches were used to span the fireboxes and the main chamber. Kiln walls (9" thick) were laid dry (without mortar) using hard brick as the hot face and backed by IFB for insulation. On an earlier, smaller fastfire kiln, Polizzi used AP Green 2300 IFB and found them to be unsatisfactory in a wood fire environment. Therefore, on the new kiln, the wall was reversed, with hard brick on the hot face and the surviving G-2300 bricks used as exterior back up. The entire kiln was raised up (Fig. 5-64 and 65) on cinder blocks to make the stoking waist high and easier, plus a catwalk was built to access the chamber for stacking.

Fig. 5—65: *Kiln raised up to allow stand-up stocking.*

In comparing the kiln's dimensions to the principles in Chapter 3, we find the kiln is within the perimeters of the principles. Kiln dimensions are based on the cube (Principle 1). Inlet flues (240 square inches) are about equal to the exit flues (232 square inches) and the total grate area of 1,800 square inches divided by 10 gives a chimney area of 180 square inches (using the 10 to 1 ratio) corresponds to the actual chimney area of 182 square inches or 13 1/2" x 13 1/2". (Principle 3) Chimney height is just under 20', conforms to Principle 5 as does the chimney diameter compared to chamber diameter in Principle 6. The kiln works well firing to a flat cone 10 in 9 hours of stoking. An observation would have used the 7 to 1 ratio on this size of kiln because of Principle 9, which allows for alteration if necessary. This kiln is locked into its dimensions, exit flue and straight shot chimney size, which are right on the limit. It takes a knowledgeable potter to stack the ware correctly, not too tight, but full; not to block the exit flue at all with kiln post or such to block the draft; and not to over stoke the kiln with wood during the transitions to high temperature.

Firing cycle:
3 hours — Candling with LP gas using two weed burners.

4 to 5 hours — Stoking with wood, damper half closed to cone 6.

3 plus hours — Aggressive, vigorous stoking using small kindling with larger pieces up to 4" thick. Damper full open.

1-plus hours — Once cone 10 is flat, soaking for evenness of temperature begins, hovering at cone 10. At this time the damper is partially closed. When finished the fireboxes are sealed tightly as is the damper slot. A slow two-day cooling period is necessary for Polizzi's glazes on the 300 to 400 pots fired.

Blakebrough Tasmanian School of Art downdraft

A 40-cubic-foot stacking envelope style downdraft fiber box kiln with a fix hearth connected to the back wall and chimney (Fig. 5-67). The kiln chamber moves in on a track over the hearth sealing against the fixed back wall. A cube was used as the basic starting point for the kiln's proportion adjusted for kiln shelves and burner channels. Interior dimensions for

Fig. 5—67: *Envelope downdraft fiber box kiln.*

the hearth are 42" wide by 54" long and approximately 52" high which allows for two 24" x 24" kiln shelves. A suspended, flat fiber roof fitting down on the three side walls, attaching to the corner legs was used (Fig. 5-68). Folded fiber blanket construction technique was used for the walls and ceiling. A 1" backup fiber blanket was used as well as fiber strips folded over onto the wall for the compression sealer against the back wall. A high-temperature 1" thick, 8 pcf Carborundum/Fiberfrax Durablanket folded to 20cm (9") was used to line the internal surface of the kiln chamber (Fig. 5-70). Refer to Chapter 2 for fiber construction. The hearth, flue channels, chimney base, and first 15 inches of the kiln chamber were built with 2600 IFB (insulation firebrick) (Fig. 5-69). Expanded metal mesh placed within the frame was used as a backing for the walls and ceiling. Two 4 1/2" flue channels, 9" apart and 6" deep funnel into a chimney flue (9" x 6") leading to a 9" x 9" chimney (Fig. 5-66). Eight floor exit flues are used. Two 4 1/2" x 6" burner ports are built into the back wall, with opposing ports built into the kiln chamber firing

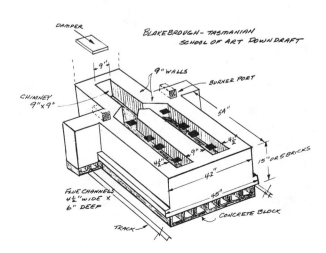

Fig. 5—66: *Drawing of floor layout.*

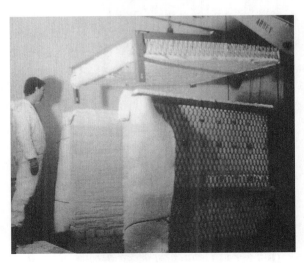

Fig. 5—68: *Roof attachment.*

Fig. 5—69: *Fixed hearth showing 4 1/2" flue channels leading to chimney base.*

down 9" side-burner channels (Fig. 5-71). Four venturi compound injector burners with individual safety and ignition are used. (Fig. 5-72)

Fig. 5—70: *Envelope wall construction.*

Fig. 5—71: *Detail of space under first shelf to allow access to exit floor flues.*

Variations of the downdraft kiln-downward draft.

There are a number of commercial kiln companies and kiln builders that produce a box kiln (flat roof) and sprung arch designs that are called downdrafts, however, I call them "pseudo" or side fire downward draft kilns. The established definition of the downdraft kiln is that the exit flue gaseous travels through the floor and into the collection channel, then to the chimney. These downward pulling kilns have been around since the 1940s but became very popular with Soldner's catenary design in the mid–50s. Whether a catenary or sprung arch, these side fire, down pulling kilns were the predominant kilns throughout the country. However, updraft kilns were introduced on the west coast in the mid-50s and became the kiln of choice for west coast schools and potters. A much later design that was first published in *Studio Potter* magazine (1976) and that became well known is the Nils Lou Minnesota Flat Top (flat roof box design) which again is a downdraft variation. In the mid-70s other downward draft kilns were first produced commercially. They are well conceived and very capable kilns and have added to the choice of kiln designs available. In fact, these kilns may change the definition of downdraft for most potters. However, for this type of configuration, "downward draft" is my term.

Fig. 5—72: *Burner assembly with ignition module and safety.*

(Photos from Les Blakebrough, Hobart, Australia.)

In the downward draft kiln designs, the exit flue is located in the back wall at floor level with the combustion channel located on the left and right side. (Fig. 5-73) It can be side-fire, back-fire or up through the floor. (Fig. 5-74) The combustion channel is normally 4 1/2" wide if firing from the bottom up through the floor. When firing from the side or from the back of the kiln, the combustion channel may have to be larger (7" to 9") depending upon the burners used. If a low-pressure venturi burner is used, then the 4" space is sufficient. However, if high-pressure burners are used, then the combustion channel may have to be increased to the larger size. A bagwall must be used when firing from the side to deflect the flame upward into the vertical combustion channel. Part of the bag-wall can be built into the floor as illustrated in Fig. 5-75. Another method is illustrated in Fig. 5-76, where a solid row of rowlock or soldier bricks are used as a bagwall and posting for the kiln shelves. Using this method the first shelf height will be either 4 1/2" or 9". Firing from the back wall into the length of the channel may require deflection bricks strategically placed to direct the flame evenly upward. In longer kilns, burners at both ends of the kiln may be necessary, as illustrated in the Blakebrough kiln.

Inlet burner ports are sized to fit the tip of the burner used and should be able to slide through the hole. This allows for the flame to pass through the hole with no restrictions and allows for secondary air. The exit flue is sized to equal the inlet burner ports in area and then adjusted smaller. A starting point for

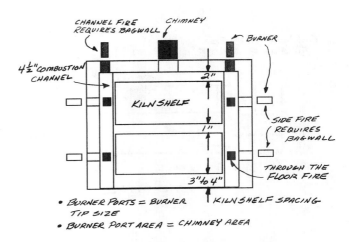

Fig. 5—74: *Floor plan with burner options.*

the chimney cross-sectional area would be to equal the inlet port area. For ease in construction the exit flue width is built the same as the chimney width, then restricted by adding a brick. The height of the chimney equals the height of the kiln or level with the top kiln frame work. A ventilation collection hood and stack take over from there. Again, it is best to be on the safe side for it is much easier to restrict than to increase in size.

The heat comes in at floor level, whether from the bottom, side or back and travels up following the wall to the top of the kiln and then down to the exit flue in the back wall at floor level. It might be pointed out here that this is also true for crossdraft kilns. Stacking of the shelves becomes an important factor in the successful firing of these kilns. If the stacking is too far forward, allowing a lot of space at the back of the kiln, it will draw directly to the back exit flue, leaving the front cold. If the stacking is too tight against the back wall and the shelves butt together, then the back can be cold. It is imperative to leave space between the shelves in back and the back wall, usually 1" to 2", a 1" space between the shelves, and a larger space in front, from 3" to 4". (Fig. 5-74) The stacking of these kilns is very similar to the fastfire stacking arrangement. In downward-pulling and downdraft kilns, a staggered setting is sometimes preferred. I have found in the fastfire kiln design, if the spacing between the back wall, and between shelves is correct, then shelf staggering is not necessary.

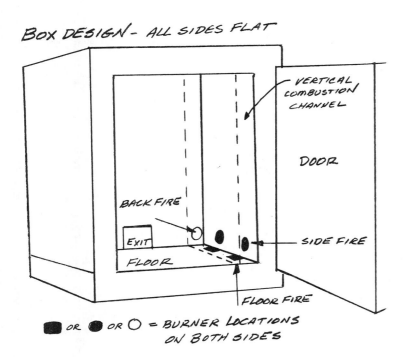

Fig. 5—73: *Box design downward draft kiln.*

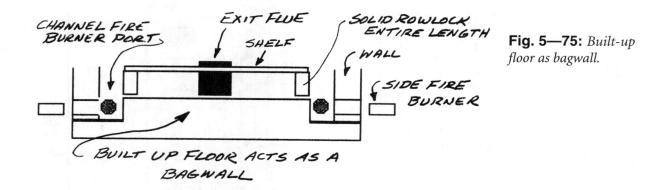

Fig. 5—75: *Built-up floor as bagwall.*

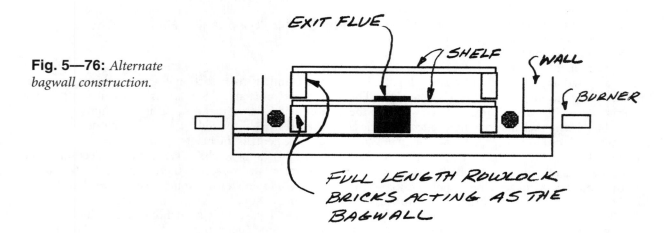

Fig. 5—76: *Alternate bagwall construction.*

Chapter 6
Updraft Kilns

A kiln that has a draft that enters through inlet flues at the bottom of the kiln, passes into the chamber, and exits through flues in the arch or dome, is an updraft kiln (Fig. 6-1). Over the centuries, primitive

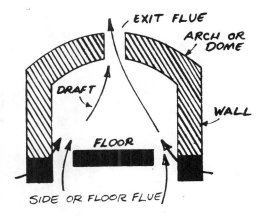

Fig 6—1: *The flow of air though an updraft kiln.*

potters realized that the more enclosed the pit kiln became, the hotter the firing and the more durable the pottery. This was accomplished by banking up the sides with clay. These early potters found that, by putting holes close to the bottom of the pit (probably to force more fuel in), the combustion was greatly improved and higher temperatures attained. Banking the walls and placing the air and stoke holes at the bottom of the pit were practices that led to the early wall updraft kiln. Fig. 6-2 shows the basic improved

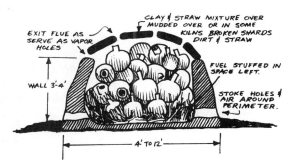

Fig 6—2: *Improved pit kiln with air-supply holes around the perimeter.*

pit kiln, with a space above the pottery to form the stoke and air-supply holes around the perimeter of the wall.

The improved pit kiln is used today in such places as Spain, Nigeria, Mexico, and in pottery villages throughout Africa, India, and South America. Sticks, grass, dung or a combination are used as fuel. The walled area is lined with fuel packed firmly into the space between the pots and wall. The pots are piled and mounded to form a dome shape. The dome may be made of broken shards, covered with dirt and straw, or plastered with a clay-straw mixture. Vapor and exit flue holes are left in the dome. The kiln is fired and stoked until the dome is red hot. In some, more fuel is thrown over the dome and burned before the kiln is left to cool.

When primitive kilns reached this stage, the next step to increase temperature was to get the fire under the pots to allow the flames to move up through them. This created a controlled updraft kiln. Potters around the eastern and southern Mediterranean Sea, and across the Middle East to North Africa and into Spain, kept building the walls higher and introduced the firebox directly under the pottery, creating a simple beehive updraft kiln. The first of these kilns was quite small because of the problem of spanning the firebox pit area under the chamber.

This problem was solved, I believe, by potters somewhere near Niger, where the baobab tree grows. The baobab has a thick trunk, with the main branches separating at a common height around the trunk. The structure of the baobab was imitated in local architecture. Branches separating off the central trunk supported ceilings. The imitation baobab construction was made of flexible branches, small trunks and bundles of fagots tied together and shaped into the support structure. This was then reinforced with clay and plastered with clay plaster. Local potters borrowed this technique from builders and constructed a baobab-type structure to hold up the kiln floor. This umbrella-style kiln spread to other areas, including Spain.

UMBRELLA KILN

The umbrella kiln is still being fired in Moveros, Spain, today. The kiln consists of a small chamber, about 5' in diameter, and an umbrella floor built off a central trunk with the firebox below (Fig. 6-3 and photo 1 and 2). Granite rocks are mortared together

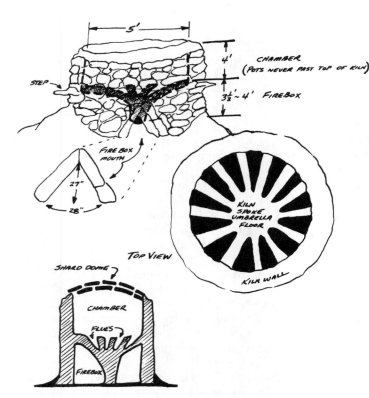

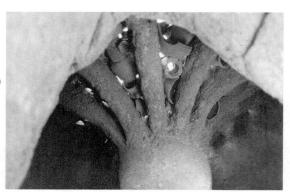

Fig 6—5: *View of umbrella floor supports through the firebox.*

Fig 6—3: *Lower left: early updraft "baobab" kiln; above: umbrella kiln in current use, Monveros, Spain.*

Fig 6—6: *Interior view of ware chamber with shard buffers.*

Fig 6—4: *Walls are built of mortared granite rocks.*

Fig 6—7: *Overall view of umbrella kiln.*

in 18" to 24" walls (Fig. 6-4 & 6-7). The firebox and chamber interiors are plastered with clay. Spaces between the spokes of the floor are filled with pot shards to absorb the direct flame shock and to keep the pots from falling through. The kiln is piled full of pots to the level of the top, then shards are stacked over the pots to form the roof.

The kiln is fired with heather and any available brush. The firing is started at the firebox mouth, then after two hours, brush is pushed farther into the fire-

box and stoked faster for about six hours. When flames come out the top of the kiln, the firing is done. Coals from the firebox are put on top of the kiln during the firing, and at the end, ashes and coals are poured into the kiln for flashing effects.

The Greeks enclosed the more primitive kiln with a dome, and added a door — a sophisticated innovation. Unknown potters through the years developed a domed floor for spanning greater distances and developed refractory blocks made of a clay that was more

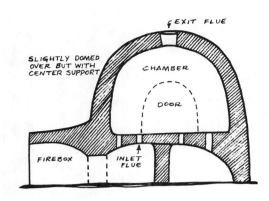

Fig 6—8: *Early Greek updraft kiln.*

refractory than the pots fired. The fired clay bricks and the domed floor made it possible to build larger kilns that could reach higher temperatures (Fig. 6-8).

The primitive updraft kilns came with definite advantages. Heat could be controlled, achieving slow-burning embers or intense flames. The domed chamber contained the heat, allowing the temperature to rise quickly and to new heights. Because of the new temperatures reached and the control of the flame to gain these temperatures, a great advancement in pottery took place — the development of ceramic glazes. Ceramic glazes originated around 5000 B.C., probably in settlements and cities near the Nile and Euphrates rivers. These early glazes were, for the most part, used only on tiles. Glazes were first used on pottery and functional ware after 2500 B.C. Sometime later, saggars first appeared to protect the pottery from the residues of combusted fuel.

EARLY MUSLIM LOW-FIRE GLAZE KILN

An efficient early updraft kiln still in use is Mansimran Singh's low-fire glaze kiln in New Delhi, India. The updraft kiln, built by Singh's father, is a Muslim

design dating to antiquity (Fig. 6-10). It is used to fire Delhi Blue glaze decorative tiles and low-fire glazed pottery. Everything except the tiles are saggared. They are stacked on end in rows separated by wads of clay.

The firebox requires about five hours to warm up, then the actual firing takes about six to seven hours. To warm the kiln, small amounts of wood are burned in the firebox and the coals shoved down into the pit bottom (Figs. 6-9 and 6-11). Slow build up of coals in the pit allows the chamber temperature to gradually

Fig. 6—10: *Mansimran Singh's low-fire glaze kiln, New Dehli.*

Fig. 6—11: *Logs are fed into the firebox.*

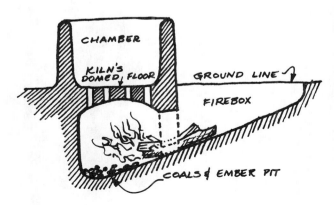

Fig. 6—9: *Coals from firebox are shoved into the pit beneath the chamber.*

increase to 260°C, thus ensuring the safety of the wares.

Large hardwood logs by stoking standards (from 2" to 6" diameter) are used. These give a relatively short flame and long coal life. The type of wood (hard or soft, branch or log or kindling) plays an important

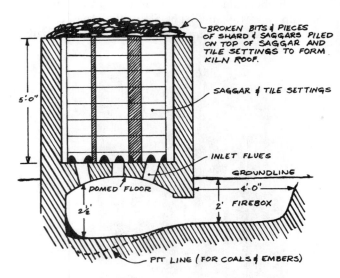

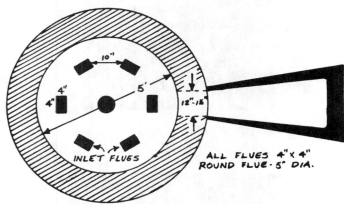

Fig 6—12: *The early Muslim low-fire glaze kiln.*

Fig. 6—14: *Detail of kiln roof during firing.*

role in controlling the temperature rise, the actual flames in the chamber and the chamber's atmosphere. Hardwoods, for example, give short flames, intense local heat and good coals. Softwoods explode quickly, giving an extremely long flame and moving heat quickly into the chamber. Figure 6-12 shows the kiln layout; Figure 6-13 illustrates stacking, and 6-14 shows the kiln roof during the firing.

Peruvian Primitive updraft

In a 1994 trip to Peru, Phil Cornelius and I visited the Tombs at Sipan, an excavation of an ancient pre-Columbian burial site. Living close by were some folk potters; one potter doing large pottery jars in a most primitive manner for daily use (Fig. 6-15) and the other potter making decorative style vessels, cups etc., for folk craft stores (Fig. 6-16). Both potters used woodfired, updraft kilns, but they were considerably different. The first potter used a kiln base

Fig. 6—13: *Placing shards atop the potter stacking for protection.*

Fig 6—15: *Sipan folk potters' ware, large storage jars.*

with a fire pit under the channels (Fig. 6-17), set the large containers upside down on the channels and built up adobe walls around the perimeter and used

Fig 6—16: *Updraft kiln using common house wall with kiln.*

Fig 6—17: *Kiln base with stoking underneath, old kiln behind.*

Fig 6—18: *Delivering clay by donkey to pottery, kiln in background.*

shards over the top. Clay was dug a few kilometers away and transported by donkey to the pottery. An outside work area was used (Fig. 6-18).

The second potter's kiln was a permanent structure actually built into the side of his house with a common wall. Using the house wall as the left kiln wall was an interesting idea (Fig. 6-16). An ash pit was built using the channels with pass-through flues between them that served as grate bars for the firebox above. A large arched-over firebox was built with exit flues built into the arch that lead to the chamber above. An exit flue leading to the chimney from the ware chamber was incorporated into the building wall as was the chimney. The chamber was approximately 2/3 bigger than the firebox. On the other side of the common kiln wall was the enclosed studio space.

Both kilns were built with adobe clay just as they have been for the past two centuries. The work featured good craftsmanship and the fire quality of the pieces show an understanding of their updraft kilns. It would be hard for me to believe that a modern kiln design could improve their ware or their productivity. If they were to change, it would have to come from within first, because their whole way of life would change — their marketing, their ware, their method of getting clay and their tools. Gone would be the folk craft approach to making pottery.

NINODAGUIA PRIMITIVE KILN

The Ninodaguia kiln, located in northwest Spain, is an interesting example of a primitive updraft kiln still in use in a commercial pottery (Fig. 6-21). The kiln is made with common building bricks used throughout Spain. The floor is a dome of bricks laid in circular soldier courses in a very shallow rise to a

12" stone key. The 1 1/2" holes in the bricks act as inlet flues for the chamber. Figure 6-19 shows the firebox. One thing worthy of note is that the firebox and the chamber are approximately equal in height and width.

Pots are stacked on raised round setter tiles, as shown in Figures 6-19 and 6-20. The kiln holds 2,000-3,000 small pots, or about 1,000 large pots. Shards stacked over the top of the pots enclose the chamber. The kiln is fired with pine bark. Needless to say, this kiln is inadequate for a commercial operation. The potter told me he wanted a gas tunnel kiln like his neighbor's.

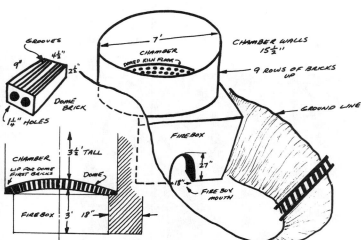

Fig 6—21: *Ninodaguia kiln, northwest Spain.*

MIROVET MEDIEVAL KILN

The old-style medieval kiln can be found in a few folk pottery areas in Spain, such as Mirovet Village (Figs. 6-23). This particular kiln is unique because the proportions fit almost perfectly the principles of kiln design we discussed in Chapter 3. The kiln is based on three equal-sized cubes, joined to form the chamber, sub-chamber and firebox. A kiln chamber cube with a domed roof is a perfectly proportioned downdraft chamber. The lower sub-chamber is also a cube, less the thickness of the floor arch containing the inlet flues. In front of the sub-chamber, which is used for stacking pots, is the firebox cube, which acts as the firing chamber and ash pit all in one. No grates are used in the firebox.

The four corner flue holes in the chamber dome act as exit flues and as control flues. By damping or closing selected flues during the firing, the heat can be channeled to the flues that are open. When encountering a cold area in the kiln during firing, pull out a plug to draw the flames and heat to that section.

Fig 6—19: *Raised setter tiles on floor of kiln.*

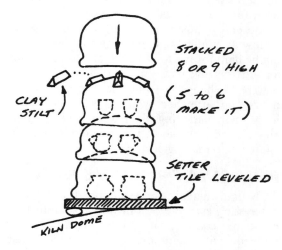

Fig 6—20: *Method of stacking pots on setter tiles.*

Fig 6—22: *The stacked kiln: literally thousands of pots fill the chamber and sub-chamber.*

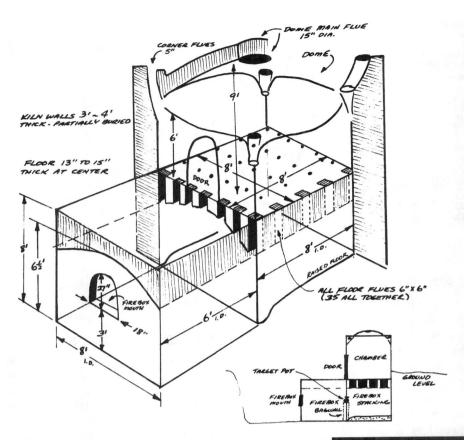

fuls at a time, are stoked at about 4- to 5-minute intervals, until the sub-chamber glazed target pot turns darker than the pots next to it. Then the fuel is changed to wood chips (Fig. 6-25). Six shovels full are stoked at a time, slowly building up to 30 shovels full at the end of the firing. Supplementary fuels are bundles of wood include grass, slash, slats and dehydrated olive pits. Sufficient time between stoking must be allowed for oxidation, determined by the time it takes for the fuel to burn down and clear the atmosphere. The firing lasts until the target pots in the dome flues are "done." Firing times with this type of kiln vary from potter to potter. The Mirovet kilns fire in about 28 to 32 hours.

Fig 6—23: *Diagram of the Mirovet medieval updraft.*

Pots are stacked one upon the other, until the kiln is plumb full. Thousands of pots can be stuffed into the kiln chamber and sub-chamber, as shown in Fig. 6-22. Specially glazed pots, called target pots, are placed on the sub-chamber bagwall and in a visible spot near the dome flue holes (Fig. 6-24). During the initial firing, the two front dome flues closest to the firebox are closed. Long pieces of wood, several arm-

Fig 6—24: *Target pots visible in the center dome flue during firing.*

Fig 6—25: *Firing the huge Mirovet kiln.*

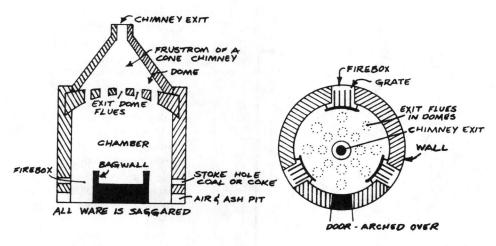

Fig. 6—27: *Circular updraft kiln, Germany, circa 1700.*

ENAMEL OR RAKU KILN

I came across Bernard Leach's original notebook in Tomimoto's studio one day. It contained a sketch that he had done in 1915 of an early Japanese enamel kiln. This Kin-Gama, or gold kiln, was probably the type Kenzan used in firing his overglaze enamel pottery. Kenzan (1663-1743) was a potter renowned for his overglaze enamel designs on raku. He worked with great restraint, and his work possessed a richness of brushwork that was unequaled until Tomimoto (See Appendix for further information).

This enamel kiln design, shown in Fig. 6-26, dates back to the earliest days of the Sung Dynasty (950-1250) and could, in fact, be the first use of a muffle kiln. An extremely interesting feature is the muffle chamber. Muffles can be defined as a total kiln saggar, a clay chamber-shaped lining which fits into the kiln. Many kinds of pottery, such as lead-glazed wares, various glaze colorants that are sensitive to reduction, and overglaze enamels, must be protected by the muf-fle from direct flame contact and combustion gases. Today most muffle kilns for such wares have been replaced by electric kilns, which are superior.

CIRCULAR UPDRAFT KILN

A circular updraft kiln developed by Boettger in Germany around 1700 greatly influenced European kilns. The kiln is basically a cylinder, with three evenly spaced fireboxes for coal and coke at its base (Fig. 6-27).

The dome contains evenly spaced exit flue holes leading into a frustrum of a cone, which acts as a chimney. The main improvements in this updraft kiln were:

1. Introduction of refractory bricks, making higher temperatures possible.
2. Improved firebox design and the use of cast-iron grates.
3. Introduction of coal and coke as fuel.
4. Frustum of a cone chimney, which increases the draft and fuel-burning capacity.

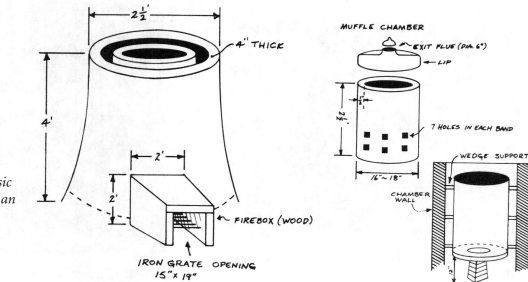

Fig 6—26: *Classic Kensan design for an enamel kiln.*

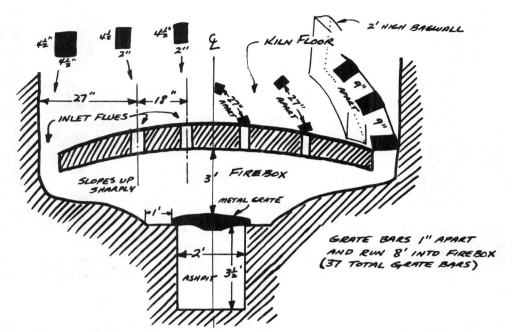

Fig 6—29:
Detail of the fire-box, ash pit and inlet flue area.

BREDA BOTTLE KILN

A number of potteries using the old-style bottle kilns developed in the Seventeenth century are located near Barcelona in the town of Breda. Some of the kilns are relatively old. However, the local clay supplier built a new bottle kiln for producing domestic earthenware in August of 1979. The kiln shown in Fig. 6-28 is located at Segra Pottery.

Normally, this kiln design did not have an ash pit below the firebox. Notice how small the firebox is, compared with the Mirovet kiln's double-cube firebox and sub-chamber. Because the firebox is only three feet or so to the floor dome, and the sides slope, the kiln has a tendency to choke and thus retard the firing. With the advent of smaller fireboxes, the frustrum of a cone was used atop the kiln to act as a chimney, in effect drawing a greater draft. Good idea, but the ash buildup in the firebox chokes the kiln and must be raked out in order to resume firing. The Breda potters arrived at the same remedy as did other potters using this design in Europe — incorporating a grate, with an ash pit below, into the firebox (Fig. 6-29). This improved the firing and the firing time. Note that the volume directly above and below the grate is equal, a design factor that is critical (see Chapter 7). The ash pit collects the coals and ashes and preheats the air for a free breathing grate. At the end of the firing, all coals and ashes must be thoroughly cleaned out of the pit. Otherwise, the metal grate bars will deform and oxidize when the firebox is sealed.

Pots must be stacked off the floor, leaving a dead air space between inlet flues and the stacking. A 2-foot-high bagwall is built just inside the perimeter inlet flues to baffle the direct flames. The firing is done with chestnut slats 3 feet long, and uses about 1,800 kilos of wood. The firing begins with a slow pre-heating period of about 3 to 4 hours. Stoking is then

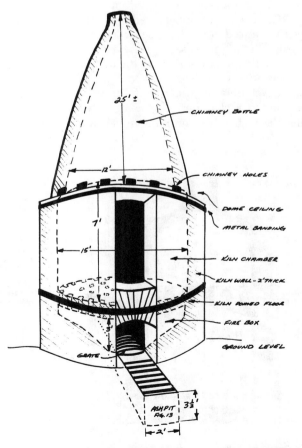

Fig. 6—28: *Bottle kiln, Segra Pottery, Breda Spain.*

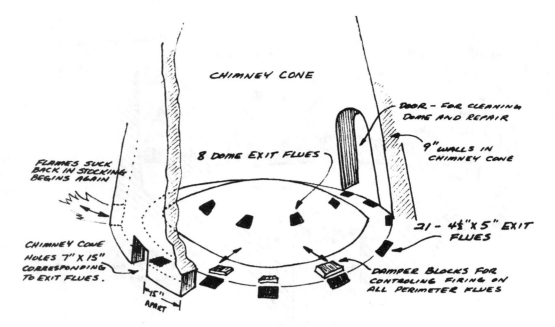

Fig 6—30:
Detail of the dome flues and chimney cone.

increased, building to a 4-minute-interval stoking rate at the end of 7 hours. The stoking interval is determined by the flames coming out of the chimney cone holes (Fig. 6-30). When they suck in, you stoke. The total earthenware firing takes about 10 hours. Evenness of firing is controlled by damping and opening the exit flues on top of the dome.

There are a lot of overfired pots, underfired pots, overly reduced pots (they use lead glazes) — in other words, a lot of seconds.

Gradual developments in the design of the bottle kiln eventually resulted in a two-story kiln. It grew in size, developing the frustum of a cone chimney into a second-story chamber (Fig. 6-31). The bottom was the glaze chamber and the upper was the bisque chamber. Production kilns were so large that the bisque chamber entrance was on the second floor of the pottery. Saggars were used to stack the ware in the kiln.

While the bottle design offers advantages, it also has shortcomings:

1. The added weight of the second chamber and chimney makes huge wall sections and heavy external iron bracing necessary.

2. A tremendous amount of fuel is consumed just to heat the brickwork.

3. The cost of masonry is high.

4. Firing evenly is impossible.

5. There is a very long firing and cooling cycle.

CONTEMPORARY UPDRAFT KILNS

The updraft kiln remained at a virtual design standstill until the twentieth century, with the exception of its use in combination with a downdraft kiln, as in Milton's two-chamber design. Then, insulating lightweight refractory bricks were introduced, as well as the use of oil, natural gas and propane as fuels for firing kilns. Fuel burners were perfected also. These factors revolutionized the building of pottery kilns, and industrial kilns as well.

I designed and patented a series of gas updraft kiln kits, ranging in size from 12 to 120 cubic feet of stacking space, called the Olsen Kiln Kits (Fig. 6-32, 33, and 34). The kiln kits are the basis for the ensuing discussion (for more information, write to: Olsen Kiln Kits, 60250 Manzanita 205, Mountain

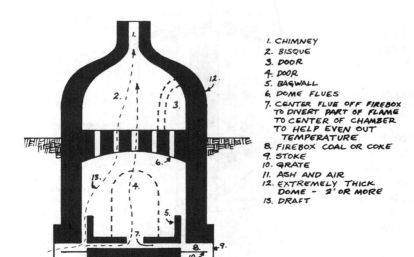

1. CHIMNEY
2. BISQUE
3. DOOR
4. DOOR
5. BAGWALL
6. DOME FLUES
7. CENTER FLUE OFF FIREBOX TO DIVERT PART OF FLAME TO CENTER OF CHAMBER TO HELP EVEN OUT TEMPERATURE
8. FIREBOX COAL OR COKE
9. STOKE
10. GRATE
11. ASH AND AIR
12. EXTREMELY THICK DOME - 2' OR MORE
13. DRAFT

Fig 6—31: *Two-story bottle kiln.*

Fig 6—32: *The Olsen 24 gas updraft kiln (Pat. 251249).*

Fig 6—33: *Olsen 16 kiln used by Jan Peterson.*

Fig 6—34: *Olsen 72 car kiln.*

Fig 6—35: *Bob and Sandy Kinzie's Olsen Kiln kit with an even firing (Kinzie photo).*

Center, CA 92561). The discussion of updraft kilns assumes the use of lightweight insulation bricks (IFB) and gas fuel. If the three requirements listed below are followed within a reasonable tolerance, the kiln design will be effective.

Three basic requirements for efficient forced-draft updraft kilns:

1. A cube is the best all-around chamber shape for a kiln (i.e., height equals width). Keeping the width close to the height is important for an even-firing kiln, while the length can be any dimension (i.e., tunnel kilns). There can be about a 25 percent greater height deviation factor from the equal-width-to-height rule, without undo concern for an uneven firing kiln. An Olsen 16 kiln kit has a 25 percent height deviation and, as the picture illustrates, fires quite evenly (Fig.6-01). The cube chamber shape holds true for small kilns, or large updraft kilns like Jun Kaneko's 500-cubic-foot car kiln he designed (Fig. 6-36 and 37).

2. A forced draft can be accomplished by using natural, propane or butane gas which is delivered under pressure to the kiln. This can be low-pressure or high-pressure gas.

3. The chamber design must accommodate heat direction and ease of flame movement to allow a natural flow up and through the ware. This is best accomplished by using floor inlet burner ports.

Remember that increasing the height of the cube chamber by more than the 25 percent factor with a fixed width and length decreases the evenness of a normal length firing (between 8 to 12 hours). That is because you cannot maintain an even temperature throughout the kiln with just bottom floor-level burners, unless long protracted soaking periods are used during the firing.

An efficient, popular size using simple atmospheric burners, is a 3' or 4' cube (inside dimension) with a 1-1/2" rise arch on top of the cube. A mini-

Fig 6— 37: *Enrique Sanchez's Olsen 36 car kiln.*

mum burner or combustion area of 4 1/2" around the stacking space is normal. If side fire channels are used, the combustion area is also 4 1/2" wide. This is based on the normal 2 1/2" burner tip size. A larger burner tip would require a larger space. For instance a 3" burner tip needs a 6" space. Notice the space in back and in front of the shelves (Fig. 6-38), which allows for good heat circulation around the ware setting. Many of the updraft designs use the side fire channels because of the ease of configuring the burner and safety system to meet safety standards required by some locals (See the Chapter 8, Fuels, Combustion, and Firing Systems, for details). This size kiln can handle a maximum of six perimeter atmospheric burners and one bottom burner (optional), each rated at 35,000 to 54,000 BTU per hour.

The perimeter burners should be placed a minimum of 9" and a maximum of 12" from the corners and then equally spaced at 9" to 12" intervals (Fig. 6-31). When using the side fire channels, the burners can be placed from 1" to 6" from the corners and then evenly spaced from 9" to 12" along the channel on both sides.

For large updraft kilns, such as Jun Kaneko's (8' tall, 9' deep, 8' wide with the cart 7" wide), perimeter burners are recommended. Kaneko's kiln uses 32 atmospheric burners, 10 per side and six in the front and back. A 9" burner combustion width was used with standard spacing for the burner ports. Notice the suspended door on the overhead I-beam using a trolley. A detail of a similar suspended kiln door is pictured. Two, Yale half-ton trolleys rode the overhead I-beam using U-bolts and eye-bolts to suspend the door (Fig. 6-39). Using this suspension system allows

Fig 6—36: *Jun Kaneko's large updraft kiln.*

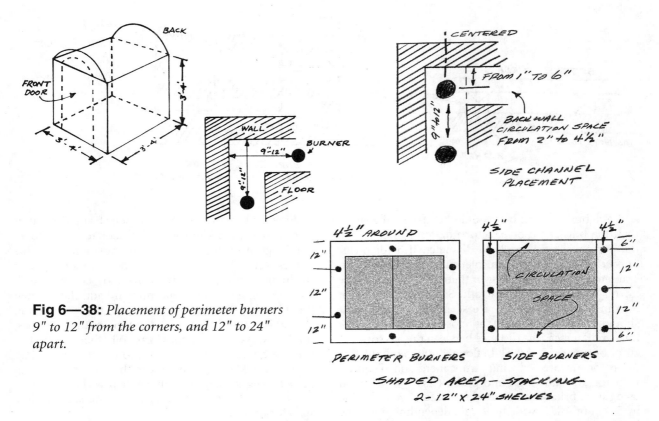

Fig 6—38: *Placement of perimeter burners 9" to 12" from the corners, and 12" to 24" apart.*

the door to be sucked into the door jambs using spring tension latches. Kaneko's kiln is fired extremely slowly, allowing for a long soaking rise in temperature over a long period of days, depending upon the size of the pieces being fired.

The temperature at the bottom of the kiln can be raised by using the bottom burner or burners, but in most cases they will be used to facilitate reduction by introducing excess gas. The way the bottom shelves are supported affects the efficiency of these burners; adequate clearance of 2 1/2" must be maintained. The number of bottom burners and the shelf size help to determine the setter shelf supports arrangement. Arrangements that work extremely well for 12" x 24" or 12" x 18" shelves is the rectangular "S" and for a single bottom burner. For either a perimeter or channel combustion area, use the "X" configuration (Fig. 6-40). The arrows indicate the flame direction each burner must take to escape from beneath the setter shelves. If the bottom burners are enclosed by the shelf supports, back pressure will result in the loss of heat circulation into the kiln chamber and cause damage to the burner tips.

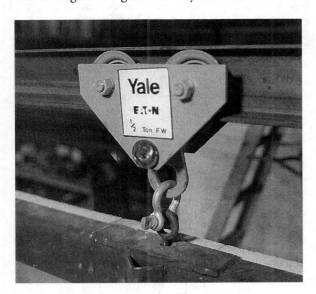

Fig 6—39: *Trolley and suspended kiln door construction.*

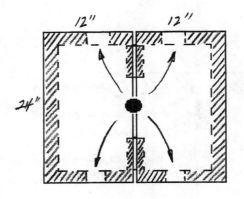

Fig 6—40: *One bottom burner arrangement.*

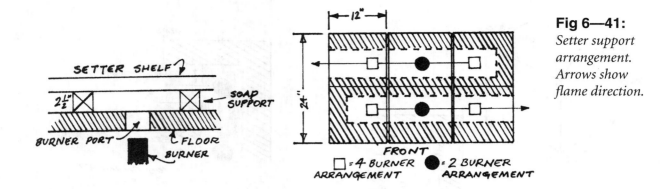

Fig 6—41: *Setter support arrangement. Arrows show flame direction.*

The burner portholes should be just a trifle larger than the burner tip or injector nozzle. In most cases, the ports will be 2" to 3" in diameter. If 3" diameter burner tips are used, then inlet flues should be 3" in diameter. If they are any bigger than that, reevaluate the normal combustion area width. Square holes are not uncommon because of the ease in brick laying, but should be adjusted to fit as closely as possible the burner diameter. The distance between the ejector nozzle or burner tip and the kiln floor should be about 1/4" or so for a more reducing atmosphere and up to an inch for an oxidizing atmosphere (Fig. 6-42). When using hard bricks, the portholes would be 4 1/2" wide by 5" tall or 4 1/2" wide by 9" tall, depending upon the burners and the number of burners used per port. These sizes are common brick-laying sizes, however, custom burner blocks could be made to fit any size needed. Being able to control the amount of secondary air is important for atmosphere control within the kiln.

The exit flue area in an updraft kiln is based upon the total square area of the inlet flues. In my experience I find that this rule is more than adequate for kilns 40 cubic feet and under in size. In these sizes of kilns, I usually make the exit flue holes slightly smaller, then fire the kiln to determine if the exit flue area is correct (so far, it has always been correct). This

is done by backing off the damper at any time after bisque, when the kiln should immediately go into an oxidizing atmosphere. If it does not, and exit flue flames still remain when the damper is totally open at the higher temperatures (cone 8 or so), check to see if you are using too much gas pressure and then (when the kiln is cold) enlarge the exit flue. Reduction should be caused by partial damping of the exit flues, not by excessive amounts of gas. Whether it is best to use one big exit flue or two or more is determined by proper bricklaying. There can be no free-floating bricks along the key brick flue hole row (Fig. 6-43).

I would suggest these approximate starting flue sizes for updraft kilns.

— 16 cubic ft. (stacking space): 40.5 sq. inches
— 24 cubic ft. (stacking space): 45 sq. inches
— 50 cubic ft. (stacking space): 90 sq. inches
— 100 cubic ft. (stacking space): 120 to 140 sq. inches

I use these flue sizes in my kiln kits of the same cubic foot size. I have found that in the larger kilns (above 50 cubic feet in stacking) that the exit flue sizes will be larger than the inlet flue area. The 24-cubic-foot kiln has eight perimeter burners and two bottom

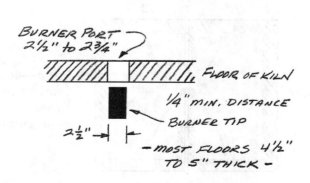

Fig 6—42: *Burner distance from floor.*

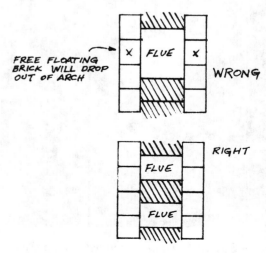

Fig 6—43: *Spacing exit flues in the arch.*

burners for a total inlet area of 50 square inches and an exit flue area of 45 square inches. A larger exit flue of 50 square inches can be used, but the kiln would have to use the damper to block the extra area. The equal or slightly smaller exit flue area, in relationship to the inlet port area, works on my kits up to 36 cubic feet of stacking space. From 50 cubic feet (stacking space) on up, I increase the exit flue area by about 20 percent. For example, on the 100-cubic-foot kiln the inlet flue area is 100 square inches. However, the exit flue area is 120 square inches (minimum) and could be up to 140 square inches. It seems that the larger kilns over 50 cubic feet with the greater input of Btu require larger exit flues in order to fire evenly, quickly and efficiently in oxidation or reduction.

The damper platform area and the seal become very important in controlling the firing and in the cooling of an updraft kiln. The exit flues should be made slightly smaller or equal to begin with, but with the option to enlarge them if necessary. If the exit flues are made on the large size, then it is important to have a good damper system. When using an arch a flat platform area has to be constructed around the flue holes to allow for an effective damper seal. A flat roof design already contains the flat platform for easy construction of a damper seal (Fig. 6-44). Again, make all areas easily changeable. Remember that exit flues are easily made bigger, but difficult to make smaller even when using IFB refractories. If the kiln is located above 5,000 feet in altitude, use equal areas for the inlet and exit flues for kilns 40 cubic feet and under. For the larger kilns, plan for the 20 percent exit flue size increase.

The iron angle bracing shell for an updraft kiln must withstand the weight and pressures of expanding inside brickwork (Fig. 6-45). I suggest the following iron bracing sizes for a kiln with outside dimensions of 5' x 5' x 6' tall (The suggested sizes are also good for smaller kilns, but for economical consideration the tie braces could be 3/16s. Larger kilns

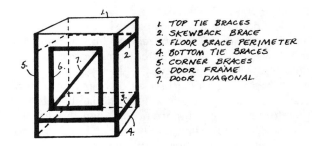

1. TOP TIE BRACES
2. SKEWBACK BRACE
3. FLOOR BRACE PERIMETER
4. BOTTOM TIE BRACES
5. CORNER BRACES
6. DOOR FRAME
7. DOOR DIAGONAL

Fig 6—45: *Angle iron bracing for 4' x 4' kiln.*

may need a thicker gauge angle iron especially for the floor and possibly the door components):

— 4 corner braces 3" x 3" x *1/4"*
— 4 top tie braces 2" x 2" x 1/4"
— 4 bottom tie braces 2" x 2" x 1/4"
— floor perimeter bracing 4" x 4" x 1/4"
— floor joist bracing 2" x 2" x 1/4"
— door frame 3" x 3" x 1/4"
— skewback brace 2" x 2" x 1/4"

These angle iron braces can be larger (stronger), but not smaller for this size kiln. Special care must also be taken in sizing the door and door frame angle iron. If the angle iron is undersized and the door extremely heavy, the weight will torque the arch and cause it to break its bond. Angle iron components should be kept away from direct flame, reflected flame, and intense heat. Otherwise, metal failure can result. When the frame is welded up, make sure that the welds have good long beads and are not just spot welded.

The door bracing for the Olsen kiln designs has a 12" seal distance between the hot face and the metal of

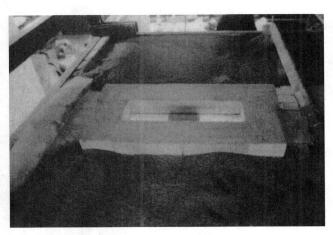

Fig 6—44: *Kiln flue and damper seal.*

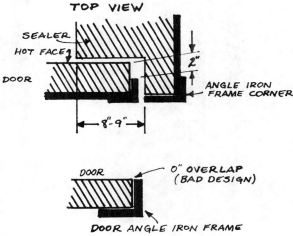

TOP VIEW

SEALER
HOT FACE
DOOR
2"
ANGLE IRON FRAME CORNER
8"-9"

DOOR
0" OVERLAP (BAD DESIGN)
DOOR ANGLE IRON FRAME

Fig 6—46: *Poor door frame construction.*

the door frame. I have seen professionally built kilns that had door frames enclosing the bricks, as in Fig. 6-36. The seal distance between the hot face and the frame was 2 1/2" or less. After numerous firings, the door frame was burning away and warping.

When using a fiber blanket or boards, it is difficult to get good permanent door and jamb seals. It is therefore extremely important to design the seals for easy replacement when totally compressed. I do not use a fiber blanket or boards in my kiln kits (Fig. 6-47 shows why). However, if I did design a kiln for fiber construction, I would follow the folded blanket or the compressed module construction techniques shown in Chapter 2.

Floor joist failure is usually caused by leaving the ring pilot or ignition match on a perimeter burner manifold during the firing. This can cause excessive heat and, combined with the weight of pottery on the joists, can cause metal fatigue. If the temperature reaches 316°C to 427°C (600° to 800° F) under the kiln where the burners are located, metal fatigue and deflection of the floor joists will occur. Under no circumstances should a ring pilot or ignition match on a perimeter burner system be allowed to burn under the kiln during firing. If the ignition match or ring pilot is properly designed and heat shielded as not to cause overheating under the kiln, then it can be left on. See Chapter 8 for an explanation of an alternative system.

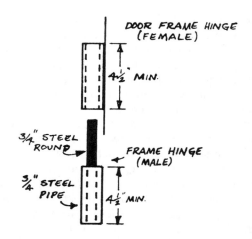

Fig 6—48: *Post-and-sleeve hinge installation.*

The door hinges and door lock assembly are extremely important, and are, too often, not strong enough. For a door 4' in height by 4' in length, I recommend 3 hinges, at least 9" in length. The hinges I used on the Olsen Kiln Kits are a simple but immensely strong post-and-sleeve arrangement (Fig. 6-48). The door lock is similar to the hinges. When the elliptical end is rotated, pressure is applied and the door locks to the frame, tight against the sealer wall (Fig. 6-49).

(**CAUTION:** Kiln doors should never be closed and cinched down extremely tight because of expansion during firing, which can cause the brick door jamb to collapse. The elliptical end and the corner jamb of the frame must be close (1"), or the steel rod can bend and break the seal loose. (See Fig. 6-50.)

When using insulation bricks, a 7" kiln wall is sufficient. The wall is constructed with a rowlock course of low-duty bricks or a 2" insulation low-duty fiber board and a hot-face stretcher course of high-duty brick. Featheredge firebricks are used for the skewback construction.

Fig 6—47: *Compete failure of bracing and seals in fiber construction.*

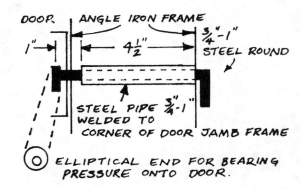

Fig 6—49: *Proper door lock installation.*

Fig 6—50: *In a badly designed lock, the rod will bend and break the seal.*

In bricking, the floor is laid first, then the door. Then the interior of the kiln is laid with the door closed and bolted so the bricks can be butted exactly to the door, thus ensuring a perfect seal. The arch is laid last and covered with an insulation blanket or vermiculite/clay mix for added insulation.

A metal damper guide can be made to act as a slide for the kiln shelf damper. A flat, smooth area around the exit flue holes on top of the arch is made for the damper slide (Fig. 6-51). The damper shelf should not grind against the flat area used, but be close enough to have a good tight fit when closed.

Flat Roof Updraft

Some updraft kiln designs use a flat roof instead of a sprung arch. The proponents for the flat roof maintain that it is easier to build and adjust the height of the flat roof to increase the kiln's volume, and reflects the heat in the same manner as the flat side walls and therefore outperforms the arch in heat distribution. Flat and arched roofs each have their problems when it comes to construction. A special independent frame for the flat roof must be constructed and designed to be either bolted or welded together. In some designs rod holes are drilled through each row of bricks across the span and bolted to the outside perimeter frame. In other designs the corner bolts are cinched down from both directions, putting the spanning bricks in compression. Normal wear and tear of expansion and contraction can grind the bricks down and make them loose. Thus, they require constant surveillance.

When building an arch, the frame to hold the arch is already in place. An arch frame must be built and inserted that matches up to the featheredge parallel rows and the arch laid. Both construction methods take time and special care. I consider it a draw.

A major advantage with the flat arch is the adjustability of the roof height to allow for taller pieces. However, this could become a disadvantage if allowed to become excessive and affects the quality of firing. As far as the heat distribution of an arch versus a flat roof, I am sorry to say I'm not a combustion physicist, but I would bet that the arch would win the contest. I do not believe an arch has a "lens" effect and concentrates the radiant heat into a lower center focal line. Remember, the arch is not in a vacuum or a static environment where this could be possible. I feel the arch produces more natural, aerodynamic flow across the top of the arch and circulates the flow down and around. The flat roof produces a hot spot and stress point at the places the flame hits the flat roof and is deflected. I have seen flat roof kilns (especially wood-fired kilns) where this is very noticeable due to the spalling and slagging that occurs there. I believe this translates to gas kilns also. In the gas kiln, if marginal IFB were used, this would be the spalling area and the hot spot or area of uneven heat distribution.

Industry is going to the flat roof designs using the fiber materials, which are lightweight and reduce construction cost while making the firing more economical.

In the end, an arch versus a flat top becomes a draw. Only personal choice and preference are important.

The contemporary updraft kiln is the most efficient design possible because:

1. It has the lowest cost per cubic foot of construction.

2. It has the lowest cost per cubic foot to fire.

3. It has the most usable stacking space in the chamber.

4. It is easily adaptable to hood envelope, sliding envelope, car kiln and tunnel kiln. (Updrafts are dominant in the ceramic industry.)

5. It has an extremely even firing quality with good atmosphere control when designed and built correctly.

Fig 6—51: *Metal damper guide for a kiln shelf damper.*

Chapter 7

Multi-directional Draft Kilns

Olsen's multi-directional draft kiln design originated from the combining of two wood-fired kilns — the anagama-derivative style kiln and a modified groundhog kiln. The purpose of the kiln design was to develop and explore a new technique of firing with greater control over temperature, atmosphere and the quality, plus create a totally new look in kiln design.

Traditional kiln designs allow for the draft to flow in one main direction, from the inlet flues and/or firebox, to the exit flues of the kiln and then into a chimney system or into the atmosphere, as in the case of updraft kilns. The anagama design, featuring a moderately wide, long tube, was used as the starting point for creating the multi-directional kiln concept. Depending upon the length of the tube and the design of the side stoke areas, the anagama kiln can be difficult to fire evenly. The kiln can be easily put into a reducing mode and quite easily choked. Uniform results and evenness may not be a major concern for the potters who have an anagama kiln, but if they were, then how to remedy the design?

The American groundhog kiln, on the other hand, as developed in the southeastern United States, is an understated kiln design with tremendous potential for innovation (See Gulgong racer, Chapter 4). The groundhog kiln fires evenly with good control, unless the kiln is too long and without side stoke holes. The kiln is more difficult to put into reduction because of the tremendous amount of air supply built into the firebox and the lack of dampers in a large chimney.

A combination of these two kiln styles bisecting each other would create a new innovation for wood kiln designs (See Fig. 7- 1). Therefore my multi-direc-

tional draft kiln design uses the two separate cross-draft systems in one kiln. Melding these two crossdraft configurations at right angles to each other would create a very large firezone that both systems must pass through, thus producing an evenness of temperature throughout the whole kiln (See Fig. 7-2).

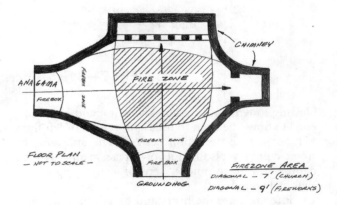

Fig. 7—2: *Combination kiln floor plan.*

Controlling the direction of the draft from two different sides of the kiln can create overlapping firing patterns and ash deposits never before seen. By firing one firebox and the opposite chimney alone to a high temperature or low temperature, then soaking for a period of time, you can set the flashing patterns and ash deposits as developed by the stacking and draft rate for that side. Switching over to the other firebox and chimney and firing it to a lower temperature or higher temperature and soaking sets up an overlaying flashing pattern and ash deposit from the right angle cross draft that is created. Alternating fireboxes and rhythms of stoking, or using one firebox with both chimneys in various combinations, can create innovative results.

The differences in the pulling power provided by these two chimneys are essential to controlling the atmosphere and manipulating the draft, and overall kiln performance. By controlling the pulling power of each chimney, the cross drafting is produced. However, since the normal groundhog chimney can be so overpowering, it was segmented into thirds, with each chimney flue having its own passive air and shelf damper. The chimney could be left fully open for

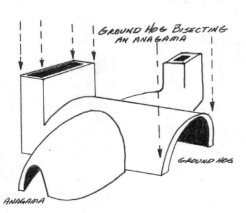

Fig. 7—1: *Groundhog-anagamagama combination.*

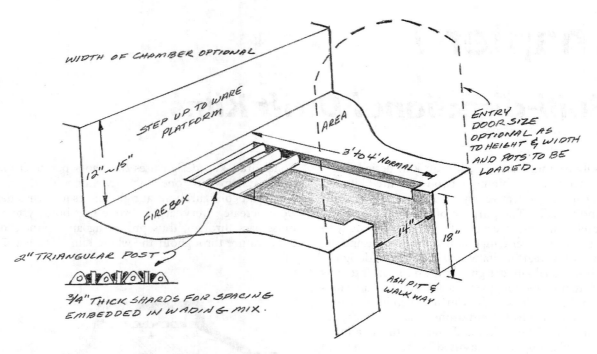

WIDTH OF CHAMBER OPTIONAL

STEP UP TO WARE PLATFORM

12"~15"

FIREBOX

AREA

3' to 4' NORMAL

ENTRY DOOR SIZE OPTIONAL AS TO HEIGHT & WIDTH AND POTS TO BE LOADED.

14"

18"

ASH PIT & WALK WAY

2" TRIANGULAR POST

¾" THICK SHARDS FOR SPACING EMBEDDED IN WADING MIX.

Fig. 7—3: *Firebox design.*

blasting to temperature quickly or it could be dampened to draw the draft to the right, center, or left flues only, or any combination desired. The anagama, or single chimney, also had its own passive air and shelf damper. Both chimneys were of equal height and slightly tapered.

Fireboxes are the heart and breath of a kiln and determine if the kiln has the capability to reach temperature. Each firebox has an opposing chimney and functions as the door to the kiln's chamber. Consequently, the firebox size determine the size of pieces that can be loaded into the kiln's chamber (Fig. 7-3).

Designing the firebox requires that all these factors are considered:
— Overall firebox size/area
— Overall grate bar area
— Ash pit depth and width
— Step up to the chamber floor
— Air supply for the ash pit, grate and firebox floor level and the stoke hole level
— Entrance width and height

Abundant air supply is one prerequisite for overall kiln performance, but it is how the air is supplied

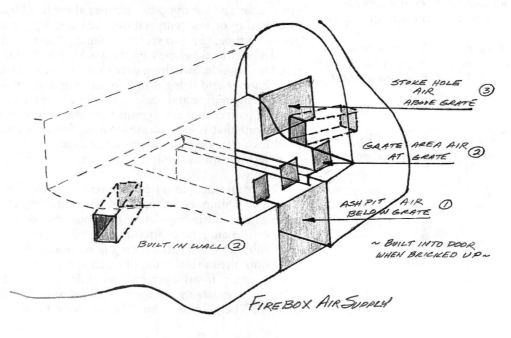

STOKE HOLE AIR ABOVE GRATE ③

GRATE AREA AIR AT GRATE ②

ASH PIT AIR BELOW GRATE ①

BUILT IN WALL ②

~ BUILT INTO DOOR WHEN BRICKED UP ~

Fig. 7—4: *Firebox with adjustable air supply.*

FIREBOX AIR SUPPLY

that becomes extremely important. To achieve maximum performance, the air sources should be: (1) below grate level, (2) at grate level, (3) at stoking level and all should be able to be opened or closed as desired (Fig. 7-4). This results in good firebox management which gives the tools for blasting, choking, maintaining, and atmosphere control. The two prerequisites for kiln performance, as discussed above, are the relationship of the air supply and firebox to the chimney design.

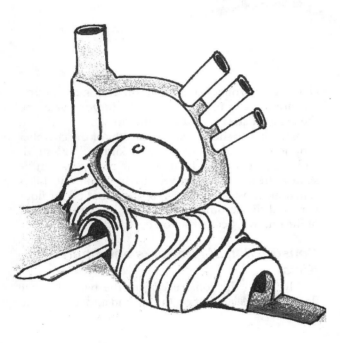

Fig. 7—5: *Edmonton fireworks kiln, version 1.*

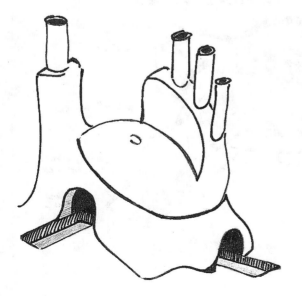

Fig. 7—6: *Edmonton fireworks kiln, version 2.*

Since the single chimney was smaller in overall area, I made the anagama firebox the largest with the most firebox stacking area. It would be the starting firebox for taking the kiln up slowly to a soft stoneware temperature. The groundhog firebox was made with a smaller entrance size, more directly into the stacking and capable of blasting through the firezone quickly.

This kiln design allowed for creativity in the firing method, and more control over temperature and ash deposits. For potters who enjoy firebox pieces, there are two such areas to work within this design. Another goal of the design was to create a more architectural and free-formed kiln capable of being a kiln but appearing to be something more distinctively sculptural and unusual.

There were two multi-directional drafting kilns built in 1998 at workshops I conducted in Canada and Denmark. They represent the beginning of my new style of kiln designing.

Edmonton Fireworks Kiln

During the 1998 Edmonton International Ceramics Fireworks Seminar at the University of Edmonton, Alberta, Canada, the "fireworks" kiln was built in a pre-conference workshop in four days, fired to cone 10-plus and opened for the conference closing on Sunday, for a total of a seven-day event. This uniquely designed freeform, wood-fired kiln introduced to the 40 workshop participants was so unusual and different that a sigh of relief and excitement was heard when it was announced that it would not be just another box kiln or catenary. Also, the fact that it would be the first multi-directional draft prototype kiln to be built contributed enthusiasm to the project. There were no plans for the kiln, just my two drawings to choose from and follow. Drawing 5, with its angular chimney, was deemed too complicated for the three-day window. Drawing 6 was posted next to the kiln site for all to follow during construction (Fig. 7-5 and 6).

Church Kiln

A few months later, after my participation in the Lithuanian 1998 Panevezys International symposium for clay artists, I was invited by Danish clay artist Nina Hole to lead a kiln-building workshop for the newly created International Ceramic Center in Skaelskor, Denmark. The project was to build one Olsen 36 gas kiln and one special wood kiln. Nina and her American husband, Larry, a furniture designer, live in a small village a few miles from the art center. Fifty meters up the road from their home/studio is an old Danish church, stark white in color and of a very bold design. A perfect kiln, I thought! (Fig. 7-7) Therefore, the Skaelskor kiln design would incorporate the stark whiteness and have a bold look. The kiln was the second multi-directional design with the smaller firebox

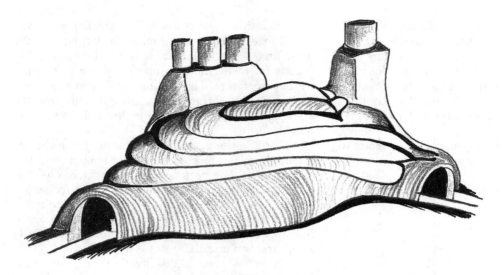

Fig. 7—7: *Danish church kiln.*

(24" wide) facing the groundhog-style chimney and the larger firebox (36" wide) facing the single anagama chimney. Part of the outside roof design was shaped like an inverted Viking long boat, flowing and integrating into the chimneys and fireboxes. The kiln was completely whitewashed to give it a stark, bold, appearance. An explanation of construction methods and materials used follows. Because the kilns are similar in design and only different in size (interior volume), the description will cover both.

The firezone was approximately 9 feet in both directions for the fireworks kiln and 7 feet for the church kiln. Both kilns were approximately 3 1/2 feet tall to the vertex of the ceiling. The kilns had slightly different firezone shapes, depending upon the perim-

eter stacking zones leading into the chimney and firebox areas. Refer to Fig. 7-1 for the firezone area and the areas of stacking around the firezone, which can be extended or shortened. The height of the chamber is optional, and depends upon the kiln builder's needs and the pieces to be fired. The firezone area can be shaped freely and creatively to best suit the kiln's function. Illustration Fig. 7-8 of the basic kiln floor plan and the accompanying photos give an overview of the following construction description.

Construction of Fireworks and Church Kilns

To begin the construction of the two kilns, the floor plan was laid out on the ground and the sod and

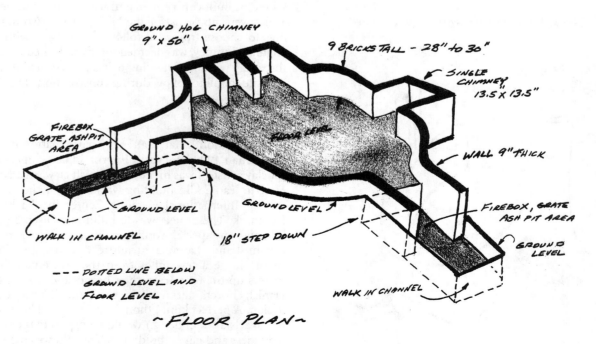

Fig. 7—8: *Danish church kiln floor plan.*

Fig. 7—9: *Laying out floor plan and digging out fireboxes, making sure castable will be sufficient.*

topsoil was removed. A grid pattern was drawn on the ground to represent the bags of castable for the dome shape and make sure the kiln was the right size for the amount of castable on hand (Fig. 7- 9). Next, both the firebox/entrance channels were dug out to a depth of 2 feet below the floor level, and the perimeter wall and chimney footings were dug down two bricks deep from the floor level. The firebox ash pits were built and bricked up to the grate level (Fig. 7-10). A leveling bed of sand was put down followed by the sub-floor (Fig. 7-11). Once the two firebox walls were built up level with the sub-floor, the main floor, perimeter walls and chimneys were simultaneously started (Fig. 7-12).

On the fireworks kiln, notice the method of using angle cut bricks to span a greater distance than the length of the brick (Fig. 7-13). Arching of the two fireboxes was finished and the side walls, along with the double chimneys, was continued up to the 10th row — approximately 26" (Fig. 7-14). The last two

Fig. 7—10: *Laying perimeter wall. Fireboxes laid to ware platform level.*

Fig. 7—11: *Laying floor on bed of sand within the perimeter wall.*

Fig. 7—12: *Building wall and chimney.*

Fig. 7—13: *Spanning the chimney flues for the groundhog side.*

Fig. 7—14: *Building firebox arches and continuing walls.*

rows, the eighth and ninth, were laid with K-26LI insulating firebricks to make a transition from hard, dense, brick to the insulating castable that was used in the free-formed dome. The last three rows were also tilted into the chamber to form the proper angle for the skew brick to achieve the dome form (Fig. 7-15).

Once the firebox arches were integrated into the side walls and the chimneys were well above the walls, a wooden platform was built inside the kiln at the level of the skewback row (Fig. 7-16). Dirt was piled upon the platform and roughly shaped into the desired form (Fig. 7-17). A layer of sand was applied and smoothed out, then the total form was covered with plastic in preparation for casting (Fig.7-18). The castable was mixed using the hand and ball test for proper consistency. (Make a softball size ball out of the castable, toss it into the air— 2 feet or so — catch it and if it crumbles, add water. If it flattens out, add dry castable. If it retains its shape, it is the proper consistency.) We slap troweled the castable onto the dirt form, starting at the bottom and working around the form. (Do not overwork or smooth out the castable or it will begin to sag. When applying the castable, make a ledge pointing down into the form to receive the next layer, at the same time keeping the thickness at a minimum of 4 1/2" to 5". See Fig. 7-19).

Once the cast was finished, the castable was covered with wet towels and then plastic and left to cure for 24 hours. Before removing the dirt and form from inside the chamber, the side wall was buttressed with rock debris, concrete blocks, and rubble, and mixed with cement to support the weight of the casting . After or before removing the form, the shaping of the kiln form can commence with an adobe mix applied over the cast dome shape. This can be done creatively or just as insulation (Fig. 7-20).

At the same time the stacking of these kilns commenced, the decoration was being finished. Sitting in the anagama firebox of the fireworks kiln, Warren Mackinsie, Alfred Schmidt, and I checked out the dome and the size of the kiln. The stacking started from each chimney and moved toward each firebox with the builders keeping in mind the fire channels needed for each firing direction. As one backs out of the kiln, the firebox area is stacked. Grate bars were laid over the ash pit spaced 3/4" apart (Fig. 7-28). Air holes were built into the door at grate level, and the ash pit entrance was left completely open on both fireboxes. A 9" x 9" stoke hole

Fig. 7—15: *Walls built up and skewed in to receive castable. Chimneys are built up past wall. Fireboxes are arched over.*

Fig. • 7—16: *Making plywood and wood platform level with wall.*

Fig. 7—17: *Piling dirt on top and shaping platform.*

was left in both firebox doors. Although there was a 9" to 12" rise from grate area to the floor of the kiln, it was designed to have the collecting coals fall into the front stacking. Care must be taken not to over-toss or cause the wood to hit the pots directly in the firebox stacking.

The initial firing of the fireworks kiln was a bit on the wet side. As the kiln was building up temperature and the rain kept coming down, we hit a point where we were generating our own clouds. Never missing a beat, the kiln climbed just as it was designed and we reached cone 10 during the height of the storm.

Fig. 7—18: *Dirt form reaches final shape before being covered with plastic.*

Fig. 7—19: *Finishing casting.*

Fig. 7—20: *Slap troweling casting form.*

Fig. 7—21: *Castable covered with wet towels and plastic for 24-hour cure.*

Fig. 7— 22: *Plastering and final buttressing of the kiln before final shaping with adobe mix.*

In the groundhog firebox, the draft can be pulled to the left or right of the chimney, or graduated to one side or the other. This helps in distributing the heat to all the stacking zones. Patience in maintaining a stoking pattern and rhythm for long time periods with one firebox is essential for exploring the possibilities of cross-directional overlaying of ash and flashing. When the switching of fireboxes occurs, the new firebox should be blasted for a short period of time to

Fig. 7—23: *Finishing shape of chamber and beginning chimney.*

Fig. 7—24: *Nina Hole shaping the keel of the Viking boat.*

Fig. 7—28: *Grate area of completed church kiln.*

Fig. 7—25: *White washing kiln.*

Fig. 7—27: *Unfinished ware ready to be fired.*

Fig. 7—26: *A look into the interior volume.*

build coals on the grates. At the same time, the other firebox is allowed to burn down, then maintained to keep the grates covered with large pieces (logs) and with the air supply severely restricted to allow the slowest possible burn rate. It is imperative that during the cycling between the fireboxes the kiln is allowed to cool a bit and then brought back up to temperature and held from the new firebox. The other firebox is allowed to cool. The firebox zone stacking is allowed to cool, while the firezone is brought back to temperature from the other firebox.

There seems to be an overwhelming urge to blast both fireboxes at once to make a spectacular chimney flame show. This is fine once in a while, but the rhythm in firing the two fireboxes, one hot and the other cold, is important for producing the cross-directional effects.

Our fire-lighting ceremony was started about 8 p.m. with a small fire outside the single chimney firebox at the ash pit entrance. This fire was maintained all night and the next morning was moved up onto the grate bars and stoked to maintain a steady rise in temperature to cone 9/10 by evening. The burn was maintained through the night and the next morning the other firebox was started and fired at a rapid pace while first firebox was maintained. Hours of off-and-on burning followed using alternating fireboxes. All the time, water was steaming out of the kiln. The kiln fired beautifully with total control of temperature rise and atmosphere. All enjoyed the experience and the pots that were produced when the kiln was opened.

Chapter 8

Fuels, Combustion, and Firing Systems

FUELS

Whether it burns wood, coal, oil or gas, the heart of any kiln is the firebox. When fuel is ignited and the kiln roars, smokes and gets hotter and louder, the firebox is breathing properly. But if the fuel is ignited and the kiln smokes and roars hour after hour with no increase in temperature, it is likely that the firebox is improperly designed and is not breathing.

A firebox must be designed to fit the fuel used. Wood fireboxes are larger than coal, and coal larger than oil. Gas requires the least space of all.

Solid fuels, such as wood and coal/coke, need a system that exposes maximum area to oxygen, thereby allowing the fuel to be ignited and give off its combustion energy quickly. Thus, wood, coal or coke should be burned on grates made of either fireclay or iron, with enough space below the grate to allow proper air supply and ample space for the ashes. Coal and coke grate bars are placed closer together than wood grate bars because of the size difference.

The simplified diagram in Fig. 8-1 illustrates how carbonaceous or cellulose fuels are reduced into a solid residue (coal and wood ashes, respectively) and give off heat and its exhaust gases or, in other words, how the firebox combusts the fuel. Remember that if ash accumulates on the grate bars and the fuel becomes embedded, the air supply for combustion is choked off and the fire is reduced, as is the amount of heat energy needed to raise the kiln temperature. If the ash pit is too close to the grate, the accumulation of ash may also choke off the air supply and cause the iron grate bars to bend from excessive heat.

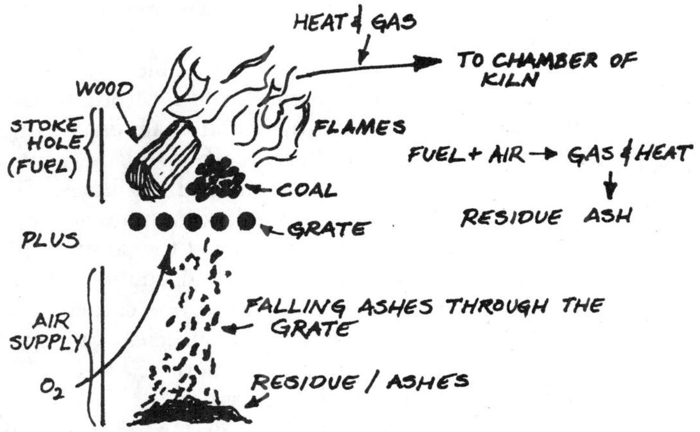

The kiln chimney is responsible for maintaining a constant draft, continuously sucking fresh air through the firebox for combustion. As long as the fuel is replenished, the cycle of combustion and the resulting heat accumulation is maintained until the desired kiln temperature is reached.

Solid fuels burn from the surface and, as the surface turns to ash and falls away, a new surface is exposed to oxygen and combustion until the entire piece of fuel is consumed. A whole log gives off less heat energy than the same log split into kindling. The smaller the wood pieces, the quicker the rate of combustion, resulting in greater heat release and a longer flame. The larger the piece of wood, the slower the rate of combustion, resulting in a shorter flame with less heat release. When firing a wood kiln with a cold top, smaller kindling is used to get the longer flame; if the bottom is cold, larger pieces that burn with a short flame are used, thus allowing the heat intensity to remain lower longer.

Softwoods are best for firing a wood-burning kiln because they have less density or weight in pounds per cubic foot, and thus burn more readily. For example, a soft pine may weigh only 25 lb./cubic foot, while a hardwood, such as oak, weighs from 50 to 59 lb./cubic foot. Pine, spruce, fir and hemlock are excellent woods for firing a kiln, for they release their energy quickly. White pine, for instance, develops 5,085 kg-cal/gm or 2950 Btu/lb. or about 9,400,000 Btu/cord. Allow wood to dry out for one year before using as fuel in a kiln. Wood with an excessive amount of moisture will cause steam to form, creating a cooling action and nullifying heat release.

Wood produces an enormous amount of smoke. In stoking my chamber kiln, one 1" x 1" x 24" stick will, upon exploding, produce a billowing cloud of smoke for almost 15 seconds. It is best to use a well-ventilated wood kiln in the country, or somewhere with ample open space. When firing with wood, the rate of stoking must be maintained and gradually increased. The amount per stoking, and the time between each stoking, determines the kiln's atmosphere. In firing oxidation, stoking is done after the clearing of the atmosphere within the chamber. Reduction stoking is done as soon as the flame disappears from the blow holes. Wood requires long tedious hours of stoking and preparation.

Fig. 8—1: *Combustion of solid fuels.*

Coal is a sedimentary rock produced from plant remains by partial decomposition in the absence of atmospheric oxygen. The net result of this decomposition is a material having a lower amount of oxygen and hydrogen and a higher content of carbon than the original matter. The steps in the breakdown of the plant remains lead to the successive formation of peat, then lignite, sub-bituminous coal, bituminous coal and anthracite. Bituminous coal is classified according to physical properties and chemical composition, from lowest to highest grade: (1) sub-bituminous or black lignite coal; (2) bituminous coal; (3) cannel, a variety of bituminous coal; and (4) semi-bituminous, a high-grade bituminous or low-grade anthracite. Various grades of bituminous coal are used to fire kilns. A grade B bituminous steam coal (which is also used in steam locomotives) is used to fire Mr. Singh's kiln discussed in Chapter. 5. Bituminous coal burns with a long flame and increases in efficiency as the temperature exceeds red heat. Bernard Leach refers to this bituminous coal as gas coal. If it is destructively distilled and heated in the absence of air, approximately 75 percent turns to coke and 25 percent to coal gas, which corresponds to about 10,000 cu. ft. of gas per ton of coal. For firing low-temperature kilns, lignite is sufficient and produces a long flame.

Petroleum and natural gas occur in sedimentary rocks. Petroleum is a liquid with varying amounts of four types of hydrocarbons: paraffinic, aromatic, naphthenic, and cleftinic. Each grade of fuel oil contains a hydrocarbon mixture, which makes it difficult to classify them by compound, so grading is done by properties. Light oil is #1; #2 (diesel oil) is called a distillate oil and is vaporized at normal temperatures and pressures; #4 fuel oil is a blend of #2, #5, and #6; #5 and #6 are heavy, black, residual fuel offs. The content of these oils is basically carbon 86 percent + 1 percent and hydrogen 13 percent + 1 percent, with sulfur varying from 0 to 2 percent.

Natural gas has basically the same composition as petroleum, except that the hydrocarbons are in a gaseous state. Fuel oil, kerosene, propane, butane and pure hydrocarbons are all obtained from petroleum by fractional distillation. Natural gas sometimes contains fractions rich in butane, which can be separated and stored as a liquid in suitable containers by pressures of a few atmospheres (an atmosphere is a unit of pressure equal to 1.0135 x 105 Newton psi). Fuel oil and kerosene burn cleaner than coal, but are dirty and inefficient up to red heat. Natural gas, propane and butane are the cleanest-burning fuels available. When they are burned in complete combustion, there is little or no visible sign of exhaust.

COMBUSTION

Combustion can be defined as a reaction that produces detectable heat and light. Very rapid combustion can lead to an explosion. If combustion occurs in gas, a flame is produced. Solids such as coal and wood, which volatilize into gaseous materials at combustion temperatures, also produce a flame. The temperature at which a material will begin to burn is called the kindling temperature. To start combustion, however, it is generally necessary to apply a flame.

Hydrocarbons have a great affinity for oxygen and, with excess oxygen, will burn to form carbon dioxide and water, producing complete combustion. An example is the complete combustion of a simple hydrocarbon of methane:

$$CH_4 + 2O_2 \rightarrow CO_2 + 2H_2O \text{ plus heat.}$$

This chemical reaction, which liberates heat, is known as an exothermic reaction. The combustion of wood and coal produces an exothermic reaction and a gas, but leaves behind a residue or ash.

RATE OF COMBUSTION

One of the most important factors affecting the rate of combustion of hydrocarbon fuels is the intimacy of the fuel with the air supply. The highest rate of combustion is obtained when a gaseous solution is formed, such as propane and air. The least intimate mixing is obtained when a non-volatile hydrocarbon in massive form (such as asphalt or coal) is exposed to air. Fine droplets of gasoline and oils suspended in air are an example of the intermediate stage of mixture intimacy. The intimacy of wood depends upon the size and surface area exposed, and whether it is hard or soft wood. If the concentration of fuel or oxygen is too low, combustion proceeds slowly. If the fuel-to-oxygen ratio is correct, combustion proceeds rapidly.

One cubic foot of methane (natural gas) requires 2 cu. ft. of oxygen for complete combustion. For practical purposes, air has 20 percent oxygen and 80 percent nitrogen. Therefore, to obtain 2 cu. ft. of oxygen, 10 cu. ft. of air must be supplied to completely burn 1 cu. ft. of natural gas. Natural gas = 10 cu. ft. of air per 1,000 Btu (1 cu. ft. of natural gas equals 1,000 Btu). Propane = 25 cu. ft. of air per 2500 Btu (1 cu. ft. of propane equals 2,500 Btu). Within limits, it can be said that 10 cu.ft. of air is required for complete combustion of 1,000 Btu of any fuel, whether solid, liquid or gas.

If sufficient oxygen is not available, the reaction becomes more complicated. Carbon, carbon monoxide, carbon dioxide, hydrogen and steam can form. In this reducing atmosphere, carbon black soot is formed around the door jamb and spy holes. Clays and glazes are likewise affected, sometimes adversely. If a reducing atmosphere is started too soon (649°C, 1,200°F) and maintained heavily throughout the firing, the pottery will probably be carbon corded, a detriment to the clay body. If insufficient oxygen is present, the rate of temperature increase and combustion efficiency are greatly reduced.

All combustion systems are designed for their air-handling capacities. The basic requirement, 10 cu. ft.

of air per 1,000 Btu/hr., makes most combustion systems standard. For example, once a burner is designed to handle the proper amount of air for a certain Btu rating, any gas will produce the same total heat output under perfect combustion conditions just by changing the gas flow rate. The rate depends upon the different Btu value per cubic foot of the specific kind of gas.

If we have a burner system using 1,000 cu. ft. of air/hr. and 100 cu. ft. of natural gas, the result is complete combustion. But, if we want the firing to go faster or to get the kiln hotter, we turn the burner up an additional 20 cu.ft./hr. What happens? If the gas flow is increased without the additional amount of air required, then the extra 20 cu.ft./hr. of gas is wasted up the chimney or out the flue. Any increase in fuel must be accompanied by a concomitant increase in air.

A rise in kiln temperature means that the rate of combustion increases and more heat is liberated in unit time. Rising temperature also means that there is a greater loss of heat to the surroundings. One function of the kiln is to hold heat loss to a minimum. The temperature reached during combustion depends upon the rate of heat production and the rate of heat loss. The initial heating of the kiln requires a tremendous amount of heat energy. During the first firing of a new hard-brick kiln, it may be impossible to reach temperature as quickly as expected because of all the moisture in the masonry. To raise the temperature of the kiln, the refractory materials utilized and the insulating value of the kiln must be good. There must also be a sufficient supply of fuel with a properly designed delivery system to produce the Btu necessary for the successful firing.

PRIMARY AND SECONDARY AIR

Primary air is the quantity of air mixed with fuel before ignition. The air mixed after ignition begins is *secondary* air. Most combustion systems rely on secondary air to burn solid fuels efficiently. Forced-air burners use at least 60 percent primary air; atmospheric burners use 60 percent to 20 percent primary air; and raw gas burners use 20 percent. The lower the percentage of primary air, the longer and softer the flame. Pre-heating the primary and secondary air increases flame temperatures, making the combustion performance better and saving fuel. For instance, pre-heating the air of a natural gas-air mixture to (500°F, 260°C), will increase the flame temperature about (93°C, 200°F).

WOOD-BURNING SYSTEMS

Wood requires the largest combustion area and grate size of any fuel to accommodate the sudden burst of flame and heat energy, and to supply adequate air. A wood firebox should: (1) allow the air to be preheated before initial combustion — for every increase of 204°C (400°F) of air temperature, you get an increase of 37.8°C (100°F) flame temperature; (2) allow the preheated air to come up through the grate to combust, or provide secondary combustion space; (3) have enough room above the grate for maximum combustion to take place; (4) allow easy access for raking out the coals, (5) have properly sized and spaced flue holes leading into the kiln chamber.

It is important to have the main firebox outside the kiln chamber in order to pre-heat the air before combustion, thus producing maximum heat value from wood. If the firebox is inside the chamber and is too small, it will cause erratic temperature distribution and difficulty reaching maximum temperature. However, if sized properly it can be extremely effective. Examples of this include the Bizen kiln and anagama kiln, which are stacked directly in the firebox. The Bizen kiln firebox is extremely large and works well because the long duration of the firing gives time for the chamber to even out and produce the desired effects. The groundhog firebox is only for firing and is very effective.

The design for a wood kiln firebox should follow six guidelines:

1. Minimum firebox floor area should be ten times the chimney cross section. See Chapter 3 — Design Principles.

2. The grate should be placed at vertical midpoint, with half the space allotted to the ash pit (Fig. 8-2).

3. Firebox height is determined by the style of the kiln, its size and by virtue of the potter's experience. In the case of the groundhog and anagama, the firebox is contained within the chamber and is determined by that chamber's dimensions. In contained fireboxes outside of the kiln chamber, no firm rule can be stated. However, by comparing the size of the fastfire kiln, the Bidai chamber kiln, and the modern chamber kiln discussed in this section, a suitable height for a wood-burning kiln can be determined. The shortest height possible would be 12.5", with the grate height placed at 6" to 7" to fit the 12 to 16-cu.-ft. fastfire kiln. If the grate is too low, coals can build up and cause choking. I have found that for most kilns of moderate size (from 30 to 100 cu. ft.) with outside fireboxes, from 12" to 18" below the grate and the same above the grate is more than sufficient. Use a

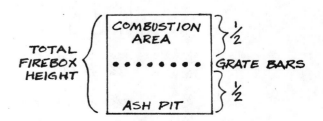

Fig. 8—2: *Position the grate at midpoint.*

graduated scale as the kiln size increases It is very important to have ample ash pit area below the grate bars and that the grate bar spacing is correct.

4. Spacing of the grate bars is extremely important to fuel and firing efficiency. If the grate bars are too far apart, large unburnt clinkers will fall through, causing the ashpit to fill up too fast. If the grate bars are too close together, clinkers cannot fall through and there is a buildup of wood on top of the clinkers. This chokes off the incoming preheated air from under the grate, and causes a drop in kiln temperature. (This is a good reason for grate combustion area air mouse holes.) To determine the spacing of the grate bars, consider the wood to be used (Fig. 8-3). Fig. 8-3 shows grate bar spacing that is at the maximum and requires a deep ash pit .

5. The ashpit must be easily accessible for raking out coals. The grate bars must also be accessible in order to rake down the wood clinkers.

6. An abundant air supply should be provided at the ash pit level, grate level, and at the stoking level. Depending upon the firebox design, the grate level air supply can be provided around the perimeter of grate combustion area. See Fig. 7-3/4 in Chapter 7.

BIDAI CLIMBING KILN

The first firebox analyzed will be the Bidai and Kawaii climbing kiln (see Chapter 4). Fig. 8-4 shows an overall view of the firebox under construction. Note the slope from the entrance (stoke and air inlets) along the firebox wall and up the side to the comer flues. Figures 8-5 and 8-6 show the relationship of the

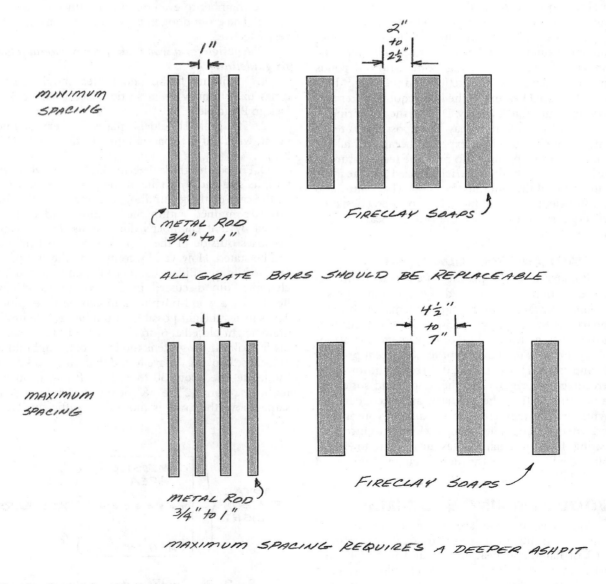

Fig. 8—3: *Spacing for grate bars.*

Fig. 8—4: *Bidai firebox under construction.*

ash pit area to the first chamber inlet flues, and the retaining wall for the earth mound and the grate bar rests. This firebox was also duplicated on the Kawaii kiln in Chapter 4. The arching-over was done with handmade tatami mat bricks, as was done on the Kawaii and Hotchkiss kilns.

Figure 8-7 provides a layout, side and top views, of the firebox, and illustrates the ash pit area and retaining wall for grate bar placement. For a larger chamber kiln, this firebox should be enlarged in proportion.

Fig. 8—6: *Slightly overhead view of ash pit.*

Fig. 8—5: *Front view of Bidai firebox.*

MODERN CHAMBER KILN

A modern wood firebox is found on the Kitade Tojilo kiln in the Kutani area of Japan (Fig. 8-8). This side stoke firebox can use long lengths of slab wood that burn on a full width grate. The ash pit is deep to accommodate the larger coals that can fall through the wider grate spacing (See layouts in Fig. 8-9). The air supply is from two sources on the bottom of the front wall. I would add more smaller-width air holes and spread them out more

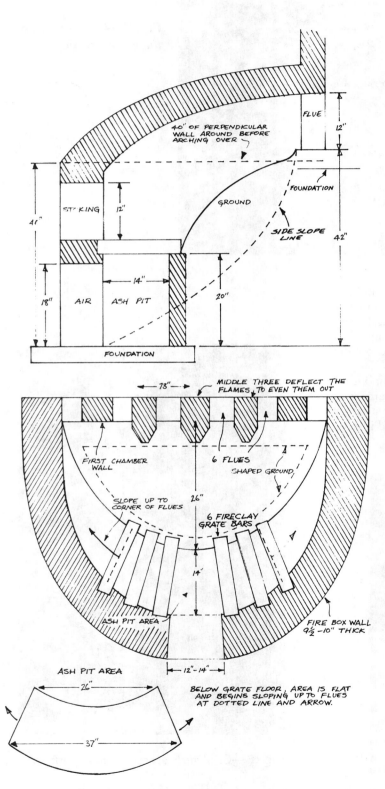

Fig. 8—7: *Bidai kiln layout. Side view on top, detail of firebox and ash pit area below.*

Fig. 8—8: *Modern chamber kiln firebox, Kitade Tojilo kiln, Kutani, Japan.*

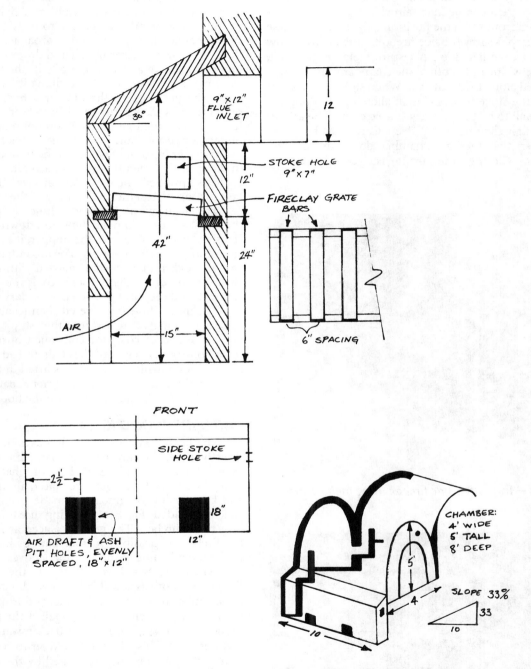

Fig. 8—9: *Firebox layout for side-stoked wood-burning kiln of Kitade Tojlo kiln.*

evenly across the chamber. The grate bars should be spaced to the minimum and I would also add grate level mouse holes that could be opened if necessary. The side-stoke firebox is good for a single person to fire because it can be maintained as the first chamber is stoked from the same position (Fig. 8-8a, b). These photographs show the side firebox, which is 18" below the first chamber floor. A fastfire metal grate 9" tall and the width and depth of the chamber is used. Air is supplied along the front wall. When stoking, the space below the stoke hole is closed, allowing air along the front wall to be the primary source of air. The ash pit in the first chamber is 15" deep. Care must be taken, however, that the first chamber does not cool too quickly. Closing the front is very important.

Fig. 8—8a: *Olsen side firebox using metal grates (pullout).*

Fig. 8—8b: *First chamber grate and ash pit.*

HOB FIREBOX

The hob firebox is simple to build, eliminates the need for grates, and uses larger pieces of wood (Fig. 8-10). There is a center hob that splits the firebox in half. Wood is laid across the hobs at a right angle to the draft. The primary air enters from the top, pulling the flames down and toward the throat arch and inlet flue. As the wood burns in half and drops into the ash pit, new logs are added to the pile in the hopper. As the embers fall into the ash pit, filling it halfway, they ignite the new logs in the hopper, which fall down onto the hobs. Care must be taken to keep the hopper full and to ensure that the ashes do not block the secondary air supply holes. All the gases released by the primary combustion of wood on the hobs are burned in the space between the bob and ash pit. The ash pit coals also pre-heat the secondary air, which is important for complete, efficient burning of the wood.

The clean-out or primary air holes, located above the hobs, are used to poke the wood down if needed. If a slab cover is used over the hopper, it becomes the source of primary air supply. The secondary air holes can be blocked or opened as needed with plugs. The clean-out holes are there in case coals must be shoveled out, and they also provide a secondary air supply.

The mouse hole is a covered channel about 2 1/2" square, running 12" to 15" into the ash pit, to supply air to the bed of coals for continued burning. This helps control the height of the coals and adds heat for better wood burning. The fire is started in the ash pit and is maintained there until sufficient coals and heat are produced to ignite the wood on the hob.

FASTFIRE WOOD KILN

The fastfire kiln uses two fireboxes of equal size directly under the kiln chamber. Basic dimensions for each firebox are 13-1/2" x 40-1/2", or what the width of the kiln is, and the boxes are placed along the front and back wall. The grates are made from 3/4" iron rod, and welded (Fig. 8-11) making sure that the grate bisects the firebox. The grate is placed as far back in the firebox as possible, so that part of it is directly under the inlet flue to the chamber above.

When the wood combusts on the grate, the flames and hot gases will roll in two directions: Into the chamber through its inlet flue, and from one-half to two-thirds down the grate, against the top of the firebox and down, around and back toward the firebox inlet flue. This allows the cold air to come in low under the grate and be pre-heated by the coals. The cold air also keeps the grate cool enough so it will not melt. It is imperative to keep the coals from building up and touching the grate bars. If the spacing is correct, this will not happen often during the firing and will only require a raking to even the coals out. Coals will never have to be removed. After the firing, the grate must be pulled out of the firebox. If it is not pulled out, the grate will oxidize and become warped. The fireboxes should be sealed up when the firing is finished.

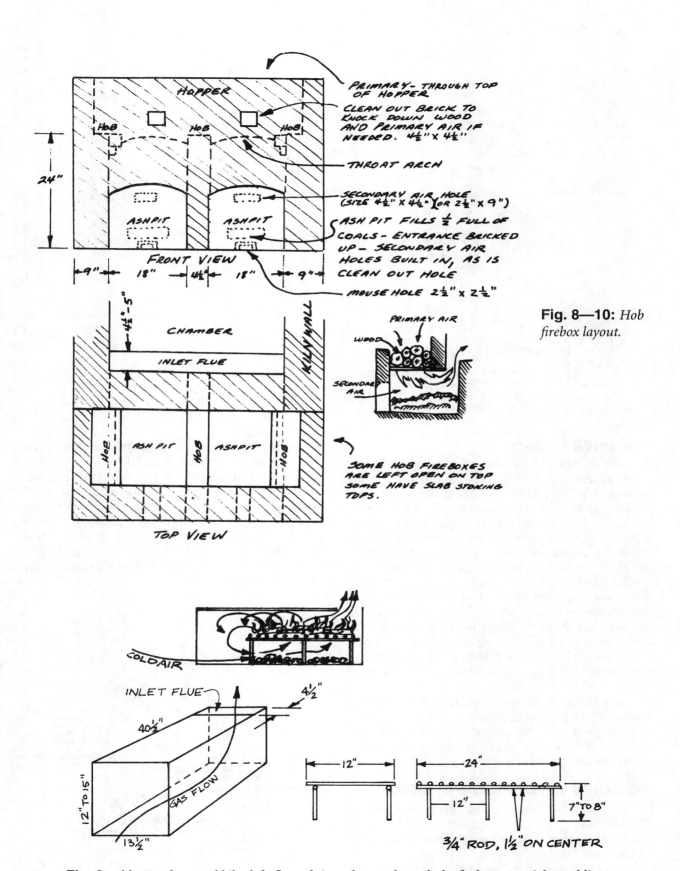

Fig. 8—10: *Hob firebox layout.*

Fig. 8—11: *Fastfire wood kiln: left, flow of air and gases through the fireboxes; at right, welding the grates.*

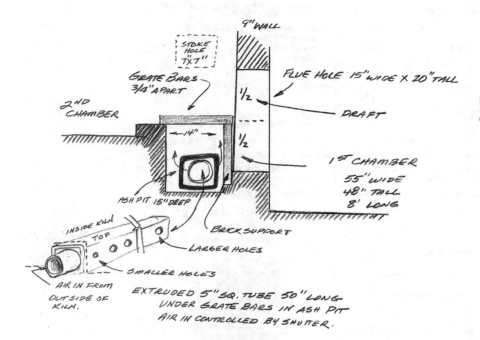

Fig. 8—11a: *Second chamber firebox.*

CHAMBER FIREBOX

The climbing kiln chamber firebox is small; only wood of about 1" x 1" x 18-24" can be used in the stoking. The first chamber of Les Blakebrough's legendary kiln in Mittigan, Australia, is shown in Fig. 8-12. The firebox channel runs the entire width of the 6' chamber. Grate bars or long soaps are wedged along the kiln wall and floor, 9" on center apart. The grate holds the wood above the air supply at the inlet flues. As the wood burns, the ashes drop to the bottom of the channel. Occasionally, a long iron poker with a hooked end must be inserted through the stoke hole to rake down the coals; otherwise, they can choke the stoke hole and retard the firing. In stoking the chamber, a few sticks are always dropped inside the door, then the long stoking — working back to the door — is done.

In a chamber without a sunken firebox, channel bricks are laid along the floor 9" on center apart between the saggar settings and the front wall (Fig. 8-13). The space created is the minimum 9", running up the entire height of the stacking.

SECOND CHAMBER FIREBOX

In multi-chamber kilns, the main air source is from the front of the kiln. Secondary air can be gotten from cracks, doors etc. Air supply can be provided during construction, but once construction is completed and there is a need for an even air distribution in the chamber after the front chamber has been closed down, then I use an extruded air tube the width of the chamber placed under the grate. When designing chambers and an in-chamber firebox, grate area and ash pit area must be taken into consideration. I use a sunken ash pit area below the inlet flue with the grate area bisecting the inlet flue. I install a 5" extruded square tube with perforated sides with the smaller holes toward the supply and larger holes at the other end. This allows for even air distribution across the firebox width and even burning (Fig. 8-11a). The air supply is controlled by a shutter on the tube outside the kiln.

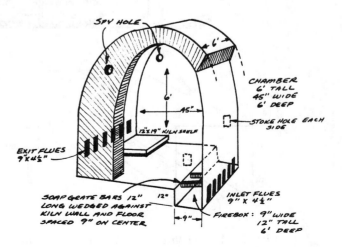

Fig. 8—12: *Chamber kiln firebox and chamber, Mittigan, Australia.*

Fig. 8—13: *Stacking arrangement of saggars in chamber kiln.*

spaced around the perimeter. A larger circular kiln should have fireboxes 6' to 8' apart around the perimeter of the kiln.

The size variation between a two-firebox and a four-firebox kiln can be seen by comparing the fireboxes in Figs. 5-6 and 5-11. Kato's kiln has 5 sq. ft. of grate area per firebox, while Singh's kiln has 4 sq. ft of grate area per firebox. Mr. Singh's kiln has four fireboxes and is larger (38 sq. ft. floor). Therefore, it can utilize the higher floor-to-grate ratio. These two kilns are a good example for planning a coal firebox (Fig. 8-14). The more fireboxes used, the higher the floor-to-grate ratio. Too large a ratio is better than too small.

OIL-BURNING SYSTEMS

GRAVITY DRIP SYSTEM

One of the cheapest and simplest oil burners is the gravity drip system (Fig. 8-15). This system, for three inlet port flues, has three plates for each flue channel — a total of nine plate-burning areas. It is my experience that three plates per flue channel are accurate for an efficient burner system. The plates are 9" x 5" and are set parallel, with a 3" height difference and a 2" overlap on a slope of about 2:9. Depending upon the viscosity of the oil used, the slope angle will increase or decrease. A slope of 2: 9 to 2 1/2:9 is excellent for diesel oil. The plates I use have a lip along the side to prevent the fuel from running off before it reaches the end. However, flat plates can be used if they are kept in a horizontal position. The plate system is built into dense or insulating bricks that are loosely laid, with loose firebricks spanning the plate channels (Fig. 8-16). In this way, they can be easily removed for adjusting, and cleaning the carbon or clinker buildup that accumulates during firing.

The firebox area inside the chamber should correspond in size to the firebox channel for side stoking the wood climbing kiln chamber. There should be a 9" minimum distance from the kiln wall to the bagwall, running the length of the chamber and up the kiln wall.

The rate of fuel feed is controlled by the three gate valves connected to the main fuel line. The gate valves drip into the funnels connected to brass tubing, which drips onto the top plates of each channel. Fuel

COAL-FIRING SYSTEMS

Coal fireboxes are illustrated in detail on the kiln plans of K. Kato's and M. Singh's kilns in Chapter 5. Coal fireboxes have, for the most part, standard dimensions, since coal needs just so much area for combustion. Coal fireboxes should have 1 sq. ft. of grate area for every 6 to 8 sq. ft. of floor area in the kiln. The number of fireboxes depends upon the chamber shape. A rectangular chamber over 7' in length will need extra fireboxes on each side. One firebox per 6' is the normal spacing. A circular kiln 7' in diameter will have from three to four fireboxes, evenly

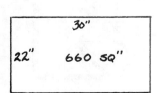

5 SQ' · 2 FIREBOXES:
10 SQ' PER 30 SQ' FLOOR
6 TO 1 RATIO
30 ÷ 6 = 5 SQ' GRATE OF
PER FIREBOX

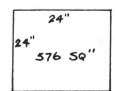

4 SQ' · 4 FIREBOXES
16 SQ' PER 38 SQ' FLOOR
8⁺ TO 1 RATIO
38 ÷ 8 = 4⁺ SQ' OF
GRATE PER FIREBOX

Fig. 8—14: *Coal-burning firebox specifications.*

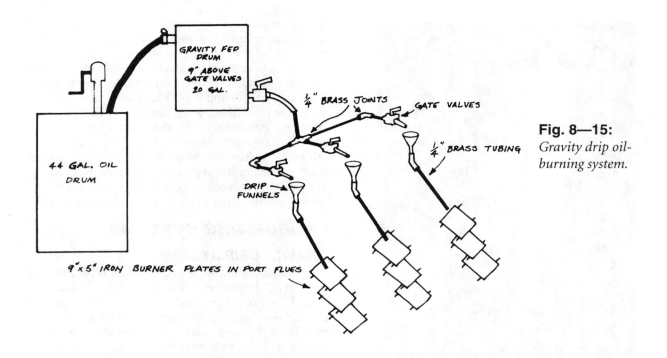

Fig. 8—15: *Gravity drip oil-burning system.*

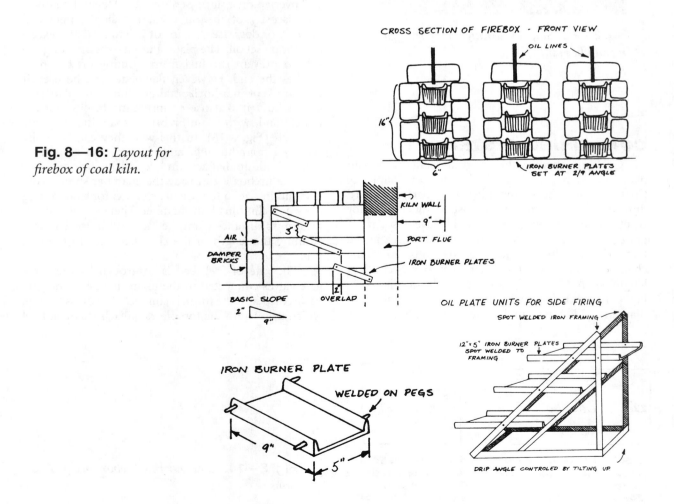

Fig. 8—16: *Layout for firebox of coal kiln.*

Fig. 8—17: *Oil-drip system on Blakebrough kiln.*

pressure is maintained by gravity feed from the overhead tank, located 10' above the plates. The oil drip system on Les Blakebrough's kiln is similar to the system illustrated except that it has six oil drip channels (Fig. 8-17).

The placement and number of oil drip ports is largely determined by the length of the front inlet flue wall. The ports are spaced 9" (or one brick) apart. Usually, one or two more ports can be put into the wall if they are started 4-1/2" from the corner, rather than 9". The maximum needed for any given kiln is one oil drip port per 9" of inlet flue wall; the minimum needed is one port per 18" of wall. A greater number of burners fires the kiln faster.

The best way to ignite diesel oil is to use kerosene-soaked rags placed at the bottom plate. Light the rags, then drip the diesel oil off the bottom plate onto the rags. A 45- to 60-cubic-foot kiln with three channel ports will, on the average, use about 60 to 75 gallons of No. 2 grade diesel oil to fire to Seger Cone 10, yielding between 132,000 and 140,000 Btu per gallon.

Care must be taken to keep the inlet flues and drip channels free of a carbon clinker buildup during the firing. This is done by breaking the carbon up with an iron rod or poker. I also pour a little water down the funnels every hour with the diesel fuel. This seems to break up the carbon buildup.

The flow of oil during the later stages of firing should be fast enough for burning to take place on all three plates. If the oil burns only on the top or top two plates, the oil flow rate should be increased.

I have seen two oil drip plates installed in 6" channel iron, as illustrated in Fig. 8-18. The channel plate system is then placed directly into the inlet flue channel of the kiln wall. The biggest problem with this arrangement is the difficulty in cleaning the carbon buildup by poking in through the air supply hole or the open end of the channel. The channel system is exposed directly to extreme temperatures and thus oxidizes away quite rapidly. Also, there is not enough plate surface area, nor spacing and overlapping of the plates. The three-drip system mentioned above is far better. This system is good for pre-firing a kiln to the temperature where a forced oil single-orifice burner can take over.

On a few occasions when money was scarce, I collected free sump oil (used crankcase oil) from filling stations and used it to fire my kiln. Kerosene and #1 diesel fuel oil are clean-burning fuels to use. However, I prefer #2 diesel fuel because of its higher viscosity and lower flashing point, which make it suitable for use in oil-drip or oil-burner systems. Its other characteristics are: 0.85 specific gravity; 132,000-140,000 Btu per gallon and 18,610 Btu per pound; 0.3 percent sulfur content.

GRAVITY DRIP AND FORCED AIR

Denis Parks, an authority on oil firing, is the designer of the modified Tuscarora drain oil diesel combination burner illustrated in Fig. 8-18a. The system is simple, effective, and able to switch from expensive diesel oil to cheap (sometimes free) crankcase oil. Water can be added to the mix just by turning on the needle valve when the kiln reaches red heat. The amount of air is controlled by the gate valve and by dampening the blower. Fuel flow is controlled by the needle valves. During cold weather the 1,000-watt engine block heater is used. Denis uses the analogy of "water in bacon grease" to explain the use of water in the fuel mix. "This violence in the firebox is spattering oil everywhere, breaking down the particle size, which in turn speeds vaporization and combustion," he said. Water helps eliminate clinker formation and helps to volatilize the fuel more effectively and cleanly. Denis increases the water mix gradually from red heat on until about 20 percent of the fuel mix is water.

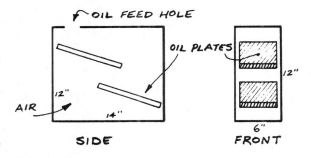

Fig. 8—18: *Alternate oil system installation.*

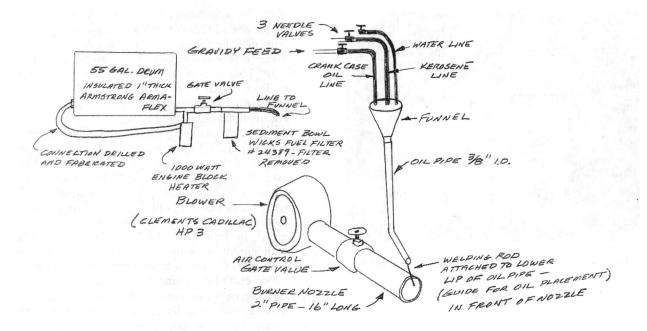

Fig. 8—18a: *Denis Park's Tuscarora with diesel/drain oil system.*

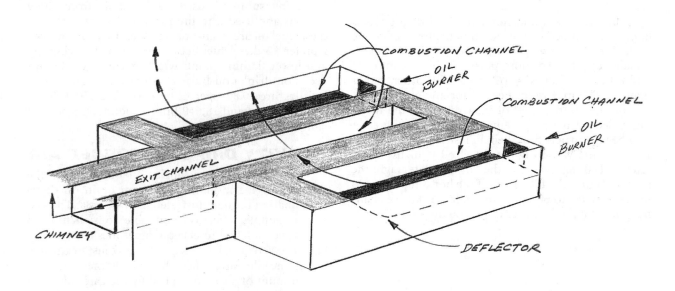

Fig. 8—18b: *Denis Park's firebox with flame deflector.*

Fig. 8-18b shows the firebox, which is 9" wide and has a curved deflector built in for the long powerful flames to heat and deflect up. The deflector helps immensely in reducing the slagging effect oil has on the refractories by lessening the impact of the blast on the target deflector and diffusing it upward (Fig. 8-18b). The difference between the Park's Tuscarora combination burner and the Denver burner is that the oil in Park's burner is supplied outside the nozzle.

FORCED-OIL BURNERS

There are two types of forced-oil burners: Air under pressure only; and both air and oil under pressure. The Denver-style low-pressure burners, which are frequently used to fire pottery kilns, are the former. Denver-type burners have been used to pre-heat and fire the Tamba kilns in Japan (see Fig. 4-9) and Bernard Leach used them to fire his chamber kiln. The oil is gravity fed to the burner from the top into an adjustable needle valve, which flows through an orifice at a point A (Fig. 8-20). The air enters at the bottom through a butterfly valve and mixes with the

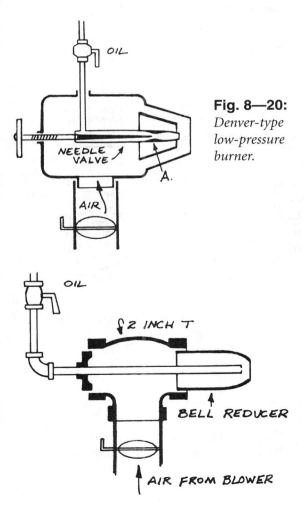

Fig. 8—20: *Denver-type low-pressure burner.*

Fig. 8—21: *Plan for a simple forced-air burner.*

oil in the nozzle to form droplets. At low temperatures, the burner is not efficient, but once the kiln reaches red heat the burner begins to become efficient. Using pipe fittings only, including a 2" T, a 2" to 1/4" plug, and a 2" to a 1" reducer or a bell reducer, a very simple forced-air burner can be made (Fig. 8-21). Paul Soldner uses a very simple raku kerosene burner, which is nothing more than a pipe with a reducer on one end and a vacuum cleaner attachment at the other end. A few inches in from the reducer a small 1/4" pipe is inserted at an angle and soldered (Fig. 8-20a). The small pipe connects to a valve and to the kerosene is gravity fed to the pipe burner. The kerosene is atomized and forced swirling through the reducer with the power of the forced air. This is pretty much a full-force burner and used after the little kiln is hot enough to take its force.

The orifice size is determined using the rule explained on page 182. The amount of air needed in CFH (cubic feet/hour) can be determined by the gallon per hour (GPH) capacity of the orifice. If a 5 GPH orifice is used, then 5 x 132,000 Btu/gal equals 660,000 Btu/hr. and will need 6,600 CFH for this one burner. If more burners are used, add their cumulative air supply when sizing for the proper blower. The air can be manifolded from the blower to each burner. Most of the blowers used with burners shown in Figs. 8-20 and 8-21 are powered with 1/3, 1/2, 3/4 hp, 2,850 to 3,600 rpm electric motors. The impellers are sized to the CFH and pressure needed. Pressures run from 4 to 48 ounces, but 4 to 10 ounces should be adequate. Too much air, or air at too great a pressure, will cause flame arresting or quenching. Excessive air cools the flame at the point of contact below the ignition point of 649°C (1,200 °F) and quenches this part of the flame. If the whole flame is cooled by excessive air below the ignition point, the flame is extinguished. Care must be taken to avoid excessive quantities of primary air and also cold secondary air. If this condition exists, you will notice an unusual odor.

The most efficient type of oil burner is the forced oil/air injector. High-pressure #2 diesel or fuel oil is introduced into a mixing chamber, along with the air under pressure, creating an atmosphere of fine droplets or mist. The mixture is extremely intimate and is a very combustible fuel. Fig. 8-22 shows a typical forced oil/air burner. The 1/8-hp, 115-V, 1,725 rpm electric motor powers the birdcage blower and the oil pump. The oil pump is a three-in-one assembly of pump, pressure regulation valve, and strainer. The pump gives 100 psi discharge pressure, but can be adjusted for a different flow rate. The pump adjustment range is from 80 to 130 psi. For example, a 3 GPH orifice can be adjusted down to 80 psi with a 2.7 GPH flow rate, and up to 130 psi with a 3.43 GPH flow rate. During firing, the increased nozzle temperature can reduce the flow rate by about 6 percent.

The ignition transformer (120 V, 60-cycle, 10,000 sec.) ignites the oil/air mist and keeps it ignited by sending a spark constantly between the spark points. The spark point gaps should be 1/8" to 5/32" apart (Fig. 8-23). The spark points should be 1/2" above the orifice hole and 1/4" ahead (Fig. 8-24). This also acts as a safety feature when used in a home heating furnace, or in a kiln.

The orifice should be 3/4" to 1-1/8" from the nozzle nose piece (Fig. 8-24). This distance depends upon the GPH orifice, but for 0.75 to 1 GPH, the nozzle should be set 3/4" from the nose piece and back as the rate increases. The best setting is that which, for any

rate, allows the flame to burn in a cone shape. If the nozzle is too far back, the rotating air stream will bend the oil spray inward so that a mushroom flame shape occurs. Be sure the oil spray does not strike the edge of the nose piece, where it will form carbon. The flame distance off the nose piece will vary from 1/2" for low rates to 1" for high rates. Adjust the air regulator so that the flame tips appear absolutely clean.

The disadvantage of this burner, using a single orifice with a constant GPH, is that it is always going full blast. It is hard to start the firing with this burner

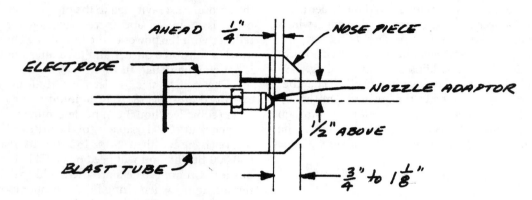

Fig. 8—24: *Nozzle and electrode locations.*

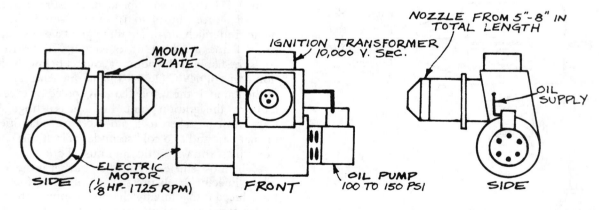

Fig. 8—22: *A typical forced-oil/air burner.*

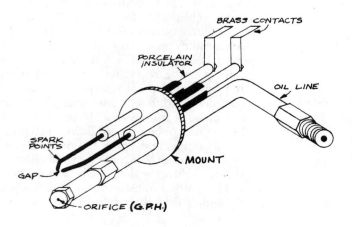

Fig. 8—23: *Detail of oil and spark system (inside nozzle).*

and maintain a gradual temperature increase up to bisque because of the lack of Btu input control. It is extremely difficult to shut down the burner, pull it out hot, and try to change the orifice to one with a greater GPH. This can be solved by using a three-stage nozzle adaptor (Fig. 8-25). Each nozzle has a different GPH orifice, controlled by different on/off valves connected to the main pump oil line. The nozzles can be used one at a time, two at a time, or all together. In fact, there are seven different GPH rate increases possible. For a kiln requiring about 924,000 Btu using two forced oil/air burners with three-stage nozzle adaptors, you might use the GPH orifice sizes.

The oil burner Btu rating is controlled by the size of the orifice used. The orifices range in size from 0.4 to 30-gallons-per-hour (GPH) and up to 100-gallons-per-hour. The orifice is very delicate in design (Fig. 8-26) because it performs two functions: (1) it determines the fuel consumption rate (GPH); and (2) it

NOZZLE SERIES	SPRAY ANGLES AND CAPACITIES (GPH)						
	30°	45°	60°	70°	80°	90°	
R*	.50 to 1.50	.40 to 3.50	.40 to 3.50	.50 to 3.50	.50 to 3.50	.60 to 3.50	SOLID
NS*	.50 to 1.50	.50 to 2.00	.50 to 2.00	.50 to 2.00	.50 to 2.00	.50 to 2.00	HOLLOW
AR*		.60 to 3.50	.60 to 3.50	.60 to 3.50	.60 to 3.50	.65 to 3.50	SOLID
PLP		2.25 to 9.50	2.25 to 30.0	2.25 to 60.0	2.25 to 100.0	2.25 to 50.0	SEMI SOLID
PL*		2.25 to 9.50	2.25 to 30.0	2.25 to 50.0	2.25 to 50.0	2.25 to 9.50	HOLLOW
HV*	1.65 to 24.00	10.50 to 60.0					SOLID NARROW

* BEST SUITED FOR KILNS; PL AND HV ARE BEST FOR HIGH GPH INPUT

Fig. 8—27: *Spray angle and GPH of standard nozzles.*

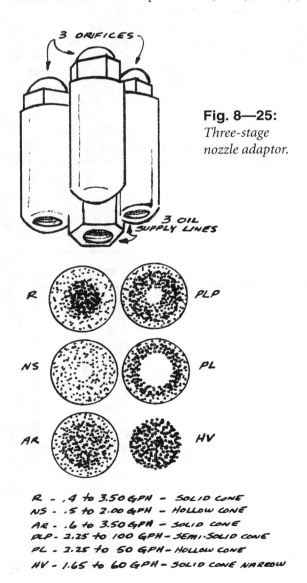

Fig. 8—25: *Three-stage nozzle adaptor.*

R - .4 to 3.50 GPH - SOLID CONE
NS - .5 to 2.00 GPH - HOLLOW CONE
AR - .6 to 3.50 GPH - SOLID CONE
PLP - 2.25 to 100 GPH - SEMI-SOLID CONE
PL - 2.25 to 50 GPH - HOLLOW CONE
HV - 1.65 to 60 GPH - SOLID CONE NARROW

Fig. 8—26: *Oil nozzle spray characteristics.*

determines the type and angles of spray mist produced (Fig. 8-27). The sprays produced are of basically two types — the hollow cone spray, designated by the letter H on the orifice, and the solid cone spray, designated by the letter S on the orifice. The angle of the spray determines the size of the cone produced.

For a long, narrow firebox within the kiln chamber, the smallest angle orifice should be used (Fig. 8-28). This is perhaps the worst firebox design for oil,

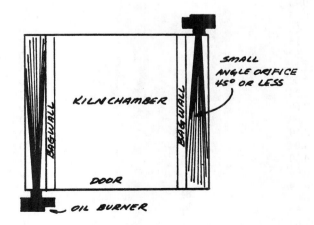

Fig. 8—28: *Small-angle or orifice is used in a long, narrow firebox.*

Table 8-1
Three-Stage Nozzle Adaptor Orifice Sizing

Nozzle	Orifice GPH Size	Btu Rating	Firing Sequence
#1	.5	66,000	#1 only: 538° C (0 to 1000° F)
#2	1.0	132,000	#1 + #2: 538 to 1016° C (1000 to 1860° F)
#3	2.0	264,000	#1 + #2 + #3: 1016 °C to finish (1860 °F to finish)
Total	3.5	462,000	

NOTE: The turn-up combinations for each burner are: #1; #2; #2 + #1; #3; #3 + #1; #3 + #2; #3 + #2 + #1. This gives the burners a very good Btu control.

but fine for gas. For a firebox outside the kiln chamber, a wide-angle spray should be used (Figs. 8-29 and 8-30).

Forced oil/air burner fireboxes must be designed with enough space for combustion (see Chapter 3). The general rule is 1 sq. ft. of combustion area to every 5 sq. ft. of floor area. When forced oil/air is used, the combustion area can be reduced somewhat due to the more intimate mixture of the fuel. For a general relationship between the GPH of the burner and the necessary firebox dimensions, see Fig. 8-31.

When using a forced oil burner, because of the extreme force of the flame and the slagging action it has on refractories, it is best to consider locating the firebox outside the chamber. The fastfire firebox under the chamber, Leach's firebox on his chamber kiln, or a converted coal firebox, using just the grate area and omitting the ash pit (see Chapter. 5), are suitable plans.

To determine the GPH for an oil kiln design, use No. 1 in Rules for Calculation of Gas Requirements. Briefly, multiply the total inside cubic footage of the

Table 8-2
Orifice size, Fuel flow rate, and BTU

Orifice Size	GPH @ 100 psi	Btu (net)
0.40	0.40	52,800
0.50	0.50	66,000
0.60	0.60	79,200
0.75	0.75	99,000
0.85	0.85	112,200
1.00	1.00	132,000
1.25	1.25	165,000
1.50	1.50	198,000
1.75	1.75	231,000
2.00	2.00	264,000
2.25	2.25	297,000
2.50	2.50	330,000
3.00	3.00	396,000
3.50	3.50	462,000
4.00	4.00	528,000
4.50	4.50	594,000
5.00	5.00	660,000
5.50	5.50	726,000
6.00	6.00	792,000
6.50	6.50	858,000
7.00	7.00	924,000

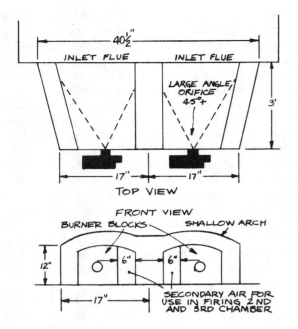

Fig. 8—30: *Firebox outside chamber, Bernard Leach's kiln.*

Fig. 8—29: *Forced-oil firebox, Leach's kiln.*

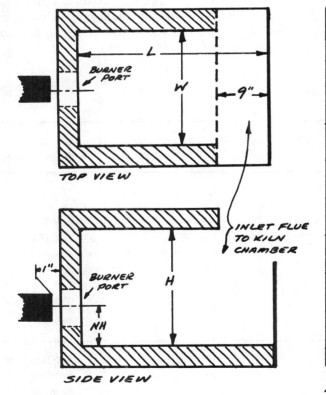

NOZZLE SIZE GPH	WIDTH (W)	LENGTH (L)	HEIGHT (H)	NOZZLE HEIGHT (NH)
1.0	12"	12"	16"	6"
2.0	16"	16"	18"	7½"
3.0	18"	20"	18"	7½"
4.0	20"	24"	21"	9"
5.0	20"	25"	21"	9"
6.0	24"	30"	24"	10"
7.0	24"	34"	25"	12"
8.0	24"	36"	27"	13"

APPROXIMATE FIREBOX SIZES NEED FOR GPH - USE AS A GUIDE

BURNER NOZZLE NOSE ABOUT
1" OUT FROM PORT - EARLY FIRING
THIS GAP SEALED WITH FIBER COLLAR.

Fig. 8—31: *Firebox size and GPH relationship.*

kiln by 10,000 Btu for IFB lining or by 16,000 Btu for dense brick lining to find the total Btu needed per hour for the kiln. The kiln design calls for two opposing oil burners. Therefore, divide two into the total to get each burner Btu capacity. Then size the orifice accordingly:

50 CF kiln x 10,000 Btu (IFB) or 16,000 Btu (firebrick)

$$= \text{Btu/burner} = \frac{\text{Btu/hr. input/}}{\text{no. of oil burners}}$$

NATURAL GAS, PROPANE AND BUTANE BURNERS

The most widely used fuel for firing kilns today is natural gas. Where natural gas is not available, bottled gas (LP) is used. Commonly known as propane or butane, LP or liquified petroleum gas has been cooled and compressed into liquid form for easy transportation and storage. Butane and propane are hydrocarbons (compounds consisting of carbon and hydrogen in a gas form. Mixtures of certain hydrocarbons (80 to 90 percent methane with ethane, nitrogen and other hydrocarbons) constitute natural gas. Two other products used for firing pottery kilns are coal gas and producer gas. Coal gas is formed by heating bituminous coal without contact with air. Producer gas is made by burning coal in a mixture of air and steam to produce largely carbon monoxide and hydrogen. When possible, natural gas, propane or butane is preferable to coal gas or producer gas. Table 8-3 gives average percentages of the compounds that make up the composition of gases by volume.

Kilns can operate with low pressure (11 WC or less) or high pressure (11 WC to 25 psi or more), depending upon the burners used. One pound per square inch (1 psi) equals 27.7 WC (water-column inches). High-pressure valves, shut-offs, regulators, gauges, etc., are much more expensive than low-pressure gas equipment and cost more to maintain. Whether you use a high-pressure small orifice or low-pressure large orifice to get the CFH needed, the kiln will reach the same firing temperature. Do not buy high-pressure equipment and try to convert it to low-pressure use, or vice versa. In either case, the burners will be extremely inefficient.

The difference between propane and butane is simply that propane boils (makes dry gas) at temperatures above minus-40°C (minus-44°F), while butane boils (makes dry gas or vapor) at temperatures above 1.1°C (30°F). Butane has a higher Btu rating than propane and propane has a higher rating than natural gas. Table 8-4 compares a few statistics of these gases. (Btu ratings will vary, depending upon the source and, in the case of natural gas, the region of its origin.)

Table 8-3
Gas Composition

Gas	C_3H_8	C_4H_{10}	H_2	CH_4	C_2H_6	C_2H_4	CO	CO_2	N_2	O_2	other hydrocarbons
Propane	100%	—	—	—	—	—	—	—	—	—	—
Butane	—	100%	—	—	—	—	—	—	—	—	—
Natural Gas	—	—	—	90.7%	3.8%	—	—	—	1.0%	—	4.5%
Coal Gas	—	—	52.5%	30.0%	0.8%	2.0%	6.8%	1.7%	3.5%	0.6%	2.1%
Producer Gas	—	—	21.1%	4.0%	—	—	19.8%	6.8%	48.3%	—	—

Table 8-4
Gas Characteristics

Gas	Specific Gravity (air-1)	BTU/ft.^{3}	BTU/gal.	BTU/lb.	Flame Temp. in Air (°C)	(°F)	Air: Gas Ratio for Complete Combustion
Natural Gas	0.65	900-1150	41,400	—	—	—	4.73:1
Propane	1.52	2516	91,690 at 60°F	21,591	1979	3595	30.00:1
Butane	2.00	3280	102,032 at 60°F	21,221	1996	3615	23.40:1

All gas burners have three main parts: mixer, burner, and controls.

1. The mixer mixes air and gas in proper ratio and delivers this mixture under pressure to the burner.

2. The burner ignites the mixture and produces a flame.

3. The controls administer the fuel input and include safety equipment.

The basic design of all burners is based upon the characteristics of gas flowing through an orifice. The orifice is a restriction and causes a pressure drop when gas flows through it:

$$Q = 1658.5 \times K \times A \sqrt{\frac{\Delta P}{d}}$$

Q = Flow in cu/ft/hr
K = Orifice efficiency
A = Orifice area, square inches
P = Pressure drop in water column inches (WC)
d = Specific gravity of the gas

The K factor is a measure of orifice efficiency, based upon its shape and approach angles against a frictionless orifice. This efficiency has a value from 0.4 to 1.3. The best atmospheric burners have a value of 0.8 to 0.85.

The pressure drop caused by the orifice is the difference in pressure between P1 and P3 (Fig. 8-32): P3 will always be less than P1; P2 will be less than either P1 or P3. Another important fact is that the flow across a given size orifice varies as the square root of the pressure drop changes. This means that, if a pressure drop from 16 WC to 1 WC occurs, the capacity will be 1/4 of the original capacity at the higher pressure. Also, increasing the orifice by, say, three times, will increase the capacity three times. Thus, it is easier to get greater variations in heat input by increasing or decreasing orifice size than by changing pressure conditions (see Fig. 8-44 and Table 8-5).

Keeping these relationships in mind, the burner design and function will be easier to understand. If a casing is made to fit the flow pattern in Fig. 8-32 and cleaned up to reduce eddy currents before the orifice and on the discharge side, we would arrive at a burner design (Fig. 8-33). The gas passes through the orifice (B1), entrains atmospheric air through the air shutter (B2) and moves into the mixer. The energy derived from P1 is almost dissipated in producing the negative pressure at P2 and inspirating atmospheric air; thus, a lower pressure at P3. For gas/air mixers, the P2 pressure must always be negative (less than atmospheric) for best operation.

For any given burner, there is an optimum orifice size at B1 for a given area at B3 which will produce the highest possible P3 consistent with the negative pressure needed at P2. This condition exists when the gas spray touches on a tangent the BT area and continues to expand into the venturi (Fig. 8-33). The area at the throat (BT) is the narrowest portion of the venturi and is one of the limiting factors in the burner's operation. Other limiting conditions are as follows:

— *B1 orifice area increased too much*: P3 pressure increases and reduces P2 pressure; thus more gas flows through B1, less air is pulled in by the reducing P2 negative pressure. The result is adverse air/gas ratio for complete combustion.

—*B3 area decreased in size*: P3 pressure increases, as does the negative pressure P2, until P2 reaches a positive pressure and forces the gas out through B2.

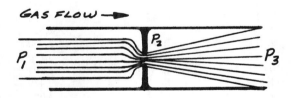

Fig. 8—32: *Pressure drop in a gas orifice.*

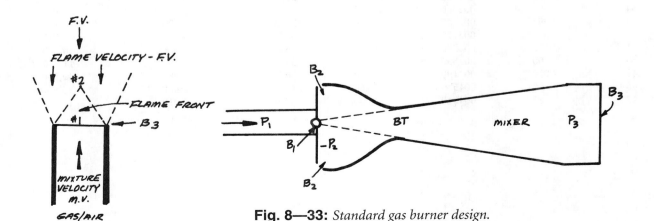

Fig. 8—33: *Standard gas burner design.*

Table 8-5
Flow of LP Gas through Standard Orifices

			Propane	Butane	Butane/Air	Butane/Air
Heating value (Btu/CF)			2,500	3,175	525	1,000
Specific Gravity (Air 1.0)			1.53	2.00	1.16	1.31
Pressure (WC)			11.0	11.0	5.0	7.0
Wire Gauge Drill Sizes	Diameter (inches)	Orifice Area (sq. in.)		Flow of Gas (Btu/Hour)		
—	.006	.000028	249	276	—	—
—	.007	.000038	333	374	—	—
—	.003	.000050	445	492	—	—
—	.009	.000064	570	630	—	—
—	.010	.000079	703	773	—	—
—	.011	.000095	345	936	—	—
—	.012	.000113	1,005	1,110	—	—
80	.0135	.000143	1,270	1,410	204	433
79	.0145	.000163	1,470	1,625	236	505
78	.0160	.000201	1,790	1,980	287	816
77	.0120	.000254	2,260	2,500	363	778
76	.0200	.000314	2,790	3,090	448	962
75	.0210	.000346	3,030	3,410	494	1,060
74	.0225	.000393	3,540	3,920	567	1,225
73	.0240	.000452	4,020	4,450	645	1,390
72	.0250	.000491	4,370	4,840	700	1,510
71	.0260	.000531	4,730	5,240	737	1,630
70	.0280	.000616	5,490	6,070	878	1,890
69	.0292	.000670	5,960	6,600	955	2,060
68	.0310	.000755	6,720	7,440	1,078	2,320
67	.0320	.000804	7,150	7,920	1,147	2,470
66	.0330	.000855	7,600	8,420	1,219	2,620
65	.0350	.000962	8,580	9,480	1,370	2,950
64	.0360	.001018	9,050	10,080	1,450	3,120
63	.0370	.001075	9,570	10,600	1,535	3,290
62	.0380	.001134	10,100	11,140	1,620	3,470
61	.0390	.001195	10,600	11,800	1,705	3,660
60	.0400	.001257	11,170	12,300	1,759	3,850
59	.0410	.001320	11,750	13,000	1,885	4,040
58	.0420	.001385	12,300	13,600	1,980	4,240
57	.0430	.001452	12,930	14,300	2,075	4,450
56	.0465	.001698	15,100	16,700	2,425	5,200
55	.0520	.002120	18,850	20,900	3,030	6,490
54	.0550	.002380	21,200	23,400	3,400	7,280
53	.0595	.002780	24,700	27,400	3,970	8,520
52	.0635	.003170	28,200	31,200	4,530	9,700
51	.0670	.003530	31,400	35,000	5,060	10,800
50	.0700	.003850	34,200	38,000	5,490	11,800
49	.0730	.004190	37,200	40,300	5,980	12,850
48	.0760	.004540	40,400	44,700	6,480	13,950
47	.0785	.004840	43,000	47,600	6,910	14,900

Table 8-5
Continued

			Propane 2,500 1.53 11.0	Butane 3,175 2.00 11.0	Butane/Air 525 1.16 5.0	Butane/Air 1,000 1.31 7.0
	Heating value (Btu/CF)					
	Specific Gravity (Air 1.0)					
	Pressure (WC)					
Wire Gauge Drill Sizes	Diameter (inches)	Orifice Area (sq. in.)		Flow of Gas (Btu/Hour)		
46	.0810	.005150	45,800	50,700	7,350	15,800
45	.0820	.005280	47,000	52,000	7,550	16,200
44	.0860	.005800	51,600	57,200	8,280	17,800
43	.0890	.006220	55,300	61,300	8,870	19,100
42	.0935	.006870	61,600	67,700	9,800	21,100
41	.0960	.007240	64,400	71,300	10,300	22,200
40	.0980	.007540	67,000	74,200	10,750	23,100
39	.0995	.007780	69,200	76,600	11,120	23,900
38	.1015	.008090	72,000	79,600	11,520	24,800
37	.1040	.008490	75,500	83,600	12,100	26,000
36	.1065	.008910	79,300	87,800	12,700	27,300
35	.1100	.009500	84,500	93,600	13,550	29,100
34	.1110	.009630	86,200	95,300	13,820	29,700
33	.1130	.010030	93,200	99,500	14,350	30,800
32	.1160	.010570	94,000	104,000	14,630	32,400
31	.1200	.011310	100,600	111,500	16,100	34,600
30	.1285	.012960	115,300	127,600	18,500	39,800
29	.1360	.014530	129,500	145,200	20,550	44,600
28	.1405	.015490	137,500	152,500	22,100	47,500
27	.1440	.016290	145,000	160,500	23,400	49,900
26	.1470	.016970	151,000	167,000	24,200	52,000
25	.1495	.017550	156,000	173,000	25,050	53,800
24	.1520	.018150	161,500	179,200	25,900	55,700
23	.1540	.018630	166,000	183,500	26,600	57,200
22	.1570	.019360	172,000	190,700	27,650	59,300
21	.1590	.019860	176,500	195,700	28,350	60,900
20	.1610	.020360	181,100	200,000	29,000	62,400
19	.1660	.021640	193,000	215,000	30,900	66,500
18	.1695	.02256	200,500	222,000	32,200	69,100
17	.1730	.02351	209,000	231,500	33,600	72,200
16	.1770	.02461	219,000	242,500	35,100	75,600
15	.1800	.02545	236,500	250,530	36,300	78,100
14	.1820	.02602	242,000	256,500	37,200	80,000
13	.1850	.02888	249,500	264,500	38,400	82,500
12	.1890	.02806	250,000	275,000	40,100	86,200
11	.1910	.02885	255,000	282,000	40,900	88,000
10	.1935	.02940	261,500	289,500	42,000	90,200

SOURCE: *Handbook of Butane-Propane Gases.* Reprinted by permission of Gas Appliances Co., Long Beach, California. It may be necessary to make adjustments to the recommended drill size for satisfactory operating conditions, since ideal size is affected by temperatures and barometric pressures in various localities. The specifications are for pressures from sea level to 3,500 feet above sea level. For altitudes from 3,500 to 5,000 feet, use one drill size larger (approximately 0.002" dia.). From 5,000 to 6,500 feet, use two sizes larger (approximately 0.004" dia.). Above 6,500 feet, use two to three sizes larger.

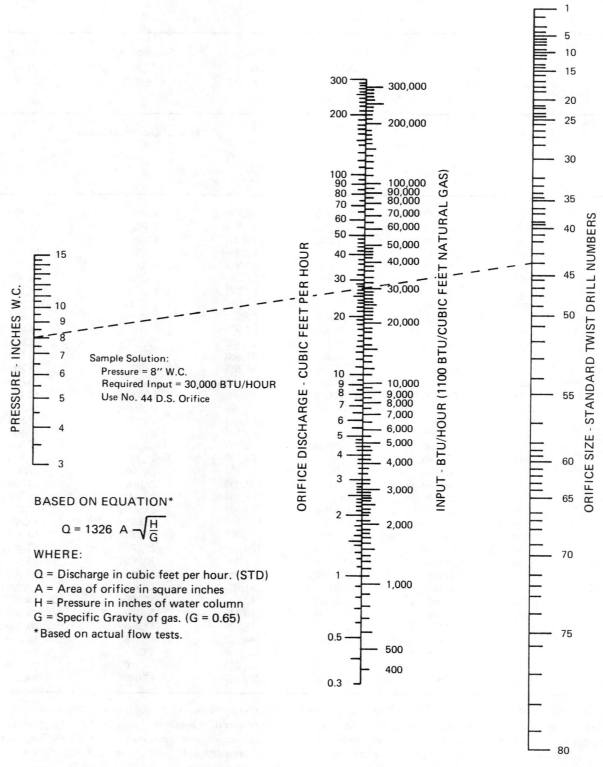

PRESSURE - INCHES W.C.

Sample Solution:
Pressure = 8" W.C.
Required Input = 30,000 BTU/HOUR
Use No. 44 D.S. Orifice

BASED ON EQUATION*

$$Q = 1326 \ A \ \sqrt{\frac{H}{G}}$$

WHERE:

Q = Discharge in cubic feet per hour. (STD)
A = Area of orifice in square inches
H = Pressure in inches of water column
G = Specific Gravity of gas. (G = 0.65)
*Based on actual flow tests.

ORIFICE DISCHARGE - CUBIC FEET PER HOUR

INPUT - BTU/HOUR (1100 BTU/CUBIC FEET NATURAL GAS)

ORIFICE SIZE - STANDARD TWIST DRILL NUMBERS

Fig. 8—44: *Gas flow chart.*

—*B3 area increased in size*: P3 pressure decreases and the negative P2 pressure increases, until the air intake dilutes the gas, resulting in adverse combustion conditions.

—*P1 pressure decreased*: P2 and P3 decrease proportionately until negative pressure at P2 is lost and venturi cannot function.

When the gas/air mixture reaches B3, it will expand and lose its velocity slowly. Once ignited, the mixture will burn from the outside across, around and through this stream at a uniform rate, moving from #1 to #2. The flame burns in a conical shape, toward the gas/air mixture. For the flame to burn at B3, a balance between the mixture velocity and the flame-burning rate or flame velocity must be equalized. If the mixture velocity out of B3 exceeds the burning rate, then the flame blows off B3 and burns at a point above that where the velocities are equalized. If the mixture velocity is too slow, the flame velocity will exceed the mixture velocity and the flame will back burn down into the mixture tube toward the mixture source. This is known as flashback. Care must be taken to use the proper burner pressure so blow-off and flashback do not occur.

Low-pressure atmospheric burners operate with 20 percent to 60 percent primary air/gas ratio in the mixture at burner B3. The most efficient, best-designed burner will use the greater percentage of entrained primary air. It is very important to use the burners within their optimum range for best results. The burner manufacturer will stipulate the capacity, turndown range, operating pressure and percentage of primary air used so you can choose the proper burner for your kiln. A burner with sufficient Btu input and with at least a 6" WC turndown range is usually adequate. The more burners used to get the necessary Btu input for the kiln design, the better the control and efficiency.

Vapor (dry) gas burners for kilns are extremely efficient, well designed and inexpensive. There are various styles of burners available, but the most popular for kilns are the simple atmospheric air mixer, atmospheric injection mixer, tempered air burner, and homemade pipe burners.

SIMPLE ATMOSPHERIC AIR MIXERS

Gas Appliance manufactures a simple cast-iron atmospheric air mixer that is efficient in most kilns (Fig. 8-34). A 2" black pipe, 8" long, is used for the flame tube. The overall length of the burner from the orifice to the tip of the flame tube is 9". Most simple atmospheric air mixers will be between 9" and 12" in length. There should be at least 1/2" gap between the cast-iron mixer and the primary air adjustment shutter for normal burner operation. When using this burner with natural gas, a No. 32 orifice is recommended to give the burner a 54,000 Btu rating per hour at 8 WC pressure. Propane would use orifice size

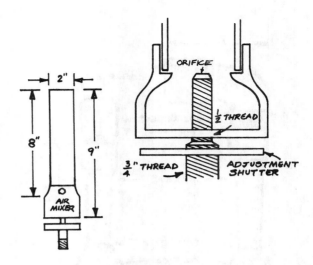

Fig. 8—34: *Efficient atmospheric air mixer.*

No. 45, giving the burner 50,000 Btu/hr at 11 WC. Butane would take orifice size No. 46, giving the burner a 57,200 Btu/hr rating at 11 WC.

When using this burner at higher altitudes, the flame may burn too far down in the flame tube, instead of at the tip. To solve this problem, first check that the orifice is sized properly for the altitude. If the orifice is the right size, then cut off 1" of the flame tube at a time, until the popping and back burning in the tube stop. Usually 2" will be sufficient.

When firing my Olsen 24 with propane, I have found that, by retaining the natural gas orifice (#32) and decreasing the water column pressure to 4, I get a softer, longer flame and better temperature distribution throughout the kiln. (This is not a recommended procedure.) The general rule is: When using higher pressure, the orifice size should be smaller.

ATMOSPHERIC INJECTION MIXERS

Figure 8-35 illustrates a small, single-casting 75,000 Btu burner from Gas Appliance with a built-in flame retention nozzle. The MR-750 burner has a range of 17,490 to 78,440 Btu while operating on a gas pressure range from 3.5" to 9.5" WC. The flame retention head is not a self-piloted nozzle; it turns the outside part of the flame back into the main flame cone, thus concentrating the flame. The effect is similar to a self-pilot nozzle and keeps the flame burning at the burner head within its pressure range. The MR750 is perhaps the best burner available in its Btu range. It is extremely efficient and quiet, with an excellent turndown range.

A more complex burner produced by Gas Appliance is a single-casting mixer and venturi atmospheric sleeve. As the gas flows through the orifice under pressure, it retains air drawn through the air

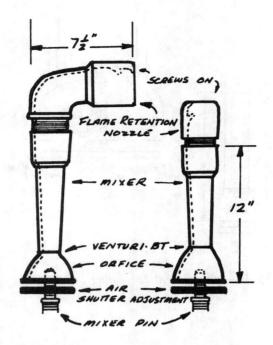

Fig. 8—35: *Single casting burner with built-in flame retention nozzle.*

shutter gap and is mixed. The venturi restriction causes a slight vacuum, which in turn draws in more air through the shutter. The gas/air mixture burns at the end of the flame sleeve (Fig. 8-36). This burner

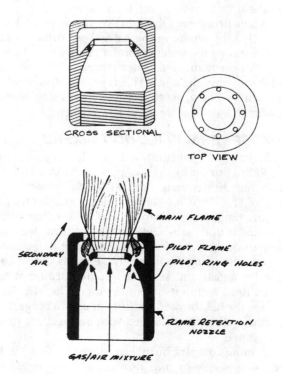

Fig. 8—36: *Single casting mixer with venturi atmospheric sleeve.*

works well at standard pressure of 8" WC and also at higher pressure with a good turndown ratio. For high pressure, a flame retention nozzle can be screwed onto the flame sleeve. The flame retention nozzle keeps the gas combustion at the sleeve head, not somewhere inside the kiln, and establishes pilot flames around the base of the burner, continuously igniting the base of the main flame. This type of flame retention nozzle is known as a "self-piloted" nozzle. The main burner mixture supplies the main flame and the pilot flame mixture. The pilot ring holes are placed low enough in the nozzle to shield the pilot flames from cross drafts and thus provide constant low-pressure flames to keep the main flame ignited. This eliminates the lifting or blowing off of the flame from the burner due to increases in input velocity.

The Gas Appliance MR-750 and the MR-100 are affordable and efficient venturi burners with flame retention features. Their Btu ratings at 8" WC are 75,000 and 100,000, respectively. These burners have an excellent turn-down range and are the choice of burners in the Olsen Kiln Kits (Fig. 8-37).

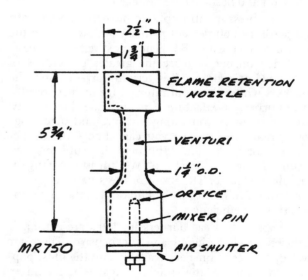

Fig. 8—37: *Standard injector burner.*

A weed burner used in Denmark for propane kiln firings is very simple in design but has high performance and output (Fig. 8-37a). A flame mixer/intensifier is set 5/8" from the lip, which is enough to give a good focal point for the flame during all increases in gas pressure.

The Eclipse Fuel Engineering Company makes a standard injector burner for gas with a 530-1200 Btu/CF rating. The mixer contains a needlepoint adjusting pin that regulates the gas flow through the orifice, thus enabling the burner to use any Btu rating up to the maximum orifice opening. However, the orifice should be of appropriate size for the gas. The

Wood-fired ceramics

The following examples show the broad spectrum of styles and temperatures used in wood-fired ceramics:

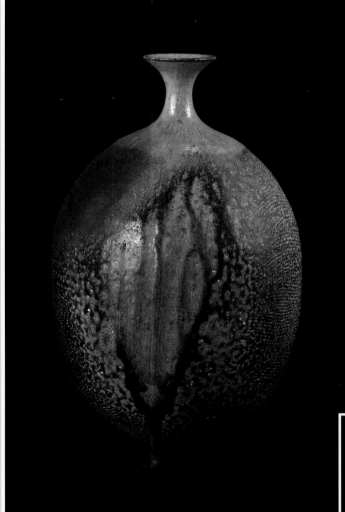

Frederick Olsen, United States, bottle, 1998, stoneware, from cone 12 reduction in front firebox area of Hollyweird tube. John Waggaman photo.

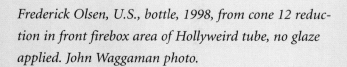

Frederick Olsen, U.S., bottle, 1998, from cone 12 reduction in front firebox area of Hollyweird tube, no glaze applied. John Waggaman photo.

Artist unknown, late Tang Dynasty, three-color lead-based glazed creature, wood fired in low-fire oxidation. From author's collection.

Reggie Meaders, U.S., jug, 1994, stoneware, cone 10 fired in groundhog kiln, clay and ash glaze. From author's collection.

Kondo Yuzo, Japan, vase, 1963, porcelain with cobalt decoration, cone 10 reduction fired in saggar in chamber kiln. From author's collection.

Tom Gaines, U.S., stoneware sculpture, 1987, reduction fired from cone 10 in the Hollyweird tube back chamber, no glaze. Tom Gaines photo.

Nina Hole, Denmark, Fire up Gulgong sculpture 1995, fired in place to cone 06.

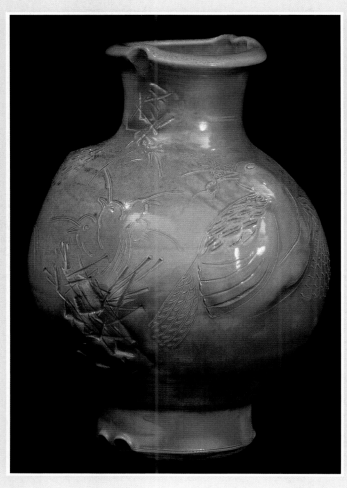

Vincent Suez, U.S., vase,1990, porcelain with incised lines and pushed-out areas, cone 10 reduction with flashing shino glaze, fired in Hollyweird tube. Vincent Suez photo.

Gas-fired ceramics

Phillip Cornelius, U.S., teapot, 1991, porcelain, high-temperature charcoal fired. Photo provided by Phillip Cornelius.

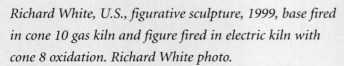

Richard White, U.S., figurative sculpture, 1999, base fired in cone 10 gas kiln and figure fired in electric kiln with cone 8 oxidation. Richard White photo.

Tom Gaines, U.S., bowl, 1998, porcelain with black slip, cone 10 reduction. Tom Gaines photo.

Giancarlo Scapin, Italy, sculpture, 1997, white stoneware, cone 10 oxidation. Photo provided by Giancarlo Scapin.

Kenji Kato, Japan, bottle, 1993, turquoise glaze, middle-fire oxidation. Photo provided by Kenji Kato.

Electric-fired ceramics

Following are some electric-fired ceramics, some of which used wood or gas for an initial firing.

Tomimoto Kenkichi, Japan, covered jar, 1961, porcelain with cone 10 limestone clear glaze, wood fired in a chamber kiln, overglaze red with gold and silver, fired in an electric kiln at low temperatures. Photo provided by Tomimoto Kenkichi.

Frederick Olsen, U.S., Afra series sculpture, 1986, stoneware with color slips and stains, cone 1 low fire.

Frederick Olsen, U.S. open vase, 994, porcelain with limestone clear glaze and underglaze blue gas fired, overglaxe enamels fired in a electric kiln at low tempeature. Photo by John Waggaman.

Mutsuo Yanagihara, Japa, vessel, 1983, mid-temperature oxidation with color stains, fired in electric kiln.

Frederick Olsen, U.S., Kecskemet tumble sculpture 2000, colored slips, multi-fired in an electric kiln at low temperature.

On the home front

Many students, artists and friends have visited the artist's home studio/pottery over the years.

Onlookers had plenty to take in at the author's 1993 kiln opening.

A big group was on hand for a 1988 firing of the author's kiln. Top row, from left: Phil Cornelius, Val Sanders, Conrad Colimpong, Donna Colimpong, Paul Frehe; bottom row, from left: Carol Spar, Otto Heino, Vincent Suez, Virginia Cartwright, Ingrid and Fred Olsen, Vivika Heino, Richie White, and Tom Gaines.

Kay Nguyen and the author check the back chamber coals on the grates of the author's home kiln.

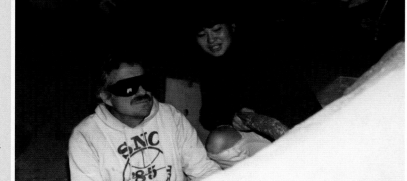

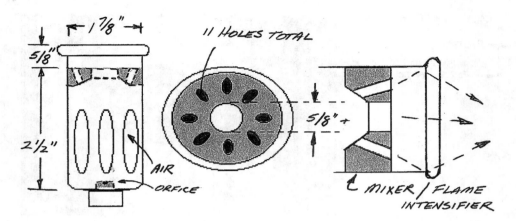

Fig. 8—37a:
Danish propane weed burner.

needle is used only for fine adjustment after numerous firings have determined the best setting for the intended use (Figs. 8-38). Using natural gas at a maximum of 7" WC, a standard injector of 2" outlet size will have a capacity of 83 CF/hour at 91,300 Btu/hour and a 3" outlet will have a 185 cu. ft. capacity at 203,500 Btu/hour. These burners are suitable for downdraft and crossdraft kilns. In updraft kilns, burners with smaller Btu ratings are appropriate because more burners can be used, thus distributing the heat more evenly. In downdraft or crossdraft kilns, burners with large Btu ratings must be used because of the limited number of inlet ports.

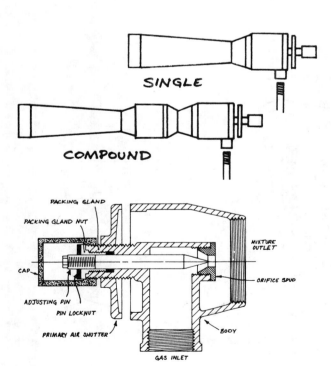

Fig. 8—38: *Standard and compound injector burners; (bottom) detail of air mixer.*

Mark Ward, of Ward Burner Systems, has a complete line of venturi burners (Gas Appliance and Ransome) with safety setups for raku and high-fire operations. The forced-air burner systems are suitable for side-firing kilns using a firing channel along the sides or under the floor. The systems are very similar to Denis Park's Tascarpra oil blower system, but for gas. The Ward systems are designed to give high output on low pressure and can be adjusted for a wide range of low pressures and Btu ratings. The forced-air systems come complete with controls for the air, 100 percent gas safety and optional spark ignition and stand.

COMPOUND ATMOSPHERIC INJECTORS

The Eclipse Fuel Engineering Company makes a compound injector burner for high-Btu gas from 1,200-3,300 Btu/CF. Compound injectors have two stage units: The second stage is added onto the standard injector to better utilize the smaller gas orifice required to handle high-Btu gas. Otherwise, the burner operates in the same manner as the standard injector. To fire my three-chamber climbing kiln (each chamber is 120 cu. ft.), I use six Eclipse 2" compound injector burners (model TR-80), producing about 214,200 Btu/hour/burner on 10" WC, using a No. 18 orifice size, for a total input at peak efficiency of 1,285,200 Btu/hour.

TEMPERED AIR BURNERS

Tempered air (TA) nozzle mixing burners manufactured by Eclipse, Job Forni and others are suitable for a wide range of operations. They are extremely good for high-temperature "on-ratio" (proper stoichiometric gas/air ratio) operations. A few kiln manufacturers are using these burners now because they offer considerable advantages:

1. They will not backfire. The TA burners have separate air and gas inlets so that no mixing occurs before the air/gas reaches the throat of the combustion block (Fig. 8-39).

2. Improved economy, due to better gas utilization.

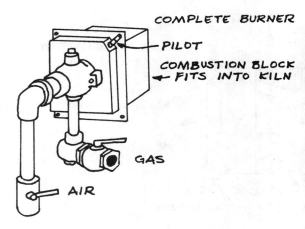

Fig. 8—39: *Tempered air nozzle mixing burner.*

Fig. 8—39b: *Mixing cylinder of Job Forni burner.*

3. The turndown range of the TA burner is considerable. For instance, for the smallest TA-53 burners the maximum Btu/hr. is 100,000 and the minimum is 20,000 Btu/hr. for natural gas at 5" WC.

4. The safety factor is excellent, due to an enclosed system and the controls used to operate the burner. However, the cost of the burners, the complicated plumbing system, the required blowers and regulating equipment make the use of these burners difficult for most potters, and unnecessary for most studio kilns.

The Eclipse tempered air burners are designed to use 100 percent primary air, thereby giving exact con-

trol in the kiln's atmosphere. The mixing block or tunnel, similar to the venturi mixer, is made of refractory material. The block interior is made in a step fashion, expanding out to the discharge end (Fig. 8-39). The step zones produce a negative pressure (P2), which tends to eddy the flames and hold them back in the step. This acts as a pilot ring of flame, keeping the main mixture ignited. The pilot flame is introduced in this area because of the low pressure and ease of ignition. Once the refractory block is hot, it provides good flame stabilization and a good turndown range. Fully aerated mixtures burn at maximum flame temperature and speed, thus flashbacking into the mixing

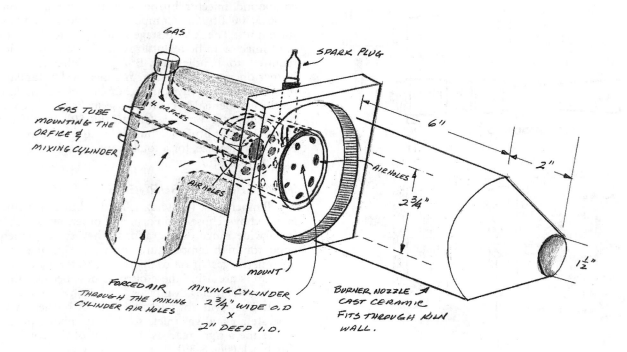

Fig. 8—39a: *Job Forni burner with nozzle.*

Fig. 8—39c: *Job Forni burner, notice spark plug.*

manifold under low input pressure is possible. This can be eliminated by using a refractory nose piece in the mixture opening. If using totally enclosed block burners, make sure that this anti-back-flashing nose piece is a part of the burner design. The Fig. 8-39a drawing illustrates a simplified cut-away view of a tempered air burner by Job Forni and shows how relatively simple it is. This style of burner allows a controller/computer to fire a predetermined schedule and maintain the proper air-to-gas ratios at all times and temperatures with complete safety and reliability.

HOMEMADE GAS PIPE BURNERS

A type of forced-air gas burner can be made at home from pipes, as shown in the step-by-step diagrams (Figs. 8-40 to 8-43). To determine the size of the blower, figure the total Btu/hr. of the burners that the blower will supply. Use the rule: 10 cu-ft of air required per 1,000 tu (see Table 8-3). A word of cau-

tion: If the blower fails, the burner is dangerous. It should have an electric solenoid shutoff valve on the gas line.

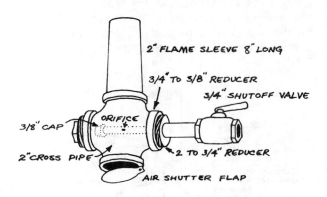

Fig. 8—41: *Detail of Alfred burner.*

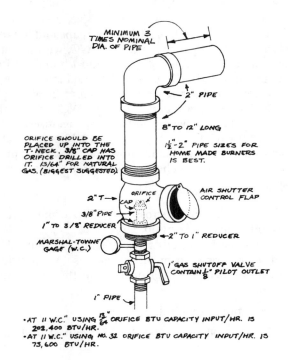

Fig. 8—40: *Homemade Alfred pipe burner.*

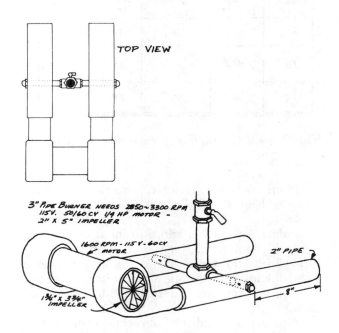

Fig. 8—42: *Forced-air gas burner.*

CALCULATING GAS REQUIREMENTS

I believe that most gas kilns are completely overpowered. I have fired a small crossdraft dense brick-kiln of about 36 cu. ft. on 6 small venturi air mixer burners rated at 36,000 Btu/hr. each in about 12 to 15 hours. An updraft kiln of 36 cu. ft. using insulation bricks will have a minimum of 10 such burners and probably fire in eight hours easily using the same gas. The only advantage to overpowering the kiln is in shortening the firing time.

I know of no standard rules for calculating gas requirements for a kiln. In fact, there seems to be an air of secrecy among gas kiln manufacturers as to how they arrive at a Btu figure for any kiln volume. One could, by charting the various gas kilns on the market by volume, number of burners, and Btu ratings, come up with a chart giving the relationship between Btu rating and kiln volume. Gas Appliance Co., manufacturers of gas burners, told me it was their understanding that local kiln manufacturers were using, as a rule of thumb, 150,000 Btu per 9 cu. ft.

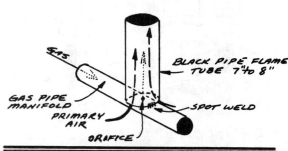

FLAME TUBE SIZE	FLAME TUBE LENGTH	GAS PIPE MANIFOLD SIZE	ORIFICE SIZE	APPROX. BTU RATING
2"	7" to 8"	1¼"	30	40000
1½"	7" to 8"	1"	32	54000
1¼"	7" to 8"	¾"	39	60000

Fig. 8—43: *Calculations for a simple pipe burner.*

From my own experience, I have arrived at the following helpful "rules" for calculating gas requirements.

Rule 1. For an IFB kiln, Btu input capacity for each cubic foot of interior volume is approximately 10,000 Btu/CF/hr. at peak burner efficiency. For dense firebrick kilns, increase Btu input capacity to 16,000 Btu/CF/hr. minimum, and 19,000 Btu/CF/hr. maximum.

Rule 2. The number of burners is computed by finding the total Btu/hr. input of the kiln (Rule 1) and dividing that by the manufacturer's Btu/hr. rating on the chosen burner. When homemade burners are

used and the Btu rating is not known, refer to Chapter 2 to find the number of burner ports required. For updraft kilns, refer to Chapter 6 for burner placement information that will help to determine the number of burners.

Rule 3. To find the Btu level necessary at peak performance for each homemade burner, divide the number of burners into the total Btu input capacity. This figure will also give the orifice size needed (see Table 8-5).

Rule 4. To find the cubic feet of gas required per hour by a given kiln size:

IFB KILNS

— Natural Gas: 9.1 to 6.4 CF of gas per 1 CF kiln volume. (1,100 Btu/CF)

— Propane: 3.9 to 2.8 CF of gas per 1 CF kiln volume. (2,550 Btu/CF)

— Butane: 3.1 to 2.2 CF of gas per 1 CF kiln volume. (3,204 Btu/CF)

FIREBRICK KILNS

— Natural Gas: 14.5 CF of gas per 1 CF kiln volume.

— Propane: 6.3 CF of gas per 1 CF kiln volume.

— Butane: 5 CF of gas per 1 CF kiln volume.

Rule 5. To find the consumption rate of gas per hour at peak flow efficiency for a single burner, divide the number of burners into the total cubic feet of gas per hour. Or, you can use the gas flow chart in Fig. 8-44: Find the individual burner input in Btu/hr. on the center column scale, then read the corresponding figure in CF/hr. on the lefthand scale.

Rule 6. To find proper orifice size, use Fig. 8-44 for natural gas and Table 8-5 for propane and butane. Normal natural gas pressure is 8" WC, with a meter capacity of 175 CF/hr. of gas for most homes. Without much trouble, the gas supplier can increase meter capacity to almost any desired cubic footage of gas per hour. However, the pressure of 8" WC will be the same. LP tanks have a standard low-pressure regulator of 11" WC. For high pressure, a 1:25 psi regulator can be used on the LP tank; however, the highest pressure ever needed will be 2 psi with proper line size.

Sample solution

Given: 20-cu.-ft. crossdraft kiln, using natural gas; IFB bricks; maximum figures.

Find: each burner's capacity and Btu input value; orifice size for each burner; peak gas consumption; establish whether it will operate on the regular gas meter.

Solution: using Rule 1:

20 x 10,000 = 20,000 Btu/hr. input at peak efficiency

Using four burners: (simple air mixer with flame tube), then:

$$\frac{200,000}{4} = 50,000 \text{ Btu/hr./burner input}$$

Using Rule 4:

9.1 x 20 = 182 CF gas required (45 CF/burner)

Knowing that natural gas has a 8" WC pressure and a standard home meter is capable of 175 CF/hr., go to Fig. 7-44. Line up 8" WC with 50,000 Btu and 45 CF/hr. and draw a straight line to give you an orifice size of 34.

The example kiln at peak efficiency would draw 182 CF/gas/hr. The meter delivers 175 CF/hr., a shortfall of 7 CF/hr. This means that neither a hot-water heater nor a range can operate at the same time the kiln is firing. But using minimum figures of 7,000 Btu, the kiln would draw 128 CF/hr. at peak efficiency, leaving 47 CF/hr. to operate a 40-gallon gas hot-water heater only.

The general rule of thumb — 150,000 Btu per 9 CF of kiln — means the example kiln needs over 300,000 Btu/hr. to fire. Peak burner efficiency is when the burner's capacity to combust fuel at the highest flame temperature is reached. Adding greater pressure or increased gas capacity will not increase the heat production of the burner, but will only increase the volume of flue gases. All manufactured gas burners have a peak Btu rating. Thus, when firing a kiln that needs gradual temperature increases, peak burner efficiency will not be reached at the beginning or during the middle of the firing, but only at the end with the last turn-up. If overpowered burners or an excessive number of burners are used, it becomes unnecessary to reach peak efficiency in order to achieve required temperature.

My rules for the calculation of gas requirements are low compared to most. Consider mine the minimum requirements needed for a gas kiln. Mark Ward of Ward Burner Systems was kind enough to allow me to reproduce his Natural Gas and Propane Btu & Orifice Table, which can be used in conjunction with the Table 8-5, Flow of LP Gas through Standard Orifices, and Fig. 8-44, Gas Flow Chart (See pages 178-181).

HIGH ALTITUDE ADJUSTMENTS

The general rule for high-altitude adjustment is: **Reduce one orifice size for every increment of 2,000 feet above 5,000 feet in altitude.** The higher the elevation, the less oxygen available per cubic foot of air. Therefore, the air-gas ratio must be increased.

GAS PIPE SIZING CALCULATIONS (WPOA 1961 UNIFORM PLUMBING CODE)

Measure the length of the pipe from the gas meter to the kiln. On Table 8-6, find that distance in the "Length" column (use the next longer length if the exact measurement doesn't appear). Read across to the necessary gas capacity for your kiln and, if it is not shown, choose the next larger figure to the right

in that line. The correct pipe size will be above the column.

If using multiple kilns, measure to the kiln furthest away from the meter; use total capacity of all the kilns, plus 20 percent to find the main gasline size. To determine individual kiln pipeline sizes, measure the distance from the main gasoline to the kiln, then use individual kiln gas demands to figure pipe size. Whether natural gas or LP (Table 8-7) is used, 3/4" pipe is considered the minimum for kiln plumbing. The equivalent distance for each elbow to be added to the overall pipe length is shown in Fig. 8-45. It is always better to use oversized pipe and have greater capacity, than too small a pipe with insufficient capacity.

PIPE DIAMETER IN INCHES	STANDARD ELBOWS & TEES					
	$\frac{1}{2}$	$\frac{3}{4}$	1	$1\frac{1}{4}$	$1\frac{1}{2}$	2
EQUIVALENT LENGTH IN FEET ADDED	1.6'	2.2'	2.8'	3.8'	4.4'	5.5'

Fig. 8—45: *For every elbow and tee used, add equivalent length in feet to overall pipe length.*

BURNER MANIFOLDS

Manifolding of burners can be done in numerous ways. However, the source gas pipe must always have the capacity to carry more than enough gas to meet the demands of the individual burners. One method of manifolding is to bring the source pipe in, then run individual burner gas lines capable of supplying only the burner orifice capacity, plus 20 percent extra (Fig. 8-46). If the capacities of burners 1, 2 and 3 were totaled, they would equal the source pipe capacity and should really be less, thus guaranteeing gas volume.

This system can be used for multi-kiln hookup where lines 1, 2 and 3 become source gas lines for individual kilns A, B and C. To size the source pipe, add the individual Btu kiln requirements and divide by the gas Btu/CF rating to obtain the CF/hr. Measure

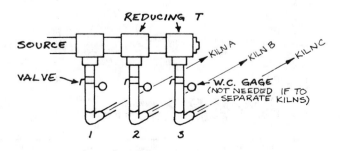

Fig. 8—46: *Gas burner manifolds.*

MANIFOLD PRESSURE	PRESSURE FUNCTION
4"WC or 2.3 oz. or 1/4 PSI	2.5000
5"WC or 2.9 oz.	2.7951
6"WC or 3.5 oz.	3.0619
7"WC or 4.0 oz.	3.3072
8"WC or 4.6 oz.	3.5355
9"WC or 5.2 oz.	3.7500
10"WC or 5.8 oz.	3.9528
11"WC or 6.4 oz.	4.1458
12"WC or 6.9 oz.	4.3301
13"WC or 7.5 oz.	4.5069
14"WC or 8.0 oz. or 1/2 PSI	4.6771
15"WC or 8.7 oz.	4.8412
16"WC or 9.3 oz.	5.0000
17"WC or 9.8 oz.	5.1539
18"WC or 10.4 oz.	5.3033
19"WC or 11.0 oz.	5.4486
20"WC or 11.6 oz.	5.5902
21"WC or 12.1 oz.	5.7282
22"WC or 12.7 oz.	5.8630
23"WC or 13.3 oz.	5.9948
24"WC or 13.9 oz.	6.1237
25"WC or 14.4 oz.	6.2500
26"WC or 15.0 oz.	6.3738
27"WC or 15.6 oz.	6.4952
27.7"WC or 16 oz. or 1 PSI	6.5788
2 PSI	9.3039
3 PSI	11.3949
4 PSI	13.1577
5 PSI	14.7107
6 PSI	16.1148
7 PSI	17.4060
8 PSI	18.6078
9 PSI	19.7365
10 PSI	20.8041
11 PSI	21.8196
12 PSI	22.7898
13 PSI	23.7204
14 PSI	24.6158
15 PSI	25.4798
16 PSI	26.3154
17 PSI	27.1253
18 PSI	27.9117
19 PSI	28.6765
20 PSI	29.4215
21 PSI	30.1481
22 PSI	30.8575
23 PSI	31.5510
24 PSI	32.2296
25 PSI	32.8942

WARD BURNER SYSTEMS

BTU & ORIFICE TABLE • Natural Gas

To determine BTUs per Hour output for Natural Gas Burners & Appliances:

Multiply the PRESSURE FUNCTION (at left) that corresponds to the manifold pressure* you are using BY the ORIFICE FUNCTION that corresponds to the orifice (drill size) on the reverse side. The resulting answer is the BTU output per Hour @ Sea level.

EXAMPLE: Using a #38 orifice with 7" Water Column Pressure. 10,711.16 (#38 orifice funct.) X 3.3072 (7"WC press. funct.) = **35,423.95 BTUs per Hour.**

To determine Orifice size used in a Natural Gas Burner:

Divide desired or known BTU output of the burner by the PRESSURE FUNCTION that corresponds to your manifold pressure . Locate the ORIFICE FUNCTION (reverse side) that is closest to your answer. The corresponding drill size is the closest correct orifice size.

EXAMPLE: Desired output of 125,000 BTUs @ 7"WC: 125,000 ÷ 3.3072 (7"WC Pressure funct.) = 37,796.32. Use a #11 orifice that has a ORIFICE FUNCTION of 37,932.60. **WARNING:** Do not increase orifice size larger than recommended by the burner manufacturer!

ALTITUDE ADJUSTMENT

As the altitude at which the burner is operating increases, the density of the gas decreases. This permits the gas to pass through the orifice with less friction loss, but reduces it's BTU value. To adjust for this; multiply the altitude factor below BY the BTU output of the burner. Do not increase orifice size at altitude to compensate unless mechanical air (blower) increases are available due to lower oxygen values.

EXAMPLE: Using 8" WC Pressure in Atlanta, GA. with a #28 orifice 3.5355 (Pressure funct. of 8"WC) X 20,508.76 (#28 Orifice funct.) X .9849 (Atlanta @ 1050 ft. altitude.) = 71,413.84 BTUs per Hour.

Altitude	alt. Factor	Altitude	alt. Factor
Sea Level	1.000	6000 ft.	.9138
1000 ft.	.9849	7000 ft.	.8999
2000 ft.	.9700	8000 ft.	.8860
3000 ft.	.9565	9000 ft.	.8729
4000 ft.	.9413	10,000 ft.	.8579
5000 ft.	.9279	11,000 ft.	.8455

* **Manifold pressure** is the regulated pressure (pressure on the line). Do not rely on gauges that measure gas flow to determine manifold pressure; they produce readings of differential pressure or pressure drop. Consult with the gas supplier if unsure of manifold pressure.

The figures on this chart are based on Natural Gas @ 60°F. with a value of 1000 BTU per Cubic Ft. and a specific gravity of .64. Natural Gas can vary in value and specific gravity depending on temperature and geographic source. Orifice figures are based on a coefficient of .80. Coefficient can vary + or - 5% depending on orifice type/burner type. Because of these variations, figures from this chart should be considered a very close estimate, not an exact reference.

We will not be liable for any loss or damage that may arise in connection with the use of this chart, including, without limitation, any indirect or consequential damages.

Distributed by Ward Burner Systems, a division of Wing & Ward Studios, Inc., Dandridge, TN. Copyright © 1995 by Marc Ward

NATURAL GAS ORIFICE FUNCTION

DRILL SIZE	AREA SQ.IN.	ORIFICE FUNCTION	DRILL SIZE	AREA SQ.IN.	ORIFICE FUNCTION	DRILL SIZE	AREA SQ.IN.	ORIFICE FUNCTION
80	0.000143	189.33	40	0.00754	9,982.96	2	0.03836	50,788.64
79	0.000165	218.46	39	0.00778	10,300.72	I	0.04083	54,058.92
1/64"	0.000191	252.88	38	0.00809	10,711.16	A	0.04301	56,945.24
78	0.000201	266.12	37	0.00849	11,240.76	15/64"	0.04314	57,117.36
77	0.000254	336.30	36	0.00891	11,796.84	B	0.04449	58,904.76
76	0.000314	415.74	7/64"	0.00940	12,445.60	C	0.04600	60,904.00
75	0.000346	458.10	35	0.00950	12,578.00	D	0.04753	62,929.72
74	0.000398	526.95	34	0.00968	12,816.32	E•1/4"	0.04909	64,995.16
73	0.000452	598.45	33	0.01003	13,279.72	F	0.05187	68,675.88
72	0.000491	650.08	32	0.01057	13,994.68	G	0.05350	70,843.00
71	0.000531	703.04	31	0.01131	14,974.44	17/64"	0.05542	73,376.08
70	0.000616	815.58	1/8"	0.01227	16,245.48	H	0.05557	73,574.68
69	0.000670	887.08	30	0.01296	17,159.04	I	0.05811	76,937.64
68	0.000755	999.62	29	0.01453	19,237.72	J	0.06026	79,784.24
1/32"	0.000765	1,012.86	28	0.01549	20,508.76	K	0.06202	82,114.48
67	0.000804	1,064.50	9/64"	0.01553	20,561.72	9/32"	0.06213	82,260.12
66	0.000855	1,132.02	27	0.01629	21,567.96	L	0.06605	87,450.20
65	0.000962	1,273.69	26	0.01697	22,468.28	M	0.06835	90,495.40
64	0.001018	1,347.83	25	0.01755	23,236.20	19/64"	0.06922	91,647.28
63	0.001075	1,423.30	24	0.01815	24,030.60	N	0.07163	94,838.12
62	0.001134	1,501.42	23	0.01863	24,666.12	5/16"	0.07670	101,550.80
61	0.001195	1,582.18	5/32"	0.01917	25,381.08	O	0.07843	103,841.32
60	0.001257	1,664.27	22	0.01936	25,632.64	P	0.08194	108,488.56
59	0.001320	1,747.68	21	0.01986	26,294.64	21/64"	0.08456	111,957.44
58	0.001385	1,833.74	20	0.02036	26,956.64	Q	0.08657	114,618.68
57	0.001452	1,922.45	19	0.02164	28,651.36	R	0.09026	119,504.24
56	0.001698	2,248.15	18	0.02256	29,869.44	11/32"	0.09281	122,880.44
3/64"	0.00173	2,290.52	11/64"	0.02320	30,716.80	S	0.09511	125,925.64
55	0.00212	2,806.88	17	0.02351	31,127.24	T	0.1006	133,194.40
54	0.00238	3,151.12	16	0.02461	32,583.64	23/64"	0.1014	134,253.60
53	0.00278	3,680.72	15	0.02545	33,695.80	U	0.1064	140,873.60
1/16"	0.00307	4,064.68	14	0.02602	34,450.48	3/8"	0.1105	146,302.00
52	0.00317	4,197.08	13	0.02688	35,589.12	V	0.1116	147,758.40
51	0.00353	4,673.72	3/16"	0.02761	36,555.64	W	0.1170	154,908.00
50	0.00385	5,097.40	12	0.02806	37,151.44	25/64"	0.1198	158,615.20
49	0.00419	5,547.56	11	0.02865	37,932.60	X	0.1238	163,911.20
48	0.00454	6,010.96	10	0.02940	38,925.60	Y	0.1282	169,736.80
5/64"	0.00479	6,341.96	9	0.03017	39,945.08	13/32"	0.1296	171,590.40
47	0.00484	6,408.16	8	0.03110	41,176.40	Z	0.1340	177,416.00
46	0.00515	6,818.60	7	0.03173	42,010.52	27/64"	0.1398	185,095.20
45	0.00528	6,990.72	13/64"	0.03241	42,910.84	7/16"	0.1503	198,997.20
44	0.00581	7,692.44	6	0.03269	43,281.56	29/64"	0.1613	213,561.20
43	0.00622	8,235.28	5	0.03317	43,917.08	15/32"	0.1726	228,522.40
42	0.00687	9,095.88	4	0.03431	45,426.44	31/64"	0.1843	244,013.20
3/32"	0.00690	9,135.60	3	0.03563	47,174.12	1/2"	0.1964	260,033.60
41	0.00724	9,585.76	7/32"	0.03758	49,755.92			

MANIFOLD PRESSURE	PRESSURE FUNCTION
4"WC or 2.3 oz. or 1/4 PSI	1.6211
5"WC or 2.9 oz.	1.8112
6"WC or 3.5 oz.	1.9855
7"WC or 4.0 oz.	2.1446
8"WC or 4.6 oz.	2.2926
9"WC or 5.2 oz.	2.4317
10"WC or 5.8 oz.	2.5632
11"WC or 6.4 oz.	2.6884
12"WC or 6.9 oz.	2.8079
13"WC or 7.5 oz.	2.9226
14"WC or 8.0 oz. or 1/2 PSI	3.0329
15"WC or 8.7 oz.	3.1393
16"WC or 9.3 oz.	3.2423
17"WC or 9.8 oz.	3.3421
18"WC or 10.4 oz.	3.4389
19"WC or 11.0 oz.	3.5332
20"WC or 11.6 oz.	3.6250
21"WC or 12.1 oz.	3.7145
22"WC or 12.7 oz.	3.8019
23"WC or 13.3 oz.	3.8873
24"WC or 13.9 oz.	3.9710
25"WC or 14.4 oz.	4.0529
26"WC or 15.0 oz.	4.1331
27"WC or 15.6 oz.	4.2119
27.7"WC or 16 oz. or 1 PSI	4.2661
2 PSI	6.0332
3 PSI	7.3891
4 PSI	8.5322
5 PSI	9.5392
6 PSI	10.4498
7 PSI	11.2871
8 PSI	12.0664
9 PSI	12.7983
10 PSI	13.4906
11 PSI	14.1491
12 PSI	14.7782
13 PSI	15.3817
14 PSI	15.9623
15 PSI	16.5226
16 PSI	17.0645
17 PSI	17.5896
18 PSI	18.0996
19 PSI	18.5956
20 PSI	19.0786
21 PSI	19.5498
22 PSI	20.0098
23 PSI	20.4595
24 PSI	20.8996
25 PSI	21.3306

WARD BURNER SYSTEMS

BTU & ORIFICE TABLE • Propane

To determine BTUs per Hour output for Propane Burners & Appliances:

Multiply the PRESSURE FUNCTION (at left) that corresponds to the manifold pressure* you are using BY the ORIFICE FUNCTION that corresponds to the orifice (drill size) on the reverse side. The resulting answer is the BTU output per Hour @ Sea level.

EXAMPLE: Using a #38 orifice with 11" Water Column Pressure. 26,777.90 (#38 orifice funct.) X 2.6884 (11"WC press. funct.) = **71,989.71 BTU's per Hour.**

To determine Orifice size used in a Propane Burner:

Divide desired or known BTU output of the burner by the PRESSURE FUNCTION that corresponds to your manifold pressure. Locate the ORIFICE FUNCTION (reverse side) that is closest to your answer. The corresponding drill size is the closest correct orifice size.

EXAMPLE: Desired output of 125,000 BTUs @ 1 PSI: 125,000 ÷ 4.2661 (Pressure funct. 1 PSI) = 29,300. Use a #36 orifice that has a ORIFICE FUNCTION of 29,492.10. **WARNING:** Do not increase orifice larger than recommended by burner manufacturer!

ALTITUDE ADJUSTMENT

As the altitude at which the burner is operating increases, the density of the gas decreases. This permits the gas to pass through the orifice with less friction loss, but reduces it's BTU value. To adjust for this; multiply the altitude factor below BY the BTU output of the burner. Do not increase orifice size to compensate unless mechanical air (blower) increases are available due to lower oxygen values.

EXAMPLE: Using 11" WC press. with a #38 orifice in Atlanta, GA. 2.6884 (Pressure funct. of 11"WC) X 26,777.90 (#38 Orifice funct.) X .9849 (Atlanta @ 1050 ft. altitude). = 70,902.66 BTUs per Hour.

Altitude	alt. Factor	Altitude	alt. Factor
Sea Level	1.000	6000 ft.	.9138
1000 ft.	.9849	7000 ft.	.8999
2000 ft.	.9700	8000 ft.	.8860
3000 ft.	.9565	9000 ft.	.8729
4000 ft.	.9413	10,000 ft.	.8579
5000 ft.	.9279	11,000 ft.	.8455

* **Manifold pressure** is the regulated pressure (pressure on the line). Do not rely on gauges that measure gas flow to determine manifold pressure; they produce readings of differential pressure or pressure drop. Consult with the gas supplier if unsure of manifold pressure.

The figures on this chart are based on propane @ 60°F. with a value of 2500 BTUs per Cubic Ft. and a specific gravity of 1.522. Changes in temperature will change the specific gravity. Orifice figures are based on a coefficient of .80. Coefficient can vary + or - 5% depending on orifice type/burner type. Because of these variations, figures from this chart should be considered a very close estimate.

Distributed by Ward Burner Systems, a division of Wing & Ward Studios, Inc., Dandridge, TN. Copyright © 1995 by Marc Ward

PROPANE ORIFICE FUNCTIONS

DRILL SIZE	AREA SQ.IN.	ORIFICE FUNCTION	DRILL SIZE	AREA SQ.IN.	ORIFICE FUNCTION	DRILL SIZE	AREA SQ.IN.	ORIFICE FUNCTION
80	0.000143	473.33	40	0.00754	24,957.40	2	0.03836	126,971.60
79	0.000165	546.15	39	0.00778	25,751.80	1	0.04083	135,147.30
1/64"	0.000191	632.21	38	0.00809	26,777.90	A	0.04301	142,363.10
78	0.000201	665.31	37	0.00849	28,101.90	15/64"	0.04314	142,793.40
77	0.000254	840.74	36	0.00891	29,492.10	B	0.04449	147,261.90
76	0.000314	1,039.34	7/64"	0.00940	31,114.00	C	0.04600	152,260.00
75	0.000346	1,145.26	35	0.00950	31,445.00	D	0.04753	157,324.30
74	0.000398	1,317.38	34	0.00968	32,040.80	E•1/4"	0.04909	162,487.90
73	0.000452	1,496.12	33	0.01003	33,199.30	F	0.05187	171,689.70
72	0.000491	1,625.21	32	0.01057	34,986.70	G	0.05350	177,085.00
71	0.000531	1,757.61	31	0.01131	37,436.10	17/64"	0.05542	183,440.20
70	0.000616	2,038.96	1/8"	0.01227	40,613.70	H	0.05557	183,936.70
69	0.000670	2,217.70	30	0.01296	42,897.60	I	0.05811	192,344.10
68	0.000755	2,499.05	29	0.01453	48,094.30	J	0.06026	199,460.60
1/32"	0.000765	2,532.15	28	0.01549	51,271.90	K	0.06202	205,286.20
67	0.000804	2,661.24	9/64"	0.01553	51,404.30	9/32"	0.06213	205,650.30
66	0.000855	2,830.05	27	0.01629	53,919.90	L	0.06605	218,625.50
65	0.000962	3,184.22	26	0.01697	56,170.70	M	0.06835	226,238.50
64	0.001018	3,369.58	25	0.01755	58,090.50	19/64"	0.06922	229,118.20
63	0.001075	3,558.25	24	0.01815	60,076.50	N	0.07163	237,095.30
62	0.001134	3,753.54	23	0.01863	61,665.30	5/16"	0.07670	253,877.00
61	0.001195	3,955.45	5/32"	0.01917	63,452.70	O	0.07843	259,603.30
60	0.001257	4,160.67	22	0.01936	64,081.60	P	0.08194	271,221.40
59	0.001320	4,369.20	21	0.01986	65,736.60	21/64"	0.08456	279,893.60
58	0.001385	4,584.35	20	0.02036	67,391.60	Q	0.08657	286,546.70
57	0.001452	4,806.12	19	0.02164	71,628.40	R	0.09026	298,760.60
56	0.001698	5,620.38	18	0.02256	74,673.60	11/32"	0.09281	307,201.10
3/64"	0.00173	5,726.30	11/64"	0.02320	76,792.00	S	0.09511	314,814.10
55	0.00212	7,017.20	17	0.02351	77,818.10	T	0.1006	332,986.00
54	0.00238	7,877.80	16	0.02461	81,459.10	23/64"	0.1014	335,634.00
53	0.00278	9,201.80	15	0.02545	84,239.50	U	0.1064	352,184.00
1/16"	0.00307	10,161.70	14	0.02602	86,126.20	3/8"	0.1105	365,755.00
52	0.00317	10,492.70	13	0.02688	88,972.80	V	0.1116	369,396.00
51	0.00353	11,684.30	3/16"	0.02761	91,389.10	W	0.1170	387,270.00
50	0.00385	12,743.50	12	0.02806	92,878.60	25/64"	0.1198	396,538.00
49	0.00419	13,868.90	11	0.02865	94,831.50	X	0.1238	409,778.00
48	0.00454	15,027.40	10	0.02940	97,314.00	Y	0.1282	424,342.00
5/64"	0.00479	15,854.90	9	0.03017	99,862.70	13/32"	0.1296	428,976.00
47	0.00484	16,020.40	8	0.03110	102,941.00	Z	0.1340	443,540.00
46	0.00515	17,046.50	7	0.03173	105,026.30	27/64"	0.1398	462,738.00
45	0.00528	17,476.80	13/64"	0.03241	107,277.10	7/16"	0.1503	497,493.00
44	0.00581	19,231.10	6	0.03269	108,203.90	29/64"	0.1613	533,903.00
43	0.00622	20,588.20	5	0.03317	109,792.70	15/32"	0.1726	571,306.00
42	0.00687	22,739.70	4	0.03431	113,566.10	31/64"	0.1843	610,033.00
3/32"	0.00690	22,839.00	3	0.03563	117,935.30	1/2"	0.1964	650,084.00
41	0.00724	23,964.40	7/32"	0.03758	124,389.80			

Chart 3

CONVERSION CHART - Inch, Decimal, and MM Equivalents which can be helpful in determining orifice size and equating to drill bit size.

Inch	Decimal	MM
1/64 =	.015625	0.3969
1/32 =	.03125	0.7938
3/64 =	.046875	1.1906
1/16 =	.0625	1.5875
5/64 =	.078125	1.9844
3/32 =	.09375	2.3812
7/64 =	.109375	2.7781
1/8 =	.125	3.1750
9/64 =	.140625	3.5719
5/32 =	.15625	3.9688
11/64 =	.171875	4.3656
3/16 =	.1875	4.7625
13/64 =	.203125	5.1594
7/32 =	.21875	5.5562
15/64 =	.234375	5.9531
1/4 =	.25	6.35

Table 8-6
Pipe Size Calculations for Natural Gas (0.65 Specific Gravity)

Length (Feet) — Maximum Delivery in CF/hr.

Length (Feet)	Pipe Size (Inches)								
	1/2	3/4	1	1 1/4	1 1/2	2	2 1/2	3	4
10	170	360	670	1320	1990	3880	5921	10,770	22,593
20	118	245	430	930	1370	2680	4189	7,619	15,984
30	95	198	370	740	1100	2150	3416	6,213	13,033
40	80	169	318	640	950	1840	2959	5,381	11,289
50	71	150	282	565	830	1610	2648	4,816	10,103
60	64	135	255	510	760	1480	2416	4,394	9,217
70	60	123	235	470	700	1350	2238	4,070	8,538
80	55	115	220	440	650	1250	2094	3,808	7,988
90	52	108	205	410	610	1180	1974	3,590	7,531
100	49	102	192	390	570	1100	1873	3,406	7,145
125	44	92	172	345	510	1000	—	—	—
150	40	83	158	315	460	910	1529	2,781	5,834
200	34	71	132	270	400	780	1324	2,087	5,053
250	30	63	118	238	350	690	—	—	—
300	27	57	108	215	320	625	—	—	—
350	25	52	100	200	295	570	—	—	—
400	23	48	92	185	275	535	—	—	—
450	22	45	86	172	255	500	—	—	—
500	21	43	81	162	240	470	—	—	—
550	20	41	77	155	230	450	—	—	—
600	19	39	74	150	220	430	—	—	—

Table 8-7
Pipe Size Calculations for Propane and Butane

Btu/hr.	CF/hr.	3/8"	1/2"	3/4"	1"
			(feet required)		
300,000	120	255	—	—	—
400,000	160	147	—	—	—
500,000	200	98	300	—	—
750,000	300	49	145	—	—
1,000,000	400	29	81	330	—
1,250,000	500	20	56	220	—
1,500,000	600	14	42	160	—
1,750,000	700	11	32	120	—
2,000,000	800	9	26	97	305
2,500,000	1000	—	17	65	200
3,000,000	—	—	12	47	—
4,000,000	—	—	—	28	—
5,000,000	—	—	—	18	—

the distance of the line from the source to the kilns and find the distance and CFH numbers in Table 8-6 for natural gas or Table 8-7 for propane. Take into consideration the number of elbows in the pipeline when calculating the gas capacity needed. For each elbow, you will have to add to the overall distance to get the proper CF/hr (Fig. 8-45). In some cases using multiple kilns, a regulator for each kiln between the tee and the valve must be installed to insure proper pressure to each kiln if all the kilns are firing at once.

A second method of manifolding is to run the same size pipes from the source to the burners (Fig. 8-47). This is the usual method where only one kiln is involved. The orifice discharge capacity will only take its fair share as long as it does not exceed the line capacity. If this happens, the burner farthest away from the source will not receive adequate gas. The

burners can be individually controlled or controlled by one valve.

In an updraft kiln, the source pipe is run through the control valves into a single manifold from which each burner taps (Fig. 8-48). Rounding the corners on the manifold will decrease the friction and create a better flow to the gas. There can be up to 20 burners tapping off a single manifold. Again, the manifold capacity is sized to accommodate all the burners, plus 20 percent. When manifolding this way, I use 1 1/4" x 1 1/4" or 1 1/4" x 2" bent (for the rounded corners) channel tubing (black pipe can also be used) for updraft kilns to 72 cu. ft. capacity. All manifolds should be pressure tested for leaks to 100 psi (plumb-

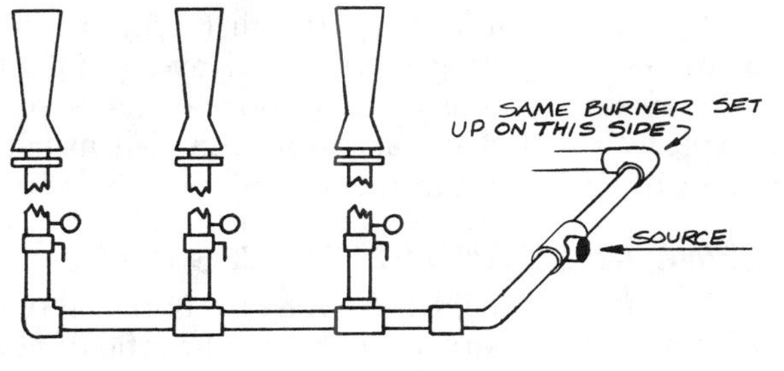

Fig. 8—47: *For crossdraft and downdraft kilns, each burner is individually controlled.*

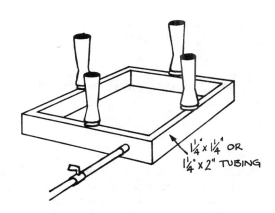

Fig. 8—48: *Manifold system for updraft kiln.*

ing codes call for 60 psi holding for one hour on all gas lines).

BURNER INSTALLATION

Never have the orifice above the burner (Fig. 8-49). In setting up or installing burners that have a right angle from the orifice to the burner tip — such as the Alfred burner or one of the single or compound injectors — the length of the arm from the elbow to the nozzle is important. To determine this distance, multiply the pipe diameter by three to get the length of the arm (Fig. 8-50). The burner tip or flame retention nozzle should not be buried or enclosed in the burner port, because of the heat generated in the burners by the ignition ring and excessive radiation or back pressure from the port. The burners must be cooled by allowing cool air to flow around the nozzle or tip; otherwise, they will oxidize and have a short life.

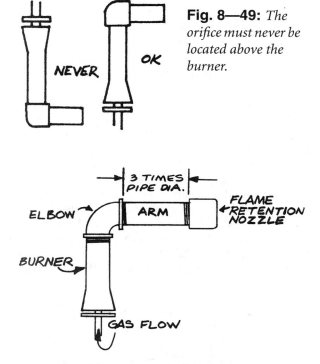

Fig. 8—49: *The orifice must never be located above the burner.*

Fig. 8—50: *Calculating length of arm from elbow to nozzle.*

Burners should be placed from 1/4" to 1" away from the porthole, depending upon the type of burners and the position (Fig. 8-51). I have found that the further distance is preferable for oxidation and the closer distance for reduction. Distance also depends upon the amount of secondary air needed to com-

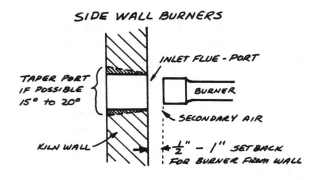

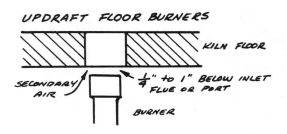

Fig. 8—51: *Spacing burners in relation to flues.*

plete combustion. In some cases, if the kiln is under constant reduction and will not climb in temperature easily, the portholes can be widened to provide more secondary air for combustion. At the same time make sure that the exit flue is not too small. However, most of the time the burners will have oversized orifices, thus throwing off the air/gas ratio for proper combustion. To solve this problem, replace the orifices with smaller ones. (Normal orifices for low-pressure burners are between 28 and 32 for natural gas, 38 and 42 for propane.) For high altitude, decrease the orifice one size for every 2,000 feet over 5,000 feet when using propane or natural gas. Porthole openings in the walls or kiln floor should be slightly larger than the diameter of the burner tip or nozzle (Table 8-8).

I recommend that you flare sidewall burner ports by 15° to 20° into the combustion chamber whenever possible. In floor burners for an updraft, the flaring is not necessary.

The installation of tempered air (TA) burners is complicated, requiring mounting flanges built into the frame and combustion blocks or nozzles be built into the wall. Manufacturers supply complete installation instructions with their equipment.

SIZING INLET AND EXIT FLUES

Inlet flues: The inlet flue for each burner should be sized to fit the burner nozzle tip. The ratio of nozzle size to port or flue opening is shown in Table 8-8. The burners entrain their own primary air and the secondary air needed is supplied at the flue opening (see Fig. 8-51).

Table 8-8
Ratio of Burner Tip Size to Port Opening

Tip Size (inches)	Port Size (inches)
1 1/2	1 3/4–2
2	2 1/2–3
2 1/2	3–3 1/2
3	3 1/2–5
4	5–6 1/2
6	7 1/4–9

Exit flues. There are three methods of determining exit flue sizes:

1. Add the total inlet flue areas (ports) to find the exit flue area.

2. A rule of thumb for exit flues is 2 1/2 sq. in./CF kiln space.

3. I find that 7,000 Btu burner input requires 1 sq. in. exit flue area, regardless of the burner system used. A kiln requiring 1,000,000 Btu burner input will need an exit flue of 143 sq. in., or 12" x 12".

It is always better to have flues on the large side than to have them small and choke the kiln. When the flues are too big, they can be made smaller easily. Of the three methods, I use No. 1 and 3, then build the flues accordingly.

PRESSURE REGULATORS

Regulators reduce a high inlet pressure from a street gas main or a propane tank to a usable outlet pressure for the particular appliance. To determine the regulator needed for your kiln, find:

1. The inlet pressure from your natural gas service (gas line or meter)

2. The WC (water column inches) rating of the kiln's burners

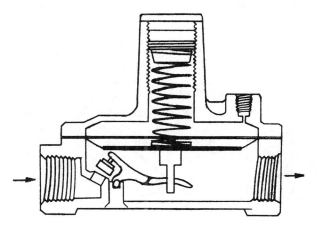

Fig. 8—52: *Maxitrol pressure regulator.*

3. CF/hr. needed to operate the kiln at peak efficiency

4 The necessary gas line size for the main line to the kiln

For instance, if the gas pressure at the meter is 2 psi, the burners are rated 8" WC, the kiln needs a 1" line, and its fuel consumption rating is 500 CF/hr., we could use a Maxitrol 325-5 pressure regulator with an E (HO-1) spring. It is a high-performance regulator that can be used as a single-stage regulator, reducing the pressure from pounds down to the burning pressure (Fig. 8-52). It can handle inlet pressures up to 25 psi with outlet pressures from 2" WC to 3 psi with a capacity of 675 CF/hr. Note the spring in the regulator which adjusts the range of outlet pressure within certain limits. The spring adjustment is set at the factory to a certain pressure. Use different springs to provide different outlet pressures (Table 8-9).

Table 8-9
Maxitrol Spring Pressure Regulations

Spring Number	Pressure Range
D (standard)	2-6" WC
E (HO-1)	4-12" WC
G (HO-1)	15-30" WC
H	1-2 psi
J	2-3 psi

Pressure regulators are available in all standard pipe sizes. When using propane, the standard tank regulator (11 WC) may be sufficient for firing most kilns, so long as the number of bends in the pipe and the distance between the tank and kiln are not too great. However, I recommend a two-stage setup, using an adjustable regulator such as the Rego LP Regulator, with outlet pressure set at 5 psi. This regulator can handle up to 400 psi inlet pressure, with an outlet pressure range from 0 to 30 psi. For the second stage, use another regulator at the kiln to drop the pressure to the burners' operating pressure (Fig. 8-53). This maintains a constant pressure at the kiln. In a single-stage line, factors such as cold weather, number of bends, length, usage, etc., can cause a drop in pressure when it's most needed.

SAFETY EQUIPMENT AND PROCEDURES

SHUTOFF VALVES

Safety shutoff controls serve several purposes: Eliminating the possibility of burner flame-out due to loss of pressure in the gas line or due to gas stoppage,

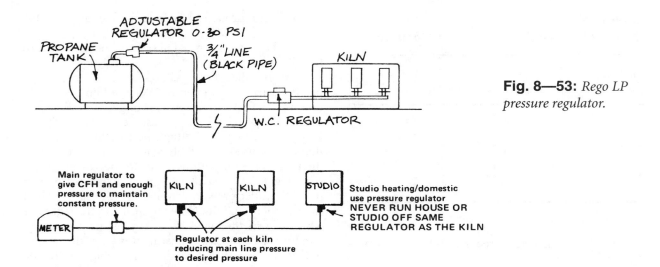

Fig. 8—53: *Rego LP pressure regulator.*

and eliminating burner flame-out due to sudden drafts or gusts of wind at the beginning of the firing when the kiln's temperature cannot reignite the burners. If there is loss of pressure or a gas stoppage during a firing and the operator is not there to turn the valves off, a potential bomb exists. When the gas resumes, and re-ignition either by the heat remaining in the kiln or by hand takes place, an explosion could occur. Ventilation is extremely important during these occurrences.

Johnson/Penn Controls, and ITT General Controls make safety shutoffs for gas fired kilns. Choosing the proper safety shutoff control for a kiln depends upon the gas line size at the kiln (usually from 3/4" to 1-1/4") and the CF/hr. needed. Not only does the regulator output have to be greater than the CF/hr. capacity, but so does the capacity of the safety shutoff control valve and the on/off valves for the burner controls.

Operation of these two safety shutoff valves is basically the same. Electrical current from the thermocouple or pilot generator energizes the thermomagnet to hold the valve open after manual reset. Loss of current to the thermomagnet due to low pilot flame, pilot outage, or limit switch operation at preset temperature causes the thermomagnet valve to snap closed, shutting off the gas flow (Fig. 8-54). Each safety shutoff valve has matching thermocouples with corresponding millivoltage specifications. To light, depress and hold the red button. This forces the valve to open and the arm to come into contact with the magnet. Light the pilot; after 60 seconds, release the red button; the pilot will have heated up the thermocouple enough to energize the thermomagnet and hold open the valve.

A simple and effective safety system for sidewall-fired downdraft or crossdraft kiln installation, where the burners are manifolded together and operate off one valve, is shown in Fig. 8-55. The pilot is extremely

sensitive to any drop in gas line pressure, gas stoppage, or draft which would cause the pilot to go out long before affecting the burners. It cools the thermocouple, which breaks the thermomagnet connection and shuts down the gas line. It is critical to put the safety shutoff valve first in line so that the pilot gas is shut down, too. The effectiveness of this system

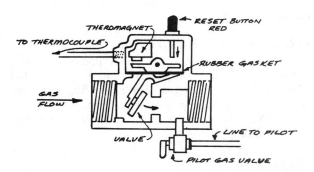

Fig. 8—54: *Safety shutoff control.*

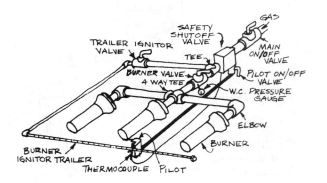

Fig. 8—55: *Downdraft burner setup with shut-off installation.*

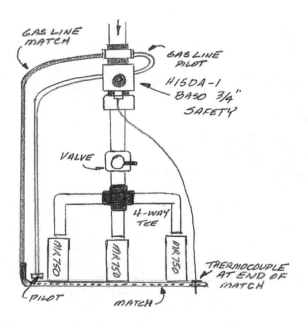

Fig. 8—55a: *Complete safety using continuous burning pilot/match.*

depends upon the sensitivity of the pilot. The recommended pilot and thermocouple for the particular safety shutoff valve must be used. It is important to periodically check millivoltage output of the thermocouple and milliamp dropout range of the safety shutoff valve to keep the system within the manufacturer's specifications for safe operation. (Fig. 8-55)

To alter this safety system to be 100 percent gas safe, run the pilot and the match line off the initial side plugs of the Baso valve, and run the thermocouple to the end of the match line. A continuous burn

ignition match with end of line proof to maintain burner ignition has been approved by the American Gas Association for in-line manifolding. For the H15DA-1 valve to open, the thermocouple must proof the end of the match line for flame and thus all the burners will ignite and stay ignited as long as the match is proved. A pilot re-ignition system can be installed, but then electricity must be used, which complicates a simple system (Fig. 8-55a). An alternative method would be to use individual safeties on each burner as pictured (Fig. 8-55b photo). The burner setup on each side of a downdraft kiln must have its own safety system.

Figure 8-56 illustrates the standard safety system used by manufacturers in updraft kilns with floor burners. It is extremely important never to leave the trailer ring on (not even for pre-heating), because metal floor joists will deflect and lose their strength above 2,040°C (400°F). With a load of pottery in the kiln, it will cause the floor to drop. This safety system will only protect from the loss of gas pressure or outage, and if the pilot blows out the system will shut down. To make it 100 percent safe, give each burner an individual safety system or redesign the manifold system to allow for a continuous burning match system.

The simplest, least-confusing safety system is always best. Inevitably someone will bypass the safety system (Fig. 8-55c photo) because the firing must go on or it's too much trouble to fix or beyond the budget. ***Therefore, the greatest safety precaution of all is a kiln fired only by someone who understands how the kiln works and is present during the entire firing cycle.***

Fig. 8—55b: *Individual safety on each burner.*

Fig. 8 . 55c: *Safety bypass.*

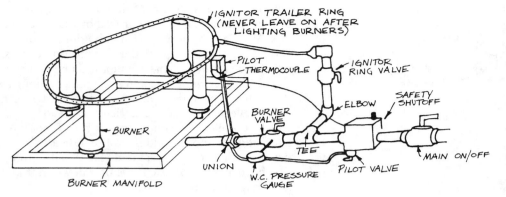

Fig. 8—56:
Standard safety system in updrafts with floor burners.

There are other exotic flame safeguard controls designed for large commercial and industrial kilns that require precise operating conditions and procedures. Two such products from Electronics Corp. of America (Fireye(R)) are the Ultraviolet Monitor (UVM) and Photocell or Flame Rod Monitor (TFM) commercial flame safeguard controls. These are usually set up with a spark ignition system similar to that used on the forced oil/air burner. The UVM control uses an ultraviolet-sensitive gas discharge tube to visually monitor radiation from gas and light oil flames. The TFM control uses either a photocell or a flame rod (the same method as the thermocouple) to monitor gas and light oil flames. The controls can monitor both pilot and main flames and will not allow the main gas valve to open for burner ignition until the pilot flame is proved. If the main burner doesn't light within 12 seconds, the gasline is closed. For the controls to operate, they need the burner motor, ignition transformer, pilot fuel valve, main fuel valve, lockout alarm, limit and operating controls, (depending upon the burner blast gates), blower, mixers, combustion air flow proving switches, and lots of plumbing (Fig. 8-57).

Fig. 8—57: *TFM safety controls, requiring a great deal of equipment and plumbing.*

The problem with these exotic systems in the pottery studio is that they are too expensive, and too many things can go wrong. For example, a normal 50-cu.-ft. downdraft kiln would require $3,500 or more for the parts and installation. And, a loss of electricity or an out-of-tune spark gap can render the system useless. There are new controllers by major companies — Minneapolis Honeywell, Partlow, Pixsys (Italian out of Padova) — that have gotten smaller, more versatile, and cost considerably less than a few years ago. The more sophisticated and modern the safety system, the more that can go wrong. The simplest system, with common sense, can do basically the same thing as elaborate, costly equipment.

KILN VENTILATION

Inadequate ventilation causes more kiln mishaps than any other problem. If the kiln is fired with natural gas inside a building, there must be proper ceiling ventilation, such as a flue exhaust hood for an updraft, or a chimney for a downdraft or crossdraft. To ventilate an updraft kiln, the hood should cover the entire top of the kiln and vent it as directly as possible to the outside. The exit flue temperature of an updraft kiln is approximately 954°C (1,750°F). Four feet above the kiln in the stack, the temperature is approximately 399°C (750°F). According to the Uniform Building Code for ventilation, the updraft kiln is a medium-temperature appliance. When venting an updraft kiln to the outside, use heavy-gauge sheet metal to withstand the temperatures above the flue, and use the proper roof jack (Fig. 8-58).

When using propane inside a building, have proper floor ventilation leading directly outside on at least two opposite sides of the kiln. Never use propane to fire a kiln in a basement. Propane is heavier than air and it is impossible for the gas to escape or disperse in the event of a leak. If the burners of the kiln are lower than the ground or floor line, the burner pit must be ventilated so the propane can flow downhill to the outside and away from the kiln. Also, vent the exhaust gases out through a chimney or a ventilation hood for an updraft kiln.

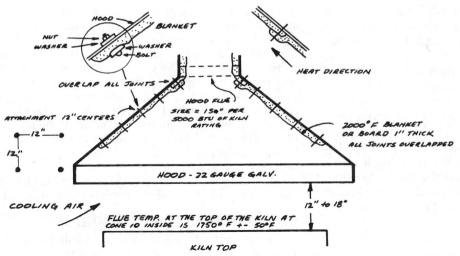

Fig. 8—58: *Installation of vent for an updraft kiln.*

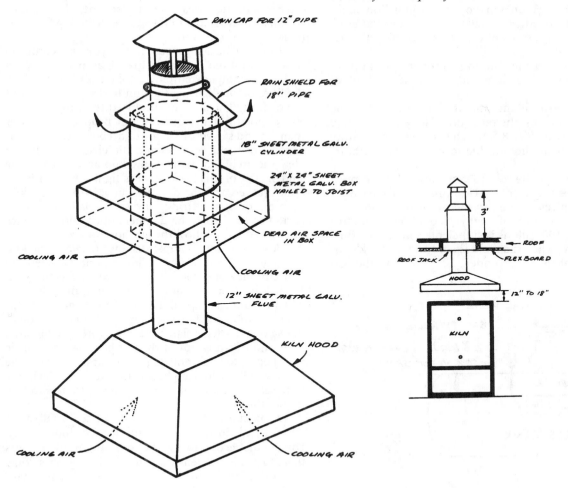

The hood can be insulated by using the cheapest 1,100°C (2,000°F) fiber blanket or board to line the inside. Construction details are shown in Fig. 7-58. Attach the blanket or board to the hood with nuts and bolts or sheet metal screws on 12" centers. If the ceiling is low, then also insulate the flue pipe.

It is very important to use the proper roof jacks. The main exhaust flue pipe (12" diameter) is enclosed by another liner, 18" in diameter, which pulls in air to cool the main exhaust flue. The 18" liner is supported by the dead air box or roof jack, which is attached to the ceiling joints. To figure exhaust ventilation for the kiln, use 1 sq. in. per 5,000 Btu of kiln input. One also has to be concerned with intake air ventilation, windows that open, doors that open or built-in floor and ceiling vents. If the kiln room or area gets too hot and you can smell exhaust flumes, then there is a problem with the intake and exhaust ventilation. Additional fan-driven roof vents might be necessary and more intake space allowed, but consult with a heating and air conditioning expert.

Remember, the arch flue temperature at the damper when the kiln is at cone 10 inside is about 954°C (1,750°F). Four feet above the kiln in the hood, the temperature reaches about 399°C (750°F). Proper exhaust ventilation is a must, as is the intake air supply.

LP GAS TANKS

LP tanks come in a variety of sizes and can be bought or leased. For a kiln 24 to 40 cu. ft. in size, I suggest a 500-gallon tank or two 250-gallon tanks manifolded together. Smaller tanks can be used. There are a few points of caution concerning the use of LP gas tanks:

1. Always set the tank in its proper upright position; otherwise, you'll withdraw liquid instead of vapor.

2. Never overfill the tank. It is designed to hold 80 percent liquid with the remaining 20 percent allotted to vapor space (Fig. 8-59). This allows temperature expansion of the liquid, due to outside temperature increase.

3. Regulator freeze-ups are caused by the presence of moisture in the fuel. To prevent this, have the LP dealer inject a little dry methyl alcohol into your tank. About 1 ounce of methyl alcohol per 20 lb. fuel or 1 pint to 100 gallons is sufficient. Sometimes, during the firing when the night is cold and the tank's liquid content is low (under 30 percent), the gas pressure will decrease and the tank will start to freeze up on the outside. When this happens, all you can do is pour hot water over the tank until the firing is finished. Manifolding two tanks together will solve this problem. In some colder climates withdrawing liquid propane maybe necessary. Consult the propane company as to the set-up and liquid propane burners and/or get a hold of the *Practical Guide to LP-Gas Utilization*, Earle A. Clifford, Harbrace Publication, 1969. (Also refer to Nils Lou, *The Art of Firing, A & C Black,* London/Gentle Breeze Publishing, Oviedo, Florida.)

4. Tanks should be placed 35 feet from the kiln or kiln building and preferably downhill and downwind.

GENERAL SAFETY PRECAUTIONS

Never vent a kiln into exhaust ventilation ducting. Never put the ceramic kiln room in the basement or on a floor above ground level when using gas, oil or wood; never put kilns in the classroom (provide an outside kiln shed area). Never place the kiln chimney or exhaust vents next to the air conditioning fresh-air intake vents on the roof.

Gas can be dangerous, but if you use common sense precautions, it is safe. I recall an instance when an LP gas company employee told a student to bleed the lines before lighting the kiln in order to clean out the orifices. The student did bleed the propane lines and cleaned out the orifices, but propane is heavier than air and stayed in the lower firebox area. The student then lit the burners and the ensuing explosion blew the arch and door off the kiln and knocked the student flat on his back. Always light a kiln with the door cracked and the damper open. When a gas kiln goes off during a firing, always be patient. Wait a period of time with the dampers open and spy holes unplugged, then follow the ignition procedure.

Always maintain a safe distance between the kiln roof and the roof of any buildings, and between the kiln chimney and roof (use the proper flashing). In 1963, John Chappell and I were firing his salt-glaze kiln in Domura, Japan. The roof over the shed was made of corrugated plastic sheeting. Halfway through the salting — with flames leaking through the arch door and bursting out of the salt ports — the plastic roof began to melt and sag closer and closer to the kiln arch. The roof caught fire and we had a devil of a time salting and ripping off burning plastic sheeting to save the kiln.

Against my advice, a friend once installed an Olsen 24 kit in his studio with a low 7-foot ceiling. During the second firing, the roof caught fire. He was there to put it out before any major damage was done, but both of these stories illustrate the most important safety precaution: *Use **common sense.***

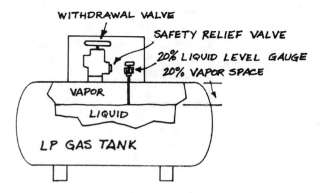

Fig. 8—59: *LP tank in proper perspective.*

Chapter 9

Electric Kilns

Electric kilns have very little in common with the fuel-burning crossdraft, downdraft and updraft kilns discussed in the preceding chapters. Electric kilns do not rely on a direct fuel for energy, on combustion for heat, on a draft through the kiln, or on the second through eighth rule of the principles of kiln design.

The electric kiln is a product of the Twentieth Century and could prove to be the fourth most important innovation in kiln-building history. The first was the building of the fundamental kiln container in which pots were placed. The second was the development of high-temperature refractories both in the Orient and Europe, along with the introduction of fossil fuels in Europe. The third was the development of lightweight insulation bricks and related refractory materials during the 1930s. The fourth is the electric kiln, an original concept in the firing of ceramic ware, using completely different principles of design, combining the laws of electricity and electrical wiring with lightweight insulation refractories.

PLANNING AN ELECTRIC KILN

An electric kiln can be defined as a no-draft kiln, relying upon radiant heat produced by the conversion of electrical energy into heat energy in resistance elements.

SHAPE

The first principle of kiln design states that a cube is the best all-around chamber shape for a kiln. The principle holds true for electric kilns. Electric kilns depend upon heat radiating from the walls toward the center of the chamber. If the chamber width is too great, it becomes difficult to heat the center. Thus, there is a relationship between chamber width and the efficiency of the kiln. A cube of 30" x 30" x 30" (15 cu. ft.) is the largest that will retain maximum efficiency in heating the center. The largest width I know of is a 45" in an electric car bottom kiln. The kiln measured 8' 10" long by 45" wide and 49" tall, with elements located in the sides, door, and floor. An example of large electric car kilns is found in the Jiesie Bone China Factory in Kaunas, Lithuania (Fig.9-1p, 2p-photos). The roll-away carts use neoprene wheels and a German shelf and post system. For most large electric kilns of 8 cu. ft. and up, the width will usually fall between 22" and 26" in order to accommodate standard 20" to 24" kiln shelves. To increase the cubic-foot capacity of an electric kiln once the width is

Fig. 9—1 photo: *Jiesie Bone China kiln.*

Fig. 9—2 photo:

Jiesie Bone China factory kiln is an example of a large electric car bottom kiln.

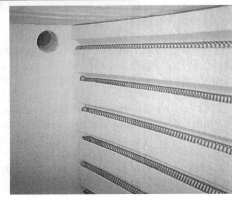

Fig. 9—2 photo 2: *Job Forni grooved board wall.*

established, simply increase the length or the height. To enlarge the capacity of kilns over 20 cu. ft., the length is increased because it simplifies the construction tremendously by making the kiln a top loader. On the other hand, top loaders are bad on the back. Therefore, larger electric kilns tend to be car kilns or feature two doors on each end.

The four most popular styles of electric kilns are: top loader, front loader, polygonal top loader, and sectional polygonal top loader (Fig. 9-1).

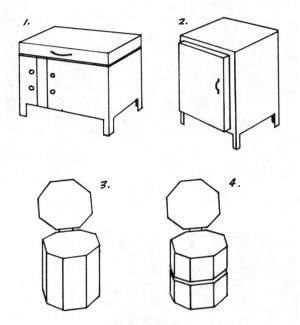

Fig. 9—1: *Electric kilns: 1. top loader; 2. front loader; 3. polygonal top loader; 4. sectional polygonal top loader.*

BRICKS

Particular care is essential in selecting a high-quality insulation brick that is to be in contact with the heating elements. Bricks used in an electric kiln should meet these specifications: (1) contain at least 40 to 45 percent alumina; (2) iron oxide (Fe_2O_3) content must be under 1 percent; and (3) low alkali (such as Na_2O) content of 0.4 percent or less. For temperatures not exceeding Cone 9 or 1,260°C (2,300°F) a 2300 insulation brick could be used. Temperatures from Cone 10 to 11 or more require 2,600 insulation bricks. The old Babcock and Wilcox K-26 brick contains 2.4 percent Fe_2O_3 and 0.4 percent alkali and thus does not meet these specifications. The Thermal Ceramic JM-26 insulation brick and the Thermal Ceramic K-26 insulation brick, however, do meet the specifications with a 0.8 percent Fe_2O_3 and a 0.1 percent alkali content. A high Fe_2O_3 content is extremely bad for element life and must never appear on the contact surface between the bricks and the elements.

In fact, it is recommended that all surfaces coming into contact with the Kanthal element be coated with alumina or a high-quality refractory cement. High-quality bricks must be chosen because the durability of the resistance elements depends on the formation of a protecting oxide layer. This is done naturally by the element's reaction with oxygen in the air. Foreign materials — iron oxide, alkalis, vaporization or splashing of enamels and glazes — coming in contact with the elements usually interfere with the formation of the oxide layer and reduce element life.

ELECTRIC ELEMENTS AND GROOVES

The kiln construction methods discussed in Chapter 2 will suffice for the building of electric kilns, with one important addition: Grooving the bricks to hold and support the elements. The two basic groove shapes are the square notch and the cylindrical shape (Fig. 9-2). Both can be made quite easily. The square notch is made in the middle of the brick by sawing parallel grooves 1/4" apart to the proper depth, then breaking out the remaining upright slivers (Fig. 9-3). The cylindrical groove can be made exactly and easily using a drill press and proper size bit to drill down through the 9" length close to the corner edge or in the middle. The hole is opened to the proper size by sawing (Fig. 9-4). Both grooves must allow enough room to assure free radiation toward the interior of the kiln and enough space beyond the coil wire diameter to exchange elements easily.

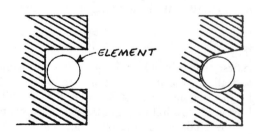

Fig. 9—2: *Square and cylindrical notches to accommodate elements.*

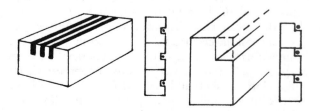

Fig. 9—3: *Square notch in corner or middle for elements.*

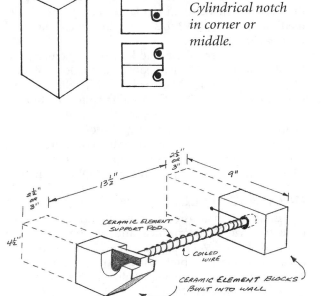

Fig. 9—4: *Cylindrical notch in corner or middle.*

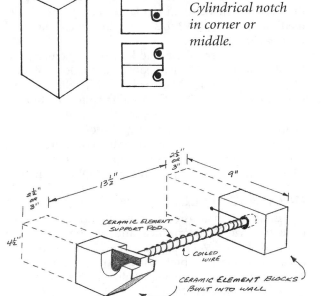

Fig. 9—4a: *Ceramic element blocks.*

Fig. 9—4a photo: *Door construction.*

The ceramic element blocks that can be built into the brick work to hold the supporting element ceramic rod are used in commercial kilns. They allow for complete radiation around the element into the kiln and also prolong the life of the elements (Fig.9-4a, Fig.9-4ap-photo). Another advantage is that high-iron bricks or impure insulation bricks can be used,

since the elements never come into contact with the refractories, only the high-quality element blocks.

The formula for the size of the groove in relation to coil size is: Rd = 1.25 D, where D is the diameter of the coil width, and Rd is the diameter of the groove or notch in the brick (Fig. 9-5). Care must be taken not to recess the coils too deeply or to restrict the opening.

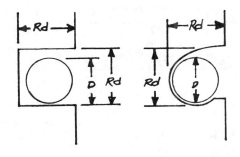

Fig. 9—5: *Determining groove size for a given coil size: Rd = 1.25 D (Reprinted with permission from The Kanthal Handbook).*

Spacing between elements in a kiln depends upon kiln size, the wire size and related groove size, and the number of element groups. Element groups should be spaced as equally as possible throughout the kiln. The usual spacing between element groups is one brick width or 2 1/2" (Fig. 9-6). In some smaller kilns, the group elements may be spaced as close as 3/4" between grooves with a brick, or 2 1/2" spacing between element groups (Fig. 9-7). Chang-

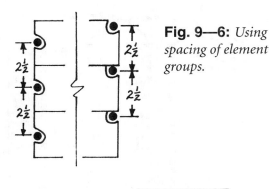

Fig. 9—6: *Using spacing of element groups.*

Fig. 9—7: *Some smaller kilns use 3/4" spacing.*

ing from one element row to another is simply a matter of grooving the transition brick with a 45° groove to the next row (Fig. 9-8). To change direction in a floor element, a hairpin turn is used (Fig. 9-9).

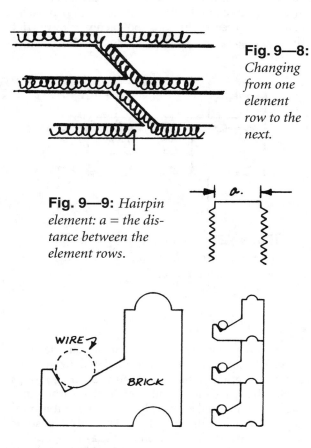

Fig. 9—8: *Changing from one element row to the next.*

Fig. 9—9: *Hairpin element: a = the distance between the element rows.*

Fig. 9—10: *Element support bricks, manufactured by Kanthal.*

Kanthal Corporation manufactures special element support bricks for large-to-medium, medium-to-small, and small-to very-small furnaces. The spacing between elements in the large category is 3", the medium category is 2 1/2", and the small about 1" (Fig. 9-10).

One commercial electric kiln manufacturer, Job Forni, Cartigliano, Italy, grooves a single wall unit (Thermal Ceramic M-Board), using the recommended spacing of 2 1/2" and a hairpin turn hidden within the butt corner joint, for their Hobbyker line of front-loading kilns (Fig. 9-2 photo). All the kilns are extremely well insulated with a louvered heat shield and dead-man air space built into the 6" wall. (For further U.S. information contact Olsen kilns.)

ROOF AND WALLS

Electric kiln construction is very straightforward once the size is determined and all the bricks are grooved. Figure 9-11 shows three 7" wall constructions: (1) using 4" of high-temperature M-board with 2" back-up insulation board plus 1" dead-man air space with louvered metal shell, (2) 2 1/2" of block insulation and a stretcher course, and (3) a K-20 backup with the stretcher course.

These walls should not exceed 48" in height unless tied back to the frame of the kiln. Usually, kilns under 20" x 20" x 20" have 4 1/2" walls with a metal (stainless steel) backing. The polygonal kilns that fire up to cone 6 have rowlock walls of 2 1/2". Most electric kilns have some type of venting hole arrangement, either in the top of a side wall or in the ceiling.

A flat roof, rather than an arch, simplifies construction and cuts cost. Figure 9-12 illustrates a typical flat-roof construction for a top loader that can be increased or decreased in size to fit any kiln plan. An angle iron frame is basic for electric kiln construction.

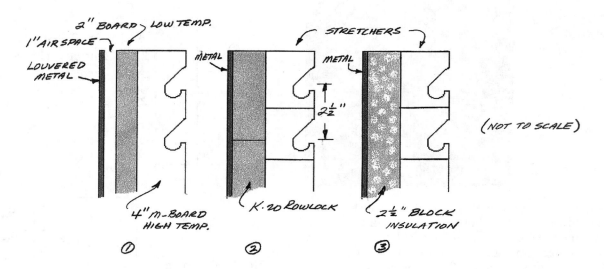

Fig. 9—11: *Three 7" wall constructions.*

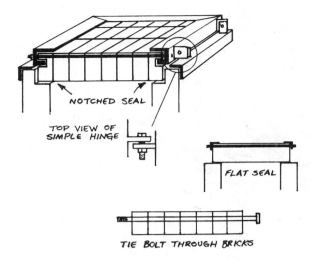

Fig. 9—12: *Typical flat roof construction for top loader.*

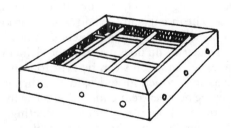

Fig. 9—13: *Joints for welding angle-iron frames.*

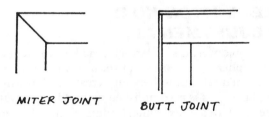

Fig. 9—14: *Cast roof with reinforcing bars.*

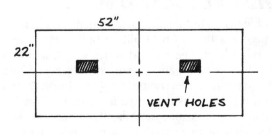

Fig. 9—15: *Venting a large top-loading kiln.*

Rows of ring bricks are held in place by tie bolts running through the bricks.

Either a miter or butt joint can be used to weld together the angle iron frame (Fig. 9-13). The miter joint is used when only one or two kilns are going to be constructed. The butt joint should be used when manufacturing a large quantity. The butt joint can be cut in a metal press cutter, thus saving torch cutting time, and is far stronger and more accurate. Flat roofs can be cast in angle iron frames containing crossbar reinforcing rods (Fig. 9-14).

For any kiln over 8 cu. ft. a vent hole should be cut into the roof to allow moisture to escape. On a kiln lid measuring 22" x 52", a vent hole 2 1/2" x 2 1/2" should be placed in each half of the lid (Fig. 9-15).

POLYGONAL KILN CONSTRUCTION

Polygonal top loaders and sectionals use either 2 1/2" rowlock or 4 1/2" stretcher walls, depending upon maximum temperature use. The kilns may or may not have back-up fiber insulation, but are reinforced with stainless steel banding.

The polygonal kiln design layout is based on a 9" brick module. Select a diameter for the kiln based on need and the available shelf size. Determine wall thickness. Lay out two circles (or a portion of their

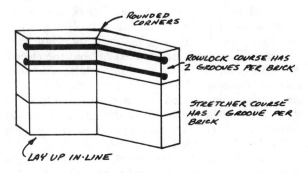

Fig. 9—16: *Establishing brick silhouette for polygonal kiln.*

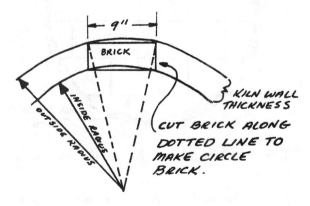

Fig. 9—17: *Element grooves for polygonal construction.*

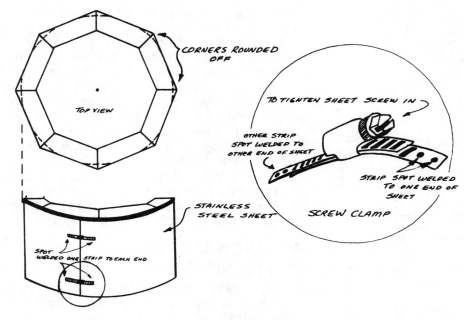

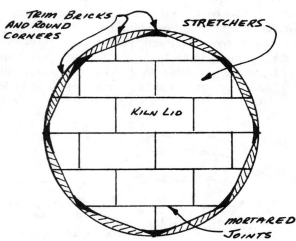

Fig. 9—18: *Weld hose clamps to tighten steel bands.*

Fig. 9—19: *Mortared and banded polygonal lid.*

arcs) using the inside radius and the outside radius of the kiln wall. Mark off a 9" segment touching the outside wall radius, and place a brick silhouette in place.

Stretch a string from the center to each outside 9" corner of the brick silhouette and mark (Fig. 9-16). To make the circle brick template, cut off the corners marked by the string line across the brick silhouette.

Each brick must be grooved to hold the electric elements before the final banding is done. The outer corner joints should be rounded off (Fig. 9-17). The circle bricks are banded together with stainless steel sheet material in the width of the kiln or sectional. Bands are tightened by welding on hose clamps (Fig. 9-18). There is no need for mortar.

The lid is made from bonded stretchers in the shape of the polygon, mortared and then banded (Fig. 9-19).

REDUCTION KILN ADJUSTMENTS

To convert a standard electric kiln for reduction atmosphere, you must introduce smoke into the static/neutral atmosphere and create a draft through the kiln. This is accomplished by building an outside firebox with a fine channel leading to inlet flues in the floor of the kiln and out through an exit flue leading into a chimney (Fig. 9-20). The firebox and chimney are opened when reduction is to begin. A steady rate of stoking kindling is begun, filling the kiln with smoke, allowing it to clear a bit, then repeating the sequence. The intent is not to add heat to the kiln, but to keep the atmosphere in a reducing, smoky state. A reducing electric kiln does decrease the elements' normal life expectancy. This can be kept to a minimum by alternating reduction and oxidation firing, or by bisque firing between reduction firings. The life of the element depends upon the protective coating formed by the element in an oxidizing atmosphere. Therefore, the alteration helps to rebuild the coating on the element.

ELECTRICAL MEASUREMENTS AND CALCULATIONS

Electric current is measured in amperes. An ampere is a flow of 6.25 billion billion electrons per second. Water, gas, air and other substances can be put under pressure and measured in terms of pounds per square inch. Electric power is also under pressure, and this pressure is measured in volts. Amperes alone or volts alone do not describe the actual amount of power flowing in a wire. Similarly, gallons per minute tell nothing about the amount of work involved in pumping water unless the pressure is also known.

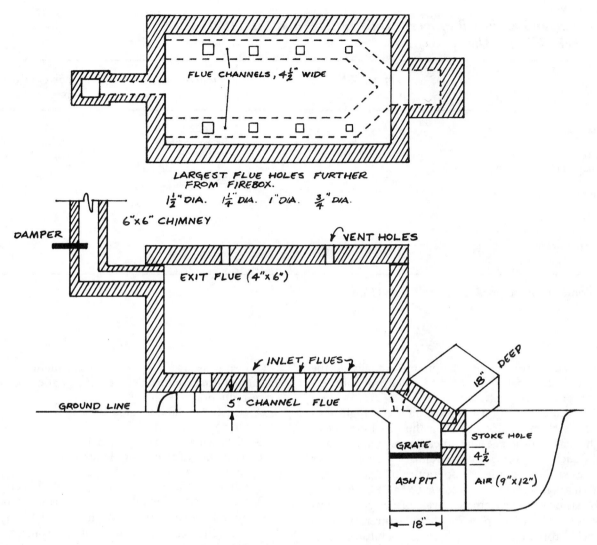

Fig. 9—20: *Reduction kiln adjustment.*

When amperes and volts are considered together, they describe the power flowing in the wire, or watts. Thus, amperes x volts = watts. One kilowatt is 1,000 watts.

Resistance is an equally important factor in controlling the rate of electric current. As the rate of water flow in a pipe depends upon the amount of pressure behind it, it is also governed by the amount of resistance offered to the flow. Smaller diameter pipes offer greater resistance than larger diameter pipes. Long pipes offer greater resistance than short ones. Smooth-walled pipes offer less resistance than rough-walled.

Some materials also conduct electricity better than others. Therefore, remember that the electrical resistance of a wire depends upon its length and diameter, and the materials used in its composition.

The current (I-amperes) passing through a conductor, such as wire, depends directly on the pressure (E-volts) and inversely on the resistance (R). Therefore:

$$I = \frac{E}{R}$$

SELECTING ELECTRIC ELEMENTS

This chapter will provide general knowledge on the building of an electric kiln. I would stress that there is no substitute for experience when it comes to creating proper element designs. The best designs will always be developed by experienced electric kiln builders or manufacturers. If, however, you want the experience of building an electric kiln, it is advisable, once your design and element calculations are completed, to consult a professional kiln builder or element manufacturer. It is also advisable, when connecting the elements to the proper switches, circuit breakers and power source, to have an electrician

Table 9-1
Physical and Electrical Properties of Kanthal® and Nikrothal® (Nickel-Chrome) Alloys

Alloys	Kanthal A-1 percent	Kanthal A percent	Nikrothal 8 percent
Analysis	5.5 Al Cr 22 0.5 Co 72 Fe	5 Al Cr 22 0.5 Co 72.5 Fe	80 Ni 20 Cr
Form	Wire and strip	Wire and ribbon	Wire and strip
Maximum recommended temperature temperature continuous use	2505°F	2425°F	2190°F
Resistivity at 20°C (microhms per cm^3)	145	139	108
Resistivity at 68°F (ohms per cm^3)	872	837	650

Reprinted by permission from *The Kanthal Handbook.*

double-check your circuit design and actually do the hookup. All things considered, you are probably better off buying an electric kiln.

A major reason for the growing use of high-temperature electric kilns has been the development of high-quality, heat-resistant, metallic resistance materials, such as Kanthal alloys. Kanthal elements have increased the operating temperature of electric kilns to past sagger cone 10, or 1,285°C (2,345°F). There are two basic types of elements available: For low-temperatures, a variety of wire manufacturers make a nickel-chrome element; for high temperatures, Kanthal elements are used. Table 9-1 gives physical properties of the two types of elements.

The service life of resistance heating elements depends upon:

1. heat resistance property of the element
2. operating conditions, such as oxidation or reduction
3. element size and length
4. temperature of the kiln
5. surface load in watts per sq. in.
6. frequency of switching element on and off
7. construction of element
8. refractory material used to hold the elements

Most wire sizes for kilns used in firing ceramic ware will fall between Brown & Sharpe (B&S) gauge 16 to 5. In choosing an element, it is important to remember that the operating temperature of the element is directly related to the wire size and dependent upon the kiln's atmosphere. A realistic starting point for kilns operating up to Cone 6 would be between

Table 9-2
Recommended Operating Temperatures

Wire Diameter (inches) B&S Gauge	0.0403 18	0.1285 8	0.1285 and heavier 8 and heavier
Kanthal A-1	1224°C–1349°C (2235°F–2460°F)		1375°C (2505°F)
Kanthal A	2143°C–1299°C (2145°F–2370°F)		1336°C (2425°F)
Kanthal D	1099°C–1199°C (2010°F–2190°F)		1286°C (2335°F)
Nikrothal 8	1963°C–1149°C (1965°F–2100°F)		1199°C (2190°F)

B&S 16 to 12 and, for kilns operating up to Cone 10, B&S 12 to 5, both of which are subject to the quality of the wire chosen and other factors. Larger kilns need a heavier gauge element than do smaller kilns. Table 9-2 gives the element and operating temperatures, with recommended wire size limits.

Wire is usually selected over strip or ribbon for ceramic kilns because of the generally better service life. Service life is relative to the minimum dimension of the element. For electric kilns, the best cross section is found in wire elements.

ELEMENT SURFACE LOAD

The surface load of an element, or the watt density, is measured in watts per square inch (W/sq. in.), or watts per square centimeter (W/sq. cm.). The wear or deterioration during a given period of time is related to the surface load on the element. A higher watt density means a smaller wire size, less material and lower initial cost, but a higher deterioration rate resulting in shortened element life and higher operation costs. It is very important to use the proper surface loading for a particular wire operating at any given temperature in order to get maximum element life. A general rule is to have the lowest watts per square inch on the element and still retain the needed heat, thus gaining long element life. Figure 10-21 provides permissible surface loading for Kanthal A-1 and A wire elements. The actual surface load depends on many different factors, such as kiln temperature and

atmosphere, refractories used, the actual construction of the elements, and switching frequency, so only approximations can be given.

From 5 to 9 W/sq. in. is the normal range of surface loading for electric kilns.

KANTHAL WIRE TABLES

The columns in Tables 9-3 through 9-5 have the following values:

Ω/ft., 20°C-68°F: Given the length of the element, the resistance at 20°C (68°F) can easily be calculated. If operating temperature is to be considered, it must be multiplied by the factor C_t.

Sq. in./ft.: Given the length of the element, this will determine the radiation area of the element. Taken with the wattage, it yields the appropriate surface loading (W/in.2).

Ft./lb.: Given the length of the element, the quantity to be ordered can be calculated.

Lb./ft.: Given the length of the element, this figure yields the exact weight of the individual element.

Sq. in./Ω 20C-68F: This quantity, developed by Kanthal, guides the proper choice of element size. If operating temperature is to be considered, it is divided by the factor C_t.

DETERMINING REQUIRED KILOWATTS

The required kilowatts for any given kiln depend upon the kiln's volume temperature and the time required to reach the temperature. Basically, for stoneware temperatures, two methods can be used to give an estimate of the needed kilowatts:

1). 1.2 W/cu. in. or 2.07 kW/CF, with lower range of about 1.0 W/cu. in. or 1.5 kW/CF.

Example: 2' x 2' x 2' = 8 ft.^{3}

8 x 1.5 = 12 kW

Smaller kilns work with a higher output per cubic foot than larger kilns, which work with a correspondingly lower output. Because the variable in some cases can be as much as ± 25 percent, experience will be an important factor in determining the needed kilowatts.

2.) 5 to 7 W/sq. in. of heated wall surfaces.

The kiln walls are laid out as illustrated in Fig. 9-22 and the square inches are totaled, then multiplied by 5 to 7 W.

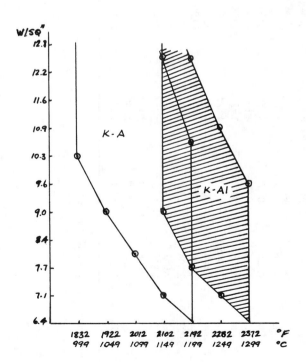

Fig. 9—21: *Maximum permissible surface loading in W/sq. in. for elements in industrial furnaces.*

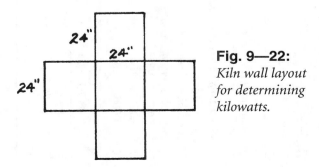

Fig. 9—22: *Kiln wall layout for determining kilowatts.*

Table 9-3
Kanthal A-1 Wire

Maximum wire temperature: 1375 °C (2505°F)
Resistivity at 20°C: 145 microhms per cm cube
Resistivity at 68°F: 872 ohms per cir. mil foot
Specific gravity: 7.1
Wt. per cubic inch: 0.256 lb.
To obtain resistivity at working temperature, multiply by the factor C_t:

°C	20	100	200	300	400	500	600	700	800	900	1000	1100	1200	1300	1350	1375
°F	68	212	392	572	752	932	1112	1292	1472	1652	1832	2012	2192	2372	2462	2505
C_t	1.000	1.000	1.001	1.002	1.005	1.010	1.017	1.023	1.028	1.032	1.036	1.038	1.040	1.042	1.043	1.044

B & S gauge	Diameter in.	Diameter mm.	Ω/ft. 68°F	sq. in./ft.	ft./lb.	lbs./M. ft.	Ω/lb.	sq. in./Ω 68°F
1	.289	7.348	.01042	10.889	4.948	202.1	0.05154	1046
2	.258	6.543	.01314	9.721	6.238	160.3	0.08190	739.4
3	.229	5.827	.01657	8.629	7.867	127.1	0.1303	522.0
4	.204	5.189	.02089	7.687	9.921	100.8	0.2072	369.4
5	.182	4.620	.02635	6.858	12.51	79.90	0.3294	260.2
6	.162	4.115	.03323	6.104	15.78	63.36	0.5241	183.8
7	.144	3.665	.04188	5.426	19.89	50.28	0.8327	129.8
8	.128	3.264	.05281	4.823	25.07	39.87	1.325	91.71
9	.114	2.906	.06663	4.296	31.63	31.61	2.106	64.72
10	.102	2.588	.08398	3.843	39.89	25.06	3.348	45.74
11	.091	2.304	.1059	3.430	50.30	19.88	5.324	32.30
12	.081	2.052	.1335	3.052	63.41	15.77	8.463	22.81
13	.072	1.829	.1684	2.713	79.98	12.50	13.46	16.10
14	.064	1.628	.2124	2.412	100.8	9.914	21.40	11.37
15	.057	1.450	.2677	2.148	127.1	7.865	34.02	8.036
16	.051	1.290	.3376	1.923	160.3	6.237	54.11	5.674

Reprinted with permission from *The Kanthal Handbook*.

Table 9-4
Kanthal A Wire

Maximum wire temperature: 1330 °C (2425°F)
Resistivity at 20°C: 139 microhms per cm cube
Resistivity at 68°F: 837 ohms per cir. mil foot
Specific gravity: 7.15
Wt. per cubic inch: 0.258 lb.
To obtain resistivity at working temperature, multiply by the factor C_t:

°C	20	100	200	300	400	500	600	700	800	900	1000	1100	1200	1300	1330
°F	68	212	392	572	752	932	1112	1292	1472	1652	1832	2012	2192	2372	2425
C_t	1.000	1.002	1.006	1.011	1.017	1.027	1.036	1.043	1.049	1.052	1.056	1.058	1.060	1.062	1.063

B & S gauge	Diameter in.	Diameter mm.	Ω/ft. 68°F	sq. in./ft.	ft./lb.	lbs./M. ft.	Ω/lb.	sq. in./Ω 68°F
1	.289	7.348	.01000	10.889	4.914	203.5	0.04909	1091
2	.258	6.543	.01261	9.721	6.195	161.4	0.07800	771.3
3	.229	5.827	.01591	8.629	7.812	128.0	0.1241	544.5
4	.204	5.189	.02005	7.687	9.852	101.5	0.1973	385.4
5	.182	4.620	.02530	6.858	12.42	80.46	0.3137	271.4
6	.162	4.115	.03189	6.104	15.67	63.81	0.4991	191.7
7	.144	3.665	.04020	5.426	19.75	50.63	0.7930	135.4
8	.128	3.264	.05069	4.823	24.90	40.15	1.262	95.67
9	.114	2.906	.06395	4.296	31.41	31.83	2.006	67.51
10	.102	2.588	.08061	3.843	39.61	25.24	3.189	47.72
11	.091	2.304	.1017	3.430	49.95	20.02	5.070	33.70
12	.081	2.052	.1282	3.052	62.97	15.02	8.060	23.79
13	.072	1.829	.1616	2.713	79.42	12.59	12.82	16.80
14	.064	1.628	.2038	2.412	100.1	9.984	20.38	11.86
15	.057	1.450	.2570	2.148	126.2	7.920	32.40	8.383
16	.051	1.290	.3241	1.923	159.2	6.281	51.53	5.919

Reprinted with permission from *The Kanthal Handbook.*

Table 9-5
Nikrothal 8 Wire

Maximum wire operating temperature: 1200°C (2190°F)
Resistivity at 20°C: 108 microhms per cm cube
Resistivity at 68°F: 650 Ω per cir. mil foot
Specific gravity: 08.41
To obtain resistivity at working temperature, multiply by the factor C_t:

°C	20	100	200	300	400	500	600	700	800	900	1000	1100
°F	68	212	392	572	752	932	1112	1292	1472	1652	1832	2012
C_t	1.000	1.017	1.035	1.052	1.062	1.068	1.066	1.063	1.062	1.067	1.071	1.075

B & S gauge	Diameter in.	mm.	Ω/ft. 68°F	sq. in./ft.	ft./lb.	lbs./M. ft.	Ω/lb.	sq. in./Ω 68°F
000	.410	10.40	.003866	15.44	2.077	481.5	.008030	3994
00	.365	9.27	.004879	13.75	2.621	381.6	.01279	2818
0	.325	8.25	.006153	12.25	3.306	302.5	.02034	1991
1	.289	7.35	.007782	10.91	4.181	239.2	.03254	1402
2	.258	6.54	.009765	9.711	5.244	190.7	.05121	994.5
3	.229	5.83	.01239	8.648	6.658	150.2	.08249	698.0
4	.204	5.19	.01562	7.702	8.389	119.2	.1310	493.1
5	.182	4.62	.01962	6.857	10.54	94.87	.2068	349.5
6	.162	4.11	.02476	6.107	13.30	75.17	.3293	246.6
7	.144	3.66	.03135	5.440	16.84	59.39	.5279	173.5
8	.128	3.26	.03967	4.844	21.31	46.93	.8454	122.1
9	.114	2.91	.05001	4.313	26.87	37.22	1.344	86.24
10	.102	2.59	.06248	3.842	33.56	29.80	2.344	61.49
11	.091	2.30	.07849	3.419	42.16	23.72	3.309	43.56
12	.081	2.05	.09907	3.046	53.22	18.79	5.273	30.75
13	.072	1.83	.1255	2.714	67.34	14.85	8.451	21.63
14	.064	1.63	.1588	2.417	85.25	11.85	13.54	15.22
15	.057	1.45	.2000	2.153	107.5	9.306	21.50	10.77
16	.051	1.29	.2499	1.915	134.2	7.450	33.54	7.663

Reprinted with permission from *The Kanthal Handbook*.

Table 9-6
Kilowatt Power Calculations

Volume (ft.³)	Kilowatts	=	Volts	x	Amps	Elements Required
1	1.800		120		15	—
2	4.600		230		20	3
	5.500		220/240		25	3
	4.600		230/208		20 (three-phase)	3
3	5.290		230		23	4
	5.060		230		22	4
	5.760		240		24	4
4	8.050		230		35	—
	11.000		208/240		26.6 (three-phase)	—
	10.800		240		45	—
5	14.400		220/240		60	—
	8.850		230		38.5	—
	7.800		230		34	—
6	9.200		230		40	5
7	16.800		220/240		70	—
	11.250		230		47	—
8	14.400		220/240		60	—
	10.350		230		45	5
	9.200		230		40	5
10	13.800		230		60	6
	26.000		240		108	—
13	30.000		220/240		125	—
	24.000		220/240		100	—
	25.000		220/240		75	—
15	34.500		230		150	6
16	36.000		220/240		150	—
	30.000		220/240		125	—
	24.000		240		100	5

If the higher values are used, then method 1 gives 8 x 2.07 = 16.5 kW and method 2 gives 2,304 x 7 = 16.1 kW. Find these values in Table 9-6; you can see that 16 kW is too high. The lower values fall in the middle. I compiled the table using manufactured kilns on the market today, comparing the volume of the kiln to its kilowatt power. Thus, the table can be used as a reference for checking your kilowatt power calculations.

Kiln voltage usually depends upon the local power voltage, which in almost all situations is enough to feed the kilns included in Table 9-6, except the three-phase kiln. However, it is advisable to have 200-amp service, which is only a small additional cost and will allow a studio or pottery enough amperage to operate.

CALCULATING WIRE ELEMENTS

In order to calculate elements for a kiln, one needs to know:
1. kiln temperature
2. amount of voltage available
3. kiln capacity (volume)
4. number of circuits

To begin a wire calculation, a few assumptions based on experience must be made. First of all, the temperature is known and C_t is found in Tables 9-3 through 9-5. The available voltage is ascertained from the service panel on the building, house or studio. The voltage required for most kilns, unless very small, is 220 to 240 volts. The kiln capacity is known, thus the kilowatts needed can be determined.

Now the two assumptions based upon experience must be made — the number of circuits needed, and the surface loading in W/sq. in. The surface loading will be 6.4 to 9 W/sq. in. for a firing temperature of Cone 10. For proper and uniform temperature distribution within a kiln, it is important to have sufficiently large heated wall surfaces. In order to accomplish this, as much wire as possible should be used — this means splitting the total kilowatts into smaller groups, connected in series. The smaller groups on the wire size will have to stay within the acceptable W/sq. in. surface loading.

There is a quick method for determining wire size, using a formula for finding the square in./ Ω, and then finding in the tables the corresponding wire cross-section matching the square in./ Ω. Knowing the amperage (I) and selecting a value for the surface loading (p) from the limits given (6.4 to 9 W/sq. in.), then:

$$\text{Sq. in.}/\Omega = \frac{I^2 \times C_t}{p}$$

or

$$\text{Sq. in.}/\Omega = \frac{\text{amperage}^2 \times \text{temp. factor}}{\text{surface loading W/in.}^2}$$

The amperage determined must pertain to a single element group, not to the total amperage of the kiln.

Given: 240 v
108 amps
26 kw
10 1/2 CF
Six element groups and six switches cone 10 firing range

Find: wire size (B&S)

Solution: six groups, equaling 108 amps, equals 18 amps per group

$$\text{Sq. in.}/\Omega = \frac{I^2 \times C_t}{p} = \frac{18^2 \times 1.04}{8}$$

Sq. in./Ω = 42.12 (Referring to tables under sq. in./Ω column and corresponding B&S column).

Wire size = B&S 10.

In order to confirm the above computations, element design calculations based upon Ohm's Law are used. Ohm's Law states that the current varies directly with the voltage and inversely with the resistance. Where:

E = volts
P = output in watts
R_h = hot resistance
R_c = cold resistance

then:

$$R_h = \frac{E^2}{P} = \frac{240^2}{4333} = \frac{57600}{4333} = 13.3$$

$$R_c = \frac{R_h}{C_t} = \frac{13.3}{1.04} = 12.8$$

To obtain the number of kilowatts needed per group, divide 26 by 6.

Thus, kW per group = 4.333
P = 4333 W output per group

Selecting the same W/in.^{2} of 8 *(p)*, then find the square in./Ω:

$$\text{Sq. in.}/\Omega = \frac{P}{p \times R_c} = \frac{4333}{8 \times 12.2} = \frac{4333}{102.4} = 42.4$$

Sq. in./Ω = 42.4 (corresponds to wire size B&S 10.) See Table 8-3.

The length of the wire per group is found by means of the table value Ω/ft.

$$\text{Element length (L)} = \frac{R_c}{\Omega \text{ft.}} = \frac{12.8}{.083} = 154.2 \text{ ft.}$$

All calculations are based on selecting 8 W/in.^{2} as the surface loading; thus, to confirm the calculations the actual surface loading must be found.

Having determined the "wire diameter, length, and watts, the actual surface loading can be found: divide wattage by wire diameter x x wire length x 12 (to convert to inches), which equals watts/in.^{2} surface loading:

$$\frac{\text{watts/wire}}{\text{diameter} \times \Pi \times \text{wire length} \times 12} = \text{W/in.}^2$$

$$\frac{4333}{102'' \times 3.14 \times 154.2 \times 12''} = \frac{4333}{582} = 7.4 \text{ W/in.}^2$$

Actual surface loading equals 7.4 W/in.-2 and, when reintroducing this actual value for p in the sq. in./Ω = I^2 X Ct/p, one finds the "wire size to be B&S 10 exactly.

ELEMENT COIL CALCULATION

The *Kanthal Handbook* states that the outer coil diameter (D) for temperatures exceeding 999C (1,830F) should be 5 to 6 times the wire diameter (d).

Thus, D = (5 to 6)d.

5 x d = 5 x .102 = .51 or $^{33}/_{64}$"
6 x d = 6 x .102 = .612 or $^{39}/_{64}$"

Averaging the two, $^9/_{16}$" or .56 coil diameter could be used.

The number of coils for an element of a given length can be found by:

$$\text{No. of turns, W} = \frac{L \text{ (length in ft.)} \times 12 \text{ (inches)}}{\Pi \times (D - d)}$$

$$W = \frac{154.2 \times 12}{3.14 \times (.56 - .102)} = \frac{1850.4''}{1.43}$$

No. of turns, W = 1293

The length of the close-wound coil (L_w) is then:

L_w = W x (d) inches = 1293 x .102 = 131.8 in. or 10.98 ft.

To find the stretched length of the coil, where the pitch of the coil is equal to twice the diameter, S (pitch) = 20, the formula is:

Stretch length of coil, L = S/d x L_w

$$L = \frac{2 \times .102 \times 131.8''}{.102}$$

L = 263.6" or 22' (approximate.)

When all the calculations are finished, you can determine: (1) whether the surface loading is reasonable for the kiln temperature; (2) whether the wire size fits the kiln temperature and W/sq. in.; and (3) if the stretch coil lengths will fit the available space for the element. (If the space is too small for the amount of wire, then the wire size must be increased to perhaps B&S 11 or 12, thus increasing the W/in.[2] and decreasing the length of wire need.)

Coiling a wire element is a difficult task, especially when done by hand and without proper equipment. Wire manufacturers wind the wire on steel mandrels rotated in a lathe. The coils are closely wound and later stretched to 2 to 3 times their diameter. For larger gauges, the wires must be heated to 700-750°C by connecting them electrically and then stretching to proper length. Uneven stretching causes unequal distribution of heat. When coiling, care must be taken to keep constant tension on the wire and to keep the feeding angle of the wire to the mandrel perfectly stable so the coils do not overlap with or separate from the preceding coil.

When installing an electric kiln, proper wire must be used from the service panel to the receptacle for the kiln, or directly to the kiln for permanent connection. Under most circumstances, kilns drawing more than 50 amps should have permanent connections. Figure 9-23 and Table 9-7 provide the proper wire sizes for given amperage and a corresponding figure for calculating the voltage drop per foot. Wiring diagrams are provided in Figure 9-24.

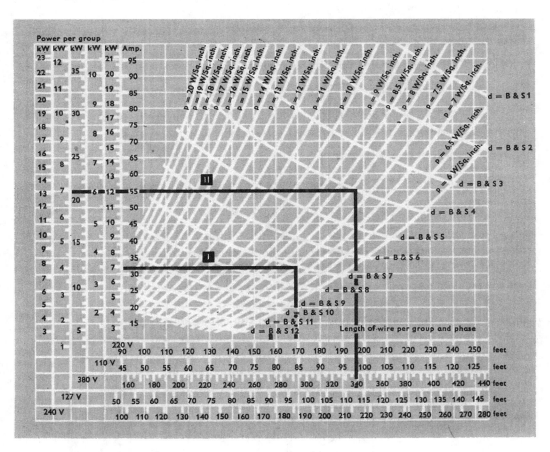

Fig. 9—23: *Kanthal D and DS wire, from B&S 1 to 12 gauge. Diameter and length of the wire and the W/sq. in., based on a 5 percent increase in resistance, can be determined. Kanthal A-1 wire: wire length minus 6 percent; surface loading plus 6.5 percent; Kathal A wire: wire length minus 3 percent; surface loading plus 3 percent (Reprinted with permission from The Kanthal Handbook).*

Table 9-7
Amperage/Wire Size

Amperage	Wire size AWG	Voltage drop/100 ft.
15	14	.4762
20	12	.3125
30	10	.1961
40	8	.1250
55	6	.0833
70	4	.0538
95	2	.0370
110	1	.0242

The electric kiln is the most difficult kiln to construct. Kiln design and bricklaying are the simplest of all kilns. However, controlling the power source in an electric kiln is most difficult. The calculation of wire sizes, resistance, length and so on depends upon so many variables and on firsthand experience that it is difficult to give general rules to follow. Therefore, if you do calculate your own elements from the data given in this chapter, be sure to have your calculations checked by either the wire manufacturer or an electric kiln manufacturer.

There is also such difficulty involved in the coiling of the wire that it is best to buy the wire pre-coiled to your specifications.Considering all that is involved, it is hard to beat the price or the guarantee of a manufactured kiln. Remember, a kiln is only as good as its designer and builder.

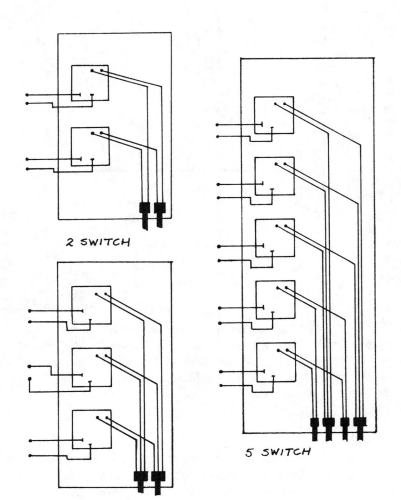

Fig. 9—24: *Wiring diagrams; on/off or high/low switches can be used.*

2 SWITCH

3 SWITCH

5 SWITCH

Chapter 10

Specialty Kilns, Innovations, Ideas, Etc.

THE WORLD'S HOTTEST INSTRUMENT

In 1996 I was invited to the International Ceramic Conference hosted by the National University of Canberra in Australia. It was imperative to build a special kiln, so I decided to build the "world's hottest instrument." Since I have no musical ability, I wrote to Brian Ransome to learn about the mechanics of building a recorder into the chimney (Fig. 10-1 and Fig. 10-2). My groundhog variation, similar in design to the Gulgong racer floor plan, was used.

The kiln turned out to be quite special, not only as an attempted musical performance piece, but also because it was the first kiln to be painted by Karen, Robert, and Regis, the children of potter Eddie Puruntatameri (1948-1995) of the Tiwi Island area in Northern Queensland. The decoration was in honor of their father, who had recently died (Fig. 10-3 and 4).

But back to the musical instrument, or as Brian named it "Whistling Flue." I separated out the chimney flue channels for the instrument and built into the remaining flue's dampers to be able to block off each flue, forcing all the draft into the two instrument flues. I built the impediment (a kiln shelf that could be removed) 7" into the two flues that were 9" by 9". A kiln shelf with a sharp, beveled edge was used as the

Fig. 10-4: *Painting kiln — Karen Puruntatameri.*

thipple and placed on just under a 45° angle that could slide back and forth in the chimney flue while adjusting to the upper corner of the impediment shelf (See fig. 10-5 and 6). The thipple and the slide angle bricks were cut on a brick saw. A total of five note

Fig. 10-3: *Layout kiln design by Regis and Robert Puruntatameri.*

Fig. 10-5: *Impediment and thipple location.*

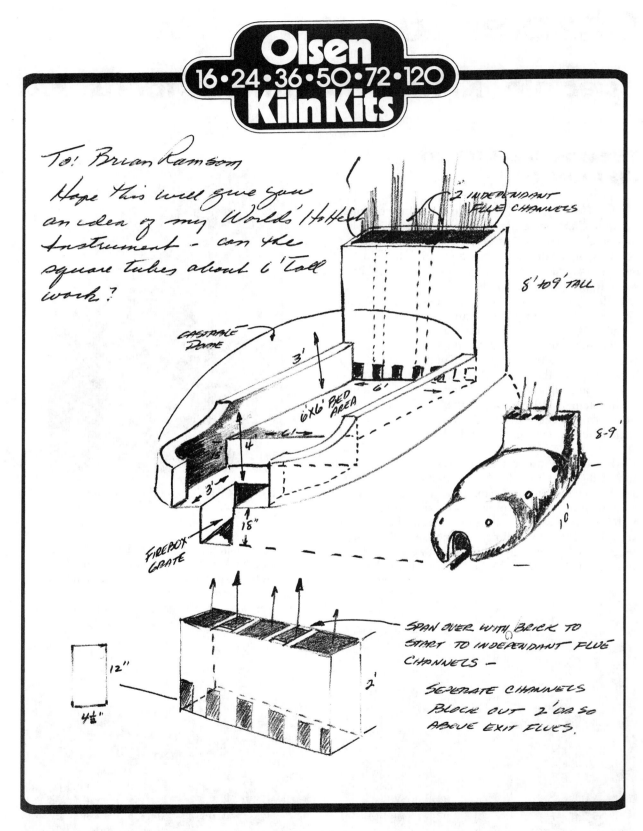

Fig. 10-1: *Letter to Brian Ransom concerning "world's hottest instrument."*

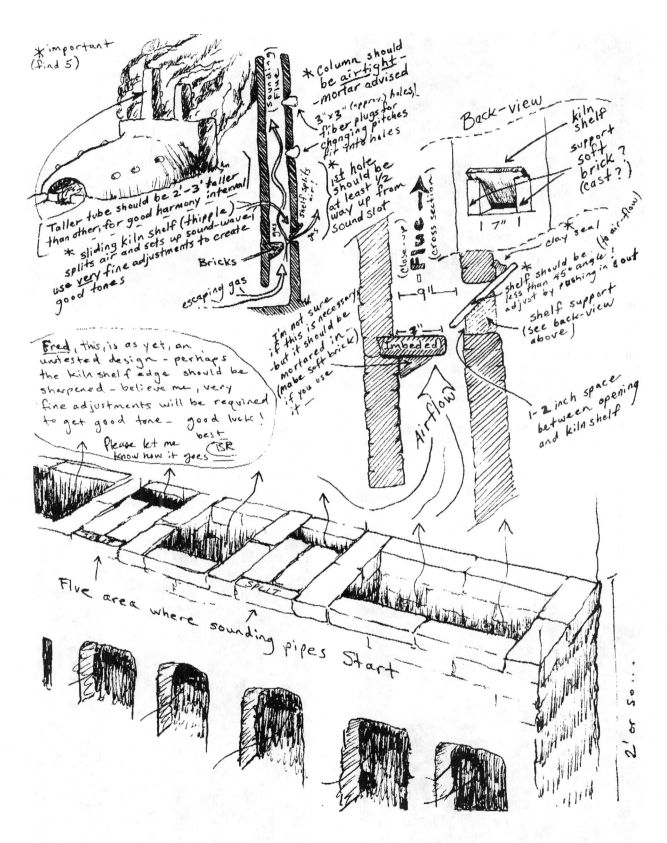

Fig. 10-2: *Letter from Brian to author on instrument.*

Fig. 10-6: *Thipple view.*

Fig. 10-8: *Firing the kiln.*

holes were placed at the recommended heights in the chimney. Someone found the two metal extension pipes we used to lengthen the flues. They were held in place with guide wires and their own weight (Fig. 10-7).

Firing the kiln initially was no problem (Fig. 10-8), but when the conference attendees and guests

arrived for the evening of music to hear me play "Happy Birthday Chester Nealie" on the world's hottest instrument, we had a bit of a problem. It didn't work. The two flues made a different, soft, musical hum. It was very noticeable if you stood next to the chimney and raised and lowered your ear past the thipple. Fergus Stewart, an accomplished potter and rock/country drummer, got his amplifier so all could hear. I admit we could not call the two hums a musical instrument, so I missed getting into *Rippley's*

Fig. 10-7: *Back of chimney finished.*

Fig. 10-9: *Playing the kiln.*

Believe it or Not, but it was a fun evening, a good kiln firing and added amusement for the conference people. Sometimes a failure can be successful, anyway, for it brought a lot of people together to watch the attempted challenge, joke and have fun at the attempt, and realize nothing attempted is nothing gained (Fig. 10-9). It can be done, however.

DOOR FRAME

Chuck Hindes, professor of ceramics at the University of Iowa, built a form to hold the entrance door bricks to the school's anagama (Fig. 10-11). It was a clever way to save and not loose the door bricks, to save time and make the job of bricking up the door so much easier.

HANGING DOOR

Carol and Arthur Rosser, of Dalrymple Heights in Queensland, Australia, have a novel solution to ease the loading and building up the door on their anagama tube-style kiln. They suspended two sectional arch forms made from bent pipe to conform to the kiln's cross-sectional chamber shape, giving them the rigid frame to line with a high-temperature fiber blanket. The lid is lightweight and strong and allows for ample access to the kiln for stacking (Fig. 10-12 and 13).

RIVER OF FIRE

Australian potter Ian Jones, who works outside of Canberra, uses the connection flue channel between the end of the anagama tube-style kiln and the chimney as a passive air damper. It is a simple matter to open the channel by lifting up the shelving on top (Fig. 10-14 and 15). The flame hugs the bottom of the channel as it races into the tall chimney with the cold air riding on top. Ian calls it the "river of fire." I used this idea in the Brockway fastfire as a perfect cooking stove to feed the stokers during and after the firing.

SOLDNER RAKU KILN

Soldner's Quonset hut raku kiln has a rollaway chamber that slides over the ware platform and the two side firebox channels (Fig. 10-16 and 17). The abutment

Fig. 10-11: *Door form for door bricks.*

Fig. 10-12: *Hanging door closed.*

Fig. 10-13: *Hanging door open.*

Fig. 10-14: *Back of tube.*

Fig. 10-15: *"River of fire."*

wall contains two side-fire burner ports 4 1/2" tall by 4" wide at the floor level that align with the side firebox channels, which are on each side of the ware platform. The naturally bent sheet metal is attached to the floor plate angle iron mounting the wheels that run in an inverted angle iron track (Fig. 10-18). Kaowool blanket lines the bent sheet-metal form and the back wall panel. A 2" blanket or 1" blanket doubled up can be used. Kaowool B, Cerawool, or Kaowool having a continuous use limit of 1,800°F and in the case of Kaowool of 2,300°F can be used. An exit flue involves nothing more than cracking open the rollaway chamber.

Paul Soldner's ideas are well known around the world. The Soldner mixer and the Soldner potters wheel (now handled by ART) are a few. His work in clay, especially raku and low-fire salt, also stands out. His intuitive, common-sense ideas are simply executed, which means they are well engineered and

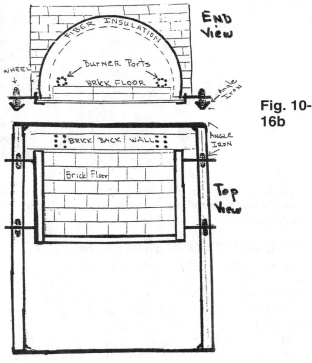

Fig. 10-16b

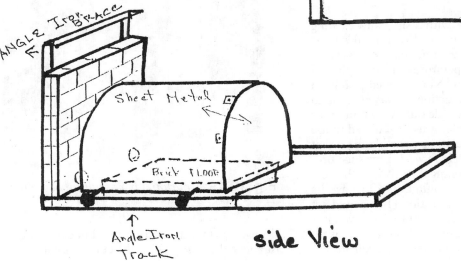

Fig. 10-16: *Soldners illustration of raku kiln.*

Fig. 10-17: *View of raku kiln.*

Fig. 10-18: *Wheel detail.*

practical for all to use. In the case of this raku kiln, his design is easy to build just by looking at the drawing and pictures.

CHARLOTTENBORG SCULPTURE KILN

Improvising a kiln structure around a ceramic sculpture piece is challenging, especially when it must be completed at a precise time. This was the case when I helped Nina Hole of Denmark fire her Charlottenborg ceramic sculpture in Copenhagen in October of 1998 (Fig. 10-19).

The obvious problem with using any existing ceramic sculpture is finding a way to turn the basic sculptural form into a kiln volume that can be evenly fired to a reasonable temperature for strength and durability. In the sculpture Nina created using an open-weave clay wall construction, it was possible to fire the sculpture from the inside out. After numerous faxes and conversations, a plan was formulated to use fast-fire fireboxes incorporated into the platform that the sculpture was built on. There were three such fireboxes with the inlet flue opening directly into the bottom of the sculpture. Each volume had to have its own firebox. The tall, vertical section (14') would act as the chimney for the whole sculpture. However, it is difficult to fire a straight chimney because there is no restrictive volume to act as the heat reservoir. In the

Fig. 10-19: *Charlottenborg sculpture by Nina Hole.*

14' tower form, a restriction was built into the piece just above the point where the curved second volume joined the tower at its lowest point. The restricted opening, or exit flue opening, was placed to the inside of the tower thus forcing the draft to the inside of the form (Fig. 10-20). The curved, joining form had a restrictive exit flue into the chimney tower just above the tower restriction. This created the bottom 2/3 of the sculpture into volume area necessary to build temperature.

The kiln shell would be constructed using Kao-wool blanket, 36" wide and 1" thick. Steel reinforcing mesh was cut into strips and wired together to form an acute angle, then placed at each corner, running up the full height of the sculpture. The object was to keep

Fig. 10-20: *Restricting shelf placement.*

Fig. 10-22: *Finished wrapping.*

Fig. 10-21: *Wrapping sculpture.*

Fig. 10-23: *Sculpture at temperature.*

the fiber blanket away from the walls as much as possible so the heat circulation could penetrate through the wall and along the outside as well as inside. Fiber blanket strips were cut to a length to cover half of the length of the sculpture. Chicken wire was bent around the ends of the blanket and secured by using wire and cut squares of sheet metal. The sheet metal squares kept the wire from pulling through the fiber blanket. When all the lengths were cut and secured with chicken wire, the sculpture was wrapped starting from the bottom (Fig. 10-21). The matching blanket ends were sewn together with a single wire (pull wire), interlocking the two halves together from bottom to the top. On top of the last side (seventh) row, a flat piece with a 4" by 5" chimney exit flue hole was placed over to form a flat roof for the kiln (Fig. 10-22).

Once the kiln was to temperature and ready to unwrap (Fig. 10-23), the pull wire connecting the ends of each row was pulled down, freeing the sides to fall away. Unwrapping the sculpture took seconds as each row fell away, leaving a glowing, sparkling sculpture (Fig. 10-24 & 25).

Nina Hole's Charlottenborg sculpture was built, dried out, fired in the rain and opened precisely at 9 p.m. during "Cultural Night" in Copenhagen before a huge crowd that applauded during the unwrapping.

Fig. 10-25: *Glowing sculpture.*

SLOT EXIT FLUE/CHIMNEY SWINGING DOOR

A key step in designing a two-car downward draft shuttle kiln was to incorporate the exit flue and chimney within the back swinging door frame work. An example of this style of kiln is the Port-o-kiln of Dandenong, Victoria, Australia (Fig. 10-26). The light weight of IFB refractories and ceramic fiber blanket

Fig. 10-24: *Unwrapping.*

Fig. 10-26: *Port-o-kiln shuttle kiln.*

Fig. 10-27: *Door exit flue.*

and boards has made this construction possible and very simple. A slot exit flue is used in the door. The flue is normally a long and very narrow space positioned at the bottom of the door, bisecting the collection channel under the bottom shelf setting on the car platform. Between 2/3 and 3/4 of the slot is below the floor level (Fig. 10-27). A slot exit flue is sized according to the rules for inlet and exit flue areas, with a rowlock brick as the given height (4 1/2") of the slot in most kilns up to 100 cu. ft. The slot exit flue is channeled through the door and into the slot chimney flue (of the same size), which runs up to the top of the door at the top of the kiln (Fig. 10-28). A top damper is placed at this point. A collection hood is placed over the slot chimney to vent the exhaust gas up and out of the kiln room or shed. When using forced-air gas (T.A.) burners or high-pressure gas venturi burners, the chimney normally goes to the top of the kiln and stops. A collection hood continues the venting of the kiln to the outside.

A CAST WOOD-FIRED SALT KILN

Suvira McDonald is an inspired master student who attended Claysculpt 1995, saw the Gulgong racer and attended my master class at the National Ceramic Conference in Canberra, Australia. She returned to Southern Cross University (Australia) and began her masters kiln project under Professor Tony Nankervis. Suvira decided to build a groundhog derivative kiln based on the Gulgong racer and a groundhog derivative I built in Canberra. The Kiln was for multi-purpose use, including salting. (Fig. 10-29).

What made this kiln interesting was that she used castables for the entire hot face surface of the kiln (Fig. 10-30). The perimeter wall was cast with Pyro-

Fig. 10-28: *Slot exit flue channel and chimney built into door.*

Fig. 10-29: *McDonald kiln.*

CROSS SECTIONS

1st Cross Section

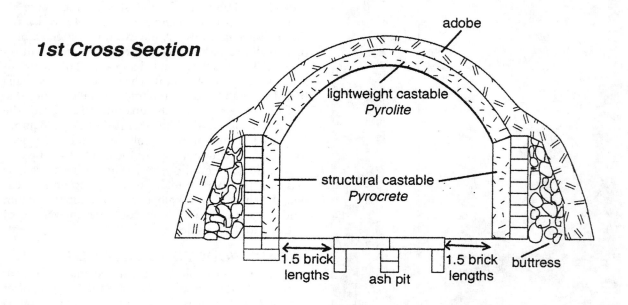

adobe

lightweight castable
Pyrolite

structural castable
Pyrocrete

1.5 brick
lengths

ash pit

1.5 brick
lengths

buttress

2nd Cross Section

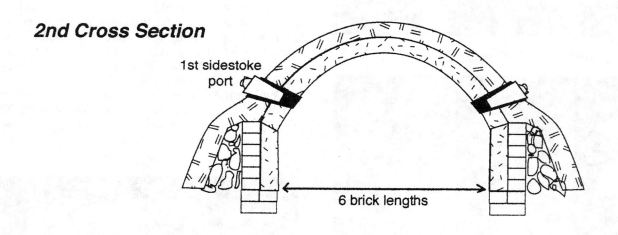

1st sidestoke
port

6 brick lengths

3rd Cross Section

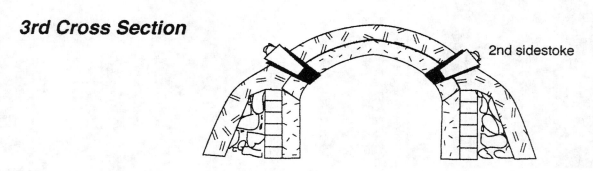

2nd sidestoke

Fig. 10-30: *Illustration of wall sections. Figures provided by Suvira McDonald.*

crete, a heavy-duty industrial castable used for load-bearing vertical walls, and Pyrolite 135, a lightweight castable suitable for crowns and arches. Both products are made by FOSECO, an Australian refractory company.

Since the ground was extremely difficult to excavate, the kiln was built at ground level, which gives the kiln an un-groundhog look. Starting from the lowest point, the ash pits, the perimeter foundations, firebox, and ware platform were constructed using fill material.

Once the wall construction began, the back-up brick wall was laid and buttressed. The cross sections illustrate the front firebox section, second and third side stoke hole sections and the exit flues. By funneling the kiln's interior shape into the exit flue back wall and into a normal style chimney, the kiln took on the appearance of a Far East tear drop kiln. Stainless steel tie pins were used to anchor the cast wall to the back-up brick and buttress walls. The ties were taped to give expansion room for the tie after the tape burned away and spaced five bricks apart in every other row. The cast walls and crown were approximately 4 1/2"-plus in thickness. The walls and crown were cast following the same procedures as discussed in previous chapters. An adobe capping mix was used over the whole kiln form.

Since this was a masters project at a university, there were concerns about toxic emissions from salt glazing in the kiln, mainly chlorine, hydrogen chloride and the normal carbon monoxide that could affect the local environment. Suvira's solution was to build a scrubbing apparatus on the chimney, until her research lead to two articles that concluded that no chloride and no HCl was detected. Ammonia and nitrous fumes were also absent in the white cloud produced from salting a salt kiln.[1] A second article concluded that the "amount of pollution directly attributable to sodium source in a kiln is negligible. Sodium chloride introduced into a stoneware temperature kiln results largely in sodium chloride being emitted. Chlorine gas is not produced and hydrochloric acid gas in significant or dangerous amounts is not an emission from a sodium chloride vapor kiln at stoneware temperatures." [2]

Therefore, based on these facts, the scrubbing apparatus was scrubbed. For years I have thought the white cloud was mainly steam, but I have not the scientific knowledge to support my thoughts.

A few of the conclusions reached by McDonald from her project that apply here are: (1) Packing or stacking the kiln can affect firing time and performance – "A loosely packed kiln resulted in a more expedient firing." (2) Maintaining the proper ember bed in the firebox affects the even distribution of heat. (3) Secondary air supply below grate, at grate and above grate are extremely important for kiln performance at the top temperatures (the control of air supply to maintain reduction or oxidation and to control the firing is essential for a good kiln design. See Chapter 8 — *Design for Wood Kiln Firebox*, rule No. 6). (4) The performance of Pyrolite 135 appears to be inadequate for the higher Cone 12 prolonged firings with or without the introduction of salt.

For a firing schedule of this kiln, refer to the Appendix — Typical firing McDonald project kiln.

FUTURISTIC KILNS?

Futuristic kiln designs will depend on how experimental, courageous and creative the new kiln designers are willing to be. My development of cross-directional drafting in kilns has opened up a new configuration of kilns. The most designs are the more architectural forms that lend themselves to sculptural compositions. Why does a kiln have to look like a kiln? It doesn't, of course, if it can still function as a kiln. Kilns by themselves could be a site sculpture. I can imagine some day where city parks could have a site specific kiln that functions once a year to raise money for public art projects and the rest of the year as a habitat/sculpture. Why does a kiln yard have to look so messy or so junky? Wouldn't it be nice to see a kiln yard that looks more like a sculpture garden? The illustrated photographs are of the courtyard and kiln yard at the International Ceramic Studio in Kecskemet, Hungary (Fig. 10-31 and 32). Although the kilns are traditional in style, the incorporation of the covering tile roof, lawn and sculptures by previous participants make the area seem like something other than a kiln yard.

Fig. 10-31: *Kecskemet court yard/kiln yard.*

1."Something in the Air" by P. Meanley, and Byers, *Ceramic Review*, 157, 1996, p.16.
2."Salt and the Atmosphere" by G. Stengel, *Ceramics Technical*, No. 7, Nov. 1998, p.8.

Fig. 10-34: *Catholic church in Hungary.*

Fig. 10-32: *Kecskemet courtyard/kiln yard.*

My fascination for expanding the look of kilns, buildings and sculptures has become very important to me. Every time I see architectural structures, like the famous pueblo style church outside of Taos, New Mexico (Fig. 10-33), and a Catholic church on the road between Kecskemet and Pecs in Hungary (Fig. 10-34), I imagine them as possible kiln designs. These two examples lend themselves to becoming a kiln and I shall use their inspiration to create my next kiln

building project. The fascination is in how to build them, how to fire them, and how to solve the problems to make them work.

One possible method of initiating a new kiln design is to scribble a five-second sketch and then turn it into a kiln. I have thought this would be a good class project because it would dispel the notion that kiln designs have to be tied to strict formal rules. It could also loosen up the creativity of the class. The instructor would then have to lead the class through the principles of kiln design, formulate and follow the building techniques required and then develop the firing system to fit the scribble and make it work.

It is not exactly a scribble, but Fig. 10-35 is a drawing by Sten Lykke Madsen, a ceramic artist at Royal Copenhagen Porcelain Factory. It depicts his interpretation of future Skaelskor church style kilns.

Sten participated in the building and initial firing of the church kiln in August of 1998. His humorous renditions of the cross-drafting style kilns exhibit a freedom that serious kiln builders and designers have a hard time acknowledging, much less exhibiting themselves.

Creating kiln sculptures that are built and fired on site and have

Fig. 10-33: *Taos church.*

Fig. 10-35: *Sten Madsen drawing.*

Fig. 10-36: *Olsen drawing.*

a dual purpose will become my main challenge over the next few years. So will creating specialty kilns with unusual shapes and innovative firing systems. Fig. 10-36 shows an anagama derivative with some styling, unusual curves and interior chamber shapes that direct flame patterns through undulating roof channels. The white and shaded areas would be colored adobe capping mix. In the same mode, a hill-climbing sculpture idea by Richard White uses my cross-directional draft with a figure form coupling the two tubes together with the fir-

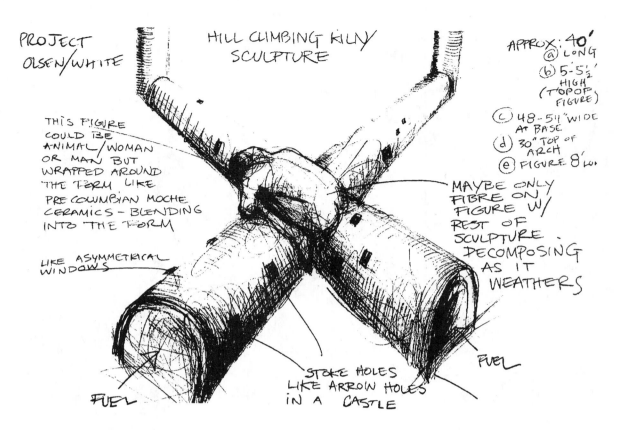

Fig. 10-37: *Richard White drawing.*

ezone beneath the figure (Fig. 10-37). Using architectural forms, specifically the Taos Church, a groundhog derivative-style kiln could be constructed, perhaps in the manner of Fig. 10-38. The structure would include a 600-cubic-foot tri-directional kiln with a dome and four separate chimneys. I would like the exit flue channels buried under the ground and set apart from the dome as isolated cylinder forms.

Figure 10-39 is one of my more radical kiln designs — and one that would be extremely hard to construct. A circle or donut chimney contains separate chimney flues on each side of the donut. The two chamber forms exit into the separated donut but exit at the top in

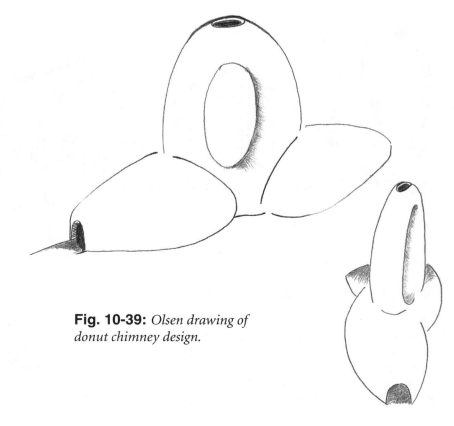

Fig. 10-39: *Olsen drawing of donut chimney design.*

one larger opening. Each chamber would contain about 100 cu. ft. of stacking space with the donut chimney system standing 14' tall. It would be possible to fire each chamber simultaneously. I would envision this kiln being built near a university ceramic department or in a city park. The kiln design reminds me of the year 2000 — two chambers connected by a big zero.

Approaching kiln designing as a sculptural statement or composition may expand the way we all perceive kilns and the possibilities that are within reach to send kilns into the new century.

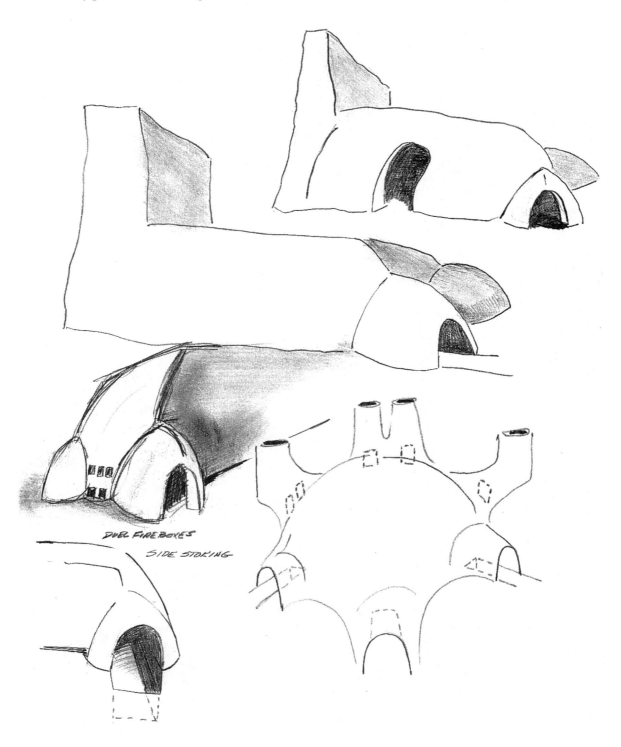

DUEL FIREBOXES

SIDE STOKING

Fig. 10-38: *Olsen drawing.*

APPENDIX

ESTIMATING DATA

The refractory industry has established tabulated brick combination tables that simplify the estimating of brick types and quantities required to construct a kiln. This section is a compendium of data relating to kiln building and design. Each revevant table to thekiln you are building should be studied carefully. Knowing what information is included and where it can be applied can save both time and unnecessary expense.

One square foot of brickwork requires the following number of 9" brick in the 2 1/2" and 3" series.

thickness of wall	9" x 4 1/2" x 2 1/2"	9" x 4 1/2" x 3"
2 1/2"	3.6	
3"		3.6
4 1/2"	6.4	5.3
4 1/2"	7.7 (headers every 5th course)	
7 1/2"	10.8	
9"	12.8	10.7
9"	14.1 (headers every 5th course)	
13 1/2"	19.2	16.0
13 1/2"	20.5 (headers every 5th course)	

One cubic foot of brickwork requires seventeen 9" straights in the 2 1/2" series and fourteen 9" in the 3" series.

One standard 9" firebrick (2 1/2" series) weighs approximately 7.6-8.4 pounds.

One cubic foot of firebrick weighs approximately 130-140 lbs.

One cubic foot of silica brick weighs 105-120 lbs.

One thousand straight 9" bricks in the 2 1/2" series, closely stacked, occupy 58.6 CF and the 3" series occupies 70.3 CF.

common brick—100	granite or limestone—165
fire clay—85	gypsum—143
loam dry loose—76	sandstone—144
loam packed—95	pumice stone—57
loam soft-loose mud—108	quartz—165
loam dense mud—125	shales—162
sand dry and loose—100	salt (course)—45
sand dry and packed—110	slate (american)—175
sand wet and packed—130	pine wood—25 to 45
gravel packed—118	maple—49
chalk—145	oak—50 to 59

Plastic firebrick weighs approximately 130 lbs./CF. Standard 100-lb. cartons are 3/4 CF volume.

300-400 lb. of mortar are required to lay 1000 firebricks.

Weights of various materials, pounds per cubic foot average, may be of interest to the potter who has to dig and haul the materials to the pottery;

In establishing the proper firebrick to use in kiln construction, Table A-1 will be helpful.

CALCULATING ARCH ELEMENTS

S = span of arch
T = thickness of arch
H = rise of arch
R = outside radius
r = inside radius
I = inner arc of arch
L = outer arc of arch
O = included angle of arch

$$r = \frac{S^2 + 4H^2}{8H} \qquad H = r - \frac{1}{2}\sqrt{4r^2 - S^2}$$

$$L = \frac{2\Pi \cdot R\Theta}{360} \qquad R = r + T$$

$$l = \frac{2\Pi \cdot r\Theta}{360} \qquad S = 2\sqrt{H[2(r - R)]} \text{ or } 2r \cdot \sin \frac{1}{2}\Theta$$

Pi (Π) = 3.1416
Circle Circumference = Π x d (diameter)

Number of bricks in L =

$$\frac{L}{2\ 1/2" \text{ or } 3\ 1/2"} \text{ (depending upon series)}$$

Total taper of bricks = L - 1

$$\text{number of tapered bricks required} = \frac{\text{taper of bricks}}{\text{of single bricks}}$$

Spacing of tapered bricks (in between straights) =

$$\frac{\text{number of bricks in L}}{\text{number of tapered bricks}}$$

The established arches will meet almost all design requirements for any given type of kiln in any size. The only decision to make in selecting the type of brick (arch, wedge, or key).

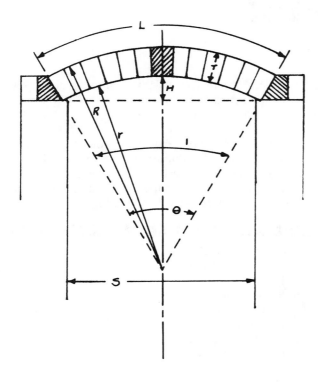

Fig. A-1
Arch element.

Arch thickness. The arch thickness depends greatly on the type of brick used, dense or insulating, and the span to be covered. One can choose from 4 1/2", 6 3/4", or 9" and over.

Arch rise. The minimum rise for an arch should be 1 1/2" per foot of span, which can be made by using a standard 9" featheredge of the 2 1/2" series, which is most commonly used. A rise of 1.608" per foot of span results in an included angle (0) of 60°, with the inside

radius equal to the span. For wide spans, it is considered good practice to have a rise of at least 1 3/4" per foot of span. A rise of 2.302" (25/16") is obtained when standard 48° side and end skew of the 2 1/2" and 3" series are used. A rise of 3" per foot of span will be sturdier than one with less rise. I recommend used as great a rise as possible within the limits. I have used, as do most chamber kiln builders, a rise of 4" to 6" per foot of span with a span of 4 feet to 8 feet.

Type of bricks. Arch thickness and the type of brick used are dependent upon each other. For instance, and arch of 4 1/2" thickness would use arch brick or a combination of arch and straight bricks. An arch of 6 3/4" thickness would use large 9" arch bricks or a combination of large 9" arch and large 9" straight bricks. An arch of 9" thickness would use wedge brick or a combination of wedge and straight bricks. Key brick, or a combination of key and straight bricks, is possible, but because of the load being on the narrow face of the brick, it is not recommended. For arches over 9" thick, 13 1/2" wedge bricks are used.

When constructing arches, it is best to use the 4 1/2" or the 9" series arch bricks with one of the four established rises (1 1/2", 1.608", 2", 2.302" per foot of span) with the corresponding skewbacks. Otherwise, for any given span and rise the formulas can be used to calculate the number of bricks required. The problem is to match up the bricks to the calculations or actually cut the bricks to size. It is wiser and easier to use the standard arches in Tables A-2 through A-7.

ROTARY KILN BLOCK TABLES

In Tables A-8 and A-9, the liner size indicates the inside and outside diameter of the circle, in inches. Thus, a 9" x 9" x 4" (72-90) liner will lay up to form a circle with a 72" inside diameter and a 90" outside diameter. The lining formed in this manner will be 9" thick and three circles or rows will be required for each foot of kiln length.

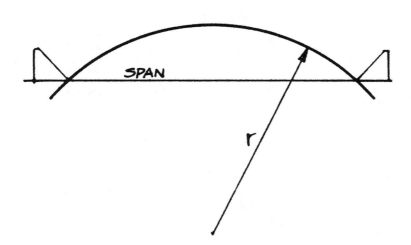

Fig. A-2
Using feather-edge skewback gives 1 1/2" ft. of span rise.

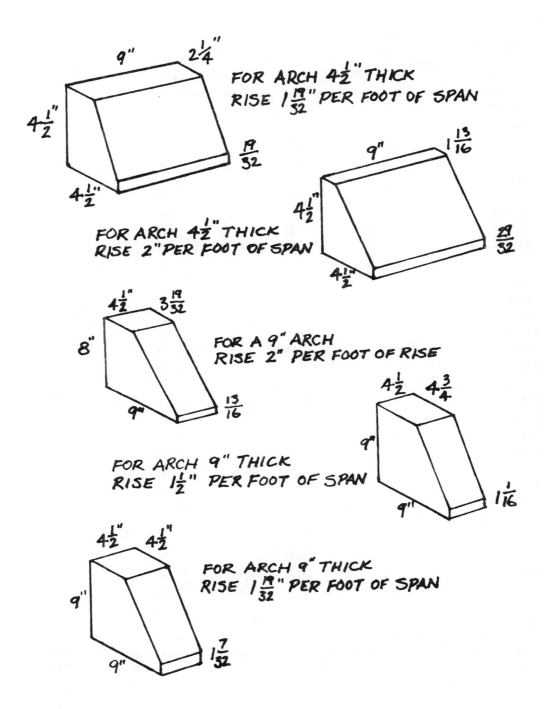

Fig. A-3
Special skewbacks for arches with an included angle of 60°.

TEMPERATURE COLOR GUIDE FOR KILNS

There are numerous times when neither pyrometric cones nor a pyrometer are available. In this situation, the potter must rely on color to judge temperature. When the right color is reached, a simple test for glaze maturity can be used. This is done by merely inserting a clothes hanger through a spy hole and observing its reflection off the pots. A mature glaze will mirror a glassy reflection. (See Table A-10).

Table A–1
Melting Points in International Temperature Scale

	°C	°F
Aluminum	660	1220
Antimony	631	1168
Cadmium	321	610
Calcium	850	1562
Chromium	1800	3272
Cobalt	1490	2714
Copper	1038	1981
Gold	1063	1945
Iron (pure)	1539	2802
Lead	327	621
Magnesium	650	1202
Manganese	1260	2300
Mercury	− 39	− 38
Molybdenum	2625	4757
Nickel	1455	2651
Palladium	1554	2829
Yellow phosphorus	44	111
Platinum	1774	3225
Potassium	63	145
Silicon	1430	2606
Silver	961	1762
Sodium	98	208
Tin	232	450
Titanium	1820	3308
Tungsten	3410	6170
Vanadium	1735	3155
Zinc	420	788
Zirconium	1750	3182

Table A–2
Values for Rises Per Foot of Span

Rise in Inches Per Foot of Span	Inside Radius (r)*	Central Angle (Θ) Degrees	Part of Circle
1″	1.54167S	37°50.9′	0.10514
1¼″	1.25203S	47° 4.4′	0.13076
1½″	1.06250S	56° 8.7′	0.15596
1.608″	1.00000S	60°00.0′	0.16667
1¾″	0.93006S	65° 2.5′	0.18067
2″	0.83333S	73°44.4′	0.20483
2¼″	0.76042S	82°13.4′	0.22840

Table A–2, continued

Rise in Inches Per Foot of Span	Inside Radius (r)*	Central Angle (Θ)	
		Degrees	Part of Circle
2.302″	0.74742S	83°58.5′	0.23326
2½″	0.70417S	90°28.8′	0.25133
2¾″	0.66004S	98°29.7′	0.27360
3″	0.62500S	106°15.6′	0.29517

*To find (r), multiply the value for the inside radius by the span.

Table A–3
Estimating Firebrick Arches

4½″ ARCH; RISE = 1½″ PER FOOT OF SPAN

STANDARD 9″ FEATHEREDGE USED FOR SKEW

Span	Rise	Inside Radius	Bricks Required per Course			Total
			No. 2 Arch 9 × 4½ × (2½–1¾)	No. 1 Arch 9 × 4½ × (2½–2⅛)	Straight 9 × 4½ × 2½	
1′ 0″	1½″	1′ 0¾″	5	2	—	7
1′ 1″	1⅝″	1′ 1¹³⁄₁₆″	5	3	—	8
1′ 2″	1¾″	1′ 2⅞″	4	4	—	8
1′ 3″	1⅞″	1′ 3¹⁵⁄₁₆″	4	4	—	8
1′ 4″	2″	1′ 5″	4	5	—	9
1′ 5″	2⅛″	1′ 6¹⁄₁₆″	3	6	—	9
1′ 6″	2¼″	1′ 7⅛″	3	7	—	10
1′ 7″	2⅜″	1′ 8³⁄₁₆″	2	8	—	10
1′ 8″	2½″	1′ 9¼″	2	8	—	10
1′ 9″	2⅝″	1′10⁵⁄₁₆″	1	10	—	11
1′10″	2¾″	1′11⅜″	1	10	—	11
1′11″	2⅞″	2′ 0⁷⁄₁₆″	1	11	—	12
2′ 0″	3″	2′ 1½″	—	12	—	12
2′ 6″	3¾″	2′ 7⅞″	—	12	3	15
3′ 0″	4½″	3′ 2¼″	—	12	5	17
3′ 6″	5¼″	3′ 8⅝″	—	12	8	20
4′ 0″	6″	4′ 3″	—	12	10	22
4′ 6″	6¾″	4′ 9⅜″	—	12	13	25
5′ 0″	7½″	5′ 3¾″	—	12	15	27
5′ 6″	8¼″	5′10⅛″	—	12	18	30
6′ 0″	9″	6′ 4½″	—	12	20	32

4½″ ARCH; RISE = 1.608″ PER FOOT OF SPAN

RADIUS = SPAN; CENTRAL ANGLE = 60°

1′ 0″	1¹⁹⁄₃₂″	1′ 0″	6	1	—	7
1′ 1″	1¾″	1′ 1″	6	2	—	8

Table A–3, continued

4½" ARCH; RISE = 1.608" PER FOOT OF SPAN

RADIUS = SPAN; CENTRAL ANGLE = 60°

Span	Rise	Inside Radius	Bricks Required per Course			Total
			No. 2 Arch $9 \times 4½ \times (2½–1¾)$	No. 1 Arch $9 \times 4½ \times (2½–2⅛)$	Straight $9 \times 4½ \times 2½$	
1' 2"	1⅞"	1' 2"	5	3	—	8
1' 3"	2"	1' 3"	5	4	—	9
1' 4"	2⁵⁄₃₂"	1' 4"	4	5	—	9
1' 5"	2⁹⁄₃₂"	1' 5"	4	7	—	9
1' 6"	2¹³⁄₃₂"	1' 6"	3	7	—	10
1' 7"	2⁷⁄₃₂"	1' 7"	3	7	—	10
1' 8"	2¹¹⁄₁₆"	1' 8"	3	8	—	11
1' 9"	2¹³⁄₁₆"	1' 9"	2	9	—	11
1'10"	2¹⁵⁄₁₆"	1'10"	2	10	—	12
1'11"	3³⁄₃₂"	1'11"	1	11	—	12
2' 0"	3⁷⁄₃₂"	2' 0"	1	11	—	12
2' 1"	3¹¹⁄₃₂"	2' 1"	1	12	—	13
2' 2"	3¹⁵⁄₃₂"	2' 2"	—	13	—	13
2' 3"	3⅝"	2' 3"	—	13	1	14
2' 6"	4¹⁄₃₂"	2' 6"	—	13	2	15
3' 0"	4¹³⁄₁₆"	3' 0"	—	13	4	17
3' 6"	5⅝"	3' 6"	—	13	7	20
4' 0"	6⁷⁄₁₆"	4' 0"	—	13	9	22
4' 6"	7¼"	4' 6"	—	13	12	25
5' 0"	8¹⁄₃₂"	5' 0"	—	13	14	27
5' 6"	8²⁷⁄₃₂"	5' 6"	—	13	17	30
6' 0"	9²¹⁄₃₂"	6' 0"	—	13	19	32

4½" ARCH; RISE = 2" PER FOOT OF SPAN

Span	Rise	Inside Radius	No. 2 Arch	No. 1 Arch	Straight	Total
1' 0"	2"	10"	8	—	—	8
1' 1"	2⁵⁄₃₂"	10²⁷⁄₃₂"	8	—	—	8
1' 2"	2¹¹⁄₃₂"	11²¹⁄₃₂"	7	2	—	9
1' 3"	2½"	1' 0½"	7	2	—	9
1' 4"	2²¹⁄₃₂"	1' 1¹¹⁄₃₂"	7	3	—	10
1' 5"	2²⁷⁄₃₂"	1' 2⁵⁄₃₂"	6	4	—	10
1' 6"	3"	1' 3"	5	5	—	10
1' 7"	3⁵⁄₃₂"	1' 3²⁷⁄₃₂"	5	6	—	11
1' 8"	3¹¹⁄₃₂"	1' 4²¹⁄₃₂"	5	6	—	11
1' 9"	3½"	1' 5½"	4	8	—	12
1'10"	3²¹⁄₃₂"	1' 6¹¹⁄₃₂"	4	8	—	12
1'11"	3²⁷⁄₃₂"	1' 7⁵⁄₃₂"	4	9	—	13
2' 0"	4"	1' 8"	3	10	—	13
2' 1"	4⁵⁄₃₂"	1' 8²⁷⁄₃₂"	2	11	—	13
2' 2"	4¹¹⁄₃₂"	1' 9²¹⁄₃₂"	2	12	—	14
2' 3"	4½"	1'10½"	2	12	—	14
2' 4"	4²¹⁄₃₂"	1'11¹¹⁄₃₂"	1	14	—	15

Table A–3, continued

4½″ ARCH; RISE = 2″ PER FOOT OF SPAN

Span	Rise	Inside Radius	Bricks Required per Course			Total
			No. 2 Arch $9 \times 4\frac{1}{2} \times (2\frac{1}{2}-1\frac{3}{4})$	No. 1 Arch $9 \times 4\frac{1}{2} \times (2\frac{1}{2}-2\frac{1}{8})$	Straight $9 \times 4\frac{1}{2} \times 2\frac{1}{2}$	
2′ 5″	4²⁷⁄₃₂″	2′ 0⁵⁄₃₂″	1	14	—	15
2′ 6″	5″	2′ 1″	1	15	—	16
3′ 0″	6″	2′ 6″	—	16	2	18
3′ 6″	7″	2′11″	—	16	5	21
4′ 0″	8″	3′ 4″	—	16	7	23
4′ 6″	9″	3′ 9″	—	16	10	26
5′ 0″	10″	4′ 2″	—	16	12	28
5′ 6″	11″	4′ 7″	—	16	15	31
6′ 0″	12″	5′ 0″	—	16	18	34

4½″ ARCH; RISE = 2.302″ PER FOOT OF SPAN
STANDARD 9″ SIDESKEWS USED FOR SKEW

Span	Rise	Inside Radius	Bricks Required Per Course				Total
			No. 3 Arch $9 \times 4\frac{1}{2} \times (2\frac{1}{2}-1)$	No. 2 Arch $9 \times 4\frac{1}{2} \times (2\frac{1}{2}-1\frac{3}{4})$	No. 1 Arch $9 \times 4\frac{1}{2} \times (2\frac{1}{2}-2\frac{1}{8})$	Straight $9 \times 4\frac{1}{2} \times 2\frac{1}{2}$	
1′ 0″	2⁵⁄₁₆″	8³¹⁄₃₂″	1	7	—	—	8
1′ 1″	2½″	9²³⁄₃₂″	1	8	—	—	9
1′ 2″	2¹¹⁄₁₆″	10¹⁵⁄₃₂″	—	9	—	—	9
1′ 3″	2⅞″	11⁷⁄₃₂″	—	9	1	—	10
1′ 4″	3¹⁄₁₆″	11³¹⁄₃₂″	—	8	2	—	10
1′ 5″	3¼″	12²³⁄₃₂″	—	7	3	—	10
1′ 6″	3¹⁵⁄₃₂″	13¹⁵⁄₃₂″	—	7	4	—	11
1′ 7″	3²¹⁄₃₂″	14³⁄₁₆″	—	6	5	—	11
1′ 8″	3²⁷⁄₃₂″	14¹⁵⁄₁₆″	—	6	6	—	12
1′ 9″	4¹⁄₃₂″	15¹¹⁄₁₆″	—	6	6	—	12
1′10″	4⁷⁄₃₂″	16⁷⁄₁₆″	—	6	7	—	13
1′11″	4¹³⁄₃₂″	17³⁄₁₆″	—	5	8	—	13
2′ 0″	4¹⁹⁄₃₂″	17¹⁵⁄₁₆″	—	5	9	—	14
2′ 1″	4²⁵⁄₃₂″	18¹¹⁄₁₆″	—	4	10	—	14
2′ 2″	5″	19⁷⁄₁₆″	—	3	11	—	14
2′ 3″	5³⁄₁₆″	30³⁄₁₆″	—	3	12	—	15
2′ 6″	5¾″	22⁷⁄₁₆″	—	2	14	—	16
2′ 9″	6¹¹⁄₃₂″	24²¹⁄₃₂″	—	—	17	—	17
3′ 0″	6²⁹⁄₃₂″	26²⁹⁄₃₂″	—	—	18	1	19
3′ 3″	7½″	29⁵⁄₃₂″	—	—	18	2	20
3′ 6″	8¹⁄₁₆″	31¹³⁄₃₂″	—	—	18	3	21
3′ 9″	8⅝″	33⅝″	—	—	18	5	23
4′ 0″	9⁷⁄₃₂″	35⅞″	—	—	18	6	24

Table A–3, continued

4½″ ARCH; RISE = 2.302″ PER FOOT OF SPAN
STANDARD 9″ SIDESKEWS USED FOR SKEW

Span	Rise	Inside Radius	Bricks Required Per Course				Total
			No. 3 Arch 9 × 4½ × (2½–1)	No. 2 Arch 9 × 4½ × (2½–1¾)	No. 1 Arch 9 × 4½ × (2½–2⅛)	Straight 9 × 4½ × 2½	
4′ 3″	9²⁵⁄₃₂″	38⅛″	—	—	18	7	25
4′ 6″	10⅜″	40⅜″	—	—	18	9	27
4′ 9″	10¹⁵⁄₁₆″	42¹⁹⁄₃₂″	—	—	18	10	28
5′ 0″	11½″	44²⁷⁄₃₂″	—	—	18	11	29
5′ 3″	12¹⁄₁₆″	47³⁄₃₂″	—	—	18	13	31
5′ 6″	12²¹⁄₃₂″	49¹¹⁄₃₂″	—	—	18	14	32
5′ 9″	12¼″	51⁹⁄₁₆″	—	—	18	15	33
6′ 0″	13¹³⁄₁₆″	53¹³⁄₁₆″	—	—	18	17	35

9″ ARCH; RISE = 1½″ PER FOOT OF SPAN

Span	Rise	Inside Radius	Bricks Required per Course			Total
			No. 2 Wedge 9 × 4½ × (2½–1½)	No. 1 Wedge 9 × 4½ × (2½–1⅞)	Straight 9 × 4½ × 2½	
1′ 6″	2¼″	1′ 7⅛″	5	6	—	11
1′ 7″	2⅜″	1′ 8³⁄₁₆″	5	7	—	12
1′ 8″	2½″	1′ 9¼″	4	8	—	12
1′ 9″	2⅝″	1′10⁵⁄₁₆″	3	10	—	13
1′10″	2¾″	1′11⅜″	3	10	—	13
1′11″	2⅞″	2′ 0⁷⁄₁₆″	2	12	—	14
2′ 0″	3″	2′ 1½″	1	13	—	14
2′ 1″	3⅛″	2′ 2⁹⁄₁₆″	—	14	—	14
2′ 2″	3¼″	2′ 3⅝″	—	14	1	15
2′ 3″	3⅜″	2′ 4¹¹⁄₁₆″	—	14	1	15
2′ 6″	3¾″	2′ 7⅞″	—	14	2	16
3′ 0″	4½″	3′ 2¼″	—	14	5	19
3′ 6″	5¼″	3′ 8⅝″	—	14	7	21
4′ 0″	6″	4′ 3″	—	14	10	24
4′ 6″	6¾″	4′ 9⅜″	—	14	12	26
5′ 0″	7½″	5′ 3¾″	—	14	15	29
5′ 6″	8¼″	5′10⅛″	—	14	17	31
6′ 0″	9″	6′ 4½″	—	14	20	34
6′ 6″	9¾″	6′10⅞″	—	14	22	36
7′ 0″	10½″	7′ 5¼″	—	14	25	39

Table A–3, continued

9" ARCH; RISE = 1.608" PER FOOT OF SPAN
RADIUS = SPAN; CENTRAL ANGLE = 60"

Span	Rise	Inside Radius	Bricks Required per Course			Total
			No. 2 Wedge $9 \times 4\frac{1}{2} \times (2\frac{1}{2}-1\frac{1}{2})$	No. 1 Wedge $9 \times 4\frac{1}{2} \times (2\frac{1}{2}-1\frac{7}{8})$	Straight $9 \times 4\frac{1}{2} \times 2\frac{1}{2}$	
1' 6"	$2^{13}/_{32}$"	1' 6"	7	5	—	12
1' 7"	$2^{17}/_{32}$"	1' 7"	6	6	—	12
1' 8"	$2^{11}/_{16}$"	1' 8"	5	8	—	13
1' 9"	$2^{13}/_{16}$"	1' 9"	4	9	—	13
1'10"	$2^{15}/_{16}$"	1'10"	3	10	—	13
1'11"	$3^{3}/_{32}$"	1'11"	3	11	—	14
2' 0"	$3^{7}/_{32}$"	2' 0"	2	12	—	14
2' 1"	$3^{11}/_{32}$"	2' 1"	2	13	—	15
2' 2"	$3^{15}/_{32}$"	2' 2"	1	14	—	15
2' 3"	$3^{5}/_{8}$"	2' 3"	—	15	—	15
2' 6"	$4^{1}/_{32}$"	2' 6"	—	15	2	17
3' 0"	$4^{13}/_{16}$"	3' 0"	—	15	4	19
3' 6"	$5^{5}/_{8}$"	3' 6"	—	15	7	22
4' 0"	$6^{7}/_{16}$"	4' 0"	—	15	9	24
4' 6"	$7\frac{1}{4}$"	4' 6"	—	15	12	27
5' 0"	$8^{1}/_{32}$"	5' 0"	—	15	14	29
5' 6"	$8^{27}/_{32}$"	5' 6"	—	15	17	32
6' 0"	$9^{31}/_{32}$"	6' 0"	—	15	19	34
6' 6"	$10^{7}/_{16}$"	6' 6"	—	15	22	37
7' 0"	$11\frac{1}{4}$"	7' 0"	—	15	24	39

9" ARCH; RISE = 2" PER FOOT OF SPAN

Span	Rise	Inside Radius	No. 2 Wedge	No. 1 Wedge	Straight	Total
1' 6"	3"	1' 3"	11	2	—	13
1' 7"	$3^{5}/_{32}$"	1' $3^{27}/_{32}$"	10	3	—	13
1' 8"	$3^{11}/_{32}$"	1' $4^{21}/_{32}$"	9	5	—	14
1' 9"	$3\frac{1}{2}$"	1' $5\frac{1}{2}$"	8	6	—	14
1'10"	$3^{21}/_{32}$"	1' $6^{11}/_{32}$"	7	7	—	14
1'11"	$3^{27}/_{32}$"	1' $7^{5}/_{32}$"	7	8	—	15
2' 0"	4"	1' 8"	6	9	—	15
2' 1"	$4^{5}/_{32}$"	1' $8^{27}/_{32}$"	6	10	—	16
2' 2"	$4^{11}/_{32}$"	1' $9^{21}/_{32}$"	5	11	—	16
2' 3"	$4\frac{1}{2}$"	1'$10\frac{1}{2}$"	4	13	—	17
2' 4"	$4^{21}/_{32}$"	1'$11^{11}/_{32}$"	3	14	—	17
2' 5"	$4^{27}/_{32}$"	2' $0^{5}/_{32}$"	2	15	—	17
2' 6"	5"	2' 1"	2	16	—	18
2' 7"	$5^{5}/_{32}$"	2' $1^{27}/_{32}$"	1	17	—	18
2' 8"	$5^{11}/_{32}$"	2' $2^{21}/_{32}$"	1	18	—	19
2' 9"	$5\frac{1}{2}$"	2' $3\frac{1}{2}$"	—	19	—	19
3' 0"	6"	2' 6"	—	19	1	20
3' 6"	7"	2'11"	—	19	4	23

Table A–3, continued

9" ARCH; RISE = 2" PER FOOT OF SPAN

Span	Rise	Inside Radius	Bricks Required per Course			Total
			No. 2 Wedge $9 \times 4\frac{1}{2} \times (2\frac{1}{2}-1\frac{1}{2})$	No. 1 Wedge $9 \times 4\frac{1}{2} \times (2\frac{1}{2}-1\frac{7}{8})$	Straight $9 \times 4\frac{1}{2} \times 2\frac{1}{2}$	
4' 0"	8"	3' 4"	—	19	7	26
4' 6"	9"	3' 9"	—	19	9	28
5' 0"	10"	4' 2"	—	19	12	31
5' 6"	11"	4' 7"	—	19	14	33
6' 0"	12"	5' 0"	—	19	17	36
6' 6"	1' 1"	5' 5"	—	19	19	38
7' 0"	1' 2"	5'10"	—	19	22	41

9" ARCH; RISE = 2.302" PER FOOT OF SPAN STANDARD SIDESKEWS USED FOR SKEWS

Span	Rise	Inside Radius	No. 2 Wedge	No. 1 Wedge	Straight	Total
1' 6"	$3^{15}/_{32}$"	1' $1^{15}/_{32}$	14	—	—	14
1' 7"	$3^{21}/_{32}$"	1' $2^{3}/_{16}$"	13	1	—	14
1' 8"	$3^{27}/_{32}$"	1' $2^{15}/_{16}$"	12	2	—	14
1' 9"	$4^{1}/_{32}$"	1' $3^{11}/_{16}$"	11	4	—	15
1'10"	$4^{7}/_{32}$"	1' $4^{7}/_{16}$"	10	5	—	15
1'11"	$4^{13}/_{32}$"	1' $5^{3}/_{16}$"	10	6	—	16
2' 0"	$4^{19}/_{32}$"	1' $5^{15}/_{16}$"	9	7	—	16
2' 1"	$4^{25}/_{32}$"	1' $6^{11}/_{16}$"	9	8	—	17
2' 2"	5"	1' $7^{7}/_{16}$"	8	9	—	17
2' 3"	$5^{3}/_{16}$"	1' $8^{3}/_{16}$"	7	11	—	18
2' 4"	$5^{3}/_{8}$"	1' $8^{15}/_{16}$"	6	12	—	18
2' 5"	$5^{9}/_{16}$"	1' $9^{11}/_{16}$"	5	13	—	18
2' 6"	$5^{3}/_{4}$"	1'$10^{7}/_{16}$"	5	14	—	19
2' 7"	$5^{15}/_{16}$"	1'$11^{5}/_{32}$"	4	15	—	19
2' 8"	$6^{1}/_{8}$"	1'$11^{29}/_{32}$"	3	17	—	20
2' 9"	$6^{11}/_{32}$"	2' $0^{21}/_{32}$"	2	18	—	20
2'10"	$6^{17}/_{32}$"	2' $1^{13}/_{32}$"	2	19	—	21
2'11"	$6^{23}/_{32}$"	2' $2^{5}/_{32}$"	1	20	—	21
3' 0"	$6^{29}/_{32}$"	2' $2^{29}/_{32}$"	—	21	—	21
3' 6"	$8^{1}/_{16}$"	2' $7^{13}/_{32}$"	—	21	3	24
4' 0"	$9^{7}/_{32}$"	2'$11^{7}/_{8}$"	—	21	6	27
4' 6"	$10^{3}/_{8}$"	3' $4^{3}/_{8}$"	—	21	8	29
5' 0"	$11^{1}/_{2}$"	3' $8^{27}/_{32}$"	—	21	11	32
5' 6"	1' $0^{21}/_{32}$"	4' $1^{11}/_{32}$"	—	21	14	35
6' 0"	1' $1^{13}/_{16}$"	4' $5^{13}/_{16}$"	—	21	16	37
6' 6"	1' $2^{31}/_{32}$"	4'$10^{5}/_{16}$"	—	21	19	40
7' 0"	1' $4^{1}/_{8}$"	5' $2^{23}/_{32}$"	—	21	21	42

Table A–4
Number of 9″ × 4½″ × 2½″ Arch Bricks Required to Turn Circle

Diameter of Inside Brickwork	No. 3 Arch	No. 2 Arch	No. 1 Arch	Straight	Total
0′6″	19	—	—	—	19
0′7″	18	3	—	—	21
0′8″	17	5	—	—	22
0′9″	15	8	—	—	23
0′10″	14	10	—	—	24
0′11″	13	13	—	—	26
1′0″	12	15	—	—	27
1′1″	10	18	—	—	28
1′2″	9	20	—	—	29
1′3″	8	23	—	—	31
1′4″	7	25	—	—	32
1′5″	5	28	—	—	33
1′6″	4	30	—	—	34
1′7″	3	33	—	—	36
1′8″	2	35	—	—	37
1′9″	—	38	—	—	38
1′10″	—	36	3	—	39
1′11″	—	36	5	—	41
2′0″	—	34	8	—	42
2′1″	—	33	10	—	43
2′2″	—	31	13	—	44
2′3″	—	31	15	—	46
2′4″	—	29	18	—	47
2′5″	—	28	20	—	48
2′6″	—	26	23	—	49
2′7″	—	26	25	—	51
2′8″	—	24	28	—	52
2′9″	—	23	30	—	53
2′10″	—	21	33	—	54
2′11″	—	20	36	—	56
3′0″	—	19	38	—	57
3′1″	—	18	40	—	58
3′2″	—	16	43	—	59
3′3″	—	15	46	—	61
3′4″	—	14	48	—	62
3′5″	—	13	50	—	63
3′6″	—	11	53	—	64
3′7″	—	10	56	—	66
3′8″	—	9	58	—	67
3′9″	—	8	60	—	68
3′10″	—	7	63	—	70
3′11″	—	5	66	—	71
4′0″	—	4	68	—	72
4′1″	—	3	70	—	73
4′2″	—	2	73	—	75
4′3″	—	—	76	—	76

Table A—4, continued

Diameter of Inside Brickwork	No. 3 Arch	No. 2 Arch	No. 1 Arch	Straight	Total
4'6"	—	—	76	4	80
5'0"	—	—	76	11	87
5'6"	—	—	76	19	95
6'0"	—	—	76	26	102
6'6"	—	—	76	34	110
7'0"	—	—	76	41	117

This table may also be used for 13½ × 4½ × 2½ arch brick.

Table A—5
Number of 3-Inch Series Arch Bricks Required to Turn Circle (9″ × 4½″ × 3″ and 13½″ × 4½″ × 3″ arches)

Diameter of Inside Brickwork	No. 3 Arch	No. 2 Arch	No. 1 Arch	Total
1'6"	29	—	—	29
1'7"	28	2	—	30
1'8"	26	5	—	31
1'9"	25	7	—	32
1'10"	24	9	—	33
1'11"	23	11	—	34
2'0"	22	13	—	35
2'1"	21	15	—	36
2'2"	20	17	—	37
2'3"	19	19	—	38
2'4"	18	21	—	39
2'5"	17	23	—	40
2'6"	16	25	—	41
2'7"	15	27	—	42
2'8"	14	29	—	43
2'9"	13	31	—	44
2'10"	12	33	—	45
2'11"	10	36	—	46
3'0"	10	38	—	48
3'1"	9	40	—	49
3'2"	8	42	—	50
3'3"	7	44	—	51
3'4"	6	46	—	52
3'5"	5	48	—	53
3'6"	3	51	—	54
3'7"	2	53	—	55
3'8"	1	55	—	56
3'9"	—	57	—	57
3'10"	—	56	2	58
3'11"	—	55	4	59

Table A–5, continued

Diameter of Inside Brickwork	No. 3 Arch	No. 2 Arch	No. 1 Arch	Total
4'0"	—	54	6	60
4'1"	—	52	9	61
4'2"	—	51	11	62
4'3"	—	50	13	63
4'4"	—	49	15	64
4'5"	—	48	17	65
4'6"	—	47	19	66
4'7"	—	46	21	67
4'8"	—	45	23	68
4'9"	—	44	26	70
4'10"	—	43	28	71
4'11"	—	42	30	72
5'0"	—	41	32	73
5'1"	—	40	34	74
5'2"	—	39	36	75
5'3"	—	38	38	76
5'4"	—	37	40	77
5'5"	—	36	42	78
5'6"	—	35	44	79
5'7"	—	34	46	80
5'8"	—	33	48	81
5'9"	—	32	50	82
5'10"	—	30	53	83
5'11"	—	29	55	84
6'0"	—	28	57	85
6'1"	—	27	59	86
6'2"	—	26	61	87
6'3"	—	25	63	88
6'4"	—	24	65	89
6'5"	—	23	67	90
6'6"	—	22	70	92
6'7"	—	21	72	93
6'8"	—	20	74	94
6'9"	—	19	76	95
6'10"	—	18	78	96
6'11"	—	17	80	97

Table A–6
Number of 9" × 4½" × 2½" Wedge Bricks Required to Turn Circle

Diameter of Inside Brickwork	No. 2 Wedge	No. 1 Wedge	Straight	Total
2'3"	57	—	—	57
2'4"	55	3	—	58
2'5"	52	7	—	59

Table A–6, continued

Diameter of Inside Brickwork	No. 2 Wedge	No. 1 Wedge	Straight	Total
2'6"	51	10	—	61
2'7"	48	14	—	62
2'8"	46	17	—	63
2'9"	44	20	—	64
2'10"	42	24	—	66
2'11"	40	27	—	67
3'0"	38	30	—	68
3'1"	36	34	—	70
3'2"	34	37	—	71
3'3"	32	40	—	72
3'4"	29	44	—	73
3'5"	28	47	—	75
3'6"	25	51	—	76
3'7"	23	54	—	77
3'8"	21	57	—	78
3'9"	19	61	—	80
3'10"	17	64	—	81
3'11"	15	67	—	82
4'0"	13	70	—	83
4'1"	11	74	—	85
4'2"	9	77	—	86
4'3"	6	81	—	87
4'4"	4	84	—	88
4'5"	2	88	—	90
4'6"	—	91	—	91
5'0"	—	91	7	98
5'6"	—	91	15	106
6'0"	—	91	22	113
6'6"	—	91	30	121
7'0"	—	91	38	129

This table may also be used for 9 × 6¾ × 2½ and 9 × 9 × 2½ wedge bricks.

Table A–7
Number of 3-Inch Series Wedge Bricks Required to Turn Circle (9″ × 4½″ × 3″ and 9″ × 6¾″ × 3″ Wedges)

Diameter of Inside Brickwork	No. 3 Wedge	No. 2 Wedge	Total
3'0"	57	—	57
3'1"	56	2	58
3'2"	55	4	59
3'3"	54	6	60

Table A–7, continued

Diameter of Inside Brickwork	No. 3 Wedge	No. 2 Wedge	Total
3′4″	52	9	61
3′5″	51	11	62
3′6″	50	13	63
3′7″	49	15	64
3′8″	48	17	65
3′9″	47	19	66
3′10″	46	21	67
3′11″	45	23	68
4′0″	44	26	70
4′1″	43	28	71
4′2″	42	30	72
4′3″	41	32	73
4′4″	40	34	74
4′5″	39	36	75
4′6″	38	38	76
4′7″	37	40	77
4′8″	36	42	78
4′9″	35	44	79
4′10″	34	46	80
4′11″	33	48	81
5′0″	32	50	82
5′1″	31	52	83
5′2″	29	55	84
5′3″	28	57	85
5′4″	27	59	86
5′5″	26	61	87
5′6″	25	63	88
5′7″	24	65	89
5′8″	23	67	90
5′9″	22	70	92
5′10″	21	72	93
5′11″	20	74	94
6′0″	19	76	95
6′1″	18	78	96
6′2″	17	80	97
6′3″	16	82	98
6′4″	15	84	99
6′5″	14	86	100
6′6″	13	88	101
6′7″	12	90	102
6′8″	11	92	103
6′9″	10	94	104

Table A–7, continued

Diameter of Inside Brickwork	No. 3 Wedge	No. 2 Wedge	Total
6'10"	9	96	105
6'11"	7	99	106
7'0"	6	101	107

This table may also be used for 13½ × 9 × 3 arches.

Table A–8
Number of 9" × 6" ts 4" Rotary Kiln or Cupola Blocks Required to Turn Circle (6" Lining)

Diameter of Inside Brickwork	Name and Number of Blocks Required		Total
	30–42	35–48	
2'6"	15	—	15
2'9"	8	8	16
	36–48	42–54	
3'0"	17	—	17
3'3"	9	9	18
	42–54	48–60	
3'6"	19	—	19
3'9"	10	10	20
	48–60	54–66	
4'0"	21	—	21
4'3"	11	11	22
	54–66	60–72	
4'6"	23	—	23
4'9"	12	12	24
	60–72	66–78	
5'0"	26	—	26
5'3"	13	14	27
	66–78	72–84	
5'6"	28	—	28
5'9"	14	15	29
	72–84	78–90	
6'0"	30	—	30
	15	16	31

Table A—9
Number of 9″ × 9″ × 4″ Rotary Kiln Blocks Required to Turn Circle (9″ Lining)

Diameter of Inside Brickwork	Name and Number of Blocks Required		Total
	48–66	54–72	
4′0″	23	—	23
4′3″	12	12	24
	54–72	60–78	
4′6″	26	—	26
4′9″	13	14	27
	60–78	56–84	
5′0″	28	—	28
5′3″	14	15	29
	56–84	72–90	
5′6″	30	—	30
5′9″	15	16	31
	72–90	78–96	
6′0″	32	—	32
6′3″	16	17	33
	78–96	84–102	
6′6″	34	—	34
6′9″	17	18	35
	84–102	90–108	
7′0″	36	—	36
7′3″	18	19	37

NOTE: A.P. Green Rotary Kiln Liners are also available in 4½″, 7½″ and other lining thicknesses.

Table A—10
Color Test for Glaze Maturity

Color	F°	C°
Lowest visible red	475	885
Lowest visible—dark red	475–650	885–1200
Dark red—cherry red	650–750	1200–1380
Cherry red—bright cherry red	750–815	1380–1500
Bright cherry red—orange	815–900	1500–1650
Orange—yellow	900–1090	1650–2000
Yellow—light yellow	1090–1315	2000–2400
Light yellow—white	1315–1540	2400–2800
White—bluish white	1540	2800

Table A–11
Pyrometric Cone Equivalents

Cone Number	Large Cones				Cone Number	Small Cones	
	60°C	108°F	150°F	270°F		300°C	540°F
022	585°C	1085°F	600°C	1112°F	022	630°C*	1165°F*
021	602	1116	614	1137	021	643	1189
020	625	1157	635	1175	020	666	1231
019	668	1234	683	1261			
019	668	1234	683	1261	019	723	1333
018	696	1285	717	1323	018	752	1386
017	727	1341	747	1377	017	784	1443
016	764	1407	792	1458	016	825	1517
015	790	1454	804	1479	015	843	1549
014	834	1533	838	1540	014	870*	1596
013	869	1596	852	1566	013	880*	1615
012	866	1591	884	1623	012	900*	1650
011	886	1627	894	1641	011	915*	1680
010†	887	1629	894	1641	010†	919	1686
09	915	1679	923	1693	09	955	1751
08	945	1733	955	1751	08	983	1801
07	973	1783	984	1803	07	1008	1846
06	991	1816	999	1830	06	1023	1873
05	1031	1888	1046	1915	05	1062	1944
04	1050	1922	1060	1940	04	1098	2008
03	1086	1987	1101	2014	03	1131	2068
02	1101	2014	1120	2048	02	1148	2098
01	1117	2043	1137	2079	01	1178	2152
1	1136	2077	1154	2109	1	1179	2154
2	1142	2088	1162	2124	2	1179	2154
3	1152	2106	1168	2134	3	1196	2185
4	1168	2134	1186	2167	4	1209	2208
5	1177	2151	1196	2185	5	1221	2230
6	1201	2194	1222	2232	6	1255	2291
7	1251	2219	1240	2264	7	1264	2307
8	1236	2257	1263	2305	8	1300	2372
9	1260	2300	1280	2336	9	1317	2403
10	1285	2345	1305	2381	10	1330	2426
11	1294	2361	1315	2399	11	1336	2437
12	1306	2383	1326	2419	12	1355	2471

Cone Number	Large Cones				Cone Number	P.C.E. Cones	
	60°C	108°F	150°F	270°F		150°C	270°F
12	1306°C	2383°F	1326°C	2419°F	12	1337°C	2439°F
13	1321	2410	1346	2455	13	1349	2460
14	1388	2530	1366	2491	14	1398	2548
15	1424	2592	1431	2608	15	1430	2606
16	1455	2651	1473	2683	16	1491	2716
17	1477	1691	1485	2705	17	1512	2754

Table A–11, continued

Cone Number	Large Cones				Cone Number	Small Cones	
	60°C	108°F	150°F	270°F		300°C	540°F
18	1500	2732	1506	2743	18	1522	2772
19	1520	2768	1528	2782	19	1541	2806
20	1542	2808	1549	2820	20	1564	2847
23	1586	2887	1590	2894	23	1605	2921
26	1589	2892	1605	2921	26	1621	2950
27	1614	2937	1627	2961	27	1640	1984
28	1614	2937	1633	2971	28	1646	2995
29	1624	2955	1645	2993	29	1659	3018
30	1636	2977	1654	3009	30	1665	3029
31	1636	2977	1654				
31	1661	3022	1679	3054	31	1683	3061
31½					31½	1699	3090
32	1706	3103	1717	3123	32	1717	3123
32½	1718	3124	1730	3146	32½	1724	3135
33	1732	3150	1741	3166	33	1743	3169
34	1757	3195	1759	3198	34	1763	3205
35	1784	3243	1784	3243	35	1785	3245
36	1798	3268	1796	3265	36	1804	3308
37	ND	ND	ND	ND	37	1820	3308
38	ND1	ND	ND	ND	38	1850*	3362
39	ND	ND	ND	ND	39	1865*	3389
40	ND	ND	ND	ND	40	1885*	3425
41	ND	ND	ND	ND	41	1970*	3578
42	NDN	ND	ND	ND	42	2015*	3659

* Temperature approximate (see Note 3).
† Iron-free (white); made in numbers 010 to 3. The iron-free cones have the same deformation temperatures as the red equivalents when fired at a rate of 60°C per hour in air.
ND: Not Determined.

NOTES:

1. The temperature equivalents in this table apply only to Orton Standard Pyrometric Cones, when heated at the rates indicated, in an air atmosphere.
2. The rates of heating shown at the head of each column of temperature equivalents were maintained during the last several hundred degrees of temperature rise.
3. The temperature equivalents were determined at the National Bureau of Standards by H.P. Beerman (See *Journal of the American Ceramic Society*, Vol.39, 1956), with the exception of those marked (*).
4. The temperature equivalents are not necessarily those at which cones will deform under firing conditions different from those under which the calibrating determinations were made. For more detailed technical data, please write the Orton Foundation.
5. For reproducible results, care should be taken to insure that the cones are set in a plaque with the bending face at the correct angle of 8° from the vertical, with the cone tips at the correct height above the top of the plaque. (Large Cone 2″, small and P.C.E. cones 15/16).
6. Permission to reproduce all or any part of this table may be obtained by writing to the Foundation.

USEFUL CONVERSION TABLES

Table A-12
Unit Conversions

ATMOSPHERES—atm (Standard at sea-level pressure)

× 101.325	= Kilopascals (kPa) absolute
× 14.696	= Pounds-force per square inch absolute (psia)
× 76.00	= Centimetres of mercury (cmHg) at 0°C
× 29.92	= Inches of mercury (inHg) at 0°C
× 33.96	= Feet of water (ftH$_2$0) at 68°F
× 1.01325	= Bars (bar) absolute
× 1.0332	= Kilograms-force per square centimetre (kg/cm²) absolute
× 1.0581	= Tons-force per square foot (tonf/ft²) absolute
× 760	= Torr (torr) (= mmHg at 0°C)

BARRELS, LIQUID, U.S.—bbl

× 0.11924	= Cubic metres (m³)
× 31.5	= U.S. gallons (U.S. gal) liquid

BARRELS, PETROLEUM—bbl

× 0.15899	= Cubic metres (m³)
× 42	= U.S. gallons (U.S. gal) oil

BRITISH THERMAL UNITS—Btu (See note)

× 1055	= Joules (J)
× 778	= Foot-pounds-force (ft · lbf)
× 0.252	= Kilocalories (kcal)
× 107.6	= Kilogram-force-metres (kgf · m)
× 2.93 × 10^{-4}	= Kilowatt-hours (kW·h)
× 3.93 × 10^{-4}	= Horsepower-hours (hp·h)

BRITISH THERMAL UNITS PER MINUTE—Btu/min (See note)

× 17.58	= Watts (W)
× 12.97	= Foot-pounds-force per second (ft·lbf/s)
× 0.02358	= Horsepower (hp)

CENTIMETRES—cm

× 0.3937	= Inches (in)

CENTIMETRES OF MERCURY—cmHg, at 0°C

× 1.3332	= Kilopascals (kPa)
× 0.013332	= Bars (bar)
× 0.4468	= Feet of water (ftH$_2$O) at 68°F
× 5.362	= Inches of water (inH$_2$O)at 68°F
× 0.013595	= Kilograms-force per square centimetre (kg/cm²)
× 27.85	= Pounds-force per square foot (lbf/ft²)
× 0.19337	= Pounds-force per square inch (psi)
× 0.013158	= Atmosphers (atm) standard
× 10	= Torr (torr)(= mmHg at 0°C)

CENTIMETRES PER SECOND—cm/s

× 1.9685	= Feet per minute (ft/min)
× 0.03281	= Feet per second (ft/s)
× 0.03600	= Kilometres per hour (km/h)
× 0.6000	= Metres per minute (m/min)
× 0.02237	= Miles per hour (mph)

Table A–12, continued

CUBIC CENTIMETRES—cm³
× 3.5315 × 10⁻⁵	= Cubic feet (ft³)
× 6.1024 × 10⁻²	= Cubic inches (in³)
× 1.308 × 10⁻⁶	= Cubic yards (yd³)
× 2.642 × 10⁻⁴	= U.S. gallons (U.S. gal)
× 2.200 × 10⁻⁴	= Imperial gallons (imp gal)
× 1.000. × 10⁻³	= Litres (1)

CUBIC FEET—ft³
× 0.02832	= Cubic metres (m³)
× 2.832 × 10⁴	= Cubic centimetres (cm³)
× 1728	= Cubic inches (in³)
× 0.03704	= Cubic yards (yd³)
× 7.481	= U.S. gallons (U.S. gal)
× 6.229	= Imperial gallons (imp gal)
× 28.32	= Litres (1)

CUBIC FEET PER MINUTE—cfm
× 472.0	= Cubic centimetres per second (cm³/s)
× 1.699	= Cubic metres per hour (m³/h)
× 0.4720	= Litres per second (l/s)
× 0.1247	= U.S. gallons per second (U.S. gps)
× 62.30	= Pounds of water per minute (lbH₂O/min) at 68°F

CUBIC FEET PER SECOND—cfs
× 0.02832	= Cubic metres per second (m³/s)
× 1.699	= Cubic metres per minute (m³/min)
× 448.8	= U.S. gallons per minute (U.S. gpm)
× 0.6463	= Million U.S. gallons per day (U.S. gpd)

CUBIC INCHES—in³
× 1.6387 × 10⁻⁵	= Cubic metres (m³)
× 16.387	= Cubic centimetres (cm³)
× 0.016387	= Litres (l)
× 5.787 × 10⁻⁴	= Cubic feet (ft³)
× 2.143 × 10⁻⁵	= Cubic yards (yd³)
× 4.329 × 10⁻³	= U.S. gallons (U.S. gal)
× 3.605 × 10⁻³	= Imperial gallons (imp gal)

CUBIC METRES—m³
× 1000	= Litres (l)
× 35.315	= Cubic feet (ft³)
× 61.024 × 10³	= Cubic inches (in³)
× 1.3080	= Cubic yards (yd³)
× 264.2	= U.S. gallons (U.S. gal)
× 220.0	= Imperial gallons (imp gal)

CUBIC METRES PER HOUR—m³/h
× 0.2778	= Litres per second (l/s)
× 2.778 × 10⁻⁴	= Cubic metres per second (m³/s)
× 4.403	= U.S. gallons per minute (U.S. gpm)

CUBIC METRES PER SECOND—m³/s
× 3600	= Cubic metres per hour (m³/h)
× 15.85 × 10³	= U.S. gallons per minute (U.S. gpm)

Table A–12, continued

CUBIC YARDS—yd³
× 0.7646 = Cubic metres (m³)
× 764.6 = Litres (l)
× 7.646 × 10⁵ = Cubic centimetres (cm³)
× 27 = Cubic feet (ft³)
× 46,656 = Cubic inches (in³)
× 201.97 = U.S. gallons (U.S. gal)
× 168.17 = Imperial gallons (imp gal)

DEGREES, ANGULAR (°)
× 0.017453 = Radians (rad)
× 60 = Minutes (′)
× 3600 = Seconds (″)
× 1.111 = Grade (gon)

DEGREES PER SECOND, ANGULAR (°/s)
× 0.017453 = Radians per second (rad/s)
× 0.16667 = Revolutions per minute (r/min)
× 2.7778 × 10⁻³ = Revolutions per second (r/s)

FEET—ft
× 0.3048 = Metres (m)
× 30.480 = Centimetres (cm)
× 12 = Inches (in)
× 0.3333 = Yards (yd)

FEET OF WATER—ftH₂O, at 68°F
× 2.984 = Kilopascals (kPa)
× 0.02984 = Bars (bar)
× 0.8811 = Inches of mercury (inHg) at 0°C
× 0.03042 = Kilograms-force per square centimetre (kg/cm²)
× 62.32 = Pounds-force per square foot (lbf/ft²)
× 0.4328 = Pounds-force per square inch (psi)
× 0.02945 = Standard atmospheres

FEET PER MINUTE—ft/min
× 0.5080 = Centimetres per second (cm/s)
× 0.01829 = Kilometres per hour (km/h)
× 0.3048 = Metres per minute (m/min)
× 0.016667 = Feet per second (ft/s)
× 0.01136 = Miles per hour (mph)

FEET PER SECOND PER SECOND—ft/s²
× 0.3048 = Metres per second per second (m/s²)
× 30.48 = Centimetres per second per second (cm/s²)

FOOT-POUNDS-FORCE—ft·lbf
× 1.356 = Joules (J)
× 1.285 × 10⁻³ = British thermal units (Btu)(see note)
× 3.239 × 10⁻⁴ = Kilocalories (kcal)
× 0.13825 = Kilogram-force-metres (kgf·m)
× 5.050 × 10⁻⁷ = Horsepower-hours (hp·h)
× 3.766 × 10⁻⁷ = Kilowatt-hours (kW·h)

GALLONS, U.S.—U.S. gal
× 3785.4 = Cubic centimetres (cm³)
× 3.7854 = Litres (l)

Table A–12, continued

× 3.7854 × 10^{-3}	= Cubic metres (m^3)
× 231	= Cubic inches (in^3)
× 0.13368	= Cubic feet (ft^3)
× 4.951 × 10^{-3}	= Cubic yards (yd^3)
× 8	= Pints (pt) liquid
× 4	= Quarts (qt) liquid
× 0.8327	= Imperial gallons (imp gal)
× 8.328	= Pounds of water at 60°F in air
× 8.337	= Pounds of water at 60°F in vacuo

GALLONS, IMPERIAL—imp gal

× 4546	= Cubic centimetres (cm^3)
× 4.546	= Litres (l)
× 4.546 × 10^{-3}	= Cubic metres (m^3)
× 0.16054	= Cubic feet (ft^3)
× 5.946 × 10^{-3}	= Cubic yards (yd^3)
× 1.20094	= U.S. gallons (U.S. gal)
× 10.000	= Pounds of water at 62°F in air

GALLONS, PER MINUTE, U.S.—U.S. gpm

× 0.22715	= Cubic metres per hour (m^3/h)
× 0.06309	= Litres per second (l/s)
× 8.021	= Cubic feet per hour (cfh)
× 2.228 × 10^{-3}	= Cubic feet per second (cfs)

GRAMS—g

× 15.432	= Grains (gr)
× 0.035274	= Ounces (oz) av.
× 0.032151	= Ounces (oz) troy
× 2.2046 × 10^{-3}	= Pounds (lb)

GRAMS-FORCE—gf

× 9.807 × 10^{-3}	= Newtons (N)

GRAMS-FORCE PER CENTIMETRE—gf/cm

× 98.07	= Newtons per metre (N/m)
× 5.600 × 10^{-3}	= Pounds-force per inch (lbf/in)

GRAMS PER CUBIC CENTIMETRE—g/cm^3

× 62.43	= Pounds per cubic foot (lb/ft^3)
× 0.03613	= Pounds per cubic inch (lb/in^3)

GRAMS PER LITRE—g/l

× 58.42	= Grains per U.S. gallon (gr/U.S. gal)
× 8.345	= Pounds per 1000 U.S. gallons
× 0.06243	= Pounds per cubic foot (lb/ft^3)
× 1002	= Parts per million by mass (weight) in water at 60°F

HECTARES—ha

× 1.000 × 10^4	= Square metres (m^2)
× 1.0764 × 10^5	= Square feet (ft^2)

HORSEPOWER—hp

× 745.7	= Watts (W)
× 0.7457	= Kilowatts (kW)
× 33,000	= Foot-pounds-force per minute (ft·lbf/min)
× 550	= Foot-pounds-force per second (ft·lbf/s)
× 42.43	= British thermal units per minute (Btu/min)(see note)

Table A–12, continued

× 10.69	= Kilocalories per minute (kcal/min)
× 1.0139	= Horsepower (metric)

HORSEPOWER—hp boiler

× 33,480	= British thermal units per hour (Btu/h)(see note)
× 9.809	= Kilowatts (kW)

HORSEPOWER-HOURS—hp·h

× 0.7457	= Kilowatt-hours (kW·h)
× 1.976×10^6	= Foot-pounds-force (ft·lbf)
× 2545	= British thermal units (Btu)(see note)
× 641.5	= Kilocalories (kcal)
× 2.732×10^5	= Kilogram-force-metres (kgf·m)

INCHES–in

× 2.540	= Centimetres (cm)

INCHES OF MERCURY–inHg at 0°C

× 3.3864	= Kilopascals (kPa)
× 0.03386	= Bars (bar)
× 1.135	= Feet of water (ftH$_2$O) at 68°F
× 13.62	= Inches of water (inH$_2$O) at 68°F
× 0.03453	= Kilograms-force per square centimetre (kg/cm^3)
× 70.73	= Pounds-force per square foot (lbf/ft^2)
× 0.4912	= Pounds-force per square inch (psi)
× 0.03342	= Standard atmospheres

INCHES OF WATER—inH$_2$O at 68°F

× 0.2487	= Kilopascals (kPa)
× 2.487×10^{-3}	= Bars (bar)
× 0.07342	= Inches of mercury (inHg) at 0°C
× 2.535×10^{-3}	= Kilograms-force per square centimetre (kg/cm^2)
× 0.5770	= Ounces-force per square inch (ozf/in^2)
× 5.193	= Pounds-force per square foot (lbf/ft^2)
× 0.03606	= Pounds-force per square inch (psi)
× 2.454×10^{-3}	= Standard atmospheres

JOULES—J

× 0.9484×10^{-3}	= British thermal units (Btu)(see note)
× 0.2390	= Calories (cal) thermochemical
× 0.7376	= Foot-pounds-force (ft·lbf)
× 2.778×10^{-4}	= Watt-hours (W·h)

KILOGRAMS–kg

× 2.2046	= Pounds (lb)
× 1.102×10^{-3}	= Tons (ton) short

. KILOGRAMS-FORCE—kgf

× 9.807	= Newtons (N)
× 2.205	= Pounds-force (lbf)

KILOGRAMS-FORCE PER METRE—kgf/m

× 9.807	= Newtons per metre (N/m)
× 0.6721	= Pounds-force per foot (lbf/ft)

KILOGRAMS-FORCE PER SQUARE CENTIMETRE—kg/cm^2

× 98.07	= Kilopascals (kPa)
× 0.9807	= Bars (bar)
× 32.87	= Feet of water (ftH$_2$O) at 68°F

Table A–12, continued

× 28.96	= Inches of mercury (inHg) at 0°C
× 2048	= Pounds-force per square foot (lbf/ft²)
× 14.223	= Pounds-force per square inch (psi)
× 0.9678	= Standard atmospheres

KILOGRAMS-FORCE PER SQUARE MILLIMETRE—kgf/mm²

× 9.807	= Megapascals (MPa)
× 1.000 × 10⁶	= Kilograms-force per square metre (kgf/m²)

KILOPASCALS—kPa

× 10³	= Pascals (Pa) or newtons per square metre (N/m²)
× 0.1450	= Pounds-force per square inch (psi)
× 0.010197	= Kilograms-force per square centimetre (kg/cm²)
× 0.2953	= Inches of mercury (inHg) at 32°F
× 0.3351	= Feet of water (ftH₂O) at 68°F
× 4.021	= Inches of water (inH₂O) at 68°F

KILOWATTS—kW

× 4.425 × 10⁴	= Foot-pounds-force per minute (ft·lbf/min)
× 737.6	= Foot-pounds-force per second (ft·lbf/s)
× 56.90	= British thermal units per minute (Btu/min)(see note)
× 14.33	= Kilocalories per minute (kcal/min)
× 1.3410	= Horsepower (hp)

KILOWATT-HOURS—kW·h

× 3.6 × 10⁶	= Joules (J)
× 2.655 × 10⁶	= Foot-pounds-force (ft·lbf)
× 3413	= British thermal units (Btu)(see note)
× 860	= Kilocalories (kcal)
× 3.671 × 10⁵	= Kilogram-force metres (kgf·m)
× 1.3410	= Horsepower-hours (hp·h)

LITRES—l

× 1000	= Cubic centimetres (cm³)
× 0.035315	= Cubic feet (ft³)
× 61.024	= Cubic inches (in³)
× 1.308 × 10⁻³	= Cubic yards (yd³)
× 0.2642	= U.S. gallons (U.S. gal)
× 0.2200	= Imperial gallons (imp gal)

LITRES PER MINUTE—l/min

× 0.01667	= Litres per second (l/s)
× 5.885 × 10⁻⁴	= Cubic feet per second (cfs)
× 4.403 × 10⁻³	= U.S. gallons per second (U.S. gal/s)
× 3.666 × 10⁻³	= Imperial gallons per second (imp gal/s)

LITRES PER SECOND–l/s

× 10⁻³	= Cubic metres per second (m³/s)
× 3.600	= Cubic metres per hour (m³/h)
× 60	= Litres per minute (l/min)
× 15.85	= U.S. gallons per minute (U.S. gpm)
× 13.20	= Imperial gallons per minute (imp gpm)

MEGAPASCALS–MPa

× 10⁶	= Pascals (Pa) or newtons per square metre (N/m²)
× 10³	= Kilopascals (kPa)

Table A–12, continued

× 145.0	= Pounds-force per square inch (psi)
× 0.1020	= Kilograms-force per square millimetre (kgf/mm²)

METRES–m

× 3.281	= Feet (ft)
× 39.37	= Inches (in)
× 1.0936	= Yards (yd)

METRES PER MINUTES—m/min

× 1.6667	= Centimetres per second (cm/s)
× 0.0600	= Kilometres per hour (km/h)
× 3.281	= Feet per minute (ft/min)
× 0.05468	= Feet per second (ft/s)
× 0.03728	= Miles per hour (mph)

METRES PER SECOND—m/s

× 3.600	= Kilometres per hour (km/h)
× 0.0600	= Kilometres per minute (km/min)
× 196.8	= Feet per minute (ft/min)
× 3.281	= Feet per second (ft/s)
× 2.237	= Miles per hour (mph)
× 0.03728	= Miles per minute (mi/min)

MICROMETRES—μm formerly micron

× 10^{-6}	= Metres (m)

NEWTONS—N

× 0.10197	= Kilograms-force (kgf)
× 0.2248	= Pounds-force (lbf)
× 7.233	= Poundals
× 10^5	= Dynes

OUNCES—oz av.

× 28.35	= Grams (g)
× 2.835×10^{-5}	= Tonnes (t) metric ton
× 16	= Drams (dr) av.
× 437.5	= Grains (gr)
× 0.06250	= Pounds (lb) av.
× 0.9115	= Ounces (oz) troy
× 2.790×10^{-5}	= Tons (ton) long

OUNCES—oz troy

× 31.103	= Grams (g)
× 480	= Grains (gr)
× 20	= Pennyweights (dwt) troy
× 0.08333	= Pounds (lb) troy
× 0.06857	= Pounds (lb) av.
× 1.0971	= Ounces (oz) av.

OUNCES—oz U.S. fluid

× 0.02957	= Litres (l)
× 1.8046	= Cubic inches (in)

OUNCES-FORCE PER SQUARE INCH—ozf/in²

× 43.1	= Pascals (Pa)
× 0.06250	= Pounds-force per square inch (psi)
× 4.395	= Grams-force per square centimetre (gf/cm²)

Table A–12, continued

PARTS PER MILLION BY MASS—mass (weight) in water

× 0.9991	= Grams per cubic metre (g/m³) at 15°C
× 0.0583	= Grains per U.S. gallon (gr/U.S. gal) at 60°F
× 0.0700	= Grains per imperial gallon (gr/imp gal) at 62°F
× 8.328	= Pounds per million U.S. gallons at 60°F

PASCALS—PA

× 1	= Newtons per square metre (N/m²)
× 1.450 × 10⁻⁴	= Pounds-force per square inch (psi)
× 1.0197 × 10⁻⁵	= Kilograms-force per square centimetre (kg/cm²)
× 10⁻³	= Kilopascals (kPa)

POUNDS-FORCE—lbf av.

× 4.448	= Newtons (N)
× 0.4536	= Kilograms-force (kgf)

POUNDS—lb av.

× 453.6	= Grams (g)
× 16	= Ounces (oz) av.
× 256	= Drams (dr) av.
× 7000	= Grains (gr)
× 5 × 10⁻⁴	= Tons (ton) short
× 1.2153	= Pounds (lb) troy

POUNDS—lb troy

× 373.2	= Grams (g)
× 12	= Ounces (oz) troy
× 240	= Pennyweights (dwt) troy
× 5760	= Grains (gr)
× 0.8229	= Pounds (lb) av.
× 13.166	= Ounces (oz) av.
× 3.6735 × 10⁻⁴	= Tons (ton) long
× 4.1143 × 10⁻⁴	= Tons (ton) short
× 3.7324 × 10⁻⁴	= Tonnes (t) metric tons

POUNDS-MASS OF WATER AT 60°F

× 453.98	= Cubic centimetres (cm³)
× 0.45398	= Litres (l)
× 0.01603	= Cubic feet (ft³)
× 27.70	= Cubic inches (in³)
× 0.1199	= U.S. gallons (U.S. gal)

POUNDS OF WATER PER MINUTE AT 60°F

× 7.576	= Cubic centimetres per second (cm³/s)
× 2.675 × 10⁻⁴	= Cubic feet per second (cfs)

POUNDS PER CUBIC FOOT—lb/ft³

× 16.018	= Kilograms per cubic metre (kg/m³)
× 0.016018	= Grams per cubic centimetre (g/cm³)
× 5.787 × 10⁻⁴	= Pounds per cubic inch (lb/in³)

POUNDS PER CUBIC INCH—lb/in³

× 2.768 × 10⁴	= Kilograms per cubic metre (kg/m³)
× 27.68	= Grams per cubic centimetre (g/cm³)
× 1728	= Pounds per cubic foot (lb/ft³)

POUNDS-FORCE PER FOOT—lbf/ft

× 14.59	= Newtons per metre (N/m)

Table A–12, continued

× 1.488	= Kilograms-force per metre (kgf/m)
× 14.88	= Grams-force per centimetre (gf/cm)

POUNDS-FORCE PER SQUARE FOOT—lbf/ft²

× 47.88	= Pascals (Pa)
× 0.01605	= Feet of water (ftH₂O) at 68°F
× 4.882 × 10⁻⁴	= Kilograms-force per square centimetre (kg/cm²)
× 6.944 × 10⁻³	= Pounds-force per square inch (psi)

POUNDS-FORCE PER SQUARE INCH—psi

× 6.895	= Kilopascals (kPa)
× 0.06805	= Standard atmospheres
× 2.311	= Feet of water (ftH₂O) at 68° F
× 27.73	= Inches of water (inH₂O) at 68°F
× 2.036	= Inches of mercury (inHg) at 0°C
× 0.07031	= Kilograms-force per square centimetre (kg/cm²)

RADIANS—rad

× 57.30	= Degrees (°) angular

RADIANS PER SECOND—rad/s

× 57.30	= Degrees per second (°/s) angular

STANDARD CUBIC FEET PER MINUTE—scfm (at 14.696 psia and 60°F)

× 0.4474	= Litres per second (l/s) at standard conditions (760 mmHg and 0°C)
× 1.608	= Cubic metres per hour (m³/h) at standard conditions (760 mmHg and 0°C)

STOKES—St

× 10⁻⁴	= Square metres per second (m²/s)
× 1.076 × 10⁻³	= Square feet per second (ft²/s)

TONS-MASS—tonm long

× 1016	= Kilograms (kg)
× 2240	= Pounds (lb) av.
× 1.1200	= Tons (ton) short

TONNES—t metric ton, millier

× 1000	= Kilograms (kg)
× 2204.6	= Pounds (lb)

TONNES-FORCE—tf metric ton-force

× 980.7	= Newtons (N)

TONS—ton short

× 907.2	= Kilograms (kg)
× 0.9072	= Tonnes (t)
× 2000	= Pounds (lb) av.
× 32000	= Ounces (oz) av.
× 2430.6	= Pounds (lb) troy
× 0.8929	= Tons (ton) long

TONS OF WATER PER 24 HOURS AT 60°F

× 0.03789	= Cubic metres per hour (m³/h)
× 83.33	= Pounds of water per hour (lb/h H₂O) at 60°F
× 0.1668	= U.S. gallons per minute (U.S. gpm)
× 1.338	= Cubic feet per hour (cfh)

Table A–12, continued

WATTS—W	
× 0.05690	= British thermal units per minute (Btu/min)(see note)
× 44.25	= Foot-pounds-force per minute (ft·lbf/min)
× 0.7376	= Foot-pounds-force per second (ft·lbf/s)
× 1.341 × 10⁻³	= Horsepower (hp)
× 0.01433	= Kilocalories per minute (kcal/min)
WATT-HOURS—W·h	
× 3600	= Joules (J)
× 3.413	= British thermal units (Btu)(see note)
× 2655	= Foot-pounds-force (ft·lbf)
× 1.341 × 10⁻³	= Horsepower-hours (hp·h)
× 0.860	= Kilocalories (kcal)
× 367.1	= Kilogram-force-metres (kgf·m)

SOURCE: Norman A. Anderson, *Instrumentation for Process Measurement and Control*, third edition. Radnor, Pa: Chilton Book Co., 1980. Reprinted by permission of the publisher.

NOTE: SIGNIFICANT FIGURES The precision to which a given conversion factor is known, and its application, determine the number of significant figures which should be used. While many handbooks and standards give factors contained in this table to six or more significant figures, the fact that different sources disagree, in many cases, in the fifth or further figure indicates that four or five significant figures represent the precision for these factors fairly. At present the accuracy of process instrumentation, analog or digital, is in the tenth percent region at best, thus needing only three significant figures. Hence this table is confined to four or five significant figures. The advent of the pocket calculator (and the use of digital computers in process instrumentation) tends to lead to use of as many figures as the calculator will handle. However, when this exceeds the precision of the data, or the accuracy of the application, such a practice is misleading and timewasting.

NOTE: BRITISH THERMAL UNIT When making calculations involving Btu it must be remembered that there are several definitions of the Btu. The first three significant figures of the conversion factors given in this table are common to most definitions of the Btu. However, if four or more significant figures are needed in the calculation, the appropriate handbooks and standards should be consulted to be sure the proper definition and factor are being used.

GLAZE FIRING, ASO PER GLUMSO KILN

The night I fired this kiln, the whiteness of the snow shone brightly in the cold air, as I began preheating to get a draught running through the kiln. As the fire burned in the chimney, I made sure the oil system was ready, the oil tank was filled, extra drums were ready for use, the burner plates were clear and ready for igniting, the wood was cut and stacked by each chamber door, and the door bricks were built well and plugged with fire clay. A half-hour later, the chimney fire was burning nicely. I tore a rag into three pieces, soaked them in fuel oil and placed them on the bottom plate of the burners at each flue porthole. Then the oil was turned on in order to saturate each plate unit well. Afterward, the flow of oil was decreased to a steady drip (Table A-13). I ignited the rags and watched the fire in the burner port flue take hold with a flicker. As the plate and flue holes became hot, a foot-long tongue of flame began to develop, hit the bagwall and disappeared into the chamber.

Two hours later, the oil was increased to a steady stream and the air supply through the burner boxes closed halfway. For the next four hours, the oil was increased periodically and the smoke was becoming

Table A–13
Glaze Firing, March 4, 1965, Aso per Glumso *Kiln*

First and second chambers, glaze; third chamber, bisque
Segers Standard Pyrometric Cones 05, 1, 7, 9, 10
No wind, cold (−7°F), snow on the ground

Time: 23½ hours
Fuel: 400 liters
Cost: 100 kroner/$15

Time	Oil Tank	Rate of Oil Drip	Air	Remarks
6:30 P.M.		—	—	½ hour preheating chimney
7:00	Full		Open	Smoking
9:00	Filled		½ closed	Smoking
11:00	Filled		½ closed	Smoking
1:00 A.M.	Filled	Adjusted up	¾ closed	Clear carbon in flues, smoking good red
3:00	Filled	Adjusted up	¾ closed	Cone 05 bending, smoking
5:00	Filled	Adjusted up	¾ closed	Reddish orange
6:30	Filled	Adjusted up	¾ closed	Clear carbon, cone 05 down (1030°C)
7:00			¾ closed	Clear carbon
8:00	Filled	Adjusted up	¾ closed	
9:00		Adjusted up	¾ closed	Clear carbon, yellowish orange
9:30		Adjusted up	¾ closed	Cone 1 down, approaching 1125°C
10:30		Adjusted up	¾ closed	Clear carbon, cone 7 bending, begin stoking, slight reduction; 3 pieces per 5 minutes
11:00		Adjusted down	½ open	Cone 7 down, cone 9 bending, heavy stoking every 4 minutes, 1250°C +
11:30		Adjusted down	½ open	Heavy stoking on left, reducing oil
12:30 P.M.		Adjusted down	½ open	Cone 9 bending, reducing, raked firebox, about 1280°C, stoking at 4-minute intervals

less dense; a dull red glow appeared up the back of the chamber. I felt it safe now to increase the oil rate to its maximum. By 6:30 a.m., the color, visible through a half-open blowhole, was a good reddish orange and cone 5 was completely down. The periodical check of the flues and burner plates showed a tremendous amount of carbon buildup, so I opened the air supply and raked the carbon coals away. There was a flash of white flame and a loud roar as the carbon exploded and flames flicked out the blowhole and through the vapor holes on top of the chamber. Peering through the blowhole at 9:30 a.m., I saw cone 1 down, thus indicating that the side stoking with wood in the fire-box should begin within an hour for reduction.

By 10:30 a.m., the kiln color was good yellowish orange. After cleaning the carbon from the flues and adjusting the oil to a low rate of flow, I began a light

stoking until 1240° (2250°F), approximately cone 7, was reached. When the cone 7 was bending, heavy stoking at four-minute intervals was begun.

An hour later, the glazes began to take on a shine, each cone 7s was down, and cone 9 was bending on the right side of the kiln. I increased the oil on the left side and continued stoking, evening up the vapor hole flame lengths in order to equalize the temperature across the kiln. After two more hours of wood stoking, I poked an iron rod through the blowhole, and could see its reflection on the pots, now bright and shiny. I then drew out the test rings through the spy hole, which confirmed that the glazes were mature and a good reduction color the clay body had been obtained.

I began to close down the first chamber at 1:30 p.m., continuing a light stoking of chamber 1 for 15

Table A–13
Glaze Firing, March 4, 1965, Aso per Glumso Kiln

First and second chambers, glaze; third chamber, bisque
Segers Standard Pyrometric Cones 05, 1, 7, 9, 10
No wind, cold (−7°F), snow on the ground

Time: 23½ hours
Fuel: 400 liters
Cost: 100 kroner/$15

Time	Oil Tank	Rate of Oil Drip	Air	Remarks
1:00	Filled	Adjusted back to drip	½ open	Reducing cone 9 down
1:30		Adjusted to drip	½ open	Glazes finished, cone 10 bending, chamber 1 finished
1:45		Adjusted to drip	½ open	Oil dripping lighter, 10-minute stoking, chamber 2
2:00		Dripping	¾ open	6-minute interval, heavy stoking rate
3:00			¾ open	Cone 1 bending, stoking same, oxidizing rate
4:00			¾ open	Cone 7 bending, cone 1 down, oxidizing stoking is the same
5:00			Open	4 minute stoking, reducing rate
5:30			¾ closed	Cone 9 bending, oxidizing 7-minute stoking rate
6:00			½ open	Cone 9 down, oxidizing 5-minute stoking rate
6:15				Glazes finished, chamber 3 good red color, bisque good
6:30				Close down tight, firebox chimney, stoke holes, and spy holes.

minutes, then plugging the blowholes. Also, the oil rate was reduced. The side strokehole stopper was pulled out and I began to stoke chamber two with three pieces of thin wood, restoking when the flames died down at the blowholes every few minutes. The second chamber, already a good dark orange color, responded immediately, and within 90 minutes, cone 1 was bending.

The firing now was too fast and there was also too much reduction. I continued stoking at 6-to 7-minute intervals, avoided the black spurts of smoke from the blowholes which indicated reduction, avoided the black spurts of smoke from the blowholes which indicated reduction, and opened up the chimney plug to reduce chimney temperature and slow down the draught.

By 5:00 p.m., the temperature rise was good and cone 7 was bending, so I plugged the chimney hole and stoked heavily for 30 minutes. At 6:00 p.m., the glazes were done. A beautiful, clear, yellowish white color pervaded the whole chamber, while chamber one was a bright, clear orange color.

After a total of 23 1/2 hours of firing, the kiln was finished. The oil was shut off and the fireboxes plugged with clay. The blowholes and chimney were closed; all wood and other flammable materials around the kiln were cleared away. I stepped out of the kiln shed, exhausted. As the cold night air relaxed me, I wondered if everything went right. Did chamber one cool too fast in the switch to chamber two? I would find out 48 hours later when the kiln became cool enough to open.

TA BURNER SAFETY CONTROL SETUPS

Figure A-4 shows several safety equipment setups. First is a multiple tempered air (TA) burner installation for operating strictly as a nozzle-mixing burner with high/low control. The high/low control is

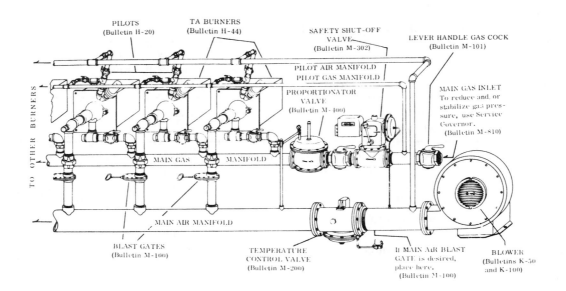

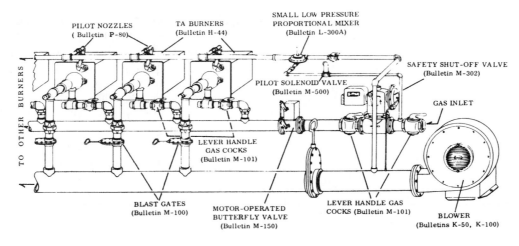

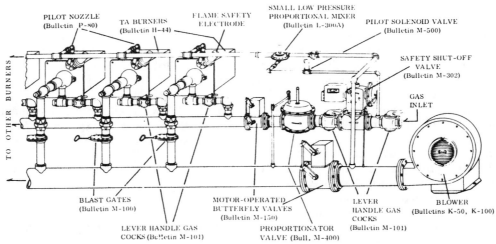

Fig. A–4
Tempered air burner control setups. Reprinted by permission of Eclipse Bulletin.

Typical Firing McDonald Project Kiln:
Preliminary: Gas burner overnight for preheating with damper closed.

Time	Front Pyro		Back Pryo	Damper
6:00 a.m.	300 C°		250 C°	90% open
7:00 a.m.	380		360	80%
8:00 a.m.	510		480	damper out
9:00 a.m.	620		600	
10:00 a.m.	740		720	
11.00 a.m.	880	commence reduction	830	50%
12:00 a.m.	990	stoke with heavy timber	940	70%
13:00 p.m.	1040	to build ember	980	
14:00 p.m.	1080		1020	60%
15:00 p.m.	1120		1065	50%
16:00 p.m.	1165	door brick out	1130	damper out
16:30 p.m.	1180		1155	
17:00 p.m.	1200	floor brick (beside	1185	
17:30 p.m.	1210	firebox) out	1200	
18:00 p.m.	1220		1230	
18:30 p.m.	1235		1240	
19:00 p.m.	1245	alternate floor bricks	1255	
19:30 p.m.	1250	salting	1265	
20:00 p.m.	1250	salting	1265	
20:30 p.m.	1250	salting- reoxidize all	1265	
20:45 p.m.	1150	air intakes open	1150	
21:00 p.m.	1050	closed	1050	closed

From 4:00 p.m. on wards the stoking pattern needs to be adjusted to maintain cmber (large pieces) or to increase temperature (smaller ones). Throughout any period of oxidizing firing, ie. with the floor level air intakes open, the stoking needs to be heavy whether with large or small timber.

obtained by using two-position temperature controller electrically connected to the temperature control value (TCV). As the air flow is reduced by the TCV, the gas flow is also reduced by the proportionator valve, thus holding a constant gas/air ratio.

Next is a multiple TA air-burner installation for automatic control of gas only. In this system, the burners are acting as excess air burners. The air flow remains constant while the gas flow is controlled automatically with the motor-operated butterfly valve.

Automatic dual-temperature control is obtained through the use of the proporionator valve and the motor-operated butterfly valves. With this system, the TA burners can operate as on-ratio nozzle-mixing burners at the desired high temperatures and as excess air burners for low-temperature operation.

THE KENZAN SCHOOL SUCCESSION

The first Kenzan, Ogata, received his *densho* from his teacher, Ninsei, a Kyoto potter. A Japanese *densho* is a document containing the clay and glaze recipes, secrets and methods of the master, and is passed to his successor or successors. The Kenzan School succession is the passing down of Kenzan Ogata's *densho*, not necessarily to another potter.

Bernard Leach and Tomimoto Kenkichi were both given the Kenzan VI *densho* by their teacher, Shigekichi Ogata; Tomimoto declined the title, but did receive — along with Leach—the *densho*. Leach accepted the succession title and became known as Kenzan VII. During my years in Kyoto with Tomimoto, we translated all the Kenzan notes into English. Among them were Leach's original notes from his apprenticeship with Ogata, and these became part of Leach's book, *Kenzan and His Tradition* (London: Faber and Faber, 1965). Bernard Leach told me in July 1976 that he would not pass on the Kenzan title, but would revert it to the granddaughter of Ogata Kenzan VI. However, the Kenzan *densho* now belongs to all who read Leach's book, and to those who have obtained copies of the translation done by Tomimoto and me.

Kenzan Ogata: Student of Ninsei (1163-1743)
Kenzan II: Edo Kenzan, Jirobe; friend of Ogata (?)
    Kyoto Kenzan, Ihachi; adopted son of Ogata, natural son of Ninsei (?-1768)

Kenzan III: Tominosuke Miyazaki; Kenzan I's natural son (1729-?)
Kenzan IV: Hoitsu Sakai; painter/historian (1760-1828)
Kenzan V: Myakuan Nishimura; amateur potter (?-1852)
    Kenya Miura; potter, refused the succession (1820-1889)
Kenzan VI: Shigekichi Ogata; potter, student of Kenya Miura (1853-1923)
Kenzan VII: Bernard Leach; potter, student of Shigekichi Ogata (1887-1979)
    Tomimoto Kenkichi; potter, declined the succession (1886-1963)
Nami Ogata: Amateur potter and artist, daughter of Kenzan VI (1899-)

Table 5-2
Fastfire Wood Firing Schedule

Time	Temperature °C	Comments
4:55		Start with 3/4 closed damper; stoking one firebox with kindling.
5:00	190	
5:15	315	
5:30	455	
5:45	580	Start other firebox. Keep stoking rhythm going: stoke, let burn down, stoke, let burn down, etc.
6:00	720	
6:15	790	Damper 1/2 open.
6:30	900	
6:45	955	
7:00	1016	Cone 6 down.
7:15	1050	
7:30	1095	
7:45	1105	
8:00	1180	Cone 5 down.
8:15	1205	Damper 3/4 open.
8:30	1235	Cone 9 bending.
8:45	1260	Cone 9 flat.
9:00	1285	Cone 10 down, push trick brick in.
9:15	1285	Damper fully open.
9:30	1285	Stoking to hold temperature to even out kiln.
9:45	1285	Firing complete, close damper and fireboxes.

Total Time: 4 hours and 45 minutes.*

*This time is slow. Les Blakebrough and I fired the same kiln design at my studio (elevation equals 6000') in 1 hour and 55 minutes to Cone 10 flat.

INDEX

C

D

Back cover photo courtesy of Paul Ames.